Class, Control, and Classical Music

Class, Control, and Classical Music

ANNA BULL

OXFORD
UNIVERSITY PRESS

Oxford University Press is a department of the University of Oxford. It furthers the University's objective of excellence in research, scholarship, and education by publishing worldwide. Oxford is a registered trade mark of Oxford University Press in the UK and certain other countries.

Published in the United States of America by Oxford University Press
198 Madison Avenue, New York, NY 10016, United States of America.

© Oxford University Press 2019

First issued as an Oxford University Press paperback, 2022

All rights reserved. No part of this publication may be reproduced, stored in a retrieval system, or transmitted, in any form or by any means, without the prior permission in writing of Oxford University Press, or as expressly permitted by law, by license, or under terms agreed with the appropriate reproduction rights organization. Inquiries concerning reproduction outside the scope of the above should be sent to the Rights Department, Oxford University Press, at the address above.

You must not circulate this work in any other form
and you must impose this same condition on any acquirer.

CIP data is on file at the Library of Congress
ISBN 978-0-19-084435-6 (Hardback)
ISBN 978-0-19-764606-9 (paperback)

9 8 7 6 5 4 3 2

Paperback printed by Marquis, Canada

CONTENTS

Acknowledgements vii
Introduction xi

CHAPTER 1. Locating Classical Music in Culture 1

CHAPTER 2. Boundary-Drawing around the Proper: From the Victorians to the Present 27

CHAPTER 3. 'Everyone Here Is Going to Have Bright Futures': Capitalizing on Musical Standard 50

CHAPTER 4. 'Getting It Right' as an Affect of Self-Improvement 70

CHAPTER 5. Rehearsing Restraint: How the Body Is Transcended 93

CHAPTER 6. 'Sometimes I Feel Like I'm His Dog': Gendered Power and the Ethics of Charismatic Authority 112

CHAPTER 7. 'Instead of Destroying My Body I Have a Reason for Maintaining It': Young Women's Re-imagining of the Body through Singing Opera 132

CHAPTER 8. A Community-in-Sound: Constructing the Valued Self 155

Conclusion 174

Appendix: Interviewees 195
References 201
Index 221

ACKNOWLEDGEMENTS

This book is based on a study I carried out during my PhD research at Goldsmiths, University of London. I had exceptional supervisors in Professors Les Back and Bev Skeggs, and I consider myself enormously fortunate to have had the privilege of their feedback on my work over the course of the thesis. I hope I have done them justice.

However, it was while working with Professor Georgina Born, during my undergraduate and master's degrees, that I started writing sociologically about classical music. I didn't find it easy, and this research would not have happened without her encouragement and mentorship. Professor Born was also immensely supportive in helping me apply for the Economic and Social Research Council funding that made this research possible.

I would like to extend very warm thanks to my editor, Suzanne Ryan, for her enthusiasm about the book. I have also been lucky to have several supportive academic networks during the process of writing this book. With the NYLON research network and NYLON alumni research network I have had honest discussions, helpful feedback, and good times. The Music and Culture reading group under the wise guidance of Anahid Kassabian has been hugely formative, and it was a privilege to be part of such an inspirational PhD cohort at Goldsmiths. More recently, I have had collegiality and support from my colleagues in the sociology team at the University of Portsmouth.

I have had an immensely supportive co-organizer and mentor in Christina Scharff, and our conversations and co-writing have influenced this work. In addition, Geoff Baker's encouragement right from the start of this project has been invaluable, and his own work remains an inspiration. Dave O'Brien has been a fantastic sounding board and supporter. I have also had formative discussions with and pep talks from other academic friends: Chloë Alaghband-Zadeh, Kim Allen, Lucy Delap, Liz Fearon, Seferin James, Clare Hall, Sarah Hickmott, Erin Johnson-Williams, Helen Keyes, Annie Ring, and Fiona Wright, among others. There have also been countless people along the way—friends, musicians, academics, students, and others—with whom I have had thought-provoking conversations; I hope this book will help these conversations to continue.

Enormous thanks to those who have read and commented on chapters: Chloë Alaghband-Zadeh, Geoff Baker, Joseph Burridge, Laura Seddon, George Ackers, Terese Jonsson, Christy Kulz, Christina Scharff, and Joe Browning, and especial thanks to Emily Nicholls for commenting on a full draft. David Hesmondhalgh's generous feedback was influential at a formative stage. Three anonymous reviewers also gave very helpful comments.

My colleagues in The 1752 Group, Antonia Bevan, Emma Chapman, and Tiffany Page, as well as being incredibly inspirational activist-academics, have allowed me to stand back from our work to complete this manuscript, and Tiffany has been an immensely supportive friend and colleague right from the start of this project. Thanks also to all my family for their patience and support during the lengthy process of producing this book. I have had unfailing support from my partner, James, who has been instrumental in making sure that I actually finished it.

Finally, my sincere thanks to all my participants, who welcomed me into their groups and generously gave their time to talk to me. I hope this account is helpful in making sense of all of our lives.

Earlier versions of some of the material in the book were published in 2016 under a Creative Commons Attribution 4.0 International licence (https://creativecommons.org/licenses/by/4.0/) as 'El Sistema as a bourgeois social project: class, gender, and Victorian values' in the journal *Action, Criticism & Theory for Music Education, 15*(1), 120–53.

An earlier version of chapter six was published by Sage in 2016 as 'Gendering the middle classes: the construction of conductors' authority in youth classical music groups' *The Sociological Review, 64*(4), 855–71.

Some material from chapters two and four were published in 2017 by Sage in an article co-authored with Christina Scharff, 'McDonalds' Music' Versus 'Serious Music': How Production and Consumption Practices Help to Reproduce Class Inequality in the Classical Music Profession, *Cultural Sociology, 11*(3), 283–301.

A section of chapter three (pages 142–153) was previously published in 'Uncertain Capital: Class, Gender, and the "Imagined Futures" of Young Classical Musicians' in *The Classical Music Industry*, edited by Chris Dromey and Julia Haferkorn. Copyright 2018. Reproduced by permission of Taylor and Francis Group, LLC, a division of Informa plc.

INTRODUCTION

As a child growing up in New Zealand, I started learning the piano at age six and cello at age seven. By my teens I was immersed in the busy life of a 'talented' musician, playing in orchestras and chamber music groups and attending courses, competitions, and masterclasses across the country. It was obvious to myself and those around me that I would study music at university, and by the time I left home at seventeen, my sense of self was fully formed into the powerful identity of 'classical musician'.

There were huge benefits to this identity. It garnered me great approval and high levels of one-to-one attention from adults. Being regularly told that I was talented nurtured a feeling of being special and important. Classical music gave me access to a social scene of other teenage geeks, at the Friday night rehearsals for my local youth orchestra and at the residential courses that I attended during the holidays. It also encouraged in me a sense of being somehow apart from the rest of the world—everyday concerns didn't touch my fellow musicians and me because we were doing something much more important than everyone else.

However, as I progressed through higher education, I started to feel doubts about my vocation. I valued classical music's strong social scene, but the manipulative modes of pedagogy I was sometimes experiencing felt toxic, and I started to feel frustrated that my whole life was organized around a genre of music that I felt was trying to shut out the contemporary world. My doubts only intensified on moving to the UK, where I studied further and worked as a musician. What I perceived as classical music's lack of social and political engagement and its values of authority and control felt increasingly unhealthy and confining to me. Not only that, but musically my classical training stifled my ability to participate in more informal kinds of music-making. I was frustrated by the lack of discussion about how gender shaped my musical experience; for example, I hardly ever played music by women composers. Coming from New Zealand, a country that was becoming more confident in its bicultural identity, I found the relentless whiteness of this tradition especially noticeable. Long before I read any ethnomusicology,

I sensed that musical practice could be a space for exploring different ways of being social, and I felt cut off from these, even while classical music afforded me many fulfilling, exciting and magical experiences. Eventually, these doubts led me to stop playing altogether.

Some of these concerns with classical music education, practice and culture are shared by other commentators (for example, Burnard 2012; Green 2003; Pace 2015a; Small 1996). However, these critical discussions have rarely been linked into a wider socio-cultural analysis of classical music's place in contemporary society and its associations with classed, gendered and racialized identities. Indeed, questions of class and socio-economic inequality are notably absent from the musical biography I have given here. This is no coincidence. Popular discussions of classical music are characterized by an impoverished language for talking about economic inequality and how it is manifested socially and culturally. Such discussions fail to address how economic inequality intersects with claims to morality and value, and how cultural inequalities are not just about economic factors but also about the social distribution of resources and power. And so, despite decades of investment in outreach programmes and education schemes intended to broaden its appeal, classical music in the UK remains predominantly a taste and a practice of the white middle classes.

To attempt to understand why this is the case, this book examines classical music within one of the cultures that produces it—white middle-class English youth—to analyse it as a social scene as well as a musical practice. Through an ethnographic study of young people playing and singing in classical music groups in the south of England, this book demonstrates that being a classical musician is a powerful social identity for the young people in this study. It explores how this identity, and the culture and practices associated with it, fits closely with the values and dispositions of the professional middle class in the south of England. Studying classical music in practice today also allows an examination of the middle classes' habitual roles: of boundary drawing around their protected spaces and of reproducing their privilege through education, both of which are camouflaged by the ideology of 'autonomous art' that classical music carries. The book also outlines how these young people's pathways through classical music education followed routes set out by their gender and class, and it describes how these pathways, and the culture and practices that they reproduce, were strongly shaped by the Victorian music education institutions that safeguard and preserve this tradition.

A sociological analysis of classical music in practice allows its bodily practices and their associations with a Protestant, imperialist white identity to become visible. Against prevailing ideas that classical music allows us to 'transcend … the bodily', as musicologist Julian Johnson argues (2002, 112), the book foregrounds classical music in this youth scene as bodily practice of control and restraint, revealing a culture where many of the conventions—wearing black, being 'faithful' to a written text, and emphasizing the organic unity of the musical work—downplay the body's role in creating sound and prioritize a cognitive approach to the music. It examines how sound works on and through the body to create powerful emotional states that do unrecognized political work. In this way, it demonstrates the ways in which learning classical music can work as a mechanism for storing value in particular bodies, thus reproducing inequality.

Key Arguments and Contributions

Classical music, or 'Western art music', has more often been studied as a text rather than a contemporary cultural practice. As Tony Bennett et al. note in their major study of class and cultural consumption in the UK:

> Those who study popular music generally use qualitative and ethnographic approaches often strongly informed by cultural studies, whilst those who study classical music are more likely to use quantitative data, focused historical studies and more 'orthodox' social theory. We badly need to bridge this divide if we are to understand the relationships between musical tastes more comprehensively. (2008, 77)

While, as chapter 1 describes, sociologists and ethnomusicologists have now begun turning their attention to classical music, this book is the first to comprehensively analyse the culture of classical music practice in relation to economic inequalities in the UK. Against earlier approaches in the sociology of music (Becker 1982), this book not only explores the social relations around the music but also asks how these socialities can be heard in the music itself. Through examining musical practice, I demonstrate how dispositions associated with a particular social position have become inscribed into the aesthetic properties of the music. One of the book's key arguments, therefore, is that inequalities in cultural production need to be understood through examining the practices that are used to create the aesthetic. In the culture of classical music analysed in this book, these embodied practices—codified and passed on through its institutions—show continuities with cultures associated with the professional white middle class in the UK and uphold white middle-class social domination.

While this book focuses on practice—what people do—it argues that the practices of classical music contribute to the formation of a middle-class form of selfhood. As Skeggs (2003), Reay (2017), and others have demonstrated, middle-class identities and culture are valued more than working-class or ethnic minority identities across a range of social institutions. Christina Scharff and I have already argued that classical music has an unspoken and uncontested value attached to it (Bull and Scharff 2017, 15). This book develops our argument by outlining the ways in which the normal practices of classical music, as observed in my research sites, form a type of personhood that is valued among the middle classes, and especially among the dominant group among my participants which I am labelling the professional middle class: those whose families have been middle class for more than one generation, and whose parents were predominantly in professional occupations (as outlined in chapter 1). I suggest that classical music is an ideal site for the middle classes to construct symbolic, cultural and economic boundaries to safeguard their privilege, as the discourse around the 'autonomy' of the aesthetic—the idea that this music exists in a separate realm from any social concerns—allows issues of inequality to be sidelined in favour of prioritizing 'the music itself'. The clear ideas of right and wrong around the aesthetic of classical music, as institutionalized in British music education, mean that any questions of how the aesthetic itself might contribute to reproducing inequalities are disallowed. Crucially, however, I link these debates back to some of the cultural institutions that reproduce and legitimize classical music's practices, and thereby its inequalities, and I suggest that it is classical music's institutions that should lead change.

As well as examining the culture of classical music within a youth scene in England, this book also uses classical music as a lens through which to examine the norms and values of different fractions of the English middle classes. This study is particularly timely given increasing levels of inequality in the UK. Recently, sociology has begun to focus on elites in the UK and US (R. Atkinson, Parker, and Burrows 2017; Khan 2012; King and Smith 2017; Rivera 2016; Savage and Williams 2008), and there is also a long tradition of sociological research looking at working-class subcultures. Within this space, the middle classes also need to be studied as political and economic actors; it is necessary to examine groups who store and pass on resources—economic, cultural or social—to be able to understand how this closes off spaces of privilege to others. Studying the middle classes is also important because their 'commonsense' norms are often universalized in social theory, government policy, and the media, and those inside this bubble are likely to be unaware that different ways of seeing the world and different value systems exist, even within their own country (Savage 2003, 536; Skeggs 2003). Critically examining the culture of the white middle classes can help to shed light on the invisible norms of this politically powerful group.

In addition, the role of institutions in storing value over time has been identified as an important way in which the middle classes retain their position. The development of classical music institutions between the 1830s and 1890s paralleled the rise of the middle classes in nineteenth-century Britain, as described in chapter 2, and the historical formation of the patterns that we have inherited today are a crucial part of the story of this book. Classical music represents the continuation of a cultural tradition forged in the nineteenth century that in many ways has attempted to eschew the technological and social changes of the twentieth and twenty-first centuries. Nevertheless, waves of institution-building during the twentieth century have influenced this tradition. In the UK, classical music could be theorized as the original post-war youth movement; the first British youth orchestra appears to be the Reading Youth Orchestra, set up in 1944, which toured Germany in 1949 (Reading Youth Orchestra 2014), and every decade since there has been a steady stream of new groups. Classical music is therefore a fascinating lens through which to examine the legacies of class and value that have been accrued and passed down through these institutions. Many of these institutions are still powerful in shaping young people's musical lives today, and the book lays out the values and norms that they reproduce.

Focusing on young people allows aspects of classical music's culture that might normally remain unspoken to become visible. In education, its norms are spelled out in pedagogic instruction from adult leaders and teachers. Examining youth engagement with classical music also foregrounds an interesting contradiction: classical music in the UK is predominantly listened to by 'older age groups' (Savage 2006, 169), and there are regular panics about the grey-haired audiences at concerts (Service 2009). Why, then, are these young people bucking this trend? Who are they, and do they represent the future of classical music?

Finally, this book contributes to ongoing debates about democratizing public funding for and access to culture (Neelands et al. 2015). In the UK, classical music—particularly opera—receives a disproportionately high level of state funding compared to other forms of culture, as outlined later in this introduction. This should be problematized and discussed more openly. By contrast, from within classical music's ranks, fears are regularly reported that it is dying out or that it is failing to reach young people. There is an urgent question to be addressed, therefore, of how to renew this cultural tradition while also democratizing cultural funding. This book will, I hope, open up ways in which changing the culture of classical music could also lead to creative renewal. This question of renewal feeds into debates about music education; music educators often hold a strong commitment to social justice, but the means to work towards this goal are not agreed on. This book shows how the everyday practices of classical music are an important part of a discussion about ethics, social justice, and respect for diverse musical cultures.

Against this backdrop, I put forward four ways in which the tradition and practices of classical music as found in my research sites form a contingent connection with the middle classes. Firstly, its repertoire requires formal modes of social organization that can be contrasted with the anti-pretentious, informal, dialogic modes of participation found in many forms of working-class culture. Secondly, its modes of embodiment reproduce classed values such as female respectability. Thirdly, an imaginative dimension of bourgeois selfhood can be read from classical music's practices, and finally, the aesthetic of detail, precision, and 'getting it right' requires a long-term investment that is more possible for, and makes more sense for, middle- and upper-class families.

Most notably, I argue that the ideology of the 'autonomy' of classical music from social concerns (Bourdieu 1984; Born 2010; Eagleton 1990; Goehr 1992; Wolff 1993) needs to be examined in historical context as part of the classed legacy of classical music's past. While for Bourdieu the apparent autonomy of high art enables boundary-drawing around taste, I follow Michèle Lamont (1992b) in theorizing this boundary-drawing as not limited to taste but including symbolic boundaries that can have moral, economic or cultural content. A theoretical intervention of this book is to suggest that we need to examine the practices of classical music alongside other forms of classed boundary-drawing such as private schools, gated communities, and suburbanization. The sonically sealed spaces of many classical music venues, insulated from their urban surrounds, enable its aesthetic of detail, precision, and dynamic extremes, and I argue that these are simply another of the middle classes' ways of closing off their protected and exclusive spaces to other groups in society. This is both an historical legacy of the institutions that we have inherited and also a tradition that is actively reproduced as a resource for recreating classed identities. But at moments of heightened social inequality, classical music's autonomy is threatened, and the moral guilt/responsibility that also characterizes middle-class identities (Reay, Crozier, and James 2011) comes to the fore, for example, through classical music's recent discovery of class inequality through the proliferation of El Sistema–inspired music education programmes (as discussed later). It is therefore necessary to examine classical music's autonomy from the social as contested, uneven and never absolute in order to make sense of many of its social and aesthetic practices today.

This book focuses on class inequality in relation to classical music education outside of school in the UK context. There is a specific historical formation to class in the UK that has sedimented into the classed identities and structures that are visible today. This means that the extent to which the arguments put forward here are also helpful for explaining patterns of inequality around classical music production in other contexts must be a matter for empirical investigation. The expansion of British music education institutions to Commonwealth countries (Johnson-Hill 2015; Kok 2011) suggests that there are likely to be some similarities in practices elsewhere, even if the meanings of these practices and the ways in which they intersect with structures of inequality may be different. In addition, rather than examining the vital issue of music within the school curriculum, the book focuses on out-of-school music education. The declining number of students receiving music tuition within schools in England (Daubney and Mackrill 2018; Scott 2018) makes it even more urgent to understand how out-of-school music education can reproduce inequalities. In this way, this book also aims to contribute to discussions of the status of music within schools.

Defining Classical Music

While for many people 'classical music' may be a familiar, commonsense term, it is currently being questioned and problematized both within and outside academia. In academic music studies, it has become the norm to use the term 'Western art music' to describe the canon of repertoire and body of practices that I am describing. However, as Laudan Nooshin argues, 'Whatever its historical legacy, clearly "western art music" is (solely) western no longer' as 'the forces of colonialism and, more recently, globalization, have afforded this music a global reach that can no longer be captured by the term "western"'. She suggests that we need a more appropriate terminology for a genre that 'has taken on a multitude of forms and meanings globally' (2011, 296) but still remains 'ideologically loaded, since it claims exclusive ownership of a cultural space whilst denying the existence of "others" who have been and continue to be central to it and who are rendered invisible by the dominant discourses' (294).

In the interests, therefore, of locating this musical practice in a particular time and space, I use the vernacular term that my participants used: 'classical music'. For them, this term had a taken-for-granted meaning that didn't require explanation. Indeed, mainstream, online and specialist media also use the term 'classical music', further confirming that there exists in public discourse a commonly understood phenomenon by this name. However, while the term is common parlance, its meaning is explored throughout the book, as is the question of what is included in this definition and what is excluded from it. The way in which 'classical music' is defined is important—and contested—because the boundaries drawn around it work to store value in this space.

Theorizing classical music as a genre with common 'orientations, expectations and conventions' (Neale 1980, 19),[1] it is possible to give a working definition drawing on existing theoretical and empirical studies (Frith 1996b; Gilmore 1987; Green 2003; Goehr 1992; Kingsbury 1988; Small 1996, 19) to identify a set of shared conventions. These studies identify classical music as a practice that reproduces from staff notation a canon of music composed between around 1750 and 1950, using acoustic instruments and tending to eschew post-1900 technologies.[2] It draws on the 'work-concept', where the performer attempts to faithfully reproduce the intentions of the composer (Goehr 1992). This reproduces a hierarchy between composer, performer and audience (Small 1996) where the composer's wishes take priority. It requires distinctive modes of adult-led pedagogy where

---

[1] In television, Steve Neale theorizes genre as 'systems of orientations, expectations and conventions that circulate between industry, text and subject' (1980, 19). For the purposes of understanding genre in classical music, we need to examine different circuits: cultural and educational institutions, texts (including performances), and musicians/audiences.

[2] Contemporary classical music and early music are distinct genres in their own right, and as such they are outside the scope of this book.

pupils usually take one-to-one lessons to learn 'musicianship'; how to interpret the composer's intentions; staff notation; and technical skill at their instrument or voice (Kingsbury 1988; Green 2003).

As well as these conventional practices, classical music is also characterized by discourses of transcendence or autonomy from social concerns (Born 2010; Bull 2009; Frith 1996b; Goehr 1992; James H. Johnson 1996; Yoshihara 2008). Indeed, as Born notes, a 'defining feature of the ontology of Western art music from the nineteenth century to the present' is 'the disavowal of music's social mediations' (40), although for David Clarke (2012, 174) this autonomy should be seen as more or less strong at different points in time. These conventions and discourses are reproduced through institutions; Simon Frith notes that 'art music discourse' has developed on the basis of its validation in academic institutions, which ensure that '[only] the right people with the right training can ... experience the real meaning of "great" music' (1996b, 39). Despite this, classical music's contemporary institutions, particularly education institutions, have received relatively little critical attention (although see Baker 2014; Benzecry 2011; Bohlman 1989; McCormick 2015). And yet, its institutions play an important role in safeguarding and reproducing this tradition. As such, this book critically analyses the 'institutional ecology' of classical music.

These institutions and practices produce classical music's distinctive aesthetic qualities. Aesthetics are commonly understood as qualities that relate to sensory beauty as distinct from social or cultural interpretations (R. Williams 1976, 32); for example, Goehr (1992, 121) describes aesthetics as a shift from 'extra-musical to purely musical criteria of value and classification'. In this book, I understand the 'aesthetic' of the music to refer to its sonic qualities, but throughout I attempt to link the aesthetic of classical music with its social, institutional and historical conditions of production.

Classical Music and Inequality: What We Know So Far

David Hesmondhalgh (2013, 4), in his manifesto for a more ambivalent music sociology, suggests that we explore ways in which the arts and culture might draw upon and reinforce patterns of social inequality, rather than reproducing arguments about the 'power of music' (Hallam and Creech 2010) that focus exclusively on its benefits. There is no simple formula for understanding the relationship between music and inequality. As chapter 1 theorizes, one of the ways in which classical music reinforces patterns of inequality is through being valued, in various ways, over other genres. Indeed, existing patterns of consumption and production of classical music as well as its unequal funding structures show stark patterns of inequality.

Data on cultural consumption from the UK shows that listening to classical music is strongly stratified by age and education level.³ A mixed-methods study of cultural consumption and class, across a variety of types of culture, found 'beyond question, the existence of systematic patterns of cultural taste and practice' (T. Bennett et al. 2008, 251). Notably for this study, the authors found that people with higher education qualifications were six times more likely to listen to classical music than those without (Savage 2006, 169). Particularly for white respondents, Bennett et al. found that 'classical music remains attuned to class', and among this group, for the working class, it evoked 'a response which is much more complex than a straight rejection or distaste for it', for example, distancing themselves from it (2008, 82–84). They conclude that 'classical music thus emerges as a mainstream, established musical field, whose appeal is somewhat broader than a narrowly defined middle class, but taste for which is highly correlated with university education' (169). For many of this group, however, classical music was viewed as 'soothing', enjoyed for its 'easy listening' qualities (86) and 'claiming affiliation with classical music denote[d] respectability' (87). Confirming this link between classical music consumption and the middle classes, Crawford et al.'s study of orchestral audiences highlighted 'the continued individualistic, middle-class, and exclusionary culture of classical music attendance and patterns of behaviours' (2014, 1) arguing that 'classical music helps make and maintain who the middle classes are' (15).

Examining those who play classical music in the UK, whether in education or professionally, reveals a similar picture, although, as Christina Scharff (2017, 41–42) notes, data on inequalities is difficult to come by and even when it is available, socio-economic data is often missing. Examining the music industry more generally (not just classical music), O'Brien et al. (2016) found that it, along with publishing, it is the most difficult of the creative industries to gain access to as a working-class person. In Scharff's (2017) study of sixty-four early-career women classical musicians in Berlin and London, she found the majority ($n = 44$) identified as middle class, with eleven more unsure of how to describe their socio-economic background. We therefore have to look to music education institutions for more data. The most comprehensive picture is painted by Born and Devine's (2015) study of tertiary education music degrees. Using admissions data from 2007–11 for music and music technology degrees in the UK (excluding conservatoires), they demonstrate that there is a clear class divide between those studying music at university and those studying music technology; the former are predominantly middle class, while the latter tend to be working-class young men.⁴

---

³ Chapter 1 will discuss ways of theorizing and measuring class. Education level is usually understood by sociologists to constitute one aspect of class.

⁴ This finding is supported by earlier research by Nicola Dibben (2006, 91), who reported that while the total number of students studying music at UK universities increased 38% between 1996–97 and 2001–2, there was no significant increase in the numbers from the lowest social classes.

These figures also reveal a genre divide between different types of musical knowledge. Music degrees tend to have a relatively large component of classical music and require the ability to read standard staff notation (Born and Devine 2015), while music technology degrees instead require knowledge of music technology software.

The dominance of middle- and upper-class young people in tertiary classical music education also extends to music conservatoires (specialist tertiary music education institutions). The Royal Academy of Music took fewer than half its pupils from state schools in 2017, and the Royal College of Music took 56.9% (Coughlan 2017; this contrasts with the 93.5% of pupils in the UK who attend state schools, the remainder attending fee-paying independent schools). Even among those pupils from state schools who attend music conservatoires, very few tend to come from disadvantaged backgrounds or areas.[5] Students and staff across conservatoires are also disproportionately white, as Scharff details; only twenty-eight, or 2% of staff at UK music conservatoires in 2014 could be identified as black or minority ethnic (Scharff 2017, 57), and black applicants were less likely to be accepted (48). Gender divisions are also striking. While roughly equal numbers of males and females study at conservatoires, fewer than a third of the teaching staff are female, and in 2014, women made up only 1.4% of conductors and 2.9% of artistic directors in British orchestras, and only a quarter of principal players (55).

These inequalities at the tertiary level are set up through unequal participation in music education for students younger than eighteen. A report[6] from the Associated Board of the Royal Schools of Music (ABRSM) found that 90% of children from AB backgrounds (the most privileged) had ever played an instrument,[7] against 74% from grades C1 and DE (lower socio-economic groups) (Hume and Wells 2014). This reflects a long-term pattern for music exams to be predominantly undertaken by the middle classes, as David Wright has described (2013, 226). The ABRSM study also found that the main reason both children and adults gave for choosing not to play a musical instrument was a lack of interest; or if they had learnt and given up, the main reason was having lost interest (Hume and Wells 2014, 18–19). By contrast, the cost of lessons was only the seventh most important factor for those who had given up playing and the second most

---

[5] In 2007–10, fewer than ten pupils per year in the UK who received free school meals (a commonly used measure of disadvantage in the UK) had attended any of the music conservatoires by age nineteen (Department for Business, Innovation and Skills 2013). Supporting this finding, data from the five top conservatoires in the UK in 2012–13 shows that only 3.9% of students came from 'low participation neighbourhoods', the lowest fifth of the UK, by area, for participation in tertiary education (Scharff 2017, 46).

[6] Because study was not weighted according to class, these figures should be treated with caution.

[7] These descriptions use market research categories to analyse class. A, B, and C1 roughly correlate with middle class; C2, D, and E roughly correlate with working class. For further discussion, see Crompton (2015).

important factor for those who had never played. This suggests that economic barriers may not be the principal explanation for why people do not play an instrument. This finding is supported by wider research in music education on young people's music-making and identity (A. Lamont et al. 2003), suggesting that the social identity of young people playing classical music is the greatest barrier to participation, working in conjunction with economic barriers.

As well as stark inequalities in consumption and production of classical music, it receives disproportionately high levels of public and philanthropic funding. Analysing the value of music in London at the end of the last century, Dave Laing and Norton York (2000) showed that classical music attracted 90% of the available public music subsidy. In 2015–18, 24.8% of total Arts Council England portfolio funding for music was allocated to orchestral music, and 57.9% was allocated to opera and music theatre (Monk 2014), a level of funding disproportionate to the size of audiences (Hodgkins 2013).[8] Antony Feeny (2016) shows that between 1946 and 2015, across all four UK Arts Councils, grant expenditure on each category of classical music has increased relatively steadily until quite recently (although other areas of the arts have increased more than classical music). By 2015, classical music (including opera) accounted for around 20% of Arts Councils of Great Britain's expenditure (Feeny 2016). Moving away from public funding, philanthropic organizations show a similar trend. In a directory of UK music education charities using 2010–11 data on their income, assets and wealth, seven out of the top ten music education charities are dedicated to classical music, opera and ballet (Arts Council England 2012a). As chapter 2 will explore, this uneven weighting of the institutional ecology of music education towards classical music is formed through the historical legacy passed on by the Victorians that shapes provision and progression routes today.

How can explain these enduring patterns be explained? While similar middle-class dominance of publicly funded culture occurs across high art genres (Neelands et al. 2015), classical music is one of the most deeply stratified forms of cultural taste and practice. This is exacerbated by the commonly held assumption that inequality within classical music is purely an access issue; it is simply that some people have not had a chance to learn to love it yet. The explanation given in media and cultural sector discussions follows this logic to suggest that this access is solely economic as learning an instrument is too expensive for working-class families, especially at a time of cuts to music education provision (see, for example, Hewett 2014; Richens 2016). While this is certainly true, it is only one part of the explanation. Against this position, this book puts forward the argument

---

[8] This trend was also apparent in the region in which my research took place. When I crunched the 2012 numbers for Arts Council portfolio funding (encompassing regularly funded organizations), I found that one pound in every five went to organizations that are dedicated to classical music. The actual proportion of funding that went to classical music was therefore higher, as some organizations supported classical music as well as other art forms, and so are not included in this figure.

that enduring patterns of unequal participation in classical music education are not solely a reflection of economic barriers but instead reflect the types of music that different groups in society enjoy and want to play.

However, while classical music in the UK is almost exclusively played and listened to by the middle and upper classes, in the last ten years there has been a worldwide explosion of music education programmes that teach orchestral instruments to disadvantaged children. Inspired by the Venezuelan music education programme El Sistema, an intensive orchestral programme that claims to rescue disadvantaged children from a life of drugs and crime through learning classical music, a worldwide movement of nearly three hundred El Sistema offshoots has grown up ('El Sistema Global Program Directory' n.d.). Geoffrey Baker's ethnography of El Sistema Venezuela, rather than finding an inspiring model of social change through music, describes predominantly middle-class children being yelled at by untrained and poorly paid teachers in a pedagogic model that would seem dated to the Victorians. Furthermore, as he notes, there is something that doesn't add up about using an inherently exclusive organization, the symphony orchestra, for a social *inclusion* programme (Baker 2014)—and, indeed, a 2016 study by the Inter-American Development Bank suggested that the poverty rate among El Sistema's intake was one-third that of wider Venezuelan society (Baker 2017a). A major evaluation produced to demonstrate El Sistema's effectiveness, as Baker, Bull, and Taylor describe, is characterized by flaws and limitations so serious that it is 'impossible to take seriously' (2018, 6).

Despite El Sistema's flawed and partial evidence base, the idea of using classical music to alleviate inequality has caught the worldwide imagination, and cultural entrepreneurs in the UK have been among those leading the charge. In the UK, Sistema Scotland's first project was set up in 2008, followed by In Harmony Sistema England (IHSE) in 2009. These programmes are 'social action' programmes first and foremost; the Arts Council England 2011 funding guidance for IHSE programmes requires that participation in these programmes lead to 'avoidance of anti-social behaviour, drug abuse, and crime' (Arts Council England 2012b, 6). As I have argued elsewhere (Bull 2016a), this assumption that without classical music disadvantaged children are headed towards a life of drugs and crime perpetuates stigmatizing stereotypes about working-class identities. In addition, the idea that disadvantaged children can change their material circumstances through learning classical music reinforces Victorian ideas that people in poverty would no longer be poor if only they acted more like middle-class people, thus diverting attention from structural and state-led solutions to inequality. This book contributes towards debates around El Sistema–inspired programmes in the UK and around the world by showing how the social identity and musical values of classical music are not neutral but fit with the identity and values of the professional middle class. This book makes visible what is at stake in such programmes by outlining how classical music's classed history shapes its conventions and practices today. If education programmes such as El Sistema drew on music's potential as a form of radical critique that could transform consciousness, as Theodor Adorno envisioned (DeNora 2003, 3), then they might serve as incubators for social change. Instead, many rely on the most conservative and authoritarian aspects of classical music culture: the symphony orchestra, the dominant conductor, and the hierarchical teaching dynamic that relies on a 'banking' model, as described by Freire (2000). As such, they are more likely to stifle critique than produce social change.

Introducing the Study

While the data just outlined on inequalities in classical music education, consumption, and work lays out patterns within the social world, such quantitative data is less useful in understanding why and how such inequalities occur. This study aims to explain these patterns through an ethnography of four youth music groups in a county in the south of England. Ethnography involves a long-term participant observation of a particular social scene. It draws on naturally occurring data by observing real events, interactions, and processes in the social world and is often combined with other methods; I also carried out interviews and drew on archival data from music education institutions.

I focused on youth classical music groups, carrying out research with four such groups between 2012 and 2013: a youth choir, two youth orchestras, and a youth opera group. The first, Cantando Youth Choir,[9] was run privately as a charity and included young people aged from around twelve to twenty-one. A further group, the Whitchestershire County Youth Orchestra, was run publicly by the county music service. I accessed these two groups through contacting them after an online search. The other two groups in my study were accessed through young people I met in Cantando youth choir. One was the New Symphony Orchestra, which was run by two of its participants and had an older demographic of up to age twenty-five. These three groups, which all rehearsed intensively for up to a week at a time during school holidays, are introduced in detail in chapter 3. The final group was a youth opera group that I have called the Young Opera Company. As it staged dramatic performances rather than concerts, rehearsals took a different form than in the other groups, so I have discussed it primarily in chapter 7. I participated as a cellist in the two youth orchestras and played as a rehearsal pianist for the Young Opera Company, but for Cantando youth choir I did not participate, instead observing rehearsals and performances. While there are differences between the rehearsal practices of choirs and orchestras, the inclusion of a variety of groups allowed me to gain a wider perspective on this youth music scene, and indeed there was a continuity of culture and membership across these groups.

---

[9] All names of individuals and organizations have been changed; in order to preserve anonymity, some other identifying details have also been changed.

In addition to these observations, I carried out thirty-seven semi-structured interviews and three focus groups with young people and interviews with nine of the adults involved in running these groups. Participants in these groups were aged between twelve and their early twenties, but interviewees were all aged sixteen or over due to ethical considerations. They had all started instrumental lessons before the age of ten,[10] and many of them had therefore been having one-to-one music lessons for at least ten years before joining these groups. Twenty-one of my interviewees were female and sixteen male. All interviewees were white other than one British Asian young man, one East Asian young man, and three mixed-race participants, all of East Asian/white British heritage. Interviewees' class position is discussed in chapter 1, and a list of interviewees is included in the appendix. All interviews were audio-recorded and transcribed verbatim with permission, and thematic analysis was carried out in dialogue with field notes from observations and participant observations.

I chose to carry out my research in Whitchestershire as there was a thriving youth classical music scene in the city of Whitchester but also high (although hidden) levels of inequality between young people across the county. This allowed me to gain a picture of the geographical spatiality of different class fractions: the professional middle classes in the town of Whitchester, and the small-town new middle classes in the county of Whitchestershire. In addition, it offered a picture of a provincial middle class that forms a contrast to recent work that has focused on London (Vincent et al. 2012b; T. Butler and Robson 2003; Jackson and Benson 2014; Reay, Crozier, and James 2011). The pseudonyms of the town and county were chosen to reflect the Roman history of the area, 'chester' and 'cheshire' being common suffixes in England, drawing on the Roman *castra*, meaning 'camp'. 'Whit' means 'a very small part or amount' or an 'iota', so together they could mean 'a small part of England'. I also like the way the name sounds quintessentially English, allowing the reader to imagine the elite provincial town along the lines of Bath, Chester, or York in which this book is set.

The discussions in this book rest on certain normative assumptions about how music could work against inequalities in society more generally, rather than perpetuating them. Pickett and Wilkinson (2010) demonstrate that economic inequality is bad for everyone, not just for those who are worse off in society, as high levels of inequality lead to adverse social outcomes such as lower trust, higher suicide rates and more crime. The question of what roles cultural production and education take in contributing to economic inequality, as discussed in chapter 1, is a complex one. I suggest that the values and ethics we practice in music and the arts, such as classical music education, affect our worldview more generally and form part of our ethics and our politics. The ethics and politics of classical music,

---

[10] Eleven had started at age four or five; fifteen started at age six or seven; and a further ten started at age eight or nine (for one further participant, the age at which they started learning was unclear).

while contested, are shaped by institutions and practices developed in the nineteenth century and retain traces of the ideals and the class politics of that era, as explored in chapter 2. One example is the curious centrality of strong authority in classical music, which I explore in chapters 5 and 6. While this mode of social organization is an efficient way of reaching high musical standards, its social consequences, as I will describe, are to reinforce normative, unequal gender positions and to discourage critical reflection and debate. However, these normative positions are always informed by the data, as this is first and foremost an empirical study that aims to reveal wider social and historical patterns through an in-depth study of a particular scene.

My perspective as a researcher is, of course, a situated one that is shaped by my own social position. Being a white middle-class woman from a Commonwealth country meant that certain aspects of this musical scene were more accessible to me than others; for example, as chapter 7 shows, young women appeared to be particularly likely to open up to me about their lives. My classical music training and experience meant that I was an insider to the musical culture of my research sites, and this was indispensable for carrying out this study. Yet I was an outsider to these particular groups and also to the world of English middle-class youth that I found myself in, and this gave me some helpful critical distance. In addition, while the ideas in this book initially grew out of my experiences studying and working as a classical musician, the book also has its genesis in my formation within elite higher education institutions. Academia, similarly to classical music, is a space of white middle-class privilege that relies on self-discipline and a separation from everyday concerns, functioning as a space where resources are passed on to others who resemble the incumbents. These similarities between academia and the classical music world may mean that there are also aspects of the world I was studying that were less visible to me. However, overall, while my positionality undoubtedly affects how I have interpreted the empirical data in this study, I draw from feminist standpoint epistemology the understanding that knowledge is always socially situated, and that this positionality can lead to a stronger objectivity than more positivistic methods (Harding 1996).

It would be possible to argue that critiques such as mine lessen the chances of lower-middle-class and working-class people experiencing what some scholars see as the emancipatory potential of classical music (Harper-Scott 2012, 17). After all, much of classical music's canonic repertoire was anti-bourgeois, even revolutionary, at the time of its writing, and for some musicologists, Western art music can bring the 'power structures [of contemporary capitalism] with immense clarity into view' (Harper-Scott 2012, 20). This position draws on an older critique by Adorno which argues that the autonomy of the musical material can create a space of critique against capitalist and neoliberal forces, including the commodification of music (Adorno and Bernstein 2001; DeNora 2003; '"Can Musical Conservatism Be Progressive?"' 2018). A more sociological defence of the potential autonomy of classical music is provided by Lucy Green, who argues that 'to dismiss the concept of autonomy ... might also lead to overlooking one of the most critical capacities made available by music', that 'music *can* cross boundaries' and take on meaning to those who are not part of its vernacular culture (2005, 91). However, she cautions 'against making any assumption about how music is understood by others' (91).

As these authors suggest, therefore, textual analyses may identify emancipatory potential. However, this does not mean that the music is interpreted in progressive ways by those who play or hear it (S. Hall 2005), and so it is crucial to examine the meanings of classical music in practice. Even if classical music does have the potential to create a non-commercialized space that defies neoliberal logics, it does not necessarily follow that this actually takes place. As chapters 3 and 7 outline, in my research sites there were ways in which classical music did form a space for positive forms of identity and bodily practice that led to flourishing, but these were not spaces of critique. Any critical potential that the repertoire may hold was not generally foregrounded in the practices of rehearsing and performing classical music. Instead, on the whole these practices contributed towards forming bourgeois subjectivities of investment, order, hierarchy and control. Therefore, I suggest that the meaning of classical music today needs to be sought within the practices that produce it. As Anamik Saha argues in his analysis of racial diversity in the cultural industries, 'a radical cultural political programme is absolutely contingent upon production strategies' (2017, 27). Indeed, critique can be present across a variety of forms of production, and commodified popular culture has sometimes—despite tendencies towards homogeneity and standardization—managed to produce progressive forms of multiculture (Saha 2017, 27). Furthermore, the intense commercialization of the linkage of classical music and social inclusion represented by conductor Gustavo Dudamel, or 'Rolex Man' as Geoffrey Baker (2017b) describes him, demonstrates that classical music is by no means alien to commodification. Rather than discussing autonomy, then, in this study I use the concept of 'articulation' to outline a more complex, contingent connection between music and the social, as introduced in chapter 1, in the hope that this will help to theorize the 'more dynamic, frictional view of musical autonomy' that David Clarke calls for (2012, 173).

Overview of the Book

This book is interdisciplinary and draws on literatures from a variety of fields. Therefore, in order to make the book accessible to readers from different disciplines, chapter 1 brings together literatures from sociology, musicology, ethnomusicology, and music education to outline a theoretical paradigm for studying music and inequality. It asks, how are musical institutions, practices, and aesthetics shaped by wider conditions of economic inequality, and in what ways might music enable and entrench such inequalities or work against them?

Drawing on Georgina Born's (2017) work on intersecting 'planes of mediation' between music and the social, I theorize a multi-scalar approach to studying music and class. I also outline the different class fractions into which most of my participants fell: the upper middle class, the professional middle class, and the new middle class.

Chapter 2 draws on the musical biographies of the young people in this study to map out the 'institutional ecology' of youth classical music that was influential in shaping their musical lives. This 'ecology' also makes visible the link between the late Victorian period and the present. I focus on the role of Victorian institutions—the conservatoires and exam boards—in consecrating classical music as more valuable than other genres by institutionalizing musical standards. I focus on the predominance of women studying in music education institutions to argue that, particularly for the exam boards, these institutions served a demand for training respectable femininity by drawing on discourses around classical music as morally 'exemplary' and 'uplifting' as well as through its requirement for daily disciplining of the body. Musical ability therefore demonstrates that the performer has acquired the bourgeois virtue of embodied restraint. The chapter concludes by examining how this boundary-drawing around the 'proper' was reproduced by my participants today, through ideas of what counted as 'serious' or 'proper' music, boundaries that I argue help to safeguard classical music's privileged status in education and funding and its association with valued class identities.

Chapter 3 continues to explore how classical music is used to draw boundaries around social groups, through examining contrasting ideas of musical standards of ability. Using close ethnographic description, it shows how musical ability is produced and recognized in and between bodies. This reveals a tension between the accepted idea among classical musicians that somebody's musical standard varies according to who they play or sing with, and a firm belief in hierarchies of ability, which could reinforce social hierarchies such as gender or age. The chapter identifies two ways in which musical standard was capitalized on by young people. First, I explore how musical standard was part of the rationale behind an exodus from the state-run music education programme by two of the groups in this study, following a wider trend of middle-class 'exit' from public services. Secondly, I map out the 'imagined futures' and aspirations of my participants, outlining a typology of three groups that shows how class and gender were highly formative in determining these young people's pathways.

Chapter 4 links the concept of musical standards discussed in the previous two chapters with the aesthetic of classical music through examining the practices required to attain ideals of aesthetic beauty within this tradition. In particular, it introduces the idea of 'getting it right' as an important component of classical music education and aesthetics. Getting it right necessitated ongoing correction, which formed the main practice of rehearsals. I suggest that this correction occurred on a symbolic as well as a musical level, as in classical music it is possible to *hear* rightness in sound, and this rightness has a moral connotation as well as aesthetic value. Getting it right musically held different meanings for young people in different class positions. Those in the new middle-class group were able fit in socially to the classical music world by getting it right musically. However, within the powerful relationship of trust that many of the young people formed with their teachers, the correction that teachers required of their students sometimes appeared to constitute emotional abuse. This chapter therefore links correction, musical standard, and gendered disciplining as formative of the aesthetic of 'rightness' of classical music.

The next two chapters examine the social experience of rehearsals. Chapter 5 analyses the structure of the rehearsal process to reveal norms of bodily practice that can be linked to theorizations of how white identities are embodied. This analysis also reveals a contradiction: the body is required to be present in order to create sound but is at the same time effaced or transcended. I explore the mechanisms through which this occurs, including 'controlled excitement', cultivating strong emotions but always keeping them under control. This is, I suggest, both an aesthetic quality and a social disposition required by/cultivated within classical music practice. The chapter concludes by suggesting that one way of reading the orchestra is as a cultural memory in which the middle-class, male leader, the conductor, is controlling and disciplining the mass or the crowd. Overall, I argue that the mode of embodiment described here can be linked to a raced, classed, and gendered hierarchy of value in which women and non-white others are associated with the bodily and white men with the cognitive, and the latter is valued over the former.

Chapter 6 continues a close analysis of rehearsal processes, this time focusing on the gendered interaction between conductor and musicians. Accounts of charismatic leadership in the arts and the craft of the conductor reveal a shift over recent decades from authoritarian to more consensual forms of leadership. And yet, among the young people in this study, the charismatic authoritative leadership of male conductors was appreciated and enjoyed. The chapter focuses particularly on the interactions which facilitate this mode of power, as well as how it inscribes itself on and affects bodies in ways that reinforce gendered norms. To this end, the construction of conductors' charisma is analysed in its workings through consensual as well as more coercive practices such as humiliation and fear. The deference and conformity that are normal within classical music practice can be read politically as trust in the authority and expertise of adult leaders that is continuous with a wider middle-class trust in institutional authority. These social relations are, in part, inscribed in the musical text.

The final two empirical chapters focus on the embodied experience of playing and singing in classical music ensembles. Chapter 7 assesses the encounter between the young women of the Young Opera Company and a profoundly anti-feminist musical text, Mozart's *The Magic Flute*, taking into account both the cultural object itself and the practices and socialities that surround it. For the young women in the Young Opera Company, singing opera was a powerful bodily practice that gave them a sense of control and embodied confidence, working against body image issues that several of them reported. Against this, the strongly gendered institutional and cultural context of classical music individualized and undermined their emergent empowered voices. Contextualizing this practice within the institutional culture of opera and its canon, and the musical-dramatic text of *The Magic Flute* itself, this emergent sense of power was contained by the powerful ideology of 'fidelity' to origins and authenticity that is normative in classical music culture. This inhibited the radical potential of this bodily empowerment through limiting the possibilities for re-imagining the musical text, thus also limiting any possibilities for changing the practices that bring the text to life.

Finally, chapter 8 describes how my participants recognized an emotional depth in classical music that they stated they did not get from other musics or activities, and that was particularly linked to the Romantic repertoire they preferred. I explore this idea of emotional depth in relation to ideas of bourgeois subjectivity. I argue that the recognition by my participants of a deep interiority both in themselves and in this music constitutes a form of interpellation of themselves as subjects who can recognize the value of this music. I suggest that in this way classical music can be seen as a cultural technology for knowing the bourgeois self. I draw on Susan McClary's (2001) argument that a mode of forward-looking, rational selfhood is inscribed within the tonal structures of classical music. Finally, I link this argument about emotional depth into the embodied and affective experience of playing in classical music ensembles and the acoustic aesthetic that facilitates transcendence of the body. I theorize this in relation to Terry Eagleton's work on the aesthetic, as the reversal of the usual condition of bourgeois subjecthood of competition and individualism. Instead, the young people experience community in sound. The sound itself does the work of opening up the individual to facilitate this connection. What is distinctive about the experience that my participants report is that this deeply personal experience is linked into institutions and social groups that possess high levels of economic, social, and cultural capital. Their emotional depth therefore has more value than other people's emotional depth, and their own sense of value is confirmed through their ability to respond emotionally to this music.

The conclusion draws together these arguments by laying out four ways in which the tradition and practices of classical music form an 'articulation' (S. Hall 1985) with the middle classes: the formal modes of social organization that it requires; its modes of embodiment; the imaginative dimension of bourgeois selfhood that can be read from classical music's practices; and the aesthetic of detail, precision, and 'getting it right'. Overall, it argues that the aesthetic of classical music does the boundary-drawing work of retaining this as a middle-class space and practice, and within these spaces, classical music cultivates a form of selfhood characterized by emotional depth that is recognized as valuable. It goes on to draw out two ways in which this book contributes to a more general understanding of the middle classes: the ways in which gender identities structure classed reproduction, and the continuing role of classical music as legitimate culture conferring institutionalized cultural capital. Finally, it lays out ways forward for classical music in policy and practice, arguing that in order to diversify classical music, we need to also change its aesthetic, and suggests that Arts Council England's Creative Case for Diversity (2011) offers an important challenge to classical music institutions that could contribute towards creative renewal and social transformation.

Class, Control, and Classical Music

CHAPTER 1

Locating Classical Music in Culture

The questions raised in the introduction have scarcely been addressed in scholarly or popular writing on classical music. Indeed, there is a dearth of research into classical music from a sociocultural perspective, which is not surprising given, as noted in the introduction, it is characterized by its autonomy from the social. Nevertheless, debates on diversifying classical music, while they are still in their early stages ('Class, Race and Classical Music' 2014; Scharff 2015), are troubling classical music's disavowal of the social. On one hand, some of the distinction of classical music lies in its exclusivity, which will be destroyed or diluted by increasing its popularity, while on the other hand, practitioners desire to share what they love with the world. In order to diversify classical music, a more sophisticated social analysis of its practices, institutions, and social significations and, through these, its value is required. Rather than a renewed justification of its extrasocial musical value, this demands an understanding of how classical music's distinctive aesthetic shapes practices that contribute towards socially valued identities, which in turn are shaped through particular class, gender, and race positionalities.

Towards this end, this chapter sets out a new theoretical argument as to how class and classical music can be analysed together. It reframes existing research on classical music by putting it into dialogue with sociological understandings of class and gender to outline what a social analysis of classical music should look like. This also lays the foundations for theorizing more widely how music might be analysed in relation to class, an urgent theoretical intervention at a time of increasing economic inequality within many nation-states. It asks, how are musical institutions, practices, and aesthetics shaped by wider conditions of economic inequality, and in what ways might music enable and entrench such inequalities or work against them? I argue for understanding music and inequality through a multi-scalar approach, going beyond the microsocial to explain how wider sociocultural discourses and practices can be traced within musical practices, and how such practices can then be heard in the aesthetic that they create.

'Class? Oh God, Who Talks in That Way Anymore?': Theorizing Economic Inequality

The preceding quote from one of my participants, Megan, sums up the perspective of many of the middle-class young people in my study who saw themselves as 'normal' (see Savage 2000, 115–16). And yet, the county in which my research took place had one of the highest levels of youth inequality in the country. It is notable, then, that many of these young people did not have a ready vocabulary with which to discuss economic inequality. Indeed, defining and theorizing the intersections between economic, social, and cultural inequality has posed an ongoing challenge to social scientists. While economists tend to analyse inequality according to purely economic categories, sociologists have instead focused on the intersection of economic, social, and cultural forms of inequality (Savage 2014). Following a theoretical lineage from sociology, in this book I draw on an understanding of social classes as groups within society who have a common position in relation to the organization of production. These groups may over time, as a result of that common position, develop shared systems of value and common social identities, as well as forming links and associations (via marriage, friendship, leisure, work, and abode) with those who inhabit similar social positions. This understanding draws on Pierre Bourdieu's (1986) work on class in assuming that class is not purely an economic category, but that social and cultural resources also play a role in allowing people to reproduce their class position. Different forms of 'capital'—economic, social, cultural, and symbolic—can be accumulated and in some cases passed through generations in order to safeguard class position. Bourdieu's approach to class as relational, rather than hierarchical, is important to understanding the boundary-drawing work that can occur through cultural practices and tastes. In this theorization, people formulate their identities against others' identities, and the wealth of some is gained from the labour of others (Skeggs 2010).

Cultural practices and tastes can contribute to class reproduction by functioning as 'cultural capital': a resource that can be converted into social or economic advantage or forms of prestige. Music has been seen as the quintessential example of cultural capital (Bourdieu 1984, 18), but the extent to which knowledge of classical music still confers cultural capital in the UK today is somewhat unclear in existing research. Studies from the US and the UK (T. Bennett et al. 2008; Sullivan 2001; Yoshihara 2008) suggest that classical music's function as a form of capital may be limited to those who do not pursue it professionally but become proficient amateurs or consumers, and whose participation takes place through prestigious institutions. In addition, the extent to which classical music functions as cultural capital is likely to differ both between and within nation-states according to whether it is recognized as a high-status signal. The setting of this study in the south of England means that, while cultural capital may work in similar ways elsewhere in the world, there may also be important differences.

Debates around whether and how classical music confers cultural capital are not aided by the lack of clarity as to precisely what cultural capital is. Michèle Lamont and Annette Lareau (1988, 155) note a contradiction within the concept in that it can be defined either as giving access to and reproducing the dominant class or, alternatively, as an indicator or attribute of class. In this study, I take this as an empirical question, by asking in what ways young people's participation in classical music is simply an expression of class position, or in what ways it actively contributes towards retaining or improving one's class position. As Christina Scharff and I have argued (Bull and Scharff 2017), classical music has an unspoken value attached to it. Therefore, one way in which it could confer cultural capital is that those who are involved with it may be able to acquire some of this symbolic value, which could be converted into economic value.

Cultural tastes and practices are associated with other social divisions as well as class. Classical music consumption varies by age; for example, it is preferred by older people in the UK (Savage 2006, 170). These age differences may be because, as Prieur and Savage (2013), among others, have argued, traditional highbrow culture is in decline, and its role as capital is being supplanted by 'emerging cultural capital'. This term refers to new practices of distinction that are no longer characterized by the Kantian aesthetic of 'withdrawal, distance and discernment' (Friedman et al. 2015, 3) but by 'a knowing mode of appropriation of culture' (Prieur and Savage 2013, 256). In this mode, cultural capital is displayed not by knowledge of culture but by the way in which one talks about culture: using irony and other new aesthetic criteria of playfulness, eclecticism, and social reflexivity (Friedman et al. 2015, 3; Prieur and Savage 2013, 257). However, possession of 'emerging cultural capital' is still clearly patterned by class inequalities, whereby the cosmopolitan middle classes—the omnivores—have wide cultural tastes, while univores, who tend to be those from working-class backgrounds, participate in and consume fewer forms of culture (Miles and Sullivan 2012; Prieur and Savage 2013; Chan and Goldthorpe 2005, 2007). This book's focus on *young* people who are enthusiastic participants in high culture therefore raises the question as to whether classical music still functions as dominant or legitimate culture, and whether omnivores still classify different forms of culture in a hierarchy of value (Tampubolon 2010).

I theorize cultural capital broadly as any form of value that can be acquired through classical music practices. This study asks, therefore, whether and how participation in classical music contributes towards forming socially valued identities for young people. This sense of being a valued person may be captured by the measures of cultural capital described by Bourdieu (1986), but it may also include other mechanisms by which young people learn that who they are and what they do is valued by dominant groups in society. This theorization draws on work by Skeggs (2003, 2010), who explores how processes of classification create differently valued identities. Skeggs asks, 'How do certain bodies become *inscribed* and then marked with certain characteristics? ... Thus, how is value *attributed, accrued, institutionalized and lost* in the processes of exchange? And how is this value both *moral and economic?*' (2003, 2). The dual focus on the economic and the moral as intertwined is particularly helpful for studying music, a practice that is often constructed as morally ambiguous (see chapter 2). Skeggs argues that this sense of value, which is marked on some bodies and not others, generates self-worth. I therefore define value as a moral quality that is read onto certain bodies as *worth* that may have economic exchange value, and that is also experienced as a sense of self-worth.

What Bourdieu fails to recognize, notes Skeggs (2003), is that people in different class (and gender) positions have different levels of resources for producing the self. These differences have become more marked in recent decades following the heightened emphasis on ideas of crafting the self (Beck 1992; Gill 2007). For example, styles of 'intensive parenting' common to middle-class groups offer children a much wider range of opportunities to develop the 'reflexive self' that is valued by and common to middle-class groups (James et al. 2010, 632); as I will describe, classical music pedagogy and practices both rely on and reproduce this form of selfhood. Cultural practices such as music are, then, a resource for *producing* the self (DeNora 2006). Rather than seeing 'classical musician' as a given identity, this study therefore looks at how the practices and social relations of classical music allow young people to form themselves into this identity—an identity that is recognized and valued by others within this scene. Indeed, classical music is an ideal site to study future-oriented, accumulative self-making strategies, as it is a form of culture that requires a long-term investment of effort and resources to acquire the necessary skill level to play the instruments and repertoire.

Boundary-Drawing and Fear of Falling Among the Middle Classes

The middle classes have proven difficult to analyse theoretically because the boundaries around them are constantly challenged and contested by those below or above (Wacquant 1991). Their common economic position can, however, lead to shared practices and values; Barbara Ehrenreich (1990) entitles her book on the middle classes in the US *Fear of Falling*, as this fear, she suggests, is shared by those who have something to lose. One way to think of the middle classes is, then, as those who have acquired resources and assets that they need to store over time (Barlow et al. 1995). The extent to which this 'fear of falling' contributes towards a common culture, politics, or set of values is, however, an empirical question that varies across time and space.[1] Other commonalities across the

---

[1] In the US, the term 'middle class' has a different meaning, and the majority of the population tend to self-define as middle class even if they are on very low or high incomes (Pew Research Center 2008). As a result, the federal government's Middle Class Task Force under President Barack Obama defined the middle class by their aspirations rather than their income or occupations (US Department of Commerce, Economics and Statistics Administration 2010).

middle classes, as discussed later, can include the shared culture and values that are acquired through working in professional or skilled occupations and through having completed tertiary education. Studying the middle classes is therefore the study of struggles over boundaries, inclusions and exclusions to protected spaces, and the formation of collective identities within these spaces.

In the UK, Reay, Crozier, and James (2011) argue that there are commonalities within middle-class culture and identity that have remained constant over time. While the middle classes are far from being a homogeneous group, they tend to share 'a strong commitment to education as key to middle-class cultural reproduction' (Reay, Crozier, and James 2011, 19), and a 'particular set of values, commitments and moral stances' constituting a 'bourgeois self' can be identified (6). These values include 'a sense of responsibility, underpinned by individualism, combined with agentic citizenship and a propensity for choice', as well as ambition, a sense of entitlement, educational excellence, confidence, competitiveness, hard work, deferred gratification, and an ability to erect boundaries, both geographically and symbolically (12). Similarly, Skeggs identifies the 'bourgeois self' as a form of selfhood that is self-reliant, future-oriented, autonomous (rather than interdependent), and focused on accumulating value (Skeggs 2003). Both individualism and choice have been particularly emphasized in the last two to three decades as attributes of bourgeois identity that have become building blocks for a preferred type of subject under neoliberalism, a new sociopolitical regime whereby 'all dimensions of human life are cast in terms of a market rationality' (Brown 2009, 40; see also Scharff 2017, 114–17). This book, rather than focusing on this more recent development of classed subjectivity, draws on a longer history, examining how classical music draws on and reproduces forms of selfhood that can be traced back to the nineteenth century and that have similarities but also differences with neoliberal forms of selfhood.

Continuities in middle-class culture and identity over time that are important for this book are their commitment to education as a way of retaining their position across generations, and their boundary-drawing practices. The latter are visible in the ways in which the middle and upper classes have created their own enclaves through suburbanization and gentrification (Davidoff and Hall 2002; T. Butler and Robson 2003; Bacqué, Bridge, and Benson 2015), as well as in education through private schooling and middle-class colonization of parts of the state school system (Benson, Bridge, and Wilson 2014; Gamsu 2016; Reay 2004c). Michèle Lamont's (1992b) research examines this boundary-drawing in a comparative study of the upper middle classes in France and the US. While Bourdieu, writing about 1960s France, argued that cultural distinction was the main form of boundary-drawing around class, Lamont also reveals two other ways in which people make judgements of others: around morality and around money. 'Symbolic boundaries' were used by her participants to classify others and give informal advantage to people like them, leading to 'the exclusion of low status individuals, to discrimination, overselection or to their self-elimination' (1992b, 178).

Lamont's work leads us to pay attention not only to forms of cultural distinction but also to other ways in which the middle classes build and maintain symbolic, cultural, and economic boundaries around their privileged spaces. As noted in the introduction, I am drawing on the idea of middle-class boundary-drawing to theorize the *aesthetic* of classical music as another mechanism—similarly to education or suburbanization—for maintaining middle-class spaces. The technical requirements of classical music's repertoire, instruments, and ideals of beauty mean that those who are unwilling or unable to make the long-term investment needed to master these are unable to participate in classical music production. However, the discourse of 'autonomous art', which positions classical music outside of any social concerns as a universal form of beauty, camouflages this boundary-drawing much more effectively than other types of social investment, as there are powerful *musical* reasons for excluding those who have not invested in intensive, long-term tuition. Furthermore, the middle classes' common commitment to education as a way to retain their social position suggests that classical music education is a particularly good way of both signalling and reproducing class position. This investment in music education is made possible by the commonalities in parenting styles that have been observed across the middle classes, and it is to these I now turn.

'Intensive Parenting' and One-to-One Pedagogy

A large body of sociological research has detailed different parenting practices between class groups (Irwin and Elley 2011; Lareau 2011; Vincent et al. 2012a; Vincent and Ball 2007; Walkerdine, Lucey, and Melody 2001). Annette Lareau (2011), writing in a US context, describes the middle-class logic of parenting as 'concerted cultivation', whereby the child is conceived of as a project to be invested in for the future, accumulating resources, skills, and experiences that will shape the adult they are to become. By contrast, in the 'natural growth' model, which Lareau argues is more associated with working-class families, the child is assumed to already be whole in themselves, not requiring extra investment. For the middle classes, the investment that good parenting requires is brought about in part through extracurricular activities, which require large amounts of parental time and money.

An antecedent of such middle-class parenting practices can be found in the Suzuki method of music education, which emerged as a citizenship education programme in post-war Japan but was soon exported to the US (Yoshihara 2008). The Suzuki method can be seen as a prototype for 'intensive mothering', an 'emotionally demanding, financially draining, labour consuming' form of child-rearing that involves organizing the life of the mother around the child's needs and wants (Hays 1998, 4). As Yoshihara (2008) describes, the Suzuki method relies on a model of the family where a parent, usually the mother, has time to invest in learning music alongside the child, requiring them to attend lessons and sit with the child while they do their daily practice. As Clare Hall describes in her study of choirboys in Australia (Hall, 2018), musical ability or talent in classical music can be understood from a Bourdieusian perspective as the economic, social, and emotional investment over time by parents and teachers that shapes a 'musical' child, which overlaps with middle-class parents' desire to see their children as special and gifted (see also Byrne 2006, 1009; Reay 2004b). While individuals may have innate musical ability, this does not have any currency in the classical music world unless it is shaped through tuition and practice. Hall describes how narratives of 'musical mothering' downplay mothers' intensive involvement in their children's education to construct the boys' musical interest and ability as 'natural', reinforcing notions of innate talent (2018, 77, 91). Beatriz Ilari, in a study of musical activity among middle-class seven-year-olds across nine countries (including England), found 'traces' of 'concerted cultivation' in parental discourses in every country (2013, 193), suggesting that this patterning of music and class is common to the middle classes beyond the UK.

As this discussion shows, classical music's mode of pedagogy shares a logic with middle-class styles of parenting, and underpinning both is a shared a form of selfhood. To make this visible, the intensively shaped, individualized middle-class self described in sociological studies of classed parenting can be mapped onto the form of musical selfhood that is shaped through classical music pedagogy. For example, it is assumed in classical music education that in order to become 'musical', it is necessary to draw on expertise and specialist tuition, usually on a one-to-one basis. The self that is inscribed through most classical music education is constructed initially as an individual and is only then able to become relational; learning an instrument on a one-to-one basis is the starting point, supplemented by participation in ensembles. The recent defence of one-to-one instrumental tuition provoked by sexual abuse scandals in classical music education institutions draws on this ontology of personhood, with music educators claiming that the intimate trust that characterizes one-to-one teaching is 'extremely precious and extremely vulnerable', an 'almost sacred relationship' (Institute of Ideas 2013). Similarly, music grade exams assume that one's musical 'voice' has to be mastered individually, with the traditional exam model involving the assessment of an individual child/musician. In recent years, even one of the more conservative music education institutions, the Associated Board of the Royal Schools of Music (ABRSM), has introduced 'Music Medals' designed for pupils learning instruments through group tuition (D. Wright 2013, 238), but both parents and teachers have been resistant to this model. Wright suggests that there is a low take-up of these exams because parents see the traditional model of grade exams as a 'better investment' (240), and indeed, it fits more closely with individualized models of achievement and investment that underpin middle-class models of parenting. The contradictions within this form of subjectivity can be made visible through examining parenting practices around classical music. Bridget Byrne found that many of her interviewees in her study of middle-class mothers in London talked of their wish for their children to learn classical music. She suggests this expressed 'potentially contradictory desires within middle-classness' between 'notions of freedom and creativity, and order and control' (Byrne 2006, 1009), a schism within bourgeois selfhood that is fundamental to the political work of the aesthetic (as discussed later in this chapter).

Through its pedagogies and practices, an accumulative, autonomous, entitled middle-class self (Skeggs, 2003) is both assumed in classical music education and also *actively formed* through its norms. Crucially, Skeggs describes how this accumulation of resources 'must be about a projection into the future of a self/space/body with value. We only make investments in order to accrue value when we can conceive of a future in which that value can have a use' (2003, 146). The social value of classical music—and those who play it—needs to be assumed in order for an investment in it to make sense. This future orientation therefore constitutes a further affinity between classical music practice and a middle-class identity. How classical music's value is constituted and recognized is, therefore, one of the key questions this book addresses.

Gendered Possibilities and Constraints

In the UK, the valued identity that classical music confers is strongly influenced by middle-class gender norms. In studies of classical music and music education, young people's identities and opportunities have also been demonstrated to be strongly patterned by gender in relation to choice of musical instrument (Green 1997; Hallam, Rogers, and Creech 2008; Scharff 2017, 51); use of technology (Armstrong 2011; Born and Devine 2015); and teachers' attitudes towards male and female students (Armstrong 2011; Long et al. 2014). In classical music, these patterns occur within a powerfully gendered canon of repertoire (Citron 1993b; Legg 2012). Furthermore, Lucy Green argues that we hear gender within the music itself, in that 'the gender of a musical practitioner plays a large, and often unacknowledged, part in the discourse on music and in musical meaning' (1997, 16). This differs between women singers and instrumentalists; Green suggests that as singers, women's music-making tends 'to affirm and reproduce patriarchal definitions of femininity' (1997, 46) but as instrumentalists, 'depending not only on the instrument and the style of music that they are playing, but also on the degree of autonomy of the music', interruption of normative femininity may occur. The tuba, for example, is more disruptive of a feminine identity than the violin (1997, 80), and these instrumental identities also have historical associations with different class positions, the violin being associated with upper-class femininity in the 1880s and 1890s (Gillett 2000) and brass instruments with the male working-class brass band tradition (Etheridge 2012; Herbert 2000). The normative femininity Green describes is a middle-class (or aspirational middle-class) one; the labels that are applied to working-class women—of excess in their sexuality, their fecundity, their noise, and their taste or style (Nicholls 2018; Skeggs 1997)—would further undermine their ability to carry off a convincing performance of any kind of 'autonomous' music. Where excess is present in classical music, such as in arias sung by operatic heroines, it often signifies madness, evil, or otherwise illegible forms of femininity (McClary 2002).

These gendered and classed associations and patterns within musical practice need to be theorized together, as the expectations and possibilities involved in being female or male are different according to one's class position (Skeggs 1997). Therefore, in this study I understand gender as an identity or set of attributes that is learned and socially ascribed *within a particular social context*. The gender norms of the middle classes are often universalized or escape attention while the perceived gender attributes of working-class people are stigmatized or made visible (Skeggs 2003). For example, respectability is a moral category and a form of judgement through which class is produced in gendered ways by labelling working-class women as sexually deviant, morally questionable, and lacking restraint (Skeggs 1997).

This book argues one of the most important ways in which classical music is associated with the middle classes in the UK is through its signification of 'respectable' femininity, in that a 'respectable' middle-class female gender identity is both required for classical music and also performed by it. The historical formations of this identity, as well as the ways in which respectability encodes racialized inscriptions, are laid out in chapter 2. Today, then, playing classical music can counter negative 'othering' of stigmatized racial groups. For example, Rollock et al., in their study of Black middle-class parents in London, found they would enrol their children in lessons on orchestral instruments to counteract the 'deficient' Black stereotype, including the gender-specific '(perceived) Black male threat constant within wider society' (2015, 137). For East Asian classical musicians, different stereotypes have to be negotiated: that of the technically proficient automaton who is unable to attain true musicality (Yoshihara 2008; Leppänen 2015; see later in this chapter for a discussion of whiteness, as well as chapter 5).

It is important, therefore, to make white middle-class gender identities visible in their specificity. In Clare Hall's (2018) research, choirboys in Australia used their middle-class status to counter gendered ideals of singing and re-frame it as an appropriate activity for boys, a re-inscription that they could pull off only because of their class position. Within the constraints of these classed and gendered expectations, it is possible to find creative fulfilment; both Scharff (2017), in her research on early-career female classical musicians, and Armstrong (2013), in her work on freelance women musicians, found that classical music could be a space where women find an expressive voice. This book re-frames existing literature on music education and gender by foregrounding the intersection of class and gender, exploring the ways in which playing classical music (particularly string and keyboard instruments) is a way for young women to perform a 'respectable' femininity, and asking to what extent the constraints and expectations of normative middle-class femininity facilitate or inhibit young women's creative expression in classical music.

Fracturing the Middle Classes

While the middle classes can be seen to have certain attributes in common, including normative gender identities, there are also important differences between middle-class fractions.[2] These divisions can be examined horizontally, whereby different groups have similar amounts of capital or vertically, dividing the middle class into fractions with more or less capital overall. Three commonly discussed divisions are between public sector and private sector employees; between the managerial and professional middle classes; or into groups with different lengths of tenure in the middle class. In addition, Bourdieu's theory of the field of cultural production can be seen as an analysis of middle-class fractions. Bourdieu describes how the artistic field, which forms a dominated fraction of the dominant class, is organized into a division between autonomous art, or 'art for art's sake', which eschews commercial values and does not seek recognition in the market, and the heteronomous pole which does seek commercial rewards. In the artistic field, people follow different rules to those who seek recognition for political or economic power (Bourdieu 1983, 319). This field is characterized, therefore, by a struggle over how artistic work should be valued. The idea of valuing artistic self-realization and expression over commercial reward made sense to many of my participants. As a quintessential form of 'autonomous' art, classical music is a way for individuals to seek status within the dominant class, but a risky one. Bourdieu's model is helpful for showing how the non-economic logic of the artistic field intersects with class reproduction. However, this book lays out how this fracturing of the middle classes is structured by gender as well as class (see chapter 3 and the conclusion).

To understand my participants' capitals on entering the artistic field, I have divided them into three groups, drawing on an amended version of Reay, Crozier, and James' theorization of vertical middle-class fractions among their research participants based on historic class location (2011, 28–29). These groups are

---

[2] Sociology has recently turned its attention to examining elites, usually defined by wealth rather than the occupational, educational, and cultural measures of class I am using in this study (for example, R. Atkinson, Parker, and Burrows 2017, 2). Two, possibly three, of my participants could have been categorized as part of the elite, thanks to their parents' occupations and their own elite schooling. However, as the majority of my participants were middle class and the research took place outside London (the main playground for elites in the UK), my sample does not allow me to focus on the elite in any detail (however, see T. Bennett et al. (2008, chap. 5) for a discussion of elites and classical music consumption).

based on participants' parents' jobs and education; their own schooling and expectations for university and career; and their subjective understanding of their class position (see overview in the appendix). Easily a majority among my participants were in the first group, which comprised children of the professional middle classes, who tended to live in or near Whitchester, and whose parents (and sometimes grandparents) had attended university. I have labelled this group the 'professional middle class' to reflect the predominance of professional rather than managerial occupations (and therefore to signal a lineage with earlier work in this area, most notably Barlow et al. (1995)). The second group was formed of upper- and upper-middle class participants. This group, as well as a few participants from the professional middle-class group, had all attended private primary schools, but these young people also had other markers of upper-class status such as attending an elite school or possessing cosmopolitan or elite social capital. A third group comprised the children of the 'new' middle class, whose parents had joined the middle class as adults. These young people were more likely to live in rural areas or small towns beyond Whitchester. Their parents had not been to university, but the young people all had at least one parent who worked in a skilled occupation or had worked their way up into a management position. In addition, one participant, Andy, could be categorized as working class, and his perspective on classical music's culture proved to be particularly insightful as this culture was more alien to him than it was to many of the others. Andy, along with others in the new middle-class group, had not been exposed to classical music at home, and for these young people it took on a particular meaning, symbolizing entry into the 'proper middle class' as brass player Owen described. By contrast, for the professional middle-class and upper-middle-class young people, playing classical music was unremarkable and did not take them out of their usual social circles. For all of these class fractions, the provincial location of this study was formative of their identities; neither the new middle-class nor professional middle-class groups in my study exhibited the 'metropolitan habitus' that Tim Butler and Garry Robson (2003) identify as typical of London's middle classes, who valued the social mixing (including across ethnic identities) available in the city. In addition, these groups revealed divisions according to the type of instrument participants played: those in the new middle-class group were most likely to be brass players, while string players were almost exclusively from the professional middle-class or upper-middle-class group[3].

---

[3] Not all participants fitted neatly into these categories; in some cases parents were from different classes, and in a few cases marriage breakdowns inhibited easy classification (although by and large my sample was disproportionately made up of young people living with both their biological parents, thirty-one out of thirty-seven, or 84%, compared to two-thirds in the UK as a whole in 2012 (Press Association 2012)). In these cases, I made a judgement based on the profession of the more educated parent, alongside participants' own education and subjective sense of class.

The relative homogeneity of the social scene of classical music, formed predominantly of those in the professional, upper middle, or upper classes, was valued by my participants, who talked about being in a space with 'like-minded people', away from the 'chavvy'[4] spaces where some of them attended school (see chapter 3). Most did not go to 'chavvy' schools, however; a disproportionate number (sixteen, or 43%, compared to 7% in England as a whole) had attended independent school.[5] Only a handful did *not* attend a top-performing school or college for sixth form. Tertiary destinations were similarly ambitious. While one of my participants was considering joining the army as a musician, the rest were all enrolled in, or planning to attend, university or music conservatoires. Ten out of my thirty-seven interviewees were at Oxford or Cambridge universities, and three more were hoping to go there, and several others attended elite universities such as Durham, Manchester, and King's College London.

How do all of these details contribute towards understanding class? Barlow et al. (1995, xii) complain that research on the middle classes describes the fragmentation of this group but stops short of explaining how they are working as political actors to safeguard their privileged position. Similarly, Reay, Crozier, and James (2011) suggest that the middle classes are no longer committed to the common good and use their privilege to instigate exclusionary practices against losing their position. By exploring middle-class institutionalization of culture in the form of classical music education, the ways in which the middle classes use culture as a mechanism for boundary-drawing and social closure can be made visible. Exploring this question in an elite provincial town rather than in an urban setting gives a picture of a middle class who are less threatened, more homogeneous, and therefore more confident in their position than researchers have described among the urban middle classes (Reay, Crozier, and James 2011). Furthermore, by using music as a lens through which to examine this group, it is possible to move beyond discursive accounts of boundary-drawing to enable non-linguistic, embodied boundary-drawing practices to become visible.

---

[4] 'Chav' is a pejorative term for a white working-class person in the UK, similar to 'white trash' in the US or 'bogan' in Australia and New Zealand (Haslam 2014).

[5] This trend of disproportionate numbers of young classical musicians in Whitchestershire attending independent (fee-paying) schools was borne out in data I collected on schooling from the two orchestras in my study. In the New Symphony Orchestra, in the 2012 group twenty-seven musicians (55%) were at or had been to state schools, nineteen (39%) had been to independent schools, and three had been to both. In the county youth orchestra (in 2013), which had a more inclusive recruitment strategy as well as putting on free transport for those living further afield, a higher number (forty-six players, 78%) went to state schools, eleven (19%) went to independent schools, and two were homeschooled. Data from 2012–13 shows that the proportion of those studying at the five top UK conservatoires who graduated from independent and international schools was at least 24.4% (Scharff 2017, 46), which suggests that my sample is not atypical.

Studying Music as Culture

Georgina Born argues that music should be understood as a form of mediation rather than as an object, drawing on Deleuze's concept of the assemblage to argue that music has no essence but has to be understood 'as an aggregation of sonic, visual, discursive, social, corporeal, technological, and temporal mediations' (2017, 44). This approach allows a shift away from the usual ontology of classical music as 'autonomous' from the social and allows a focus on practices and discourses surrounding the music. Dress, venues, technologies, reviews, post-concert chat, and divisions of labour, to name just a few possibilities, are all part of classical music's 'assemblage' and contribute to its meaning. Discourses around classical music such as its 'universality', 'transcendence', or 'pure sound' also need to be analysed as one layer of meaning among others.

This theorization of music sets out an empirical and ontological basis for studying the relationship between a social group and its music. This topic has already been extensively discussed in relation to popular music and working-class subcultures. Central to this history is the Birmingham Centre for Contemporary Cultural Studies (CCCS) (Hebdige 1981; S. Hall and Jefferson 1993; Willis 1978). Within this tradition, Paul Willis (1978) looked at the subcultures of 'biker boys' and 'hippies' and their associated musics. He describes a homology between the heavy, on-the-beat rock music that the bikers consumed, and their embodied physicalities, symbolized by their motorbikes representing physicality, solidity, and strength: 'man's domination of the machine' (Willis 1978, 61). For Willis, the aesthetic qualities of the music contribute to the bikers' embodied affinity with it.

This approach—examining music as somehow reflecting the culture that creates or consumes it—has been heavily criticized for its reductionism (see, for example, Middleton (1990)); it takes music as a cultural superstructure that is determined by the economic infrastructure, rather than allowing for a more complex, two-way relationship between the material and the cultural. A more contingent and complex connection can be captured by Stuart Hall's idea of 'articulation'. Moving away from reductionist Marxist ideas of culture as fixed to a class position, articulation 'resist[s] expressive or reductive conceptions of ideology (or culture or discourse) in which specific ideas or ways of thinking [are] identified with a particular class location' (J. Clarke 2015, 277). Hall defines articulation as

> a connection or link which is not necessarily given in all cases, as a law or a fact of life, but which requires particular conditions of existence to appear at all, which has to be positively sustained by specific processes, which is not 'eternal' but has to be constantly renewed, which can under some circumstances disappear or be overthrown, leading to the old linkages being dissolved and new connections—re-articulations—being forged. (1985, 113)

There are two key elements to this concept, as John Clarke points out: 'both its contingency and the necessity of the work of production and maintenance' (2015, 277). This approach therefore requires an historically informed analysis of the associations between cultural and socio-economic formations. As chapter 2 explores, in the UK there are three key historical moments during which articulations between the middle classes and classical music were formed and also challenged. The first was the 1830s and 1840s, when the emerging industrial bourgeoisie began to establish classical music institutions, with varying degrees of openness and exclusion. At this stage the practices of classical music, such as the distinction between rehearsal and performance, and the conductor as autocrat rather than member of the group, were starting to become codified into the forms we are familiar with today, and the relationship between music-as-art and class groupings was loosely formed and therefore still highly contingent. The second key moment was the 1880s and 1890s, when key institutions in classical music education were established and the sacralization of music as art was entrenched. Silent listening was established as the norm, and musical knowledge began to be credentialized in the form of grade exams. Again at this point, links between the middle classes and this emerging genre were contested, but the boundary-drawing practices that typify middle-class subjectivity were clearly visible in discourses, institutions, and practices. The third moment of contestation was between the late 1950s and the 1970s, when there was another wave of institution-building around music education, including the establishment of local authority music services. Coinciding with challenges to the practices and canon of classical music such as the Fluxus movement, at this point the 'articulation' with class was particularly contingent, and so it would be helpful to explore further how the articulation between the middle classes and classical music was disrupted during this period. However, the strong codification of classical music's practices and the authority of its nineteenth-century institutions were not seriously challenged, and this period of greater openness did not lead to significant changes. Instead, sub-genres of classical music such as early music and 'contemporary classical music' splintered off, with their own classed and gendered articulations, and the canonic 'greats', along with the institutions that ensured their continuing sacralization, were left untouched.

The 'articulation' between classical music and class in this brief history shows a more complex relationship than simply an homology between the middle classes and classical music. This relationship is contingent but resilient, and deeply intertwined with processes of institutionalization. It is also necessary, however, to explore the role of classical music's aesthetic in this relationship. Returning to Willis' work, despite his overstatement of the 'homology' between music and class, his attention to the aesthetic qualities of the music as part of a social analysis is an important contribution. More recently, this approach has been labelled the 'social aesthetic' (Friedman 2014a; Hanquinet, Roose, and Savage 2014; Hanquinet and Savage 2015; Olcese and Savage 2015). Along the same lines, Mark Banks has recently argued that we need to do justice to the 'internal goods' of the cultural object itself, as these 'goods' (such as the desire to make beautiful objects) are part of the justification given by cultural workers for doing this work (2017, 48, 146). Others have argued that scholarly engagement with music must also address aesthetic pleasure, examining how this is constructed and what social effects it has (Wolff 1993; Hennion 2001). Music studies has much to offer in this field, as several decades of scholars have tried to reconcile the question of how social relations can be traced in the sounds of a particular culture (Feld 1990; Middleton 1990). Neglecting the specificity of the cultural object also obscures the possibility that it might itself have agentic properties that play a role in shaping the social relations through which people engage with it; as DeNora notes, different kinds of music have their own 'affordances' such that some music might inspire people to dance while other music might be conducive to contemplation (Born 2010, 178; DeNora 2000).

Important work on what might be described as the 'social aesthetic' of classical music has been carried out by musicologists Susan McClary and Marcia Citron on the subjectivities of tonality. For McClary, there is indeed a bourgeois aesthetic; classical music is 'shape[d] in terms of bourgeois ideology', with 'its goal orientation, obsessive control of greater and greater spans of time, its wilful striving, delayed gratification and defiance of norms' (McClary 1989, 58; McClary 2001, 2002). Similarly, Citron (1993a) suggests that sonata form, probably the most widely used musical structure in classical music's canon, encodes the gendered structures of nineteenth-century white middle- and upper-class culture within its musical form. Citron describes how sonata form opens with the first or 'masculine' subject, and following this the second or 'feminine' subject introduces a new key centre. The second subject 'needs to be tamed, resolved, brought back to the original key' of the 'masculine' or primary subject whereby 'the element of Otherness is neutralized by the prevailing masculine order' (1993a, 21). The feminine is, in this way, subsumed or assimilated into the 'masculine' tonal centre of the first subject.

While for Citron, this otherness is about gender, I would suggest that it can apply to all forms of otherness from the white, masculine bourgeois self; and indeed, as McClintock (1995) has argued, gendered, classed, and racialized forms of otherness were co-produced under colonialism. Indeed, even the use of the word 'subject' to refer to musical material, as well as to the individual self around whose harmonic journey the musical material is organized, points to a reading of musical and political subjects as analogous (Citron 1993a, 21). These socio-musical readings of classical music's material can be read in dialogue with Skeggs' (2003) theorization of the resourced, entitled, accumulative middle-class self, as well as Reay, Crozier, and James' (2011) description of the boundary-drawing, individualistic, competitive, and yet hard-working and responsible 'bourgeois self', as described earlier. Does the journey of the musical subject—the models of organizing time, otherness, and subjectivity—filter through into the experience of the social subject who plays or listens to this music? These social and musical readings of bourgeois culture have not been examined empirically in dialogue with one another, but they suggest a homology between the aesthetic of classical music and bourgeois subjectivity.

As chapters 5, 7, and 8 explore, the aesthetic of classical music intersects in a variety of ways with white bourgeois subjectivities. While this can sometimes form a homology with the aesthetic material itself, following McClary's and Citron's readings, this book will outline how this occurs in uneven and unpredictable ways. However, one of the key theoretical interventions of this book is that the aesthetic of classical music can be analysed socially through examining the practices required to produce it. Over time, certain practices and forms of subjectivity that are common to the middle classes—and especially certain fractions of the middle class—have come to be codified and institutionalized into the practices required for playing (and, to a lesser extent, listening) to classical music. Its aesthetic of precision and accuracy, its modes of social organization, the difficulty of its instruments and repertoire, and the ways of working with the body to produce sound all require particular practices that have similarities with the values and dispositions, historically and today, of the middle classes.

Classical Music's Mediations of the Social

In order to examine the 'articulation' between classical music and the middle classes in more detail, Born's theorization that music can reflect, refract, or reverse social formations via four 'planes' of social mediation is generative (2012, 266; 2017, 43). In this section I discuss aspects of existing empirical research on classical music in order to draw out an emerging theorization of classical music's 'articulation' with class. In Born's first 'plane', the microsocialities of musical performance and practice in face-to-face interactions are examined. An example of this kind of analysis can be seen in Henry Kingsbury's (1988) classic ethnography of a music conservatoire in the US in which he describes how the social authority of the teacher/master is used to mediate the musical score. This authority, as Kingsbury details, is intertwined with the intimate personal relationships within with a student's musicality is developed (1988, 72). This focus on intimacy and interdependence in classical music is borne out in studies that examine the one-to-one teaching relationship (Haddon 2011; Sagiv and Hall 2015; Wagner 2015), showing the ways in which individualism—historically a bourgeois trait—is both assumed and reproduced in classical music pedagogy. However, the broader social and historical patterns that shape such interactions are not often drawn out in studies that foreground face-to-face interactions.

The second way in which Born suggests that music can mediate the social is through bringing into being imagined communities. In studies of classical music these often take the form of a utopian social ideal that is achieved through musical practice, featuring the orchestra as an idealized community. Examples include the conflict-free vision of the Middle East that is brought into being by the West-Eastern Divan Orchestra (Beckles Willson 2009), or the orchestra as creating a world free from inequality in El Sistema–inspired programmes, as discussed in the introduction (Baker 2014; Bull 2016a). Indeed, the proliferation of El Sistema–inspired programmes around the world suggests that this fantasy is an appealing one to classical musicians, and that is could be a response to living in a world where people are aware of inequality but may feel powerless to address it.

A third 'plane of mediation' between music and the social is via the 'institutional forces that provide the basis for [music's] production, reproduction and transformation' (Born 2017, 43). Classical music's inherited ecology of wealthy and powerful institutions accrues economic resources, from the state as well as through philanthropy, to guard and reproduce its value, and as such these institutions require much more critical attention from academic researchers. Existing studies of classical music's institutions often foreground contestations over value or quality, as in Lisa McCormick's (2015) ethnography of classical music competitions which describes the elaborate mechanisms used by judges for determining excellence and the vigorous deliberation among audiences. In Philip Bohlman's study of classical music in Israel, institutionalization was an important way in which classical music became central to Israeli cultural life, facilitating the European culture of this group of Jewish immigrants to become part of Israel's national culture (1989, chap. 5).

A final way in which classical music mediates the social is through 'refracting' social identity categories, including class, race, gender, religion, or sexuality; music may not form a direct relationship with social identities, but instead social identity and musical culture may inflect each other in complex ways. Studies examining social class and the culture of classical music have found, similarly to other middle-class sites such as the UK civil service and higher education (Loveday 2015; Puwar 2004), that classical musicians who are from working-class or lower-middle-class backgrounds can feel 'intimidated' or like an 'outsider' (Scharff 2017, 89–90; see also Yoshihara 2008, 137–38). However, Dibben's study of music students at a 'redbrick' university in the UK found that a strong sense of belonging could be attained if a musician from a non-middle-class background was willing to 'make a fresh start' and try to 'better oneself' (2006, 111). This process is, Dibben argues, inhibited by the Western art music curriculum, which reinforces and reproduces the norm of middle-classness (93).

Despite these complex negotiations of difference/belonging, class appears to remain unspoken; Scharff found that class was invisible to the early-career female classical musicians in her study, who spoke of the advantage of coming from a 'musical family', but implicit in this designation was that 'musical families' were also middle-class families (Bull and Scharff 2017). Similarly, in Clare Hall's (2018) Bourdieusian study of boy choristers in Australia, she found a structural 'fit' between the boys' families and the cathedral choir; parents recognized this choir as a suitable social world for middle-class boys. For Yoshihara, in her study of Asian American classical musicians, class was difficult to analyse in relation to musicians' occupational position, as 'the economic lives of most classical musicians are fraught with contradictions. As core members of the cultural elite and workers selling their labor, they possess scarce skills and expertise, but they generally have limited control in the workplace' (2008, 133). However, by examining their practices of distinction they could be seen to

> position themselves explicitly and implicitly in opposition both to those above and below them in the socioeconomic structure by articulating the emphasis they and their families have placed on discipline, education, and the accumulation of cultural capital and by distancing themselves from the materialist pursuit of wealth and commercially driven culture. (Yoshihara 2008, 165)

The sense of musicians as having a distinctive identity separate from the rest of society fits with a Bourdieusian notion of musicians as gaining capital through investing in 'autonomous' art that has a different logic to the marketplace. It also underlines the interaction of the moral and the economic in studies of class, by emphasizing the boundary-drawing by which musicians stake out a space for themselves within the middle class.

Born notes that these different levels at which the social can 'enter into the musical assemblage' are 'invariably treated separately in discussions of music and the social' (2017, 43), and much of the existing literature on classical music in practice does not address all four planes. By contrast, the approach I take in this study draws together these four levels of analysis, bringing the microsocial practices and imaginary identifications of classical music into dialogue with the meso- and macro-level patterns that can be observed across its institutions and social structures.

The Value of Classical Music

Classical music's face-to-face, imaginary, institutional, and social identity formations can be drawn together through the concept of value, by asking whose norms, tastes, and culture are valued or devalued within cultures of classical music practice. Earlier, I introduced Skeggs' concept of value to theorize classed identities. Here, I return to the question of value in relation to classical music specifically. The ways in which classical music is valued over other genres of music have been examined by Lucy Green, in her study of British secondary school music teachers in the 1980s and 1990s. She found that classical music and popular music were both taught in relation to the values which were ascribed to classical music, of its universality, autonomy from social concerns, complexity, and originality (Green

2003, 15). When popular music was taught, it was 'in ways that implicitly rendered it inferior to classical music' by focusing on its extra-musical qualities, while classical music was taught in relation to its 'inherent' musical qualities (16). While music tuition within schools in the UK has changed substantially since this research, in large part as a result of Green's own work on informal pedagogies, her findings are still relevant for understanding how classical music's value is constructed, and its classed effects. Green goes on to argue that the 'ideology that classical music is the most valuable type of music' means that it is seen 'as being equally relevant for all children, even though it clearly does not correspond with the musical tastes, values and experiences of them all' (17); indeed, the recent proliferation of El Sistema–inspired programmes suggests that this belief is still powerful.

Green's discussion of value makes sense of patterns of participation in instrumental music tuition and classical music education. As noted in the introduction, a recent ABRSM report mapped clear differences across social classes in instrumental tuition and found that the most common reason for stopping instrumental lessons was 'lack of interest' rather than financial barriers (Hume and Wells 2014, 19). For many young people, it appears that being unable to learn the types of music they value is as, or more important in discouraging musical participation than financial barriers. This is borne out in studies of young people's music-making in and out of school which have found that young people spend a lot of time listening to or playing music outside of school, but this enthusiasm often is not carried over into the classroom because the kinds of music they enjoy are not included in the school curriculum; as Stahl, Burnard, and Perkins describe, 'individuals become agentic within fields where they feel they have value' (2017, 65; Hargreaves and Marshall 2003; A. Lamont et al. 2003). These links between in-school and out-of-school music are described by Philpott as the 'double life of music education' whereby it exists both within the national curriculum and in students' leisure activities. Success within school can be therefore be boosted for those who participate in music out of school (Philpott 2010, 156).

Therefore, given that the A-level music syllabus[6] relies on knowledge of staff notation and performance and composition based on the Western classical tradition (Born and Devine 2015), knowledge of classical music is more efficacious in this 'double life' than other genres. Indeed, debates around school music education curricula can also make visible the relative value of classical music compared to other genres. In the UK in the 1980s, the introduction of a national curriculum for music led to justifications of classical music's superiority to other genres, with advocates claiming that 'not all music is equally good, equally civilising, equally humane' (Shepherd and Vulliamy 1994, 34). As Ruth Wright and Brian Davies note, in this curriculum 'the cultural capital of the middle classes was placed at

---

[6] This is the qualification taken by seventeen-to-eighteen-year-olds in England, Wales, and Northern Ireland.

the centre of the national curriculum for music' (2010, 41). The revision of the national curriculum and the introduction of the 2012 National Plan for Music Education have led to similar contestations over value. Robert Legg describes the recent changes to the national curriculum for music in England as 'a shift away from a skills-based curriculum toward one driven by the transmission of canonic knowledge' (2012, 158). Spruce argues that the National Plan prioritizes Western classical music, noting that it contains an 'almost exclusive focus on performing' (2013, 29, with musical progression framed in terms of developing performance skills rather than a focus on improvising, creativity, or composing. Within the National Plan, these skills are usually exemplified with reference to groups associated with Western musical practices such as choirs, bands, and orchestras, and case studies used are of Western art music (Spruce 2013, 29; see also Philpott and Spruce 2012).

These questions about how classical music's perceived value is upheld and how it affects the status of other genres of music within school music need to be connected into broader questions of how classical music participation signifies a valued social identity. In order for classical music's institutions to diversify and evolve, it is necessary to understand how its value is constructed. Green's (2003) identification of its discourses of universality, autonomy from social concerns, complexity, and originality points towards an analysis of how musical qualities that are perceived as valuable might also contribute towards social value. However, while some aspects of classical music's value are gained through its classed distinction, its value cannot be reduced to processes of distinction alone but needs to engage on all four of Born's levels of mediation, including the distinctive experience of listening to and playing it.

Evading Homologies: The Ideology of the Aesthetic

So far, the evidence put forward has suggested a contingent homology between the middle classes and classical music as a cultural practice. However, it is also necessary to explore ways in which this homology may be disrupted; indeed, as Born suggests, the imagined identifications of a musical scene may refract or reverse the actual social relations that are played out within it (2012, 270). These ideas require an historical detour to the turn of the nineteenth century, via Terry Eagleton's (1990) theorization of 'ideology of the aesthetic' as well as Lydia Goehr's (1992) related idea of the 'work-concept'. Goehr describes how in the late eighteenth century an ideology emerged in which a piece of music was thought to exist as a unified whole, separately from whoever performed it, who commissioned it, and the function for which it was performed. This is what she calls the 'work-concept'. Since around 1800 this concept has structured the idea of music-as-art and the power relations between composer, performer, and audience (Goehr 1992, 232).

The developments in the musical aesthetic that Goehr discusses are situated against a wider horizon by Eagleton's (1990) work. Eagleton also examines the development of 'autonomous art' or 'art for art's sake' in the late eighteenth and early nineteenth centuries and contextualizes this within the development of class society under capitalism. He addresses the question of how society hangs together under capitalism when earlier mechanisms for producing social solidarity have been lost and capitalism has undermined social cohesion through demanding individualism and competition. With earlier, more coercive forms of social control lessened (at least for the bourgeoisie), why should they continue to follow social rules and norms rather than pursue their own economic advantage? Eagleton argues that the new realm of the 'aesthetic'—autonomous art—was crucial in gaining people's consent for the new political order of class society as well as providing cohesion and meaning to the new bourgeois class. The aesthetic provided a realm of freedom outside the everyday world where the bourgeoisie could gain relief from their usual individualistic, competitive lives and experience a sense of community that bourgeois society lacks. The aesthetic does this through colonizing the senses and the body—by going outside the usual sphere of rationality within which the bourgeoisie operate—and implanting itself directly into subjectivity. However, this is experienced by the subject as 'something I just happen to feel' (Eagleton 1988, 333), not as political power acting on oneself. It feels, instead, as though this sense of 'rightness' is coming from the depths of one's own soul in responding to the beauty of an apparently universal aesthetic (333).

But, Eagleton argues, the aesthetic is not simply a handmaiden of capitalism; it also carries within it a critique of bourgeois values because it provides a vision of how the world could be different. In this way, the aesthetic (including classical music) works as a safety net or a pressure valve for upholding bourgeois values but also carries the possibility of destabilizing these values, as people experience social solidarity and embodied pleasure in the aesthetic realm which they might then carry over into everyday life, disrupting capitalism. David Clarke's argument for a more nuanced version of musical autonomy supports this dialectical position, arguing for 'a more mutable, pliable construction of autonomy' (2012, 182). In short, Clarke suggests that we *also* pay attention to the space of freedom and critique that Eagleton argues is intrinsic to the aesthetic.

Eagleton's work needs to be read critically in light of the ways in which the body has been re-theorized in social theory over the last twenty-five years (Blackman 2008). What is generative in his work for this study and is explored throughout the book, however, is his dialectical approach in which the aesthetic both upholds the hegemony of the new class society and also provides a space where its antithesis can be experienced—where all the individualism, competitiveness, isolation, and loneliness of being an independent autonomous subject can be negated and lost in communal sensory experience. This experience of 'intimately interpersonal Gemeinschaft' or community upholds the existing society by providing a safety valve where dreams of freedom, safety, ineffability, and transcendence can exist untrammelled (Eagleton 1988, 332). However, its effects are unpredictable; while the aesthetic sometimes works to uphold class society, this experience of freedom can also threaten it precisely by providing an alternative, emancipatory vision of community. In order to draw these ideas together, in chapter 8 I introduce the phrase 'community-in-sound', which describes both the sensory experience of being in sound and also the idea of community as an oppositional space to everyday socialities. This allows a theorization of classical music as having an homology with bourgeois values while also providing a space where their opposite can be experienced.

Classical Music as Bodily Practice

Eagleton ends his tour de force on the aesthetic by arguing that we need to 'think everything through again in terms of the body' (1988, 337). Classical music is, after all, a bodily craft practice as well as a practice that takes place between bodies, despite discourses that it 'transcend[s]' the bodily (Julian Johnson 2002, 112). In order to bring the body into an understanding of classical music, I use the idea of practice, or what people *do*, to foreground embodied activity. There is also a useful epistemological congruence between meanings of musical and social practice; musicians talk of 'doing their practice', the daily discipline of maintaining and improving one's skills. Practising is both a taken-for-granted part of life as a classical musician and also reveals wider assumptions about how to live one's life.

Three meanings of practice are relevant here: firstly, a nearly obsolete usage, 'to devise means to bring about (a result); ... to plan, scheme, intend' (OED 2006). This shows a link with the strategic, future-oriented identity, particularly of bourgeois parents, as identified earlier in this chapter. This is Bourdieu's theorization of practice, and he also uses the concept to theorize uncertainty, in that actors' strategies over time will have uncertain outcomes. As he describes it, 'practice is constructed in time. Time ... gives it ... its direction and meaning' (Bourdieu 1990, 98). This theorization is particularly useful for examining musical practices because of the possibility of the accumulation of skills that can be stored in the body. In classical music practice there is a strong future orientation of skills accumulation, which highlights the potential for using 'practice' strategically. Practice also assumes an actor who knows what to do within their field; for Bourdieu this 'feel for the game' (1990, 66) is conceptualized as the 'habitus', the semi-conscious sense of what is possible or not possible for someone in a particular social position. The habitus has been criticized for being over-deterministic, leaving insufficient space for transformation (Shilling 2004); I share these concerns and therefore use the concept more in the sense of a disposition (Bourdieu 1977, 214) rather than a strictly 'structuring structure' (72).

Secondly, practice refers to an ethical stance: 'to live or act according to a principle or the set of principles one advocates' (OED 2006), foregrounding the moral dimension of musical practice and the sense of self-realization and self-improvement associated with maintaining a practice regime. This sense is overlooked by relying solely on a Bourdieusian framing, but the ethical dimension of musical practice was important to the young musicians in this study, as chapter 4 explores.

A final meaning of 'practice' is 'to observe (a religious duty), to perform (a rite)' (OED 2006). This draws attention to historical similarities between religious and musical practice that can help to understand the body in classical music. Indeed, the dialogue between classical music's growing institutionalization in the UK in the nineteenth century and parallel forms of emergent bourgeois selfhood suggest that classical music could even be theorized, historically, as a Protestant sect (see also Subotnik 1991, 148). As Davidoff and Hall describe, the emergence of evangelical religion in the early nineteenth century was a formative influence on the development of middle-class values (2002, 77). Churchgoing was a predominantly middle-class pursuit, a key component of respectability (76), and religious practices inflected developing bourgeois social norms: 'religious belief gave confidence as to how to behave, how to know what was right or wrong'. While each sect drew on different fractions of the middle class and had different doctrines, the moral and social issues that were contested within these religious movements are the same as those that were at play in moral debates around music, as chapter 2 explores: pleasure, self-control, bodily decorum, and social hierarchies (92, 96).

Many of these contestations around morality related to bodily practice and can be framed within a more long-term historical shift around changing ideas of the body following the Reformation. As Mellor and Shilling argue, the medieval experience of the sacred was a sensuous one (1997, 8), but the Reformation removed the sacred from everyday life and located it *outside* the body in a sublime realm (3). Religious texts became an important mediating device for sensory experience, and emotionality 'was constrained and mediated by a thoroughgoing cognitive control' (99). This idea of the sacred as located outside the body in a transcendent realm, mediated by a written text, is crucial to my theorization of the body in classical music practice; the body must be both disciplined and at the same time effaced or transcended, and bodily experience is mediated by the written text. Yoshihara's ethnographic study of Asian American classical musicians supports this reading, describing how 'composers and compositions are grounded territorially, historically, and culturally', but the performers are 'largely disembodied' (2008, 190). Musicologist Julian Johnson, as well as suggesting classical music helps us 'transcend' the bodily, argues that 'we insist on being more than physical objects; we insist on our identity as something intangible and irreducible to physicality, even while our being is rooted in it' (2002, 112). Indeed, the reverent approach to the authoritative text of the composer, giving composers godlike or saintly status, has been noted by various authors (Leech-Wilkinson 2016; Nettl 1995).

Bodily practices in classical music practice are distinguished by the requirement for cognitive control, a process that the use of written texts facilitates or even requires. This prioritization of the 'thinker' is explored by Ruth Gustafson (2009) in her history of music education curricula in the United States. Gustafson, explaining ongoing patterns of informal exclusion of people of colour in US music classrooms, argues that preferences exhibited in music education texts for the 'thinker' and the upper body contribute to these patterns of racial exclusion. She demonstrates how the tradition of 'cultivated' listening favours immobility over bodily movement (Gustafson 2009, 1; see also chapter 5), and the bel canto aesthetic (the type of singing required for classical music) emphasizes the head as the site of vocal control while discouraging rhythmic gesturing or bodily accentuation of any kind (Gustafson 2009, 128). Through these and other mechanisms, a racialized aesthetic is created whereby 'whiteness pervades models for singing and listening' (2). This contrasts with the aesthetic values that are socially acquired by black singers in the US, who are obliged to change their mode of vocal production in order to participate in formal music education and classical music (146).

My theorization of the body in classical music is, therefore, also a theorization of how whiteness is embodied. This is a Protestant, imperialist strand of whiteness, bearing a strong resemblance to representations of whiteness in film, which, as Richard Dyer (1997) argues, draw on elements from Christianity and imperialism. He draws out the same link as Mellor and Shilling of the sacred as existing outside the body, arguing that representations of whiteness suggest that 'what makes whites different ... is their potential to transcend their raced bodies', 'a need to always be everything and nothing, literally overwhelmingly present and yet apparently absent' (Dyer 1997, 15). Dyer further posits a link between whiteness and imperialism or enterprise: 'The white spirit organises white flesh and in turn non-white flesh and other material matters: it has enterprise' (15). McClintock draws out the racialized dimensions of this quality by outlining the nineteenth-century imperialist discourse of 'idleness of the blacks' (1995, 252) which is opposed to the dynamic, enterprising spirit of whiteness. This mode of organizing, or control, can be read onto the dynamic of accumulation, investment, and future orientation which is necessary to classical music practice. As explored in chapter 4, hard work over a long period of time is integral to classical music's repertoire and instruments. This could be argued to extend to the aesthetics of the music as well; the work-concept (Goehr 1992; Citron 1993b, 122) demands a sense of control over past and future to understand how it unfolds over time.

There are, then, powerful congruences between ideas of whiteness, Christian ideas of the body, and the way the body is experienced in classical music practice: cognitive control is essential; text is supreme; the body must be disciplined; the sacred or transcendent is located outside the body; and the fleshly body does not make sense and must be effaced. This Christian 'mystery' of the body as both present and absent gives a template for the way in which classical music works as a cultural technology that disciplines but also effaces or transcends the body.

And yet, this disciplined body is still able to communicate, despite the sense that the self is bounded and autonomous. It is for this reason that it is necessary to move beyond Bourdieusian theorizations of habitus and practice and introduce a theory of communication between bodies that has come to be theorized in the social and biological sciences as 'affect'. As Gregg and Seigworth define it, 'affect is found in those intensities that pass body to body'; it 'is the name we give to those forces ... *other than* conscious knowing' (2010, 1). In classical music practice, powerful intensities are cultivated; they are inscribed into the texts of this music which musicians must bring into sound through bodily movement. The habits learnt through classical music create and naturalize the bounded autonomous subject which, ironically, should not be susceptible to these processes of affective communication. But musicians are also allowing themselves to let go of their individual, isolated self to experience being affected by these intensities. Most importantly for theorizing affect, we can then *hear* these affects in sound, externalized through our movements, our breath, our communication with the bodies around us.

Conclusion

This chapter has outlined a new socio-cultural theorization of classical music and class. While the relationship between the British middle classes and the production of classical music is contingent rather than absolute, there are also clear patterns. I theorize this link between classical music and class in terms of value, which can be both economic and moral. Music is a resource for producing a valued middle-class self that in turn reproduces structures of inequality. This builds on Tia DeNora's (2000, 2006) work on music's role in self-making at the level of the individual by analysing how these processes are embedded in broader power structures. One of the ways in which this valued self is produced is through 'intensive parenting' (Faircloth 2014). Classical music education shares a logic with middle-class parenting styles, whereby both require high levels of adult investment on an individual basis and focus on what the child will become in the future. This symbiosis can be explained because classical music's norms both assume and create the accumulative, autonomous, entitled middle-class self. This form of selfhood can be linked historically, and today, with forms of whiteness associated with Protestant imperialism, and also has distinctive gender identities associated with it, most notably 'respectable' femininity. Some of the practices and forms of subjectivity associated with this identity—particularly what I am calling the professional middle class—have been institutionalized into the practices required for playing and listening to classical music. Analysing practices as *classed* practices allows the aesthetic qualities of classical music to be incorporated into a sociological reading, through analysing the practices that are required to produce it. This analysis needs to take place in dialogue with musicological readings of classical music works that have identified bourgeois or gendered qualities in the musical material itself.

My theorization also identifies contradictions within classical music practice, including ways in which the homology between classical music and the middle classes is disrupted, and indeed it is necessary to foreground these contradictions in order to make sense of its enduring value. For example, classical music is an exemplary form of the aesthetic under capitalism, as it both upholds class boundaries and also relies on a fantasy of community. In addition, classical music both disciplines and effaces the body. Finally, classical music exemplifies the porous body as theorized in affect theory, and yet its practices help to create the experience and ideal of the autonomous, bounded individual.

Existing scholarly work on classical music has attempted little explanation of classical music's patterns of social inequality. Indeed, sociological work on music has not usually encompassed all of Born's four 'planes' of mediation. Exceptions include Yoshihara (2008) and Gustafson (2009), but while these authors start with race, my study foregrounds an intersectional, historically informed understanding of class in order to explain patterns of inequality in classical music more widely. Furthermore, by taking the UK as the setting, I provide a starting point for analysing the influence of Britain's classical music institutions across the world (D. Wright 2013; Johnson-Hill 2015). The approach I have laid out in this chapter could also be applied to other genres of music, in order to ask how musical institutions, practices, and aesthetics are shaped by, and in turn contribute towards, wider conditions of economic inequality.

Across the next three chapters, I examine boundary-drawing around class through classical music's practices and institutions in the nineteenth century and today, foregrounding the ways in which this boundary-drawing has entered the music as a sense—and a sound—of 'rightness'. Chapter 2 sets up the landscape or 'ecology' for the classical music 'world' into which my participants enter. Critically examining the historical formation of this 'ecology', it examines how the boundary-drawing around morality that was visible in the late Victorian period was institutionalized into classical music practices in the late nineteenth century, and today shapes the tradition of practice that my participants encountered.

CHAPTER 2

Boundary-Drawing around the Proper

FROM THE VICTORIANS TO THE PRESENT

Eighteen-year-old Owen's biography tells the story of a journey between two worlds. He comes from a lower-middle-class town about fifteen miles outside Whitchester, where he attended primary and secondary school. His parents are not university educated but met while training as accountants and now work for public and educational institutions. When I asked Owen what he thought his class position was, he gave an astute description of the differences between people in his home town and the people he'd met through playing classical music and through attending a sixth form college in Whitchester at age seventeen: 'We're not a particularly middle-class family I don't think. Certainly coming here to Whitchester sixth form college has opened my eyes to proper middle-class people'. By contrast, where he grew up, 'we're all very much in the same kind of boat, working-class, lower-middle-class kind of kids.... There's no real, um, I suppose you'd say proper middle-class people, certainly not in the football team anyway'.

Owen had been a keen footballer as a child, but despite growing up in a family that he described as 'not musical at all', he started learning the tenor horn at his primary school. At age thirteen he joined the local Royal Air Force band and was given a French horn to learn on the job—a pedagogic model common in brass bands that is very different to the usual one-to-one teaching model in classical music. He started going to a Saturday morning music school run by the local authority music service and joined an orchestra there. Through a friend he heard about the Junior Guildhall, a prestigious Saturday scheme run by one of the London music colleges, and auditioned when he was fifteen. When I met him, he had recently been accepted into the National Youth Orchestra and described himself as 'irritatingly passionate' about classical music. He was excited about his plans to do a music degree at a prestigious university, followed by a postgraduate course at a conservatoire which he hoped would lead to an orchestral career.

Owen was thus able to draw on considerable opportunities and resources available through what I will call the 'institutional ecology' of classical music—the framework of organizations that make up the classical music world. This had equipped him with the skills he needed to join the most elite youth orchestra in the country. Unusually for a classical musician, this had occurred without any particular parental input, a route that is more common to brass players, for whom it is possible to start learning in later childhood or as a teenager and still pursue a professional career. What is especially interesting is how Owen contrasts his first extracurricular interest, football, with his subsequent musical involvement:

> I mean football's obviously fantastic, I'm still a big supporter [of my local team], but I don't think it would've opened any doors to me, it would've just been a hobby, I would've ended up doing some other job, maybe that I hated, so I think the fact that I can, you know, I've picked up this hobby and I can actually continue it as a career, I can actually build my life around it, I think [is] better.

In this way, Owen narrates his unusual trajectory from the lower-middle-class town where he played football to the 'proper middle-class' world of youth classical music. This chapter takes Owen's story as a starting point to explore the layers of institutions that constitute this exciting world of possibilities for him and consider how the history of this 'institutional ecology' contributes towards drawing boundaries between who is allowed entry into the 'proper middle class' and who is not. An important, if unremarked, part of Owen's account is his gender, which strongly patterns instrument choice (Scharff 2017, 51) and therefore contributed to the class mobility that he experienced through classical music. This chapter foregrounds the intersection of gender and class to give an historical analysis of classical music education institutions in the UK during the late Victorian period, showing how class and gender shape the way in which classical music is read as a marker of 'respectable' or 'proper' femininity. This is, however, only one form of boundary-drawing around class that classical music's institutionalized practices support, and the chapter concludes by outlining classed exclusions that are still clearly visible in boundary-drawing around 'proper' or 'serious' repertoire today.

Mapping the Institutional Ecology of Youth Classical Music

The 'institutional ecology' of youth classical music that offered Owen such a breathtaking array of opportunities makes visible the link between the late Victorian period, when many of these institutions were established, and today. These institutions shaped the world of classical music that presented Owen with so many possibilities. As with many of my participants, inclusion in the classical music world afforded him a sense of belonging and value. The word 'ecology' is apposite because it describes an institutional landscape that appears natural and eternal, as does any successful invention of tradition (Hobsbawm and Ranger 1992). However, it is in fact a constructed environment that naturalizes a particular social and musical value system. As this chapter explores, nineteenth-century distinctions around class and morality that have been sedimented into this ecology take on the appearance of being natural, inevitable, and right; a particular value system is stored and preserved in these institutions through the kinds of musical ability that are recognized and valued, as well as the kinds that are *not* recognized or valued. In order to map out this institutional ecology of youth classical music, I have taken all the institutions, organizations, and ensembles which my participants mentioned and organized them into five categories by size, function, and history. I have labelled these the 'behemoths' (the music conservatoires); the 'standardizers' (the grade exam boards); the local authority music services; the 'informal economy'; and the 'talent scouts'.

The first set of institutions are the music conservatoires. I label these the 'behemoths' because of their Victorian origins; their architecture (heavy, stone, imposing) calls to mind the captains of industry of that period. The music conservatoires that most of my participants were attending, had attended, or wanted to attend were set up in the late nineteenth century.[1] As Ehrlich (1985, 105) notes, conservatoires proliferated in the late nineteenth century, with thirty-three existing in London alone by 1900; only a handful have survived. Today, as with other tertiary education organizations in the UK, they are public higher education institutions but have a high degree of autonomy. They also run 'Junior Departments' on Saturdays, where students get the intensive training of a conservatoire while still at school, and many of my participants attended these. The entry level required for the Royal College of Music Junior Department is a 'distinction' mark at grade five by age eleven, although for violin and piano, the most prestigious instruments, the required standard is 'significantly more advanced' (RCM 2017); these entry standards require applicants to have had several years of individual instrumental lessons. The other reason for calling the conservatoires the 'behemoths' of this institutional ecology is the huge influence they have on the rest of the ecology. Music teachers and conductors who are in positions of authority in other institutions tend to have studied at one of them, and therefore the practices that are taught at these conservatoires shape musical cultures for generations to come.

---

[1] Key institutions were the Guildhall School of Music and Drama (1880), the Royal College of Music (1882), the Birmingham Conservatoire (1886), the London College of Music (1887), Glasgow Athaeneum School of Music (now the Royal Scottish Conservatoire, 1890), and the Manchester College of Music (now the Royal Northern College of Music, 1893). The exam boards that are influential today are Trinity College London (established 1872 and started running exams in 1877) and the ABRSM (1890). Exceptions to this trend were the Royal Academy of Music (established 1822), and the Royal Welsh and Leeds Colleges of Music, which were founded in the mid-twentieth century.

The second group of Victorian institutions that were heavily formative of my participants' musical lives are the music examination boards which I have nicknamed the 'standardizers' due to their role in prescribing and credentializing musical standards of ability. The two that survive today are the Associated Board of the Royal Colleges of Music (ABRSM) and Trinity College London, both registered charities. These institutions formed part of the taken-for-granted backdrop to my participants' musical lives; all my interviewees mentioned the grade exams, for example, referring to being 'grade five standard' as a measure of musical ability. For each of the major exam boards in the UK, grades range from one to eight, with advanced certificates available subsequently. These are wealthy institutions; the ABRSM uses its income from grade exam fees from around the world to subsidize the Royal Colleges of Music (D. Wright 2013, 176) and in 2016–17 had an income of nearly £50 million a year (Charity Commission 2017). Both the 'behemoths' and the 'standardizers' have been highly influential in training musicians and shaping classical music culture not only in the UK but around the world, using their 'musical authority' to construct and export musical norms and ideologies (Kok 2011; Johnson-Hill 2015; D. Wright 2013). It is notable that across these institutions, the majority were established in the 1880s and early 1890s. This time period is therefore formative in understanding the institutionalization of classical music education, its practices, norms, values, and legacy, as explored later in this chapter.

Building on these Victorian foundations, I now move on to the twentieth century. The third group of institutions in the 'ecology' described here are local authority music services. These were publicly run until 2012, when they were restructured as commissioning rather than service delivery organizations, or 'hubs', and government funding was cut by a third (Hill 2014). It is these organizations that deliver instrumental teaching in state schools, the dogsbody work of providing beginner music lessons to children, as well as running ensembles such as the regional youth choirs and youth orchestras that many of my participants played in. Established between the 1950s and 1970s, music services initially provided free instrumental and vocal lessons within schools and ran centres where out-of-school music education took place, including ensembles such as bands, choirs, and orchestras (Cleave and Dust 1989), a system entirely separate to the mainstream music curriculum delivered in the classroom (Pitts 2000, 214). It is also precariously funded; whether parents should be charged for instrumental and vocal lessons has been a point of contestation since the 1970s, and during the 1980s and 1990 it became more common to charge parents for lessons (Cleave and Dust 1989). Despite investment in music education by the Labour government from 1999 which began to reverse the decline in local authority music service provision (Zeserson et al. 2014, 11), today there are very few local authorities that provide free or subsidized individual or small-group lessons (Rogers and Hallam 2010; Griffiths 2014). Instead, whole-class instrumental teaching is now offered on a variety of instruments such as violin and ukulele (Hallam 2016; Sharp and

Rabiasz 2016). This was first put forward by the Labour government in 2001 and was expanded by the Conservative-led Coalition government in 2012 with the introduction of the National Plan for Music Education (NPME). The latest figures show that two-thirds of the 631,000 pupils in 2014–15 who received Whole Class Ensemble Teaching were taught for a full year, with most of the remainder taught for a shorter period, usually one term (Sharp and Rabiasz 2016, 11).

The Whitchestershire county music service, which was launching itself as a music education hub during my fieldwork, was an important part of the youth music ecology locally; fourteen of my thirty-seven interviewees had started learning instruments with the county music service peripatetic teaching service (where instrumental teachers go into schools). Out of the others, two had initial tuition from a family member, and the other twenty-one started immediately on private lessons outside of school. However, by the age of eleven or twelve almost all of my participants had moved away from the lessons provided in schools to start having private lessons outside of school, a move that was seen as necessary to reach a higher standard. This reflects the wider ecology of music tuition in the UK, where a large proportion of instrumental and vocal music tuition is provided by an extensive and largely unregulated sector of private music teachers. The local authority music service was therefore widely used, but also slightly looked down on, and this has important implications for the ways in which classical music is used for social closure and boundary-drawing by the middle classes, as I explore in chapter 3.

The fourth group is the 'informal economy' of music education organizations. Through collating the different groups my participants were involved in, I amassed a bewildering array of local amateur orchestras, choirs, musical theatre groups, chamber music residential courses, and more, some of which had been operating for decades, others which had come into existence for a few years only to fade out when funding or energy ran out. The 'informal economy' therefore encompasses a miscellany of amateur, private, and charity ensembles; locally run groups or classes; and private music teachers, as noted earlier. Many private teachers are members of either the Musicians' Union or the Incorporated Society of Musicians, a membership organization that provides insurance and other services for music educators. Other groups are supported by Making Music, an umbrella body for amateur ensembles, and the National Association of Choirs. These umbrella organizations tend to be registered charities or other non-statutory organizations.

Finally, overlapping with the informal economy are the 'talent scouts': institutions or schemes that identify 'exceptional' youth 'talent' and may be funded by the government's cultural policy wing, the devolved Arts Councils, as well as drawing on extensive philanthropic funding; in 2010–11 there were 2,413 active music education charities in the UK with incomes over £500,000, adding up to a combined income of £609 million (Kane and Clark 2012). This group includes the National Youth Orchestra, Choir, and Brass Band, as well as professional cultural institutions such as orchestras that are required to have education and outreach programmes in order to qualify for public funding. The 'talent scouts' also include five specialist music secondary schools that offer intensive tuition to 'talented' young musicians, which a few of my participants had attended. These schools were established during the Cold War to train musicians who could rival those being produced by the Soviet Union (Pace 2015b). One example is the Purcell School, founded in 1962, a residential secondary school with around 180 pupils located outside London. While it is an independent school, pupils are largely funded by the government Music and Dance Scheme, along with the school's own scholarship funds (Purcell School n.d.).

Finally, as well as this ecology of musical organizations, some non-musical institutions have music education as part of their formal or informal remit and were influential in my participants' musical development, most notably churches, schools, and the military. Church choirs were often a route into singing in a more 'serious' choir such as Cantando Youth Choir. Independent (private) schools also contributed to this ecology; seven of my participants had obtained music scholarships to attend independent schools—the most direct route towards the classed self-improvement classical music education offered. In addition, as noted in Owen's story, above, the army, the Royal Navy, and the Royal Air Force were active in music education; several wind and brass players in the groups in my study were taught by army or Royal Air Force musicians and had participated in military bands.

Several features are apparent from this ecology. First, the majority of the key institutions in the first two groups, the conservatoires and exam boards, were set up in a narrow window between 1877 and 1893. These institutions appear to be highly influential on the rest of the sector, and therefore their historical origins, and any legacy this might have today, require scrutiny. Second, music education in the UK is surprisingly unregulated compared with other sectors. Unlike amateur sports, which in England is overseen by Sport England, music education and amateur music in England are not governed by a statutory body (although some organizations fall under the remit of Arts Council England). This has the advantage of allowing local groups to easily start up, leading to local variation in provision, but it means that bringing about change can be difficult, for example, in order to monitor safeguarding practices following abuse scandals in the sector (Bull 2016b). Finally, it appears that overall there is a high level of provision for 'talented' young classical musicians. This could be a result of the way in which this data was gathered, through examining the pathways of young musicians who had already reached a certain level of proficiency, but certainly it reveals that there were many opportunities available for classical musicians who had reached a high level of ability at a young age,[2] reflecting a well-developed ecology for developing youth talent in classical music.

---

[2] While there were often economic barriers to participation in these schemes, bursaries or funding schemes were available. A resourceful parent could navigate these, if they had the skills, time, and networks to be able to do so.

No wonder Owen felt amazed to have stumbled upon this musical smorgasbord of opportunities; and once he had become a proficient orchestral player he was in demand from various groups who needed players to make up their full cohort of numbers. Owen described the exciting experiences of playing in the Barbican concert hall in central London one week, then getting paid to play in the pit for another school's music theatre production the next week, then following that with a residential course with the National Youth Orchestra. For Owen, who didn't see these opportunities as normal and inevitable in the way that some of the young people in the professional middle-class group seemed to, being in demand and being chosen to be in elite ensembles created or confirmed a sense of being valued and valuable and gave him a sense of fulfilment. Being in demand in this way was in a large part facilitated by his choice of instrument, French horn, which (along with instruments such as bassoon and viola) is more likely to be in demand than other instruments such as flute, thanks to the structure of the orchestra whereby four or five horns (and only two or three flutes) are normally required, as well as the relative popularity of the flute over the French horn. This is also a valuation according to gender, as Christina Scharff's gender breakdown by instrument among members of British orchestras shows that more in-demand instruments such as French horn, bassoon, and double bass are predominantly played by men (viola, however, is equally split between men and women; Scharff 2017, 51). Instrument choice, gender, and value therefore intersect in important ways. For *some* young musicians, then, classical music's institutional ecology facilitates a two-way process of feeling valued by institutions that are seen as valuable.

What kinds of value are institutionalized and stored within this musical ecology, and how does this institutionalization take place? For instance, Owen was clear that classical music counted as *legitimate* knowledge that was worth more than other types of musical knowledge. He justified this based on its intellectual content: 'Stuff like ethnomusicology or that sort of thing has never interested me. Never. [...] Gamelan [an Indonesian musical instrument] and that kind of thing, it's never really interested me musically. I think because it's based in tradition rather than intellectual reaction'[3]. In particular, he found Romantic music to have both the 'depth' and the intellectual component that made it worthy of building his life around it. This discourse of 'serious' music—complex, worthy of detailed analysis and in-depth study—was, as I explore later, common to many of my participants (see also Goehr 1992, 121). The link between ideas of 'serious' music, legitimate musical knowledge that can be studied for its intellectual content, and moral ideas of the 'proper' were formative for the institutionalization of classical music education in the nineteenth century. This chapter now turns, therefore, to an examination of the late Victorian period, in particular the 1880s and 1890s when the 'behemoths' and 'standardizers' were set up, in order to understand

---

[3] Ellipses enclosed in brackets indicate places where I have omitted some of the interviewee's words. Ellipses without brackets indicate points where the speaker hesitated during an interview.

what kinds of values are stored in these institutions, how value is stored and recognized, and what kinds of boundary-drawing practices were required for this process. As will become clear, questions of class and morality were central to this boundary-drawing.

The Sacralization of Music-as-Art

Prior to the emergence of the institutional ecology for music education that was established in the late Victorian period, as described earlier in this chapter, an earlier wave of institution-building took place in the first half of the nineteenth century. This occurred alongside, and through, the development of a 'bourgeois' class in nineteenth-century England; music was one of the cultural practices through which the emerging bourgeoisie created their own spaces and identity. This process began in the early nineteenth century; from around 1830 onwards, Europe's major cities saw a process of the institutionalization of music-as-art, including a shift in consumption practices towards 'sacralization' whereby music would be consumed in reverent silence (W. Weber 2004; James H. Johnson 1996; Sennett 1992). During the 1830s and 1840s, as William Weber (2004) describes, in London, Paris, and Vienna, the aristocracy and upper middle class began to merge into a 'bourgeois' class. In Manchester and London, as Simon Gunn notes, 'the development of the concert-hall from the early nineteenth century was predominantly a bourgeois enterprise', and other provincial cities such as Leeds followed in the second half of the century, where bourgeois elites could see others and be seen amid the increasing social confusion of the city (1997, 223). In Birmingham, *the* elite cultural institution was the Triennial Festival, which reflected the morality of the local bourgeoisie in its heavy diet of oratorios, their depictions of the religious struggles Old Testament prophets resonating with the evangelical fervour of Birmingham's middle class (Pieper 2008, 70). Part of the way in which they did this was through expressing their musical taste, moving away from programming a miscellaneous variety of short pieces (W. Weber 2004, xxvi) towards concerts featuring whole musical 'works'—a form of classed boundary-drawing around musical taste.

This shift towards 'music-as-art' was uneven; it depended on the work of particular musical activists and was influenced by the class composition of different cities, as noted by Peter Martin (1995; DiMaggio 1986). However, by the 1870s, and in many parts of the UK much earlier, there was in place a classed infrastructure for musical life. For listening to 'serious' music, then, the overall picture is one of the middle classes acting as cultural entrepreneurs to set up institutions that served their interests or reflected their morality and world view (Gunn 1997; Talbot 2002; Ehrlich 1985; Milestone 2007; S. McVeigh 2004). This is not to say that people from other classes did not attend concerts, but rather that the cultural institutions that created an infrastructure for 'art music' were set up and run by the middle classes. When working classes were recruited into this project, it was often in order to inculcate them into practices of 'rational recreation': 'improved recreations' as an instrument for 'educating the working classes in the social values of middle-class orthodoxy', that is, engaging working-class people in morally improving activities that would keep them out of the pub (Bailey 1978, 35).

When looking at musical participation rather than consumption, a different picture emerges, and later in the century, in the 1880s, there was a proliferation of amateur music-making in England (Gillett 2004, 35). This was in part due to material considerations such as the price of pianos and sheet music coming within the range of even some working-class families (Gillett 2004), but it was also fuelled by, and reflected in, alternative forms of institution-building to the concert halls of the bourgeoisie. While it is not possible to do justice here to the many types of music-making taking place in Victorian England, one important contrast to middle-class institution-building during this period can be seen in the Tonic Sol-fa movement. Drawing on a musical training method developed by Sarah Glover in Norfolk designed to encourage participation in congregational singing, from the 1850s onwards musical activist John Curwen built up a mass musical movement based on this easy-to-learn form of musical notation (McGuire 2009). For Curwen, a Dissenter, musical participation was a means for religious and moral reform; morality was central and aesthetics came last; music was merely a means to an end (McGuire 2009, 210). After Curwen's death in 1880, his son Spencer continued the movement with a different emphasis, using music to foster social equality through the collectivist aesthetic ideal that Tonic Sol-fa allowed.

Through its pedagogy, this method militated against the idea that musical expertise was the domain of the few; a group of adults could be taught the method and would then 'evangelize' by teaching it to others. While John Curwen himself was middle class, his method became a mass movement with wide participation. It also led to debates around musical literacy. As McGuire (2009) describes, the working classes were less likely to know how to read conventional staff notation. Instead, they sang even complex pieces such as Handel's *Messiah* using alternative notation systems that were prevalent at the time, including Tonic Sol-fa. The birth of another kind of musical institution, the competitive music festival, contributed to this growth, and by 1889 'nearly every major British musical festival choir consisted of a mixture of singers of tonic sol-fa (styled the "new notation" by its adherents) and staff notation (referred to as the "old notation" by the same)' (Rainbow and McGuire, in Johnson-Hill 2015, 55). The bourgeoisie, in response to the success of Tonic Sol-fa, created new boundaries of good taste by turning away from choral music towards symphonic music concerts in order to retain their prestige (McGuire 2009, 34).

For both music-as-art and Tonic Sol-fa, morality was important, but in different ways. While temperance and religious evangelism were explicit goals of the Tonic Sol-fa movement, the moral dimensions of art music were not always as transparent. However, the moral dimension of music-as-art is one of the key ways in which classical music's association with the middle classes can be made visible. As described in the previous chapter, Michèle Lamont's work on boundary-drawing among the upper middle classes in France and the US revised Bourdieu's work through her finding that economic and moral boundaries were at least as important as taste boundaries in retaining and consolidating class position (Lamont 1992a, 181). This is about how people are valued; in drawing these boundaries, Lamont explores the nature of the criteria that are used to discriminate between worthy and less worthy persons (1992a, 1). Similarly in late Victorian England, moral as well as taste boundary-drawing can be seen clearly, and it is during this time that gendered and classed ideas around music were institutionalized in ways that are still with us today.

Gendered Morality: Music as a Problem for Respectability

With the rapid expansion of the lower middle classes in the final decades of the nineteenth century, boundary-drawing between classes intensified as the middle classes sought to defend their status (Gay 1998, 7). Gendered respectability was central to this. Simply put, for women, respectability was a signifier of *not* being working class (Skeggs 1997, 47). It was read onto women's perceived sexuality, based on the 'organizing principle' of the double standard of virgin/whore (Nead 1988, 6). For women, respectability

> was defined in terms of their location within the domestic sphere and their consequent sexual respectability. Respectability was organized around a complex set of practices and representations which defined appropriate and acceptable modes of behaviour, language and appearance; these social rules and moral codes worked to regulate both gender and class identities. (28)

Nead describes the 'anxiety and fear produced within mainstream bourgeois society by even the thought of unregulated female sexuality' (6). In this way, 'class coherence' for the middle classes 'was established through the formation of shared notions of morality and respectability' (5). Against this, working-class groups formed their own notions of respectability, 'negotiat[ing] and re-defin[ing] bourgeois beliefs and values' (36).

By mid-century, the requirements for bourgeois women's refinement meant that 'the minutiae of everyday life, their personal behaviour, dress and language became their arena to judge or be judged' (Davidoff and Hall 2002, 398). The rise of the bourgeois family involved the separation of the household and workplace, and by the mid-nineteenth century, 'work' became a problematic category for a particular group of middle-class women; reproductive work was the only kind to be socially sanctioned (Davidoff and Hall 2002, xv), and the role of housewife appeared in the census in 1851 (Nead 1988, 23). As women 'retreated to suburban homes', they came to be seen as a 'bedrock of morality in an unstable and dangerous world' (Davidoff and Hall 2002, xvi). Indeed, so important was the role of the wife in upholding the status of the bourgeois family—and, through family, the Empire—that McClintock argues that there grew up a 'cult of domesticity' whereby women's role was keeping order, raising children, and being moral regulators for household and nation. Domesticity, as McClintock argues, 'was crucial in helping to fashion the identity of the middle class', the domestic household serving as the model for both nation and Empire, as well as unifying a large class of people 'around the presiding domestic values of monogamy, thrift, order, accumulation, classification, quantification and regulation' (1995, 167–68). Women's successful performance of the role of refined, virtuous mother, daughter, and wife became the linchpin of this new bourgeois identity, upholding the future of nation and Empire (McClintock 1995). While by the 1880s and 1890s women's equality was under frequent discussion and there were political movements towards women's suffrage, 'rational dress', and higher education for women, for instance, public opinion was still far from endorsing such equality (Gillett 2000, 117).

Within these discourses, music had a contested moral status; its sensuality and intense emotionality gave it dangerous links to degeneracy, but if this sensuality could be overcome and controlled, then it could be a powerful tool for cultivating religious faith and the growth of character generally. The association of some kinds of music with degeneracy—alcohol, prostitution, and other forms of immorality—is perhaps best illustrated by debates around licensing and censoring music hall venues and acts between the 1850s and 1870s before music hall started to become respectable (Bailey 1978; Bratton 1986). As Dagmar Hoher (1986) notes, repeated questions in parliamentary and licensing reports about the status of the single women who attended London's music hall venues suggested that they were perceived as prostitutes, showing that there was, at this point, an association between music hall and the perception of sexual degeneracy. This gendered discourse also illustrates how respectability was tied to women's sexual morality. The risks of music for young women's morality are revealed in Leppert's (1995) reading of the many nineteenth-century paintings of music lessons. These tend to show a male teacher instructing a refined, attractive young lady on the piano; the chaperone dozes, and the teacher is taking the opportunity to make a move on his student. The commonalities across these paintings suggest that the music lesson has sexual associations.

Against these ways in which music could be morally risky for women, an enormously popular book by one Reverend Haweis entitled *Music and Morals* attempted to redeem music as a moral pursuit. First published in 1871 and reprinted many times until 1936, this book argued for 'the music of the great composers (i.e. the

Austro-German canon) as truly exemplary, morally as well as musically', suggesting that learning this music 'represented an uplifting and worthwhile pursuit' (D. Wright 2013, 32). (Clearly this logic didn't work for Haweis himself, who had an illegitimate daughter by one of his parishioners). The moral properties of music were also harnessed to make the case for the 'cult of domesticity', as contemporary commentator John Hullah, a close friend of Dickens' and inspector of music in teachers' colleges, argued in 1878:

> The more general diffusion of musical skills [would mean that] order, cleanliness, mutual forbearance would take—must take—the place of slovenliness, filth and mutual recrimination; and for some hours in the week the working man might exchange the hell of the gin-shop for that image and foretaste, if such be possible, of heaven—a well-ordered, cheerful home. (qtd. in Cox 1993, 33)

Absent from this description is the working man's wife, who was made responsible for rescuing her husband and children from slovenliness and filth with a genteel sing-along. Music was therefore seen as having powers of redemption for the 'degenerate' classes.

Amidst these moral discourses, there were ongoing contestations around who should, could, or needed to learn music. In true Victorian social reformer style, music education was frequently used by middle-class activists as a tool to rescue the working classes from their moral torpor (Cox 1993; McGuire 2009). This can be seen in debates around the musical training of elementary school teachers, many of whom would have been pupil-teachers who had been pauper children (Dent 1977). An inspection at Cheltenham teacher training college found that the singing practices there were having a 'refining' influence on the students involved, and the inspector, our friend John Hullah, described how music cultivated 'patience, temperance, power of attention, presence of mind, self-denial, obedience and punctuality' (Cox 1993, 16). However, at another teacher training college, trainees were not allowed to have piano lessons because the college authorities thought 'it did not become persons of their station in life' (Lynch 2010, 176).

Music not only had dangerous associations with the body and female sexuality but also threatened the bourgeois values of thrift and economy by being seen as 'wasteful' or unproductive (Leppert 1995, 26–27). The founder of the Royal College of Music, George Grove, was obliged to emphasize music's 'usefulness' in a fundraising speech to donors in the 1880s, adding that 'the College would be a place of work, and not of recreation and amusement.... Students would have to go there with the intention of ... treating music as a serious matter of life' (D. Wright 2003, 236); 'serious' and 'useful' are keywords of the nineteenth-century bourgeoisie, denoting the aspiration towards the regularity and rationality of everyday life (Moretti 2014). The contrast with music hall, in which 'pleasure is represented as an abundance', could not be more stark (Bailey 1986, xviii). However, through discourses of hard work and their associated moral connotations of respectability, the canon of 'great' music managed to escape charges of sexuality, degeneracy, and emotional excess and was able to be salvaged by the middle classes as morally acceptable, even for young women, through embodying ideals of respectable femininity around decorum and refinement of the body. As popular Victorian author John Claudius Loudon explained, 'Women's virtuosity lay in her containment, like the plant in the pot' (qtd. in Davidoff and Hall 2002, 191). The juxtaposition of 'virtuosity', a word associated with musical practice, and 'containment' suggests that this bodily disposition was a performance that could be learnt by young women who desired to demonstrate their respectability. This 'virtuosity' could then be put to its proper purpose, which was, in the words of another contemporary commentator, one Reverend Binney, to serve 'the mighty engine of masculine life' (Davidoff and Hall 2002, 118).

A 'Systematic' Finishing School: Disciplining While Denying the Female Body

George Grove, who was so insistent that the students at the Royal College of Music would treat music *seriously* and work hard, is credited with bringing the 'systematic' training institutionalized in European conservatoires (predominantly Leipzig and Paris) to the UK (D. Wright 2003). Who was subjected to this 'systematic' training? It was overwhelmingly girls and young women (Gillett 2000), and as Ehrlich (1985) notes, they were predominantly middle or lower middle class. Some of them did go on to work professionally; the number of women categorizing themselves as 'musicians and teachers' in the census rose from 900 in 1841 to 19,100 in 1891 (Ehrlich 1985, 235). These were mainly teachers (Ehrlich 1985, 119) but also some performers and composers, a 'gloriously diverse group' (Fuller 1998, 42). However, for the majority of women among the 'respectable' classes, learning music was a way of filling in the liminal period between school and marriage, leading into respectable charitable work and providing soothing entertainment to male relatives, while also learning skills that could be drawn on to earn a living if needed, an important consideration in an era of 'surplus women' (Gillett 2000, 39; Rohr 1999).

The expansion of musical tuition among the aspiring middle classes demonstrates the ways in which music was used to attain or cling to respectability, and it is at the edges of respectability or class groupings that contestations can most clearly be seen. Paula Gillett describes a newspaper editorial from the front page of the *Illustrated London News*, in 1875. Commenting on a portrait of a 'daily governess' who taught music at the homes of her pupils (Gillett 2000, 9), the editorial laments her 'erroneous views of class respectability' that lead her to cling to her position as a piano teacher rather than seeking employment as a housemaid or becoming a lady's personal attendant (10). The editorial is also concerned with the poor musical standards that it suggests this teacher is contributing towards;

the quality of Britain's music-making was seen to be tied up with questions of national prestige and the musical 'health' of the nation. The *Illustrated London News* editorial therefore neatly draws together dominant ideas around class, gender, and music from the time; for the commentators, this working-class young woman risks becoming 'above her station' through aspiring to inappropriate levels of gentility through teaching music, and yet presumably for the woman herself, teaching music is worth the fatigue and hard work as it demonstrates her status and respectability, while also allowing her to earn a living. Musical training signified membership in the respectable middle class but could also offer a way to attain respectability for those on its edges.

The piano, as one of the instruments that was seen as suitable for women to play, was an important battleground for gentility. As lower-middle-class and working-class young women started to gain access to pianos, upper-class women turned toward the violin, which became fashionable in the 1880s and 1890s (Gillett 2000, 4; Ehrlich 1985; Gay 1998). But for the lower-middle-class female pianists, a commercial infrastructure grew up to credentialize such aspirations towards gentility. Trinity College London (established 1872) and the ABRSM (established 1890) were just two among many commercial music examination boards set up around this time. Both the ABRSM and Trinity College expanded rapidly in Britain as well as in the colonies; for both, the overwhelming majority of examinees were girls and young women. By 1913, the Trinity College exam board was dealing with about 28,000 students a year, and the ABRSM around 25,000, of whom 90% were female (Ehrlich 1985, 118–19). For the conservatoires, a pattern of roughly three times as many women as men prevailed, although this varied widely between instruments.[4] While the piano was strongly associated with girls and women (Gillett 2000, 3), studying composition was only available to those who had had earlier instruction in harmony and counterpoint, which excluded most women (Seddon 2013, 25). The higher numbers of women in conservatoires did not affect men's dominance in the music profession, as men were more likely to follow informal training routes into professional work (Fuller 1998).

Moral obligations towards improving the musical standards of the nation vied with profit motives as a huge international market opened up (D. Wright 2013; Ehrlich 1985; Gillett 2000). Indeed, it could be argued that musical standards were more important; after its rapid expansion in the 1890s, the ABRSM was losing money in Australia, but it did not withdraw from this market as improving musical standards was seen as more important than making a profit (D. Wright 2013). Confirming this position, as Erin Johnson-Hill describes, at the ABRSM Annual Dinner of 1897, Victorian composer Sir Arthur Sullivan (of Gilbert and

---

[4] The National Training School for Music, during its short-lived existence, had roughly three times more female than male students (D. Wright 2005, 247). The Royal Academy of Music in 1884 had more than three times as many women as men (with thanks to Kathy Adamson from the RAM for assisting me with this archive enquiry).

Sullivan) reminded the assembled company that their work in administering music exams was part of the enterprise of empire: 'Seriously, Gentlemen, we look upon this undertaking in the light of a distinctly moral obligation rather than that of a pleasure' (2015, 29). Given the hugely disproportionate numbers of women taking grade exams, this 'moral obligation' was towards the musical standards of the women of Empire—more precisely, the bodies of the women of Empire. This moral imperative towards improving (female) musical standards forms a contrast with the Tonic Sol-fa movement, where rather than musical standard being a marker of morality, instead musical *participation* (for both men and women) would lead to moral reform.

Institutionalizing Respectability

Music is something of a paradox when it comes to respectability—the body is needed to make sound, but at the same time it needs to be carefully controlled so as not to display its sexuality. This control and discipline can be seen in the ways in which musical knowledge was codified and standardized into the content and structure of graded music exams—the musical and pedagogic materials themselves. Indeed, the discussions of the importance of musical standards to Britain's imperial project draws attention to the substance of these musical standards. To explore this, Figure 2.1 shows the ABRSM's first ever syllabus for the 'senior grade' piano exam from 1890.[5] The exam comprises scales, sight-reading, and pieces dictated by the exam board, with a separate written paper on music theory. Repertoire includes studies from Chopin, Moscheles, and Clementi; pieces by Bach, Beethoven, and Schumann; and one further piece of music of the candidate's choice. The syllabus also sternly reminds the examinee that 'candidates are informed that a large proportion of the marks required to pass will be awarded for excellence in Technical Exercises' (i.e., scales). Detailed instructions are given as to how scales should be played, including an instruction on fingering: 'N.B. the use of the third finger on the black keys is not compulsory'.

The ways in which the syllabus was interpreted will of course have varied, but comparing this syllabus with accounts of women's piano-playing from around the same time allows it to come to life. First of all, as Paula Gillett describes:

> Piano was the perfect fit for the Victorian girl and woman. The seated position accorded well with female modesty, no awkward motions or altered facial distortions were required, and there were no suggestive movements to disturb the modest female image; the pianist touched her instrument only with the extremities of fingers and toes, with the actual sound mechanism masked from view. (2000, 4)

[5] With thanks to Sara Trepte from the ABRSM for sending me copies of these syllabi.

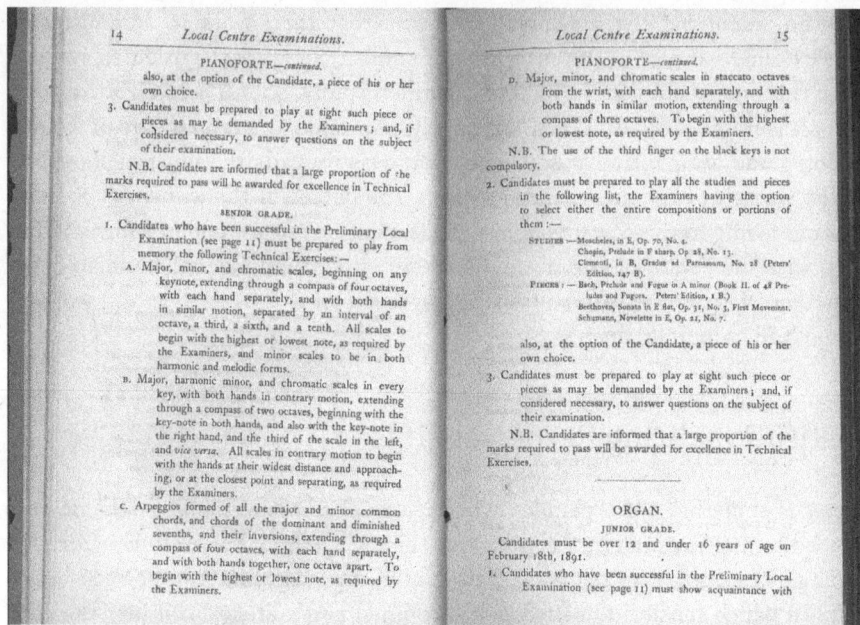

Figure 2.1 'Senior grade' piano exam syllabus, 1890, Associated Board of the Royal Schools of Music © The Associated Board of the Royal Schools of Music Reproduced by permission.

Amid the hypervigilant awareness of the male gaze, whereby women were effectively prohibited from playing wind or brass instruments due to the sexual associations that would be read into this activity (Gillett 2000), displays of musical ability had to involve careful disciplining of the body. The 'large proportion' of the marks that are awarded for scales, as well as the instruction for fingering on the black keys, can be seen as part of a broader pattern of gendered disciplining of the female body. The technical requirements of this exam, while they might be similar to the 'systematic training' that the Royal College of Music provided, have a different meaning: for young women doing grade exams, technical ability allowed a performance of respectability, by disciplining while effacing the body whereby any associations of sexuality with the female body had to be hidden in order to construct music as an appropriate occupation for bourgeois (or aspiring bourgeois) women. These exams' requirement of sustained, daily disciplining of the body in order to learn difficult instruments and repertoire entailed thousands of hours of repetitive, disciplined work to be able to render the repertoire even passably well. The aesthetic of classical music was thus dependent on years, even decades, of weekly lessons and daily practice. The emerging market in grade exams also profited from discourse around 'serious' music as morally 'exemplary' and 'uplifting' (D. Wright 2013, 32), to distinguish it from music-as-entertainment, with its associations with music hall. As such, music was used for *moral* boundary-drawing between the lower middle and working classes, and the emerging institutions around music education as both capitalizing on this economy and also fuelling it. Respectability and propriety could therefore be acquired through the successful disciplining of the body, as certified through grade exams. Musical standards were institutionalized into grade exams, to serve a demand for credentializing respectable femininity.

However, amid these discourses of classed boundary-drawing, the music itself had affordances that threatened to work against this disciplining agenda. The repertoire that women played led to the development of a particular emotional relationship with the piano. Ruth Solie's reading of the diaries and correspondence of teenage girls in this period describes the 'piano-playing contract between women and Victorian society': not only the piano as punishment or discipline from the patriarchal authority of the bourgeois family, but also as 'friend, confidant and companion', and finally as 'repository for emerging sexuality' (2004, 12, 100–113). Music therefore had a symbiosis with socially prescribed forms of middle-class femininity, but also tensions with it, in allowing women a private, expressive space. Gillett describes how fiction from the late Victorian period depicts Chopin's piano works as 'the perfect companion for the homebound woman whose life of self-sacrifice ... often produced pent-up emotions unsettling in their intensity' (Gillett 2004, 5). Indeed, Chopin's music comes up frequently in relation to bourgeois women's emotional state, for example, as the Reverend Haweis described it:

> That poor lonely little sorrower, hardly more than a child, who sits dreaming at her piano, while her fingers, caressing the deliciously cool ivory keys, glide through a weird nocturno of Chopin, is playing no mere study or set piece. Ah! what heavy burden seems lifted up, and borne away in the dusk? ... The angel of music has come down; she has poured into his ear the tale which she will confide to no one else, and *the "restless, unsatisfied longing" has passed*. (qtd. in Gillett 2000, 4; my emphasis)

The disciplining and classed boundary-drawing that classical music afforded was not, then, the only meaning that can be read from women's musicality of the time; it can also be seen as a safety valve for the emotions produced by the restrictions of the bourgeois female condition, and women's musical practices could afford them an expressive voice that they did not find elsewhere. The articulation of this emotional depth, unspeakable in other ways, through classical music is explored further in chapter 8. Similarly, the tension between music as a form of gendered disciplining or as enabling women's expression has resonances today, as chapter 7 examines.

However, it is notable that, despite over 120 years of social and musical change, including huge strides towards gender equality and the ongoing expansion of the middle classes, the ABRSM syllabus has remained remarkably similar. In the 2017–18 syllabus, the repertoire is a little broader than in 1890, but both the 2017–18 grade eight syllabus (ABRSM 2017, 26) and the 'senior grade' 1890 piano syllabus specify Bach preludes and fugues, Beethoven sonatas, and works by Chopin and Schumann. In the 2017–18 grade eight piano exam, only five out of the thirty-two options of musical pieces chosen were written after 1950, only one composer is non-European, and there are no female composers included at all (ABRSM 2017, 26). In relation to musical standards, the focus of the marking scheme appears to have shifted from prioritizing 'Technical Exercises' towards awarding the bulk of the marks to playing pieces rather than scales; but accuracy and control of notes and rhythm still feature heavily (ABRSM 2018). The wording of the 1890 instructions regarding fingering for scales has changed to state that 'candidates are free to use any fingering that produces a successful musical outcome'. The fact that this needs to be spelled out suggests that 'acceptable' fingering is still a point of contention; young women and their teachers, both in 1890 and today, have presumably been having the same correspondence with the exam board about the appropriate, 'systematic' fingering to use in scales, expecting this to be dictated by the musical authority of the exam board. These contestations are further hinted at in the lengthy instructions for how to play scales 'without undue accentuation and at a pace that is consistent with accuracy and distinctness' (ABRSM 2017, 3), a description that also outlines the aesthetic requirements for a good-quality performance.

The lack of change between 1890 and today, and the monocultural repertoire that is prescribed, suggests that the exclusion of women and other minority groups from classical music's canon is still the norm. The consistency in what is required in terms of musical standards points towards a strong tradition of practice that has been reproduced over this time period and raises questions as to what extent the meaning of classical music, for the young people who play and sing it, has changed over the intervening period. Given the dearth of research on the history of music education institutions, it is difficult to tell a coherent story about the extent to which the similarities in these syllabi point towards continuity of the tradition and culture of classical music, but they point towards the enduring legacy of the Victorians on classical music education and practice.

Boundary-Drawing around the Proper in the Present

I have suggested that boundary-drawing around class in the late Victorian period, as written onto the female body through its refinement and restraint, could be *performed* through proficiency in classical music. Music conservatoires and exam boards in the late nineteenth century proliferated to serve this demand for female respectability within an independent career. Classical music thus became a way of performing classed ideals of morality in the Victorian era by drawing a boundary between the 'respectable' and 'degenerate' classes, as well as by being a way to impose bourgeois morality on those who were feared to lack it.

What, today, is the legacy of these institutions and discourses? Is this boundary-drawing still meaningful to my participants as classed boundary-drawing, or is it simply a relic of the Victorian ideals that have been institutionalized into these practices, and that may have accumulated different meanings and associations since the late nineteenth century? While subsequent chapters examine classical music's perceived morality today, here I turn to accounts from my participants around taste boundary-drawing to demonstrate the ways in which the 'proper' is constituted as a category today. This is distinct from—but linked to—boundary-drawing around ability or musical standard. Both modes of distinction draw on discourses of the proper, or 'propriety', but today these are most clearly seen in contestations around taste and, as I will demonstrate, are central to the protected status of this musical practice, as well as working to camouflage the cultural capital that is accumulated through it.

This discourse of 'proper' music came up fairly often among my participants, sometimes with an ironic tone of voice. For example, Hannah, a singer, recounted how her school friends had asked her, 'What on earth's a music degree, do you just listen to songs?'

> HANNAH: And I'm like, no, no, a *music* degree, like proper music, so like ... [laughs]
> ANNA: What do you mean, proper?
> HANNAH: Hardcore music, Bach chorales and all of that [partly joking].

For Hannah, then, there is an ironic knowingness about seeing classical music as 'proper music'; she is aware that it is perhaps snobbish or sets her apart, but she is also proud of being able to participate in 'hardcore music'. Contestations around what constitutes 'serious' or 'proper' music denoted the boundary between music-as-art and other musics and were actively policed by some of my participants. Music by commercially successful contemporary choral composer John Rutter was the clearest dividing line, echoing the social boundary-drawing around the populism of the Tonic Sol-fa movement in nineteenth century choral singing, and when Cantando Youth Choir were singing a well-known Rutter piece, I heard complaints from several members. Francesca said that although she didn't like Rutter, her objection was not just about taste, but about how badly written it was for the sopranos, because they had to sing high in their range for long periods. (I feel this way about Beethoven's 'Ode to Joy', but the point holds for Rutter as well.) Others admitted to me that they knew they weren't supposed to like Rutter but actually they really enjoyed it; this admission usually came after I had shamelessly declared that I liked it. Rutter's music was the disputed borderland between what counted as music-as-art and what did not.

More clearly beyond the pale was Andrew Lloyd Webber's music; music teacher and conductor Roger told me that if he tried to programme Lloyd Webber, his choir would refuse to sing it. However, those in positions of musical authority could consecrate repertoire as acceptable even when it was not 'proper' music. Professional conductor Olly, who had thoroughly charmed the county youth orchestra with his genial manner and gentle jokes, chose for one holiday course a programme of film music, including medleys from *Spider-Man* and *Pirates of the Caribbean*. In his habitual didactic mode, he explained to us during rehearsals how John Williams and other film composers had drawn on classical composers' techniques, thus dignifying this music with a lineage that drew on the 'greats'. Nevertheless, he made it clear to the group that film music was in a different category to the classical canon, referring to it a couple of times as 'McDonald's' music, because it had 'no nutrition value'. It was, it seemed, acceptable to play film music as long as it was underpinned by a healthy diet of weighty, 'proper' orchestral repertoire; we had played Vaughan Williams and Shostakovich on the previous course. Indeed, as Hess (2016, 5) describes, classical music draws on discourses that it is 'good for you', like 'cultural spinach'.

Breaking these taste boundaries incurred scathing responses from some of the young people; vocal tutor Jeanette commented to me, 'Don't you find they're terrible musical *snobs*?' Cantando was singing a movement from the *Joyful Messiah*—Handel's *Messiah* arranged by Quincy Jones into a soul-inspired version. Andy was highly critical of this piece, griping to me that 'the assumption is that because it's a youth choir we want to do jazzy young choir numbers with jazz hands, you know what I mean? Cheesy. [...] Everyone hates it'. By contrast, Bernstein's *Chichester Psalms*, which they were also singing, was, he thought, an appropriate choice; although a twentieth-century composition (i.e., recent), it is a staple of the 'serious' choral repertoire, so it fits within the category of art music. Both Andy and his friend Helen spoke of their experience in Cantando as being their first exposure to 'proper [choral] repertoire', by which they meant canonic choral pieces with at least four vocal parts. Andy's and Helen's references to 'proper repertoire' echo other participants' talk of 'serious music', suggesting a common understanding in this world of what this means. This delineation of repertoire as 'proper' versus 'cheesy', 'jazzy', or 'McDonald's music' is important boundary-maintenance work, which works to safeguard the value and legitimacy of classical music. This work of reinscribing value has to be continually performed; even Tristram's mission to make sure Cantando sang a broad range of repertoire was underpinned by bringing the methods of classical music practice—of detailed, meticulous ordering—to bear on non-classical repertoire (Green 2003).

While boundary-drawing around classical music in the nineteenth century was about class and respectability, today boundary-drawing not only does moral work but also is necessary to safeguard its privileged funding status compared to other genres (as discussed in the introduction). Maybe this bias should not be surprising when the erstwhile head of Arts Council England, Sir Peter Bazalgette (2014), recently spoke of the 'civilising influence of the arts', harking back to a colonialist discourse that would be more fitting in the Victorian era than today. Classical music requires the exclusionary practices described earlier in this chapter in order to demonstrate how it is different from other genres. This justifies its special status and disproportionate public investment. As we will see, these exclusionary practices also contribute to the formation of the powerful identity that classical music can provide.

As a result, it is unsurprising that the young people among my participants were vocal in their defence of classical music and its protected status. They drew heavily on cultural preservation discourses in this defence, arguing that this music should be funded so that it will not die out, rather than because it was more valuable than other genres. Mainly, they simply told me how much they loved it. However, where a defence of classical music's value was forthcoming, it was based on a Darwinian version of universalism, and the idea that classical music's greatness would be recognized across cultures and time. This was sometimes confused with the idea that classical music is the 'Ur-music' from which all other musics derived. By contrast, the adults in my study were much more likely to draw on legitimizing discourses of the social benefits for young people of learning classical music, such as responsibility and punctuality, alongside discourses of 'great' music and tradition. These resembled the qualities propounded by John Hullah in the 1870s as being a result of participation in this music: 'patience, temperance, power of attention, presence of mind, self-denial, obedience and punctuality' (Cox 1993, 16).

Boundary-drawing around the 'proper' therefore serves a new and distinct function in the late twentieth and early twenty-first centuries: to protect classical music's special status as 'legitimate' culture and its concomitant high levels of public investment, which require these boundaries to be maintained in order to demonstrate its difference from other genres. If its value was shown to be historically contingent and tied to a particular group in society, its special status could be less easily defended.

Conclusion: Performing Respectability

The different readings of the 'proper' described in this chapter—as 'proper' or 'serious' music, for my participants today, and as respectable propriety for young women in the late nineteenth century—have both been used in drawing boundaries around classical music. As Moran and Skeggs (2003, 62) note, the 'proper' can also be linked with 'propriety' and 'property' etymologically, as the three Latin roots of this word are firstly, proper or good; second, clean or hygienic (propriety); and finally ownership or property. Common to all three meanings are the ways in which 'talk of propriety, use and exclusion is also talk of limits: of borders and boundaries', implying also a theme of invasion—'moving from order and safety to disorder and insecurity' (66). In the late Victorian period, when many of the major institutions that shaped my participants' musical lives were established, music was a site for *moral* boundary-drawing around women's sexuality and bodily propriety. In this way, women who could present themselves as respectable were morally worthy, and this respectability was a requirement for middle-class femininity. The institutions that were established in this period, particularly the exam boards, drew on these classed and gendered norms of respectability to make a profit but also to codify and reify these norms as musical standards. In this way the exam boards' business was in credentializing middle-class femininity.

This chapter has set the scene for the story to come, by showing how the historical associations between class and classical music in England have to be understood through examining the institutions that carry them. As Barlow et al. (1995) note, one of the ways in which the middle classes store value across generations is through institutionalization. The practices of classical music, as reproduced by its Victorian institutions, are one of the ways in which its value is reproduced, and around which taste and moral boundaries are drawn in order to safeguard this value. An example of an alternative way in which musical practices were institutionalized is the Tonic Sol-fa system. Much more than simply an alternative notation system, its musical practices form a contrast to the norms of classical music, for example, by flattening the hierarchy of performer and audience and downplaying the importance of musical expertise and standards in favour of access to musical participation. And yet, Tonic Sol-fa died out in the years following World War I, while many of the conservatoires and exam boards survived. Their models of music education have become dominant: individualized tuition and skill development; staff notation; and musical performance as signifying gendered respectability for women. Pointing out the contrast between classical music and Tonic Sol-fa is not to suggest that the latter is superior; each model offers benefits and drawbacks. Rather, it allows us to see the *contingency* of the musical practices that we have inherited, their historical legacies, and makes visible some of the work that has gone into reproducing these musical norms. Today's 'institutional ecology' of classical music in the UK carries a strong legacy from the conservatoires and exam boards but very little from the Tonic Sol-fa movement.

In particular, there are values carried forward from the Victorian music education institutions that, as I will argue in the coming chapters, can still be seen in classical music practices today. These include formal modes of sociality, gendered values of performing respectability, and ideas of 'proper' or 'serious' music. It remains to be seen to what extent these institutions have left a legacy of practices within classical music education that are still linked to gendered discipline, or whether the meanings of these practices have changed.

The next chapter continues with the theme of boundary-drawing, exploring ideas of musical standard among my participants today. It opens, however, with the second vignette in a triptych of accounts from working-class and lower-middle-class young men in my study. I have foregrounded accounts from these young men because it was they who found this world the most alien, and therefore their stories were often the most revealing of its paradoxes. Having begun the current chapter with Owen's story, next I introduce Andy, another musician from the New Symphony Orchestra. Similarly to Owen, Andy was amazed that through playing music he found himself in 'another world' to the one in which he had grown up.

CHAPTER 3

'Everyone Here Is Going to Have Bright Futures'

CAPITALIZING ON MUSICAL STANDARD

Andy grew up in a small town some distance outside Whitchester, in a working-class family; his mother is a school nurse and his father a builder. He went to secondary school locally, as he described it, 'just a normal state school, not particularly good'. When I met him, he was in the final year of a music degree at a Russell Group university;[1] when I mistakenly referred to him as studying at Oxford, he was pleased that he could 'pass' for being an Oxford student. He had started playing the flute at primary school with lessons through the county music service, later changing to oboe, and got into classical music through a friend at school. He described to me how there was 'no music' in his home when he was growing up—only pop music on the radio—and he felt his parents didn't really 'get' the classical music world that had come to be his life:

> They didn't understand the music world, they didn't get the idea of standard almost. [...] They didn't listen to classical music and if they did want to, they wouldn't have understood the world [...], just the actual standard that actual musicians ... it's insane, the amount of hours, and just, nothing goes wrong. It's a different world. [...] I always tease my friends and say my children will practise until their fingers bleed. Part of it is a joke, but part of it is—I do want them to play instruments, if I have children, and—I will make them practise.

Andy has even worked out what instruments his children will play: bassoon, viola, and horn, 'in that order'; if they play rare instruments, they will have more chance

---

[1] The Russell Group is an association of twenty-four prestigious universities in the UK, which includes Oxford and Cambridge.

of getting on in the classical music world. He is only partly joking when he says they will practise till their fingers bleed. But why, at age twenty-one, does he have this intense preoccupation with his imaginary future children's place in the classical music world? What is at stake for him in this struggle, that he is adamant he will *make* them practise? This chapter centres on the socially constructed concept of musical standard, or ability, an idea that Andy implies is crucial to understanding the world of classical music. It explores the ways in which musical standard is acquired, how it is recognized, and what it does for those who possess it. Musical standard, as well as being socially shaped through relationships with teachers and peers, also acts back on the social, for example, by reinforcing hierarchies of value between musicians. Its effects on the social world are not only micro-social, and I describe an example of how musical standards contributed towards the middle-class 'exit' from public services. Finally, musical standard was also capitalized on in different ways by my participants in their pathways through music education, which were strongly shaped by their class and gender positions. This chapter therefore illustrates some of the diffuse but powerful ways in which musical practices and cultures contribute towards class inequality.

'She Crafted Me': Shaping the Self in the Teacher-Student Relationship

The one-to-one relationship between teacher and student is an integral part of learning classical music. It has recently been called into question, both for pedagogic reasons (Gaunt and Westerlund 2013) and following sexual abuse scandals in classical music education (Pidd 2013). The emotional and physical intensity of this kind of student-teacher relationship can lead to great psychological damage if the teacher abuses this trust, and for a small minority of my participants, who I will discuss in the next chapter, this relationship was a negative and destructive one. Here, however, I want to focus on the ways in which the intimate experience of the teacher-student relationship was a hugely positive influence on the musical ability and identity of some of the young people in my study.

I met Megan when she was singing one of the lead roles with the Young Opera Company. She had never been in an opera before and was finding the experience somewhat terrifying, so I was doing what I could from my position as rehearsal pianist to support her—playing her melody along with her and giving her encouragement. Aged eighteen, she was in her final year of schooling at a top state school;[2] her mother was a head teacher, and her father ran a small business. She was atypical among my participants in that she wanted to go on to do contemporary rather than classical music, and she was more at home as a

---

[2] UK state schools (public schools) are ranked by the exam results their students achieve.

singer-songwriter and folk musician than as a classical musician. She had only been singing classically since she was fifteen, when she started singing lessons with Jeanette. This relationship with Jeanette had been transformational for her. Megan described how, although the singing lessons had made her sing in a less 'free' way, making her more self-critical, they also had an enormous impact on her, both personally and musically:

> MEGAN: I wouldn't be the person I was without my singing lessons [...] you go on such a personal journey with [your teacher] [...], they craft *you*. It feels like she crafted me around my voice in my singing lessons [...] I think I totally trusted her, trusted her judgement, trusted how she was teaching me. And she really got me, so ...
> ANNA: As a person?
> MEGAN: Yeah, as a person and through my voice at the same time. [...] And I don't think—I can't regret those lessons because I can't think of how I would be if I hadn't had them.

This discussion touches not only on the deep trust that Megan felt for her teacher but also on the way in which her singing voice, and through her voice her *self*, has been produced between her and her teacher. Through crafting Megan's voice, her teacher was crafting her, and Megan's voice became part of the scaffolding around which her sense of self developed.

This process meant that singing lessons, for Megan, were a 'vulnerable' space:

> Sometimes I go in and it's not linked to anything you've been doing, but I just burst into tears, so I try and sing and I just cry. It's like a space, an hour in the week where it's just you and yourself and you can't do anything else. [...] You can't hide anything, 'cause when I'm learning to sing it's quite a sensitive time.
> ANNA: Personally?
> MEGAN: Yeah, it's like an hour that is ... sacred in a way, like, I don't know, it's for yourself, and ... it's vulnerable.
> ANNA: If there's something going on for you emotionally, you can't hide it?
> MEGAN: Yeah because it's there in whether you've practised, it's there in how you sound, it's there in the emotion of the music, sometimes I'm singing a piece and I'd had like the worst week, it was like an awful week, and I was just singing the piece and my voice just cracked and I just cried, and Jeanette was just there to pick me up again.

This formation of self and voice was an intimate, vulnerable process requiring great trust in her teacher. Many of my participants, in all of the groups within my study, had long-standing, close relationships with their instrumental or vocal teachers, some of them having studied with their teachers for ten years or longer. When I interviewed another singer, Sara, she was excited at having just become godmother to her former teacher's first child. This teacher had taught her for free when she could no longer afford lessons, and they were still very close even though the teacher had moved away. Similarly, Francesca, also eighteen, had been with the same singing teacher since starting lessons at age nine. She described how '[my teacher] knows me *so* well [...] it's in the context of my voice but she knows what makes me tick and what she needs to say to get what she wants'. These relationships go far beyond the half-hour-a-week transmission of knowledge to become intimate, trusting spaces of personal development. Rather than simply musical 'knowledge' or skills being passed on, the very expressive capacities of the student—their musical voice—is moulded through the teacher's guidance and support.

Similarly, when I observed one of Ellie's violin lessons, I saw how her musical 'self' was shaped through this embodied, semi-verbal relationship of trust and openness. I'd met Ellie through playing in the New Symphony Orchestra. She had attended a top private school in Whitchester. Her father had his own business as an IT contractor, and her mother, who had emigrated from East Asia, was a housewife and also helped out with her family's business. Ellie was in the final year of a music degree at a prestigious university. As part of her degree, she was having lessons with a teacher at a music conservatoire, Roger, and she had previously told me several times how amazing he was.

I sat in on one of Ellie's lessons not long before a performance exam for her degree course. The rehearsal room at one of the London conservatoires where the lesson takes place is complete with a seven-foot grand piano, a harpsichord, and tasteful pictures of musical instruments on the pristine white walls. When we meet before the lesson, Ellie is stressed and nervous about her exam. Roger, a calm, genial man in his sixties, listens along as she plays through her pieces, starting with the Brahms G major violin sonata—a wonderfully expansive, graceful piece of music which I know very well from having played the piano part. The pianist, Tom, carefully places the first two chords to start the piece. These are simple G major chords, the piece beginning as though we have all the time in the world. His hand and arm gestures are elegant and flowing, his whole body embodying the character of the piece. After these first two chords the violin comes in. It's a gentle, lilting melody, but Ellie doesn't seem at ease in it; she is looking intently at the music, and her sound is muted, inward. After a few bars she starts to play more expressively. As he listens, Roger gestures along with the music, half conducting, half dancing. He can't keep still for more than a few seconds at a time. His whole body is involved, his legs lifting onto his toes as he sits, his body moving in circles to follow the lines his hands are making—he is living through each moment of the music as much as if he were playing it. Occasionally he picks up the violin on the table next to him and plays along with Ellie for a phrase or two, bolstering her line, the sudden vibrancy of his sound adding a burst of energy and expression to her playing. After her initial nervousness, Ellie starts to move expressively, too. She is cushioned between the relaxed support of the pianist as he provides warm, lilting lines, and her teacher's movements as he creates her phrasing with his gestures. I find myself moving along with the music as well, unable to listen in stillness.

This is how the musical 'self' is formed; through hours, over years, of this embodied communication. This is what Megan means when she says that Jeanette 'crafted me'. Her expressive voice was formed, as I am watching Ellie's being formed, through taking on the gestures, the phrasing, the encouragement, and the physicality of her teacher, as part of herself. These accounts show the encouragement and support from adults that are integral to learning classical music, by contrast with other, more peer-led or self-directed forms of musical learning. They also show how learning classical music cannot be separated from a broader sense of identity; as Megan described, her sense of self wasn't a pre-existing entity which was simply expressed through her voice, but rather her voice, and with it her expressive capability, was moulded by her teacher, within a relationship of deep trust and intimacy.

How Musical Standard is Recognized

In Ellie's lesson, her nervousness and constrained expression were gradually dissolved by her teacher's presence. Far from being a passive listener, he was actively shaping her expression in ways that directly improved her playing. This idea was supported by the common understanding among my participants that their standard improves when playing or singing with people who are more advanced than them. Several people told me they preferred to play or sing in ensembles where most people were at a higher standard than them, so that they would play better and learn more. Conversely, being in a group where they were the best player and others were not as good as them was viewed negatively. There is, then, an enabling factor to playing or singing with musicians of a higher standard, in that it becomes possible for someone to play or sing better than they would on their own.

However, alongside this idea, everyone also believed in objective, individualized measures of musical standard such as grade exams. The understanding of musical ability in the grade exam model is one of improvement comparable to climbing a ladder, getting better incrementally according to how hard you work at it. These two ideas—standard as objective, and standard as variable according to who you are playing with—are not incompatible. For example, technical ability usually improves with hard work, contributing to improvements in standard, which may then be enhanced or diminished by the musical company you are keeping. However, the assumption that objective standards existed was a hugely important part of the commonsense understandings that shaped the social and musical world of my participants. The idea that musical standard is quantifiable, individualized, and hierarchalized was therefore given greater weight than the idea of musical standard as variable according to the standard of people you are playing or singing with.

As with the example of Roger, who drew more expression and confidence from Ellie by moving along as she played, musical ability was transmitted from teacher to student through non-verbal processes of communication such as movement, breathing, energy, and listening. With peers as with teachers, such interactions could enhance or diminish an individual's playing within a group, or inform judgements of others' standards of ability. Ellie told me how this occurred with her desk partner in one of the orchestras she played in:

> ELLIE: If my desk partner is good, then I will play much better, if he inspires me to play better.
>
> ANNA: How does that communication happen, if someone's really good, how can you tell?
>
> ELLIE: You can hear it, it's weird, you just feel it when you're sitting next to them.
>
> ANNA: What are you getting?
>
> ELLIE: It's like a weird kind of connection, you might look at each other and smile because you realize that you've just done something exactly the same, exactly the same feeling. For example, we were doing Brahms One last night, my desk partner was this guy called Tim, really good violinist, really incredible, and the reason he is such a good leader is because he is inspiring to listen to and to watch, like everything he does is like 'this is what I'm going to do, follow me' [...]. He always does it in a way that's not commanding, 'you must do this', it's always an invitation. For me sitting next to him, he's one of the best desk partners I would ever sit next to, because I feel like he will give as much as I give him, it's equal.

The kind of leadership Ellie described has resonances with the way the conductors in this study described their role as inviting rather than commanding (as explored in chapter 6). The welcoming gesture was one that Ellie could not help but follow, and that she felt made her play better. This kind of non-linguistic communication also took place among the choral singers. They would pick up signals from their fellow singers that were simultaneously used as information for fitting into the group, as well as to position others as 'talented', similarly to how Ellie labels Tim as 'incredible'.

Musical ability is perceived in what Tia DeNora (1995, 8) calls an 'interpretive act': using very subtle signals of breath, movement, or lack of movement to judge whether someone is a good musician. It is, therefore, variable according to who you are playing or singing with, but within this relationship, judgements of ability are made through subtle, non-verbal signals. Despite common understandings of musical ability being a property of the individual, it is these interpersonal, social judgements that work towards creating it.

'In Orchestras, It's Set Out by Hierarchy, It's Made on a Hierarchy': Musical and Social Hierarchies

While musical ability was, in part, recognized and labelled through the kinds of processes described earlier in this chapter, in orchestras it was also clearly visible through being demarcated by seating position, with the best players seated closest to the conductor and the less able players further away. While in the two orchestras examined in my research, this was usually a relatively relaxed negotiation, for those of my participants who played in the NYO it had become a crucial marker of hierarchies of ability. Despite their inconsistencies, these hierarchies were immensely important to the identities of many of the young people, particularly the orchestral musicians. As well as hierarchies between individuals, there were also hierarchies between groups, where the strong disinclination, almost fear, from some of the advanced orchestral players of playing in groups of a lower standard was palpable. When the Whitchester County Youth Orchestra lowered the standard required for entry, Owen commented scathingly that 'they let *anyone* in now'.

This fear of loss of standard, and defence of the hierarchy of musical standard, was captured in debates around changes to the NYO. A new chief executive had been appointed who wanted to abolish hierarchy in the string sections. Cellist Fred, who was incensed by this, told me:

> [The new manager] always said that there should not be a hierarchy in NYO, but there's always going to be a hierarchy. [...] In orchestras, that's the thing, [it]'s set out by hierarchy, it's made on a hierarchy. [...] When you come into NYO, it's the process of moving up, like, how do you measure progression in an orchestra? Each year, you go from [desk] nine, to seven, to whatever, to move up from desk nine, that's the natural progression. Say, oh, it's my second year, I'm fifth desk, next year I really want to be like desk three, desk two, that's my aim. You come back next year, desk seven, no explanation. Is that the way to motivate ... ?

As with most members of the NYO I spoke to, Fred and his friend Jack were both intensely loyal to the orchestra and so were furious at the changes to repertoire, personnel, and social arrangements that the new manager had brought in. Fred and Jack had more to lose than most players. They were part of a 'joke group' (as they described it) called the 'Alpha Males', which was formed of seven of the young men in the orchestra who had had 'hoodies' (hooded sweatshirts made for themselves saying 'Alpha One', 'Alpha Two', and so forth. The manager told them they were not allowed to wear these to rehearsals. This incensed them, because, as one of the young men told me, 'I think the whole orchestra knew it was a joke, we took it as a complete joke'. Despite being a 'joke group', the Alpha Males were clearly asserting their social status—they were tall, male, and among the oldest members of the orchestra. In this way, powerful social hierarchies within the orchestra existed alongside musical hierarchies.

The example of the Alpha Males suggests that musical hierarchies and social hierarchies might reinforce and legitimize one another. Others echoed this idea. Ellie described:

> Like with everything, the NYO had a hierarchy, social groups in the orchestra, and that's how it works, you have your leader, you have your principals [section leaders] and they are the top people, and they're decided by the violin professors and they know what they're doing.

There is no separation of 'social groups' and musical ability in this statement. Ellie simply refers to the 'top people', conflating musical and social status, and suggests that the hierarchy of the NYO is about 'social groups in the orchestra'. She went on to assert that 'it's not even possible' to make the orchestra non-hierarchical. From both Ellie's and Fred's accounts emerge the trust in the judgement of the adults who make these decisions; the 'violin professors ... know what they're doing', asserts Ellie. This trust in authority was integral to the functioning of this social world; respect for elders and tradition was a sine qua non, and musical authority trumped other kinds of authority.

What is at stake in judgements of musical standard, therefore, is one's position in this social and musical hierarchy. This affected social groups in the orchestra as well as one's own identity. The young people in these groups tended to be friends with other musicians who were of a similar standard to them. These friendships were important; most of my participants also said that their closest, most intense friendships were with the friends they had met through music, and for a few, *all* of their friends were musicians. In addition, out of the nine people who mentioned romantic relationships to me, only one was in a relationship with a non-musician. Consequently, young musicians come to know themselves—their identity and status within the group—through hierarchies based on musical ability. This is a key way in which musical and social norms formed an homology; hierarchies of musical ability were paralleled in social hierarchies.

'Being with Such Like-Minded People': Finding a Congenial Social Space

I have described hierarchies of musical ability as occurring on the micro-social level of interactions within Whitchester's youth music groups; however, these hierarchies also contributed to wider social identity formations around class. For these young musicians, the fear of playing in a group of a lower standard is not just about music but equally about the loss of hard-earned status; about how you perceive yourself and how others perceive you; and about who you are likely to socialize with or have sex with. The powerful identity formation that is occurring through these processes can therefore be seen to be linked with young people's social trajectories, that is, the different social worlds that they encounter throughout their lives. For example, the young people in my research were likely to spend time with other white middle-class people because of the schools they attended and the extra-curricular and family activities they participated in. As Bourdieu (1987) describes, the sense of 'like-mindedness' or 'affinity' that draws people with similar backgrounds towards one another means that people with similar social trajectories reinforce their resemblance, in a recursive process.

Confirming the links between social and musical hierarchies in this scene, young people gave me both social and musical reasons for their participation in classical music groups. Often, social reasons were paramount, as their involvement in classical music groups gave them a congenial social space outside of school in which they formed close friendships. Indeed, conductor Adam averred that what the young musicians in this scene had in common was being sociable; another conductor, Olly, declared that all classical musicians were geeks. This was a space, therefore, where it was acceptable to be a (sociable) 'geek', an identity that could be difficult to carry off in school (Francis, Read, and Skelton 2012). Being able to inhabit this identity was particularly valued by two of my participants who had been bullied at school and found in classical music a scene where they felt they fitted in. For another, Lisa, classical music was a place where she felt at home, away from her 'chavvy' secondary school; there was a clear understanding that youth classical music spaces did not overlap with 'chavvy' spaces. Similarly, Hannah explained that she loved being in Cantando Youth Choir because of 'being with such like-minded people':

> We're all young, most people have been through [the top state school in the area], and it's all kind of Whitchester people, you've always got some link from some other ensemble, so it's nice to all come together and just being with everyone who's sort of . . .

Everyone who's sort of what? Hannah runs out of words just at the point of articulating her commonality with the other young people in Cantando. Being lost for words at this moment is significant, in that it points towards something that is not usually or readily articulated—the shared social space which is recognized but does not usually need to be described. This shared social space is constituted by what Bourdieu calls 'a structure of affinity and aversion between [individuals]' that draws them together or apart (1987, 6–7). This simply means that people feel they have things in common with those in similar class positions to themselves. Indeed, studies from the UK show that both children and adults tend to make friends with those who share their class position (Vincent, Neal, and Iqbal 2015), and most people marry or partner with others from the same class (T. Bennett et al. 2008, 220). The similar conditions of the young musicians in these groups have led them to seek out others who resemble themselves and reproduce this 'structure of affinity', which they recognize even if they cannot necessarily describe it.

'Fitting in' was therefore not just about musical skills, as Richard, the conductor of Cantando, described in relation to the benefits of the 'self-selection' processes in the choir:

> And obviously it is word of mouth [for recruiting new members] at the moment, but in a way, that is a little bit better than having all comers because the people who are in the choir know the sort of calibre of person that should be [in the group], so it is quite self-selecting. It's quite limiting, because you don't have a wide pool of people to choose from, but it does mean that the people who come forward are usually, more often than not, just going to fit straight in.

For Richard, the benefits of having a self-selecting group appear to outweigh the costs. His use of the word 'calibre' to describe the type of person he is looking for—people who are going to 'fit straight in'—suggests that he is talking about someone's character and personal qualities rather than solely their musical skills.

Selection into the Whitchester classical music scene cannot, therefore, be seen as a purely musical concern. Indeed, through the descriptions presented here, it is clear that trying to separate musical ability from social relationships is not possible; the social groups young people are in determine how likely they are to join this musical world, and their musical ability and capacity for expression are shaped through their social relationships with others. The ways in which musical standard is enhanced or diminished by playing with others mean that it cannot accurately be described as a property of an individual. Furthermore, the subtle interpersonal ways in which it is judged demonstrate that it is not a solid foundation on which to build hierarchies of value. There are tangible social and material consequences to such judgements of standard, those made both by peers and by adults. These judgements label people as having a particular 'calibre' or not, but as discussed in chapter 1, in many ways they are simply an outcome of someone's class position through the investment over time that parents and teachers have made in building the child into a musician. People then come together with 'like-minded' others to form groups that reinforce their likeness. This is one way in which classical music practice can reproduce class, as the next section goes on to explore.

Musical Standards and the Flight from Public Services

These notions of musical standards have an effect on music education and class formation on a wider social scale. Soon after starting my fieldwork, I heard from several people the story of Cantando Youth Choir's defection from the county music service. 'It was basically a parental coup', Jeanette, one of the tutors involved with Cantando, told me:

> There was a fallout, I think, between Richard [the conductor] and the music service, and Richard said he was going to quit, and the music service said, [...] fine we'll find someone else to take the youth choir, and I think the word got out [...] so the parents turned to Richard and me [...] saying, would we take over the choir and run it privately?

The choir had been started some years previously by music teacher and conductor Gregory. When Jeanette came on board, before the 'coup', she found that the young people in the group had

> an enormous sense of snobbery. Oh my god! They were all, you know, 'we are very good at what we do and you're not coming in this choir unless you're as good as us' [...] people who think they're wonderful sight-readers and have the right to be in the choir.

When Jeanette and Richard took over from Gregory, the 'training choir' of less experienced singers had just been combined with the main youth choir. As Jeanette described, 'There'd been a lot of hostility about that, because the people who felt that they were really good were really sick about being combined'. Richard's abilities as a conductor soon made the choir even better than it had been before, despite the apparently lower ability of the members. Hence it was a serious matter when the choir seemed about to lose him, as the standard of the group would drop. Parents of choir members stepped in, and the choir was re-convened as a privately run ensemble.

The second defection from the county music service, that of the New Symphony Orchestra (NSO), was more discreet. Helen and Andy, who ran the NSO, had in fact met and become friends while singing together in Cantando. Lamenting the low standard of the Whitchesterhire County Youth Orchestra (WCYO), they decided to form a better orchestra for young people locally. Helen described how it had come about:

> We were all having a drink after a concert, and we were saying, [...] the County Youth Orchestra is shocking, you know the standard is

dropping every single year, they're way too ambitious, it's so expensive. [...] So we were having this age-old conversation of, isn't it a shame, there are so many great players in Whitchester, and they're all our friends and wouldn't it be so much fun if we just got together and played some music. [...] We met up a month later, and sat down and came up with a name for the orchestra, came up with lists of players.

And in this way the NSO was formed. Players were recruited through friends and friends of friends, with an older demographic than in the WCYO, longer courses, and more ambitious repertoire. Helen's low opinion of the WCYO was shared by other members of the NSO; Jonty described how 'it's become a feedback loop, because they're not thought to be that good [...] the county ensembles don't attract good people'.

The commonalities between these two vignettes help to illustrate what musical standard can do on the level of wider social formations. On one level, these are simply stories of people wanting to play in the best group, with the highest standard. This was the 'common-sense' position of my participants, one which needed no explanation or justification. On another level, however, they describe stories of the exit from public services by those who feel entitled to a higher quality of music-making than they are getting, and who have the resources, contacts, and skills to make these groups happen without public support.[3] Zooming out even further, these narratives reveal some of the assumptions behind classical music practice that are so taken for granted that they may not even be seen or discussed by those involved; or where they are revealed, they are fiercely defended. One assumption is encapsulated in the attitude that, as Jeanette described it, 'you're not coming in this choir unless you're as good as us', the idea that it is important to sing or play with people at the same standard as yourself, rather than having mixed-ability groups.[4] Jeanette challenged this attitude

---

[3] As well as being about musical standard, there had been complaints about the inefficient administration of the county music service (which, to be fair, ran an enormous number of projects with a very small team). This raises the question of who should do the administration for these groups; it was usually women, sometimes paid, sometimes not (see Vaugeois 2014, 135, for an historical account of women's voluntary labour in classical music).

[4] While the best ways to group students are currently being investigated among education researchers (Francis et al. 2016), research from sociology of education within schools has to date found that mixed-ability classes rather than setting or streaming are, on the whole, better for the majority of students as they encourage 'pupil responsibilization'. As Diane Reay describes, this means that 'teachers don't teach to the whole class but pupils can go along at their own pace more' and learn from others as well as from the teacher (1998, 551). However, as will become clear in chapter 6, the pedagogy of large ensembles works almost entirely on a model of teaching to the whole class, and there is very little opportunity for 'pupil responsibilization' as the learning model of these groups works on a top-down, unidirectional model from conductor to musicians, a model which is consistent across amateur, professional, and educational environments of classical music ensembles (one-to-one lessons,

by letting in singers with a lower standard of sight-reading, despite complaints from the pre-existing choir. It's notable that it is the adult tutors—Jeanette and Richard—who were trying to make the entrance requirements less strict, while the young people and their parents in both Cantando and the NSO were the fierce defenders of the status quo and tighter standards of entrance. While this was a way of defending the legitimacy of the system which had rewarded them, it was also because the young people wanted to have the best possible musical experience for themselves. Playing with better musicians means that it is possible to play more difficult repertoire, more quickly. By contrast, in other musical scenes, such as the English folk scene that I have played in, or in Dueck's (2013) ethnography of the working-class music scene in Manitoba, people of different abilities and standards routinely play together, with the more able musicians accompanying less able musicians to allow them to have a musical experience they couldn't have otherwise. However, in these classical music scenes, such intermingling of people with different standards was not valued, unless it was between teacher and student.

As well as avoiding mixed-ability groups, another assumption that underlies these two narratives is the overall aim of raising the musical standards or 'excellence' of the group as a whole. This was an aim shared by young people and adults in these groups. Working towards the highest musical standard was an unquestioned good, trumping any other considerations around access, affordability, diversity, or the importance of remaining within a public system. Even when Jeanette and Richard opened up Cantando to a more mixed-ability group, this was a step towards building a bigger choir with a better sound; the quality of the performance would in the end be stronger, and those who were not as good at sight-reading would just have to work harder to keep up. Similarly, the formation of the NSO in order to have a better-quality orchestra was so obvious as to not need justification.

This common-sense idea of musical 'excellence' assumes that widening access and increasing the diversity of participants will compromise the musical standards or quality of the musical product. However, this mode of thinking has been challenged by England's national public arts funding body, Arts Council England, in its Creative Case for Diversity (Arts Council England 2011), which argues that diversity within the creative process produces artistic innovation (as discussed in the conclusion to this book). This approach would mean that making music with a group of 'like-minded' people of the same 'calibre', rather than enhancing the artistic product, will work against innovation and creativity and in this way will inhibit 'excellence' of outcomes.

In the examples discussed here, classical music ability magnifies social differences, particularly of class. The defections from the county's publicly funded

however, have the potential to be more pupil-directed). The main aim is usually a good-quality performance, and learning objectives for the young people tend to remain undefined.

music service by the NSO and Cantando show how the slow process of embodied shaping of musical ability described at the beginning of this chapter becomes magnified when people with similar trajectories in social space meet each other and discover their 'affinity'. Furthermore, the exit from publicly run music services that can be seen in Cantando's history and in the NSO's formation fits clearly into a broader pattern of the middle classes carving out protected enclaves for themselves in education and in cities. The closest examples to the processes I am describing of middle-class secession can be seen in research on social class and school choice. One of the battlegrounds in education under the British New Labour government (1997–2010) was to try to persuade middle-class parents to keep their children in state (publicly funded) schools, rather than sending them to private school. Policies such as 'gifted and talented' schemes were introduced into state schools towards this end (Reay 2004a). In effect this was a mechanism to avoid middle-class flight from the public sector by re-imposing hierarchical structures within the state sector, which reinforced classed and racialized hierarchies in education. The reconfiguration of Cantando and the NSO as privately run groups therefore shows how the idea of musical standard works on a wider political level. The formation of these groups brought people together to become organizers and activists on the basis of a shared sense of entitlement to a particular kind of musical experience for themselves or their children. This exit from the county music service fits a broader pattern middle-class secession from public services such as education or healthcare. This process was about musical standards, and quality of administration, but at the same time it was also, and equally, about class.

However, this is not a straightforward picture of the middle classes pulling up the ladder beneath them. Cantando's administrator, Linda, herself from a working-class background, along with conductor Richard and the rest of the committee, had recently set up a programme of choirs in primary schools in the city, including in working-class areas. This network was intended to create access routes for children to come through these choirs and eventually join the main youth choir. The social processes involved in selection and self-selection for Cantando suggest that this project is not likely to be highly successful in widening access. However, the commitment to social justice that was demonstrated by this programme complicates the picture described earlier.

The exodus of Cantando and the NSO from the county music service demonstrates how ideas of musical standard and the social affinities that these reinforce can have a wider political effect that intersects with class structures. But these social processes are camouflaged by occurring within music education. The ideals of musical ability and excellence that provide part of the rationale for this exodus appear to be separate from social processes because of assumptions that musical standard is the measurable property of the individual. However, the effects are social as well as musical: to safeguard the 'social mix' of 'like-minded people' of similar 'calibre'.

Uncertain Capital: What Does Musical Standard Do?

After the young people in these groups have been 'crafted', invested in, criticized, praised, and ranked, what do they aspire to do with the musical ability that they have accumulated over their ten or fifteen years of practising? The amount of effort, time, and money that parents and young people put into the pursuit of classical music suggested they expected some return on their hard work, as does the huge investment by private schools in the UK in resources for classical music (Tregear et al. 2016). These rewards were clearly distributed according to young people's gender and class positions, which mapped closely onto the ways in which they imagine their futures. They fall into three groups: the 'bright futures', the 'masters of the musical universe', and the 'humble and hard-working'.[5]

The 'bright futures' group acquired their name from a comment Bethan made when I interviewed her the summer before she started a degree at Oxford. When I asked her what she had in common with the other members of the New Symphony Orchestra, she responded:

> Well I guess everyone here is very disciplined, you know, they're all clearly working very hard and going to have bright futures [laughs]. And I think—I've been practising the violin every day since I was six—not that I practise every day [laughs] but it's a good way to get into that kind of mindset where you just keep going and what you do pays off.

I was struck by her earnest confidence in the 'bright futures' that were in store for her and her fellow musicians. She didn't mean a bright future as a musician—at least, not for herself, as she had never had any inclination to become a professional musician—but rather a general sense of faith in the future rewards of present effort, towards the professional careers that their parents had followed.

Bethan went on to describe how the mindset of 'what you do pays off' helps with schoolwork as well. This is an attitude whereby discipline and hard work, which Bethan pinpoints as two of the characteristics that make up this group, will lead to success. This shows a congruence between what is required to succeed in classical music and within the education system. Indeed, disciplined work with a view to future proficiency, pleasure, praise, or other rewards is a value that permeates classical music education. Such a value requires having a strong enough sense of an imagined future that it makes sense to invest in that future. As Skeggs notes (2003, 146), this is about imagining a future self that is valued by society. If the

---

[5] As most of the young people in my study were white, I have not attempted to analyse this data in terms of racial inequalities, although chapter 5 discusses the role of whiteness in the classical music practices I observed. Given Yoshihara's (2008) and Scharff's (2015) findings about discrimination and low representation among classical musicians from minoritized racial groups, this issue requires more attention.

future that is imagined is precarious, uncertain, or 'blocked', then investing in it makes less sense (Skeggs 2005, 90). This is related to class because it is about the ways that different groups in society are valued differently. The middle-class habit of long-term investment in a successful future self is a requirement for learning classical music. In turn, learning classical music reinforces this habit in young people.

The 'bright futures' group encompassed mainly those who came from the professional middle class and who had, similarly to Bethan, decided not to pursue music as a career. They saw themselves as 'normal', and indeed they were normal according to the circles they moved in; their parents were lawyers, academics, vicars, teachers, research scientists, or architects or ran their own companies. Some of these young people had seriously considered following a career in music, but they had made what Fred described as a 'difficult decision' not to pursue music. This had clearly involved a process of soul-searching for him, but he eventually decided to study business at a prestigious university. He described his choice as a personal preference, but it is no coincidence that retaining his middle-class position would be much more likely if he did a business degree than if he did a music degree. The effect is that he followed the path that reproduced his class position. When I interviewed him, in the summer between his first and second years of university, he was in the process of setting up a business with a friend at another top university whom he had met in the National Youth Orchestra. His musical contacts had 'set me up hugely', he told me, with 'people I've met along the way that have gone on to do other things that I have as a contact that are going to be useful'. His friend Jack, who was studying history at a top university and wanted to go into politics, agreed that 'the social side [of music] will always be important'. One of the key assets of the middle classes is their 'social capital', the wide social networks that they use to share knowledge such as to find employment or the best schools. For Fred and Jack and others in the 'bright futures' group, classical music was setting them up with networks of other middle-class professionals that they would be able to draw on in the future.

For Alice, as for Fred, it was a difficult decision not to study music at university. Alice's mother had started her on the violin explicitly to teach her the discipline of daily practice and hard work. Indeed, it had already paid off; Alice had obtained a music scholarship to a private school, which, she told me, had meant she had got better exam results than she would have done if she had stayed in the state system, and as a result she had got into a better university. Rewards such as these were already piling in for many of these young people; no wonder it was a difficult decision not to follow a career in music. And yet, none of the 'bright futures' group seemed to regret this decision. Fred said he would find an orchestral career boring if he had to do it for too long; others said they weren't prepared to put in the amount of work they knew would be necessary. Learning classical music, for this group, was part and parcel of the normal practices of people in their class position; there were rewards in the form of social networks, international travel, and access to even more exclusive spaces, but they were similar to the types of experiences that they would accrue anyway. Learning music had not made a transformative difference to their lives in the way it had for those from lower-middle-class groups, such as Andy, with whose story I began this chapter, who found that classical music introduced them to an entirely different social world.

The second group are the 'masters of the musical universe'. This was a much smaller group, exclusively male, also of those from professional middle-class backgrounds. By contrast with the 'bright futures' group, they *had* decided to become professional musicians, but only because they had been promised a high status within the classical music world. Toby, at age sixteen, had already been singled out as a future 'master of the musical universe' by being selected to start a music degree at the junior conservatoire programme he attended, while still at school. With his sights set on a classical music career, he was on the way towards a high status in the musical world, maybe as a composer, which was his main interest. This group also included the two young conductors of the NSO, Adam and Will, both in their early to midtwenties, and already occupying positions of authority with ease. Adam had studied music at Oxbridge and described how

> when I got towards the end of university [...] I looked back at the competitions I'd won, and positions I was being given over other people, and I thought, this is something that's worth putting all my energy into pursuing professionally. I'm aware that by the time I reach thirty, I could not have made it [...] and then if it doesn't work, I can convert to law and sell my soul, you know. [...] There are lots of things that I could earn some money doing.

Like Adam, those in this group felt that they had options for alternative careers if they did not reach their musical goals. It is significant that this group were exclusively male. As Christina Scharff (2015) found in her study of equality and diversity in the classical music profession in the UK, men disproportionately hold positions of power in classical music. Only 1.4% of conductors working in the UK are women, and the winners of the British Composers' Awards have until recently been predominantly male; in 2013 no women were even shortlisted for an award. The ease with which Adam, Will, and Toby occupied positions of prestige—and expected to continue to do so—shows that this identity is already formed by the mid-teens, and that class as well as gender plays a part in making this role seem natural to these young men.

The third and final group is the 'humble and hard-working' group. It comprised those from lower-middle-class families, as well as some of the young women from professional middle-class backgrounds, the sisters of the more privileged brothers. Young people in this group wanted to make a career out of music, aiming to become either orchestral players or opera singers. They did not expect, or want, to occupy positions of power within the industry. They not only had internalized the identity of being a classical musician, but had invested their whole lives in it. This was an exciting prospect for them; this group includes Owen, whom we met in the previous chapter, as well as Andy and Ellie, who told me her career plans involved continual learning and improving, hence the label 'hard-working':

> I'd love to be in an orchestra, to be at the back of an orchestra and be told what to do. Because I feel a lot of the time I'm always at the front and I already know what to do. I want to learn [...] I don't want to be a leader, I don't have any aspirations in that—earning money or being the soloist or whatever, just having the sense that I'm learning constantly.

Unlike the 'masters of the musical universe', she disavowed any ambition to be a leader. However, the identity of being a musician, for Ellie, was total. All of her friends, her housemates, and her boyfriend were musicians, and for her it was a whole world: 'I never feel like I'm missing out on the rest of life because ... I've got music. [...] We're in our own little world, I have no awareness of what's happening outside this world'. Furthermore, with the exception of Megan, whose account was presented near the beginning of this chapter, all the participants I have included in this category were adamant they wanted to be classical musicians, even if they played other genres as well.[6] Many of this group named experiences of youth music, such as being in the National Youth Orchestra or a Young Opera Company production, as being critical moments in deciding to pursue music as a career.

Some young people subverted these categories. One example was Jenny, whose mother was adamant she would be a professional musician and had worked hard to get Jenny into a specialist music secondary school. Jenny left the school at sixteen, having found it stressful and difficult, and decided not to go to music college, as she was convinced that she was not a good enough player to make a career. This decision led to conflict with her mother. However, towards the end of my research, Jenny was overjoyed to find out that she had made the grade to take up a place at a prestigious university to study music. Her mother had been trying to shoehorn her into the 'humble and hard-working' group, but Jenny rejected this to move into the 'bright futures' group; a degree from Oxford or Cambridge, no matter what subject it was in, would give her many more options, not least greater future earning power, than a music performance degree.

These three groups demonstrate how the young people's gender and class positions shaped their imagined futures. Those in the 'bright futures' group would often seriously consider going on to be a professional musician, but somehow they almost always decided against it, and I would hear on the

---

[6] However, when I caught up with percussionist Lisa a year later as she was finishing music college, she had decided to try and make a career in pop rather than classical music.

grapevine that so-and-so had won a place on a prestigious management training scheme. Gender was crucial here, however, as many of the young women who came from professional middle-class families might go on to do music, but their brothers would not; Ellie's brother Jack was in the 'bright futures' group, while she was in the 'humble and hard-working' group. This difference needs to be read in light of the previous chapter's description of music conservatoires in the UK as institutions of gendered discipline. This historical reading that was given as to why there were more women than men at music conservatoires appears to remain relevant today; classical music is still a much more appropriate pathway for middle-class young women than young men, and the implications of this for understanding the middle classes more widely is discussed in the conclusion to the book.

Conclusion

This chapter began with Andy's account of what is at stake in ideas of musical standard: the chance of being included in this world of opportunity. As I have shown, musical standards of ability are formed socially within the trusting one-to-one relationship between teacher and student. Furthermore, standard is not fixed or absolute, despite being measured by mechanisms such as grade exams or auditions. Instead, people's musical ability varies according to who they are playing or singing with, so playing or singing with people better than you means that your own ability is enhanced. Within these musical relationships, judgements are made of musical ability based on subtle, non-linguistic interactions and are reified in hierarchies such as seating position in orchestras. These judgements have powerful effects in the world, amounting to an homology between the social hierarchies within young people's friendships and social groups, and the musical hierarchies of ability within and between groups. As Tia DeNora argues, 'There is much more to learn about how value and extraordinary ability emerge as recognizably "real" entities' (1995, 191), and Mark Banks highlights the 'ineffability' of judgements of talent involved in selection into arts higher education institutions (2017, 76). The inclusions and exclusions, hierarchies, and competition are all premised on musical ability being the property of the individual which leads to rewards for the individual.

I have described how the young classical music groups in this study drew together 'like-minded' young people who were identified as being of similar 'calibre'. This indicates that there is a judgement of social value being made rather than strictly musical ability. These groups of like-minded people are the basis of class formation and reproduction. What is being reproduced here are the social boundaries of the professional middle class. This was made visible through the defections of Cantando Youth Choir and the New Symphony Orchestra from the county music service: an example of 'middle-class secessionism' (Bacqué, Bridge, and Benson 2015, 20) from public services to establish and protect their own spaces, following similar patterns to education and housing. This raises an ethical question around ideas of musical excellence: At what point does pursuit of excellence begin to detract from the wider social good? I suggest that ideas of musical excellence should be called into question when they can be seen to magnify other social inequalities, in this case, class, and this point is taken up in the book's conclusion.

This reproduction of inequality within and through music education can be clearly seen in the three groups I have described that my participants fell into according to their class and gender positions and their aspirations or imagined futures. These three groups demonstrate the different ways in which young people draw on the investment that has been made in their musical ability to shape their futures. The patterns of young people's imagined futures by class and gender demonstrate that classical music confers an uncertain type of capital (Bourdieu 1984; T. Bennett et al. 2008; Bull 2018). For those already in positions of privilege (the 'bright futures' group), playing classical music works as an expression of their social position, rather than adding substantially to what they already have. By contrast, for those coming from working-class and lower-middle-class backgrounds, it can be a mechanism for social mobility, but it is highly uncertain whether this will pay off or not. Another factor to be taken into account in this uncertainty is how class and gender work together to determine young people's trajectories. Class inequality in classical music only makes sense when examined together with gender; out of those of my participants who wanted to pursue a career in classical music, only the middle-class young men expected to occupy positions of power and prestige.

Overall, this chapter has shown that despite the individual benefits from positive relationships with teachers that some of my participants recounted, overall for the young people in this study, being involved in classical music reproduced and entrenched the class and gender inequalities from wider society, rather than working to negate them. The rhetoric of musical standards as the overriding goal worked as a disavowal of the social, even though for many of the young people in these groups the social scene was the main reason they were involved in youth music. And yet these standards are socially formed, in part through the powerful institutional ecology set up in the late nineteenth century when Britain's musical standards were a matter of national prestige (Johnson-Hill 2015; Kok 2011). The conclusion to this book will discuss ways to deal with this institutionalized legacy. However, the next chapter focuses more closely on the affects and effects of correction and accuracy that classical music's aesthetic demands, opening with a third and final account from a young man who felt himself to be something of an outsider to classical music culture.

CHAPTER 4

'Getting It Right' as an Affect of Self-Improvement

Jonathan's trombone had cost £5000. He'd bought it when he started music college at age eighteen, having previously played one he borrowed from the county music service. In order to pay for the trombone he had used the money his grandmother had been saving for him since he was four and applied for grants for smaller amounts, as well as getting a tax exemption. He still owed money on it, three years later, and to pay it off he was working in retail during the summer holidays while he was playing with the New Symphony Orchestra.

Sporting a hipster haircut, Jonathan stood out as stylishly dressed, in contrast with the other young men in the orchestra, who tended to wear public-school label Jack Wills, their shirt collars turned up at the back. He described his background as working to middle class; his father held down two jobs, working as a firefighter as well as doing quality assurance at a factory, and his mother was an accountant; neither had been to university. Despite all these jobs, his family had struggled financially over the years. Jonathan had also struggled with depression, he admitted, which affected his motivation at times, but having a rigorous daily practice regime helped:

> JONATHAN: I had a few downers this year. This year's been the most I've been focused and motivated, but as I said, no one likes to practise, but if you can get yourself into a routine it's hard to get out of it. But likewise if you're out of that routine it's hard to get back into it, and that's where I am at the moment [...]. I think on the whole I work hard and I know that a lot of my laziness does come through and I need to work on it, so.
> ANNA: It's like you can always work harder.
> JONATHAN: Yeah. Every performance I do I'm not happy with. I think every solo performance I've done is not good at all.

The result of this self-critique and sense of his own 'laziness' was that he would spend eight hours a day in a practice room with his trombone. Jonathan's instrument, like those belonging to many of my participants, had a history and an identity of its own, as well as being a part of his own sense of self. This identification was evident in a dream that he told me about in which his trombone had become crumpled as though it was made of paper, the texture of the metal creased and scrunched up. I was struck by the resemblance to a recurring nightmare that I have had for years, in which I have to rescue my cello from a life-threatening situation such as a burning building, a bomb scare, or a car accident. For both of us, our instruments appear to have become a psychic symbol for our sense of self. Jonathan's dream of a crumpled trombone seemed to be mirroring his sense of never being good enough, no matter how hard he worked. Like Andy, who was introduced at the beginning of the previous chapter, Jonathan's account was one of precarious belonging—of never being quite sure of his place in this 'world'. If hard work could get him there, then he would do it. Practice, improvement, and making mistakes were common themes among this group—the humble and hardworking—particularly among those who came from working-class and lower-middle-class positions.

This chapter draws on these accounts to discuss how the aesthetic of classical music in my research sites was mapped onto a morality of 'getting it right' both musically and socially. It draws on current sociological debates on class and hard work to explore how the labour required to reach the high levels of accuracy and technical proficiency that this musical tradition demands was experienced differently by people in different class positions. Becoming proficient was dependent on the one-to-one relationship with a teacher, which the previous chapter described as enormously formative of my participants' sense of self. Here, I analyse accounts of what happens when this relationship becomes abusive, even while my participants defended such bullying behaviours as helping them to attain high musical standards. Overall, this chapter demonstrates ways in which the aesthetic of classical music inflected the social relations and subjectivities of my participants, showing how the music itself is not a 'neutral mediator' (Lambeau 2015, 1) of the social, nor is it deterministic; it interacts with the existing culture and norms of those playing it, while bringing its own affordances.

'The Satisfaction of Doing Something Right': The Ethics of Aesthetics

Andy was the only person I met in my fieldwork who could be described as objectively working class.[1] Thanks to this position as a semi-outsider, his perspective

---

[1] This is due to his parents' occupations.

on the classical music world was particularly astute; he would notice things that others didn't. One example was his take on the ethical or moral connotations of the experience of playing classical music. When I asked him what he enjoyed about playing in an orchestra, he replied:

> I don't know, I suppose the satisfaction of doing something right, to be honest. I know that sounds like a really silly thing to say, but when you're playing in a wind section and you have an entry and it's really in tune and you all come in at exactly the same time, the unity of that is just so powerful, like such a good feeling, to make something communally.

Andy talks about the satisfaction of 'doing something right', not just playing something right, suggesting that there is an ethical sense of rightness associated with musical accuracy. Furthermore, getting it right together has, for him, a powerful unity, represented in the musicians all playing an entry exactly in time and in tune with each other. This is powerful on an affective level; it can be felt as well as heard. This affect of rightness was also described in relation to choirs. Conductor and chorus master Gregory suggested that when the singers breathe at the same time, their pulses synchronize to the same pace. Tristram, the conductor of Cantando, told the choir that if they were breathing right, they would then get a difficult rhythm right, saying, 'I want the audience to be moved by seeing you all breathing together'. This multi-sensory unity has great affective power, or, as Andy describes it, 'such a good feeling', an affective sense of rightness that carries over into everything that occurs in these musical spaces, and into classical music culture more widely.

According to Simon Frith, there is indeed a link between the ethical and musical aesthetics of 'rightness'. In popular music, he suggests that 'it is in deciding—playing and hearing what sounds right ... —that we both express ourselves, our own sense of rightness, and suborn ourselves, lose ourselves, in an act of participation' (Frith 1996a, 110). Elsewhere, Frith draws on work from John Miller Chernoff, who suggests that 'among African musicians an aesthetic judgment (this sounds good) is necessarily also an ethical judgment (this is good) ... the quality of rhythmic relationships describes a quality of social life' (Frith 1996b, 275). In the previous chapter, this sense of rightness or 'making music ... as a way of living ideas' (Frith 1996a, 111) was explored in the way that musical and social hierarchies mirrored each other; social status became externalized and knowable in ideas of musical standard, in a 'fit' between oneself and one's friends. Making music becomes a way of living ideas in terms of hierarchies of perceived musical-social calibre of value.

This idea can be put in dialogue with Skeggs' argument (1997, 90) that 'rightness' is also a classed disposition. Her working-class female participants could 'never have the certainty that they are doing it right [socially] which is one of the main signifiers of middle-class dispositions'; this 'lack of certainty means they cannot make use of social space in the same way' as those whose confidence and ease in dominant spaces means that they are not taking social risks by entering these spaces (Skeggs 1997, 10). One thing that is at stake in getting it right socially, therefore, is access to middle-class spaces. For Andy, getting it right musically was his ticket to the middle-class spaces of classical music, in which he learnt to fit in socially. Classical music was a way for some of the lower-middle-class young people in my study to improve their class position, whether through getting music scholarships to private schools, going to courses and making friends with 'proper middle-class people', or gaining admission to high-status universities. However, in classical music rightness can be heard and known; or rather, you ought to be able to hear it, and if you cannot, you are demonstrating your ignorance by playing it wrong. It is necessary to prove that you can make judgements of right and wrong, in tune and out of tune, together or not quite together. Both in getting it right, and in making judgments of whether you (or someone else) has got it right, the work of learning to make these judgments is being performed.

As well as Frith and Skeggs, a third writer on 'getting it right' is Richard Sennett, who draws on his background as a classical musician to explore the idea of craftsmanship. Sennett describes how young string players learn to hear and produce the right sound and tuning in the body. For Sennett, musical technique is produced through a dialectic between doing something the correct way and the willingness to experiment; as a musician, 'I have to be willing to commit error, to play wrong notes, in order to eventually get them right' (2009, 160). He uses the process of learning to get it right musically as a metaphor for learning craftsmanship, 'the skill of making things well' (8), which is 'an enduring, basic human impulse, the desire to do a job well for its own sake' (9). While Sennett focuses on 'unity of head and hand' (178), in this chapter I take a different perspective towards understanding how the 'correct way' to do something musically occurs in the body by foregrounding the social context in which musical technique is developed. Classical music's ideals of beauty require a long-term investment of hard work, and as this chapter goes on to explore, through this requirement the aesthetic itself contributes to the social relations around classical music.

Constructing Rightness through Respectability and Hard Work

In one of my interviews with Andy, I asked him to explain why he had said his classical music friends were more similar to him than his school friends. To my surprise, he put forward the idea of classical music as indexing a middle-class morality:

> ANDY: I think music is ... often linked to, like, not even intelligence level, but kind of a moral level of what is right and what is wrong, do you know what I mean?
> ANNA: I'm not sure ...
> ANDY: Like I mean chav culture has a different set of morals as, like, white middle class, and I think—you know I very much consider myself—even though my parents are very working class, all my university friends would say, oh you're completely middle class, I'm like, I'm not.

The association of getting it right musically with what he described as a 'moral understanding of what is correct behaviour and what is okay' was powerful for him. It was also racialized; this sense of right and wrong that he felt was inextricably linked to classical music was also part of a 'white middle-class morality'. Andy suggested that this was a gendered morality linked to women's promiscuous sexuality, but when I questioned this, he reflected that many of his classical music friends were just as promiscuous as the 'chav culture' he was trying to set them against.

However, this reading of sexual morality onto middle-class morals, as expressed through classical music culture, is an important piece of this puzzle. Chapter 2 set up the historical argument regarding female sexuality as marker of classed respectability in the Victorian period. 'Chavvy' culture, including its gendered associations of shameful female sexuality as exemplified by the moniker 'slut' or promiscuous female, was commonly understood among my participants not to have any overlap with classical music culture. This was referred to only occasionally. For example, in the pub one evening Helen told her friends that her boyfriend had been teasing her about having 'chavvy' vowels. She told this as a funny story, but it was not risky for her to tell it as there was absolutely no way that anyone could read anything other than respectability onto her. Indeed, her friends all reassured her, amid indignant laughter, that her vowels were in no way 'chavvy'.

When this vignette is examined alongside classical music's boundary-drawing practices of classical music, its associations with white middle-class morality, and its modes of 'respectable' dress and embodied restraint, playing classical music comes to be seen as an expression of classed respectability. As Nicholls (2018) describes, respectability still forms an important part of the currency of British femininity. However, it only becomes visible when it is transgressed, and there were very few transgressions in my fieldwork. Where they did occur they were subtle, for example, during a concert with the NSO, the girls were required to wear 'long black', with long skirts or dresses covering elbow and knees; but, the organizers told us for the 2012 concert, 'since it's so hot you don't need to wear stockings'; the requirements of respectable femininity would, it appears, usually require all flesh to be covered. We all wore modest but elegant clothing, except one young woman who stood out for having very high wedge heels and bright peroxide blonde hair, drawing attention to how soberly dressed the rest of us were. Indeed, for that concert I had put on unobtrusive earrings and pinned my hair up, trying to fit in with what was acceptable in that space. We were so far in social distance (Bourdieu 1987) from 'chavvy' or non-respectable femininity that there was rarely any need to spell out these requirements.

As well as female sexual respectability, a further link between classical music practices and classed morality is the requirement for 'rational labor' to avoid idleness (McClintock 1995, 119). This discourse can be dated to the Victorian period, when it was a key axis around which the emerging middle class asserted its identity. As McClintock describes, this was a way in which members of the middle class could distinguish themselves both from the aristocracy and from the unrespectable working classes, each of whom 'spent, sexually and economically, without moderation and who preferred not to work' (1995, 100). Nick Taylor draws out links between such ideals held by Victorian social reformers—that 'members of the working class and underclass (and those of other races) lacked foresight and a certain work ethic'—and contemporary political rhetoric, demonstrating the contemporary power of such discourses (2018, 406). Indeed, as Mendick, Allen, and Harvey argue, in the UK there has been a shift over recent years towards a 'hard work zeitgeist' (2015, 174) whereby 'hard-working' has become a moral category that separates those who deserve state support or other economic benefits from those who do not. This language has sedimented into common-sense categories of 'hard-working families' or 'strivers' versus 'shirkers' and 'skivers'. These terms have migrated from political rhetoric to popular culture such as the new television genre of 'poverty porn' (Jensen 2014).

Classical music is a prime site in which to observe discourses of hard work as it is very labour-intensive. The most obvious example of the hard work required in playing classical music is daily individual practice, which elicited strongly contrasting discourses from my participants. Jonathan's view, echoing some others, was clearly one of duty: 'I don't think *anyone* wants to practise [...] doing the nitty-gritty, having to do the really boring stuff and forcing yourself to do it'. Others gave more nuanced accounts, such as Jenny, an eighteen-year-old string player, who loved the hard work but also felt an obligation to do it in the right way. Jenny came from what she described as a 'poor but middle-class' family, in which her mother had very strongly encouraged her to learn music. Following her mother's research into musical opportunities, Jenny had attended a specialist music secondary school on a scholarship. She described how, as a child,

> I really enjoyed practising and my mum really encouraged me, [...] and I really wanted to try and improve [...]. Until I went to [the specialist

music school] I played because I loved it, and I practised for four hours, [...] two hours in the morning, two hours in the afternoon.

This was at age ten. 'But', Jenny went on to describe,

> [I was] practising as in running through pieces, playing how I wanted to play it, not looking ... not taking it apart at all, and so I did improve I think quite a lot but not nearly as much as if I'd done better practice. And then when I got to [the specialist music school] I did get told, you must do this, these are the ... you need to work on shifts et cetera, all those little things to do with technique, and my technique improved a lot. And how to practise, like taking a bar and adding two then adding two, et cetera [...] you'd never get it really really good unless you really do the detailed practice.

This passage gives a glimpse of the labour that goes into becoming proficient on an instrument. Similarly, Izabela Wagner's (2015) ethnography of virtuoso violinists in training details their endless hours of practising scales and technical exercises. Rather than 'playing how I wanted to play it', Jenny had to learn to 'take it apart' and 'do the detailed practice'. She doesn't finish the phrase in the first sentence: 'playing how I wanted to play it, not looking ...'. Not looking for errors? Practising 'properly' means looking for what is wrong and correcting it, then repeating it over and over again to make sure that it will be correct every time you play it. This contrasts with Sennett's discussion of craftsmanship, in which music practice is an exploration. The sense of playful curiosity that is central to his account was absent from descriptions of practising among my participants.

This idea of repetitive scrubbing away at what is wrong uncovers the implicit analogy with dirt in the way that musicians sometimes talk about mistakes. The metaphors of 'cleaning up' or 'fixing' mistakes are common parlance; for example, Ellie's teacher, in a lesson that I observed, commented that she just needed to 'clean up' the tuning a bit in one section. Similarly, in 'sectionals' in orchestra rehearsals (when each section of the orchestra goes off together to practise their parts) we used a 'cleaning-up' process similar to the one Jenny describes in her personal practice. During one of these sessions with the NSO, the leader of the cello section led us through a difficult section, putting the metronome on and first playing it very slowly, then moving the metronome up one notch faster each time we played it. If someone made a mistake, we would stay on the same speed or slow it down again until we got it right, then continue edging the speed upwards again. It was tedious work, and entirely unmusical, but the passage did improve, and at the end of the session we could play it not perfectly but better. When the young musicians in my study described hard work, this was the kind of labour they were talking about: making it unmusical in order to be able to play the music, and often far from attaining the 'unity of head and hand' that Sennett (2009, 178) describes as the ideal craft experience.

This labour is both collective and individual; as chapters 5 and 6 examine, large-group rehearsals are characterized by high levels of discipline and concentration. On the individual level, examining differences between the ways participants in different class positions talked about hard work in their own personal practice, it was possible to distinguish between musicians who felt they needed to work hard and those who felt this less acutely. It was those who were closer in social space to groups labelled as 'lazy' or as 'skivers' or 'shirkers' (Jensen 2014) who felt they had to work especially hard. The level of hard work they disclosed depended partly on whether they wanted to go on to be a professional musician, but, as described in chapter 3, these aspirations were related to their class position: the lower-middle-class participants I spoke to all wanted to go on to be orchestral musicians or opera singers; those who were from professional middle-class families, especially the young men, either didn't want to be musicians (instead wanting to be diplomats, lawyers, academics, or teachers or go into business or politics, among other possibilities) or wanted to study music but as conductors, academics, or composers. For those who wanted to be performers—none of the young men in the most privileged class positions—this ethic of hard work was more pronounced.

However, the following exchange illustrates the nuances of this discourse of hard work. Thomas and Sam were friends who were at Oxford together doing music degrees. Both of them had considered becoming musicians, although in the end neither took this route. Thomas was from a middle-class, state school background and had won a music scholarship to a very exclusive public school for sixth form, finding himself surprised that he had ended up at Oxford. By contrast, Sam had gone to private schools since the age of seven and had always been headed for Oxford or Cambridge. I asked them about practising, and they told me:

> SAM: One thing I have never been particularly fond of is practising. [...] To be honest, if I practise an hour a day, I feel like that's been a good day for me.
>
> THOMAS: Yeah, same for me. When I'm at home, I try to practise at least an hour a day. [... While at Oxford] I decided to do a diploma to kind of focus my practising. [...] So I just did it whilst—just to make sure. There's so many times at Oxford you think, I have an essay due tomorrow, and you spend the whole evening doing it, spending half an hour practising seems a waste of time, whereas if you're doing a diploma, or any kind of thing that's marked properly [it doesn't].

Thomas agrees with Sam that an hour's practice a day is a good day, but he reverses Sam's formulation, to say 'at least an hour'. Even so, to give himself the incentive to ensure that he practises, Thomas decides to do a diploma (a post-grade eight qualification offered by the exam boards) 'just to make sure'. It is unclear what he is trying to 'make sure' of, and why he needs to keep improving and working on his playing when he doesn't need it for his career. He says he wants a diploma because it's 'marked properly'—an external validation of his standard, suggesting that he feels he needs the credentialism offered by the grade exam boards in a way that Sam doesn't. The difference in class position between Thomas and Sam, I suggest, can help to make sense of this difference in attitudes towards practise. For Thomas, it is important to keep improving, and to keep proving his worthiness to be part of this social group of privately educated Oxbridge students. For Sam, this is a familiar culture in which he doesn't have anything to prove; there is no fear of losing his place. Practice as hard work is therefore doing performative, place-marking work for Thomas, which it isn't for Sam.

Among my participants, then, discourses of hard work were not uniformly adopted but could be mapped onto their class positions. Those who were part of the professional and upper middle classes did, for the most part, appear to work hard but had less to prove, while those in newer or more precarious middle-class positions performed more conspicuously the hard work that is required in classical music. Practising therefore performed a moral function of proving that you were not lazy and therefore feckless or 'chavvy', and this labour was audible to oneself and others in the sound produced. However, this hard work had to then be performed with an air of ease in order to produce a convincing musical performance, as the next section outlines.

'If It Sounds Easy You're Doing It Right': Concealing Labour

In the youth music groups in my study, we not only had to get it right but also had to perform 'ease', to look relaxed, and to 'look like you're having fun!' as the tutors and conductor on the county youth orchestra course kept instructing us. Throughout my fieldwork and interviews, statements about enjoying the hard work recurred. Simon, a singer, liked being in Cantando Youth Choir because of 'actually spending time being really focused in rehearsals and doing hard work—feeling tired at the end of the rehearsal is nice'. Many people told me how hard they work in National Youth Orchestra courses, with Jenny's comments being typical: 'I really enjoyed it, it was fantastic, it was really hard, I found it really hard'. These accounts denote a common mindset among young people in my study of thriving on the difficulty of the repertoire and enjoying the sense of achievement when it was mastered. However, sometimes it seemed as though the enjoyment or fun was a compulsory part of narrating this experience; Megan commented on how much fun it had been being in the Young Opera Company production, before telling me how she had sometimes wanted to run out of the rehearsal room crying, then finishing her account by emphasizing that 'it's been really fun'.

These discourses of striving and hard work versus ease and enjoyment were sometimes presented in aesthetic terms. Laurence, a singer who had won a choral scholarship to Eton and then to Oxford, described the type of sound he liked in his or other people's voices as 'easy, if it sounds easy you're doing it right, [...] I hate it being difficult'. This ease, for Laurence, occurred on the level of both the aesthetic and the technical (in terms of singing technique) and required concealing the labour that had gone into producing it. He elaborated:

> I think my main goal is to make everything easy, then I view it as being the right way to do it. I don't like it when it seems like an effort. I've done so much singing, obviously when it's extremely high it's still quite a challenge but it doesn't stress me at all to sing for long periods of time—if you're doing it the right way then it shouldn't be difficult, that's how I feel, and people might disagree, but ... it's not ever straining or ...

Laurence also uses the language of 'rightness' in describing 'the right way to do it'. For him, most of the hard work was put in when he was aged seven to thirteen, as a choral scholar, doing (he estimates) eighteen to twenty hours of music a week, living in as a boarder at the cathedral school. Maybe he really had forgotten what it was like when it was an effort, but nevertheless his statement belies the amount of labour that goes into creating the kind of musical performance he is describing. Laurence's account echoes the discourse of 'effortless achievement' of the 'ideal student' identified in studies of education (Mendick et al. 2018, 43) whereby hard work is only required for those who are less intelligent (Mendick, Allen, and Harvey 2015, 161).

While Laurence's comments need to be read within a discourse of the voice being natural and 'ease' as a pedagogic rhetoric that is emphasized in voice training, they also show that he had a different orientation to hard work to some of my other participants. While Jonathan constantly felt like he needed to work harder, Andy set ambitious practice regimes for himself, and Thomas enrolled in an exam to make sure he practised, Laurence's way of tackling the craft of singing is instead similar to Sennett's account of craftsmanship. This involves emphasizing not hard work but a sense of ease, or if there is resistance or difficulty, the expectation of being able to overcome it. This expectation can be traced to a common position of privilege which means Sennett and Laurence are more likely to have been (at least sometimes) successful in their achievements.

This difference is also apparent in the visibility or invisibility of the work they need to put in. Unlike Jonathan, who emphasized the hard work that he needs to do, Laurence doesn't want his labour to be audible. This reveals a contradiction: it is necessary to prove your place in the middle class through performing labour, while at the same time concealing that labour through ease of performance. It is hard work, but it has to sound easy; labour exists in the value of the product/

performance, but it must be concealed. The rhetoric of 'exceptionally talented young musicians'—a common phrase among the 'talent scout' organizations I described in chapter 2—also helps to hide this labour by suggesting it is about talent rather than work. In addition, as Clare Hall (2015) describes, the parents of choristers in her study minimized the amount of work they had put into their sons' musical education in order to emphasize the 'naturalness' of the boys' musicality. The intensive bodily investment and shaping that I described in chapter 3 is concealed, and the 'talent' becomes the property of the individual rather than the outcome of the labour of teachers, parents, conductors, and others investing in this body.

However, the aesthetic of ease that Laurence, among others, preferred needs to be contrasted with an account from Gregory. He was the chorus master for the Young Opera Company, a semi-retired music teacher who had grown up on a council estate and gone to grammar school, then music college. He described his background as 'aspirational but cautious' and in narrating his musical preferences noted, 'I like a bit of striving in my music', for example, the 'angst, with resolution' that could be found in Brahms. This was 'striving' in terms of the harmony, rather than in terms of the sound quality, as Laurence is describing. This striving appeared to fit with the ethic of labour and hard work that was common to the 'humble and hard-working' group described in chapter 3, which could also describe Gregory's class of origin. Classical music made sense to this group because they could work hard and perform their morality of hard work and, for the young women, their successful disciplining of the body into gendered respectability. The concealment of labour in the 'fetish' of the performance or product was more fraught for them than for those who didn't need to perform their morality, such as Laurence, whose place in this world was secure. He had only to choose whether he wanted to take it up; he didn't need to perform or demonstrate his worthiness for it. By contrast, the striving of Jonathan, Andy, and Thomas to be good enough was something that needed to be heard and known. Indeed, for Gregory, striving had become a source of aesthetic pleasure. In this way Laurence and Gregory each emphasized *musically* qualities that they also described existing in their wider lives, demonstrating in this instance an homology between musical and social dispositions.

Such classed differences in the ways hard work is narrated form a contrast with recent studies, which have drawn attention to a shift in such discourses (S. R. Khan 2012; Littler 2017). Khan and Littler both describe how elite groups are no longer relying on their habitual discourses of ease or entitlement, but instead are using a performance of hard work to legitimize their positions of wealth or power. This allows them to sustain a belief in meritocracy because, they argue, their hard work has earned them their positions of privilege. For example, in Khan's ethnography of an elite boarding school in the US, we would expect that the upper-class pupils would feel the 'assured optimism' and ease that their social status confers on them (Forbes and Lingard 2015). Instead, Khan (2012) found that they put on a constant performance of hard work. He argues that this is evidence of elites trying to prove they are worth their status by laying claim to the notion that their wealth is deserved and earned. Similarly, Jo Littler's (2017) cultural analysis of British celebrities finds them emphasizing the ways in which they appear to have earned their status through hard work.

These ways in which privileged groups justify their status were not visible among my participants. This difference from Khan's and Littler's findings can be attributed to my participants' lack of awareness of inequality. Despite living in a county with one of the biggest gaps between rich and poor among young people in the UK, my participants appeared to have little knowledge of this. As a result, the more privileged among them did not feel the need to justify their status through a performance of hard work; their social circles appeared to include predominantly others like them, so there was no need for them to justify their status. Making mistakes, while still shaming and unwelcome, was therefore less fraught for this group than for those who needed to prove their worth. For the lower-middle-class young people, the link between labour and 'rightness' meant that getting it right musically was also a way of performing the labour that has gone into accuracy. Andy described how 'accuracy in terms of notes is constant work, you're always working on getting the notes'. In playing and performing classical music, therefore, as well as performing your knowledge of what sounds right and wrong, what is also being performed is the labour that has gone into this practice. For some, such as Thomas, demonstrating their proficiency and therefore their worth is more important than for others, such as Sam. In this way the ethic of getting it right/doing something right is linked to the aesthetic of classical music. 'Getting it right' is a way of performing the thousands of hours of disciplined labour—from parents and teachers as well as the young people themselves—that are required to learn an instrument: the accumulated investment that becomes audible in a few bars of a solo. In this way, homologies between the aesthetic and the social reflect the ways in which the practices required to create the aesthetic are formed through classed values.

Affects of Rightness and Wrongness

As well as the one-to-one practice that classical music requires, in the collective practice of rehearsals, the main substance of the work of rehearsals is correction (Weeks 1996; P. Atkinson 2006). The conductor stops and starts the musicians throughout a rehearsal, giving detailed instructions about dynamics, tuning, ensemble, or phrasing. But as well as correction from the conductor, there is also a constant process of self-correction going on. Indeed, with most mistakes, the conductor will assume that players can correct them themselves, or the mistakes will be so small he won't have heard them.

As one's standard of playing improves, smaller and smaller details become perceptible as mistakes. In rehearsals, when I got all the details of tuning, bowing, and ensemble as well as all the notes exactly right, I would feel a pleasant sense of self-righteous superiority, a sense of satisfaction that could easily become addictive. But, especially in a youth orchestra, it was rare to get this sense of 'rightness' as the possibilities for error were legion. First, there were the mistakes that the whole orchestra would hear; in one NSO rehearsal I came in on the conductor's upbeat rather than downbeat, playing an unintended solo in front of the whole orchestra that meant we had to stop and start again. A second level of wrongness is when your whole section hears your mistake and the conductor might also hear it but chooses not to mention it as he assumes you will correct yourself the next time. The next level is where only you and your desk partner notice something. Finally, there are the mistakes that no one else notices but yourself, which are myriad—the chord which you suspect probably isn't quite in tune but you can't hear clearly; the quick adjustment to a bow going in the wrong direction; holding a note too long and starting the next phrase ever so slightly late; as well as all the intentional faking that even professional string players do deliberately in passages which are close to impossible to play accurately (A. McVeigh 2016).

All these levels of mistakes or not-quite-right-ness are audible. As a musician, your standard—that is, your calibre and your moral worth—is made transparent through the sound you make, or fail to make, since silence or playing timidly is also a mistake. Bethan and Rebecca, two string players in the NSO, described the fear they felt when their section in the orchestra had a solo. Grade exams were described as 'terrifying'. The worst judges are one's peers, despite the strong affinity with them described in chapter 3. As Andy described:

> If I'm playing in front of Tommy [another player in NSO] I'll crap myself. It's to do with putting yourself out there and having someone say, *this is wrong, this is wrong, this is wrong*. I think that's what it's about for me. And I think you have to have the confidence to overcome their criticism. (my emphasis)

The sense of being judged that Andy describes is almost overwhelming. This culture of fear is the corollary of the correction that forms the substance of rehearsals; the strength of the feeling of 'wrongness' that Andy describes necessitates these corrective practices. This is explored in close detail in a rare academic intervention into youth orchestra rehearsals: Peter Weeks' (1996) conversational analysis of the language of correction in a youth orchestra rehearsal in the US (notably, also showing a continuity of practice between the US and the UK). One of the most common modes of correction is what Weeks calls 'contrast pairs' (1996, 269). In this mode of correction, the conductor gives two examples of a musical passage, the first one 'embodying the failed performed version of a given musical passage, the other exemplifying the conductor's prescribed version'. Weeks notes that the first version 'was often sung in an exaggerated and faulted way, with a mocking tone, or done in a hasty offhand way, whereas [the preferred version] tended to be articulated more forcefully, clearly, and perhaps at greater length' (274). This mode of correction was instantly recognizable to me from my own musical education, bringing with it a powerful memory of the shame of being mocked in the 'faulty' version that would exaggerate the 'wrongness' in order to contrast it with the rightness of the correct version. The shame of playing it wrong is not only that the musician's failed attempt is amplified for the whole group to hear, but that the person whose expertise gives them the power to designate right and wrong overlays their own mockery on top of your already inadequate attempt.

There is thus a powerful affective dimension to getting it right or getting it wrong. Getting it right feels good, as the quote from Andy at the start of this chapter described; 'doing something right' together is 'such a good feeling'. After orchestra rehearsals, I often wrote in my field notes about the pride in getting it right: in counting the bars exactly and then coming in clearly and confidently with the next entry, in tune and in time; the surprise and pleasure that it all comes together and sounds good; and taking time over a bar line, the sense of satisfaction in all watching the conductor and following him precisely, as though the orchestra is all breathing together. George, the cello tutor in the county youth orchestra, referred to this in a cello sectional rehearsal when we practised a difficult passage together. We worked on it until we got it exactly together, and he said, 'Doesn't it feel good to get it right like that?'—and it did sound and feel good.

When it was wrong, ever-present was the fear of humiliation that came with being corrected. But possibly the most powerful affect of wrongness is shame. This was most often connected with tuning; Andy could have spoken for most of us when he said 'My tuning is the one thing that I stress about the most'. Sara Ahmed (2004, 103) describes shame as about exposing something that should be kept hidden. With playing out of tune, it is about exposing something that is wrong and should be corrected. If you play out of tune, it might be because your technique has failed you and you missed a shift, or—even worse—it might be that you can't even hear that it's out of tune. In a rehearsal for the county youth orchestra, conductor Olly made a very small hand gesture towards me, very respectfully, to suggest that my note was a touch under and I needed to come up a bit. This tiny interaction stuck in my mind because I felt ashamed not to have heard that it was ever so slightly out of tune. Similarly, in Ellie's lesson, as described in the previous chapter, there was a moment where she had a high, long note, played very quietly. As she was playing it, her teacher gestured towards her, his finger pointing up to indicate that the note needed to be pitched higher. Ellie didn't see this gesture as she was looking at her music, so when she stopped at the end of the piece and he was giving his comments, one comment, very gently given, was to 'be careful' of that top B as it was 'under', it was 'almost a B flat'. It is less that I noticed Ellie looking ashamed at having played out of tune, than that I felt the shame with her and for her. Earlier in the lesson she had commented that she needed to 'sort out her intonation' (tuning) in a particular piece, possibly as a pre-emptive strike before her teacher made any comments. Indeed, he commented that she was very hard on herself about tuning, which I had also noticed, but maybe not too hard on herself, as I'm not sure if you can ever be too hard on yourself about tuning. Nevertheless, I felt shame in the room, and from her teacher's particularly gentle manner in pointing it out, it seemed that he did too. He had no choice but to mention it, but as he did so, there became visible underneath his gentle, avuncular demeanour a sterner, stricter teacher who wouldn't baulk at mentioning things that his students would find it difficult to hear about their playing. Tuning was a spectre in the background throughout the lesson, as it is throughout everything every string player does. Ellie's uncertainty and self-consciousness showed in her facial expressions as she played; she would wince slightly if she suspected her note was a smidgeon out of tune, sometimes even when it was fine. Indeed, as I wrote in my field notes, it starts to seem nothing short of miraculous that string players bring themselves to play anything at all.

A refusal to play or sing did come up in my fieldwork, as part of a recurring narrative of fear of improvisation, or refusal to improvise. This inability to improvise was something that had given me a deep sense of inadequacy as a classically trained musician; I was unable to make a sound without being given music to read. This response can be easily explained: in improvising, there is no clear right and wrong, therefore, the entire ethical and practical framework of making a sound is removed, paralysing musicians and singers into silence. This was apparent from interviews and discussions with many of my participants; not only couldn't they do it, they didn't want to. Katherine is a typical example:

KATHERINE: I hate the whole concept, I just can't do improvisation. I just freeze and think, just kind of lose any musicality in me at all, and I'm just like, I can't do it. I don't know what.
ANNA: I guess this is common for classical musicians, because we're used to using the score.
KATHERINE: Yeah, I'm very classical, I'm not ... yeah.
ANNA: So is it something you find scary, or that you'd like to do, or ... ?
KATHERINE: It's something that I admire in people that can do it but I don't really have any interest in doing it.

Conductor Gregory described how he'd tried to get his choir to improvise and was frustrated because they either wouldn't or couldn't. However, a few people on more progressive music education programmes were learning elements of improvisation. Susanna had learnt jazz improvisation at one of the Saturday junior conservatoire programmes. She described how she 'absolutely hated the thought of doing it, I was just terrified of it [...] I just refused to do it, but they suddenly just made me do it and ever since I've just done it, and not really looked back at all'. However, she went on to say that at music college, she was not going to do any more jazz or improvisation because she did not think it would be useful for her career, which she saw as being strictly within classical music; the improvisation was helpful, she said, only because it improved her classical playing. This refusal is therefore not in any sense a lack or a failure, but a positive strategy that Susanna, Katherine, and others employed, of eschewing something that has no value in this culture. They didn't need to learn to improvise to do well as classical musicians; in fact, the emphasis on getting it right and the potential shame involved in making a mistake made refusal the obvious strategy.

These powerful affects of shame and fear at getting it wrong, or community and togetherness when it was right, demonstrate the ways in which getting it right musically has powerful social effects. In this way, the precision and detail that, as Kramer describes, 'matter a lot' in classical music (2009, 22) cannot be seen as purely *musical* factors. The ways in which they inflect the social will vary according to the wider socio-cultural context. In other words, the aesthetic does not fully predetermine the social meanings it will acquire, even though it carries with it certain preconditions such as a long period of training. However, as I have demonstrated earlier, in a culture with high levels of inequality where hard work is a marker of social worth, musical practice—and through this the musical material itself—becomes inflected with the wider social meanings that are circulating.

The Social Distribution of Fear and Confidence

Getting it right came at a cost for some of my participants. While Richard Sennett describes the practice of professional musicians as a process of 'investigative repetition' (2012, 16; 2009, 157), for young people in my study the social relations of authority in classical music education meant that the element of curiosity and investigation that Sennett describes was quashed by instructions from teachers of 'you must do this'. In Sagiv and Hall's research on music conservatoires in Israel, they describe how teachers argued that 'the never-ending series of instructions and constant technical demands can also be experienced as empowering by the learner' as it helped them to develop greater bodily awareness (2015, 119). However, neither Sennett's nor Sagiv and Hall's studies include the voices of young people narrating their experience of this process. The accounts in my study from Jenny, Andy, Jonathan, and others show an uncomfortable ambivalence: they wanted to improve, but this improvement often came at an emotional cost. Furthermore, this cost was not equally distributed across social location. Sam and Laurence, who were both privately educated before attending Oxbridge, did not need to perform the labour of practising or showing they deserved their place in this world. By contrast, those from less privileged class positions such as Jonathan, Andy, and Jenny had to work hard and perform their belonging.

This was a labour that they welcomed and sometimes enjoyed, but they also felt that they had no choice but to accept correction—even if it came in the form of bullying, as discussed later—as it would lead to their improvement.

Sennett's descriptions of craft match those of my most privileged participant, Laurence, more closely than the others. However, Sennett's evocative writing on the development of technique through 'a dialectic between the correct way to do something and the willingness to experiment through error' (2009, 160) omits an examination of the social context that creates and legitimizes correctness or error, for example, through tradition and authority. Sennett rightly recognizes that fear is part of the classical musician's emotional repertoire, noting that 'diminishing the fear of making mistakes is all-important in our art' and suggesting that 'the confidence to recover from error is not a personality trait; it is a learned skill' (160). While this is certainly true, it is only part of the picture. By contrast, the account I have given focuses on how this fear or confidence is learned within a social environment. Among the young people in my study, fear and confidence were not equally distributed between those in different social positions. While most, if not all, classical musicians are likely to feel fear when performing, the social causes and consequences of that fear are different; for Andy, making mistakes could lead to losing his social position in this group, whereas others with more confidence appeared to feel less shame at making a mistake.

Therefore, while Sennett takes fear as a seemingly natural part of musical or craft learning, I think it would be possible to have a musical learning environment where fear is not such a pervasive part of the experience. Developing an embodied craft through play and curiosity, as Sennett's view of the ideal conditions of craft practice describes, cannot happen in an environment where high levels of external control engender a fear of making mistakes. Even for those young people with extremely positive relationships with teachers, fear could still be a paralysing force. While Sennett gives beautifully observed accounts of his own experience of being a classical musician, the voices of the young people in my study demonstrate that his experience is not necessarily shared with those in other social positions. This highlights the importance of analysing the social distribution of fear and confidence as part of the musical/craft experience.

'He Really, Really Broke Me... Which I Really Needed'

The data in this chapter so far has demonstrated how participants carried the dispositions related to their class location into their musical practice, and these dispositions entrenched or exacerbated the inequalities that were already present. However, the most striking accounts of fear were descriptions of bullying in the one-to-one teaching relationship. Four of my participants told me about experiences that verged on emotional abuse by their instrumental teachers.² While only two of the young people who described these experiences were under eighteen at the time they occurred and therefore covered by this statutory guidance, these accounts point towards a culture where bullying and humiliation are a normalized, accepted part of learning classical music, as illustrated by the following account from Miriam:

> MIRIAM: My teacher at music college ripped me to shreds on a weekly basis, but in a good way. At the time I thought he was really mean and he was just bullying me, and actually you look back on it now, actually nothing he said to me was a lie, and he was just pushing me.
> ANNA: But did you feel like ...
> MIRIAM: Yeah, and at the time I think I was a lot more young-minded and I wasn't ready to take things on board, I took it all as a sort of personal attack, but it wasn't, it was a way of trying to get me to advance as quickly as possible, under pressure, and by the end of the year it was working.

Similarly, Jonathan describes his first year at music college:

> JONATHAN: I had a really tough first year actually, I had a real bastard of a teacher [...] but I've come to realise that he's an amazing player [...] but he really, really broke me. But I persevered ...
> ANNA: By being really critical?
> JONATHAN: Really critical to the point of insulting critical, and I do actually appreciate him breaking me down, because the trouble is, when you start becoming a better and better player very often it's the case [...] you start to get big-headed [...] and he really knocked me down which I really needed. I needed to have that humility brought to me, so I could realize this is where I am, and I have this potential to be a lot better than what I think I am, so whilst it did depress me, I persevered.

Both Jonathan and Miriam describe their gratitude towards their bullying teachers for pushing them really hard so they would improve as much as

---

² The UK government's definition of emotional abuse of children is 'the persistent emotional maltreatment of a child such as to cause severe and persistent adverse effects on the child's emotional development. It may involve conveying to a child that they are worthless or unloved, inadequate, or valued only insofar as they meet the needs of another person. It may include not giving the child opportunities to express their views, deliberately silencing them or "making fun" of what they say or how they communicate. It may feature age or developmentally inappropriate expectations being imposed on children. These may include interactions that are beyond a child's developmental capability, as well as overprotection and limitation of exploration and learning, or preventing the child participating in normal social interaction' (HM Government 2015, 92).

possible. Jonathan is more critical than Miriam, in that he names his teacher as 'a real bastard'. He then frames his account in terms of his own perseverance in overcoming this barrier. This narrative of hard work and perseverance as overcoming obstacles was echoed in Miriam's interview. She was very alert to ways in which her position as a lower-middle-class woman playing a brass instrument presented obstacles in terms of economic barriers as well as sexism. However, she positioned herself as having overcome these hurdles, and similarly her account of dealing with her bullying teacher focuses on what she sees as the positive aspect of this behaviour: that her playing eventually improved under this treatment.

A third account, from Jenny, was similar, but she was younger when she experienced bullying from a teacher. She started at a specialist music school at age eleven and stayed till she was sixteen, and while in some ways she loved her time there, she also found it very difficult:

> I think I was probably the worst violinist in my class and, um ... I don't know. There was a lot of pressure from my teacher, which obviously he wanted me to progress. I think emoti ... I mean, matu ... my maturity level wasn't as good as it should have been so that I could develop more, as in practice-wise I didn't ... I didn't take ... I don't know ... my practising wasn't very efficient and I didn't do enough to try and change it, I think. But now I hope I have, a lot, I'm much better at ... [...] I got quite upset about ... that he was quite angry with me at times, quite a lot of times. But I mean, I'm not angry at him, I don't resent him for it, because I needed to improve, but it didn't really work, his method of trying to make me practise [...] so I got quite, quite upset and he wasn't very happy with my progress. It wasn't an incentive, it was sort of quite unfailing, and that's why I didn't really do well, until I left.

In the first part of this quotation, Jenny struggles to articulate what was going on. Her teacher would get angry at her, but she is adamant that this was only because he wanted her to improve, and she tries to take responsibility for this herself, but she can't quite get the words out for what she was doing wrong. She does not appear convinced that his behaviour was her fault, but it is clearly not an option to blame him so she struggles to articulate what happened. What is striking about these accounts from Miriam, Jonathan, and Jenny is that they all emphasized how good these bullying teachers were, and how their teachers were right to pressurize and humiliate them in these ways. Common to all three accounts is accepting, and even being grateful for, the treatment that they have received. They all blame themselves for being too immature to be able to deal with these bullying teachers. Even Emily, who was bullied by her cello teacher as a young teenager until she stopped playing, took responsibility for her teacher's behaviour:

I think I sort of assumed it was my fault, which looking back on it I don't think it was 100% my fault, probably I was slightly to blame. [...] Maybe I just wasn't good at cello.

Notably, all four of these accounts came from people who were in different ways unsure of themselves in terms of their class position. Emily attended a top private school and had an upper-class father but a working-class mother, this 'in-between' class position meaning that, in her words, she always felt 'insufficient'. Jenny's family were middle class but poor, as she described it. Jonathan and Miriam were both from lower-middle-class families; Jonathan said his family were maybe 'working to middle class', and Miriam's parents had worked their way up from working-class and immigrant backgrounds. Like Jonathan's family, they were unable to help pay for instruments or courses or extra activities, something that Miriam described as putting her at odds with her friends at music college.

The common social positions of these young people suggest that the ethic of correction that is central to classical music practice is experienced more intensively by those who are somewhat marginal to this world. It is possible—indeed likely—that some of my participants from more middle-class positions also experienced bullying but that it was only those in marginal class positions who spoke to me about it. The preceding accounts reveal ambivalence in that these young people all described wanting correction because they felt they needed to improve. None of them labelled this behaviour from their teachers as bullying; instead, they accepted it as normal. The similarities across these four accounts suggest that this is not about individual teachers so much as an accepted culture of practice within elite classical music education. However, the hints of ambivalence in these accounts suggest that these young people realized that something was not right, even if, other than Jonathan, they couldn't name it.

It is also necessary to scrutinize the social context that enables this bullying. As discussed chapter 3, the one-to-one teaching relationship can be characterized by an intimacy that shapes young musicians' sense of self and expressive voice. It is not surprising, then, that when it became negative, there were powerful effects on young people's social and musical identity. Part of the power of this relationship must be traced back to the ethic of correction that I have described as central to classical music pedagogy, and also to the strong relations of hierarchy and authority towards teachers, composers, and conductors (Goehr 1992; Kingsbury 1988; Small 1996). Discussing the film *Whiplash* wherein the conservatoire music teacher bullies a jazz drum student, Ian Pace describes how the teacher uses 'the old lie that he is pushing students to get the best results' (2015a), echoing the accounts of my participants. Pace describes elite musical training as characterized by 'a systematic pattern of domination, cruelty, dehumanisation, bullying and emotional manipulation from unscrupulous musicians in positions of unchecked power, of which sexual abuse is one of several manifestations' (2015a). Surprisingly, while a body of research on one-to-one music teaching is now being built up (see, for example, Gaunt 2010; Haddon 2011), there is almost no research evidence on abuse in music education, either sexual, emotional, or physical abuse, across classical or other genres of music education, as compared to over twenty-five years of research and policy innovations addressing abuse in sport education (Brackenridge 1997; Lenskyj 1992; Brackenridge and Fasting 2002). This suggests a denial of the problem within classical music more widely. While there is no reason to believe that there are higher levels of abuse within music education than within any other field of activity, there are likely to be distinctive ways in which abuse occurs and is enabled, such as particular gendered patterns or enabling social environments. Ways forward in this area are discussed in the conclusion to the book, but any solutions must certainly take into account the wider culture of practice in classical music education and the profession, as well as patterns of inequality that leave students from minority or marginalized groups particularly vulnerable to harassment and abuse (Cantor et al. 2015).

Conclusion: Classical Music as a Means towards Classed Self-Improvement

For the young people playing classical music in this study, rightness and wrongness in classical music were not only about getting it right musically but also about getting it right *socially*. In particular, musical 'rightness' or 'correctness' intersected with a classed morality of hard work and gendered respectability so that, for example, pulling off a successful musical performance would, for young women, also involve presenting themselves as appropriately respectable. This musical 'rightness' is seductive and compelling for many reasons: the praise from adults, the social recognition, and the embodied sense of achievement that it brings. However, overall, in classical music being able to *hear* rightness (one's own and that of others) allows musical judgements to become social judgements.

Indeed, classical music offers fertile soil for this kind of labour because it is necessary to work extremely hard over a long period of time to become proficient. This can be immensely satisfying when one's improvement can be heard, and known, in sound. The possibility of continuing to practise and improve can, for many people, lead to deep satisfaction and a path towards self-realization. For others, it can exacerbate the lack of self-worth that comes with being an outsider, as illustrated in Jonathan's statement that 'every performance I do I'm not happy with'. While this kind of self-criticism can be experienced in many kinds of social and aesthetic practices, classical music offers institutional support and validation for the kinds of labour described here, with its clear boundaries around who is included and who is excluded, its modes of credentialism, and the constant need to keep performing one's proficiency. Getting it right in one exam/audition/performance still leaves open the possibility of making an egregiously shaming mistake in the next one.

To add to the ambivalent meanings associated with classical music practice, for some young people it was a route towards classed self-improvement. For Jenny, the impetus for this came from her mother, who had done a lot of work behind the scenes to gain Jenny a place within its institutional ecology. For others, such as Andy, it was their own efforts that gained them their place within this world. Revisiting the triptych of working-class to lower-middle-class young men whose accounts opened this and the previous two chapters offers a way of drawing out these themes. For Owen and Andy, in particular, classical music was an escape route from the provincial or rural small towns where they went to school, to urban areas. For all three of them it was their ticket into what Owen called the 'proper middle class'. Notably, Owen didn't talk about correction in the ways I have described in this chapter. This could be because he was still at sixth form college, while Andy, Miriam, and Jonathan were already at music conservatoires, a much more demanding and intensive environment, or it could be because Owen's background had in some way given him a confidence and adaptability that allowed him to feel he belonged in this world. However, for Owen, rather than critique being directed inwards towards himself, judgements could emerge outwards towards others in funny but scathing comments about anything that he didn't find musically up to scratch.

As well as providing an escape from their lower-middle-class, rural home towns, classical music was a route towards class mobility in other ways. Andy, in particular, had successfully learnt the moral and social codes and the bodily dispositions—ways of speaking authoritatively and dressing conservatively—that allowed him to fit in to the classical music world. Whether or not he succeeded in his chosen career as an orchestral musician, these dispositions would stay with him as embodied capital. He had also learnt to imagine a different life from that of his parents. His 'plan B' was to work in music administration, and he had already proved his ability in this area to himself and others by running the NSO for three years while at university. His imagined future, as well as his accent, taste, and dress, had become congruent with those of his friends in this world.

I have foregrounded Andy's, Owen's, and Jonathan's accounts in these three chapters because the experiences of the lower-middle-class young men in this world are particularly revealing. These young men do not have the assurance, ease, and authority that the professional and upper-middle-class young men exhibited. They were also negotiating a musical scene that has historic and contemporary connotations with gendered respectability and femininity. It is therefore doubly difficult for them to negotiate a successful identity in this space. Their accounts demonstrate how the classical music world is both an exciting site of possibilities and a precarious space of potential pitfalls. They were able to see, and describe, this world more clearly than other participants because it was more difficult for them to negotiate.

The affective experiences of classical music, as well as the intense friendships and connection that these experiences facilitated, demonstrate why people participate in this scene. The next two chapters continue to explore affective experiences, focusing on the social relations of rehearsals to examine the embodied, affective communication that is occurring. Chapter 5 unpicks the taken-for-granted logic of the rehearsal structure, to interrogate the rationale behind the mode of correction I have described in this chapter, beginning with an affect that has an important classed history—pleasure.

CHAPTER 5

Rehearsing Restraint

HOW THE BODY IS TRANSCENDED

On one of the New Symphony Orchestra courses we played a lush Rachmaninov symphony, a piece that the whole idea of an orchestra could have been designed for. In the first movement the cellos play a melody of Dr Zhivago–esque stomach-dropping gorgeousness. Every time this part came around, I looked forward to it. The rest of the orchestra would fade away as we—the cellos—lingered on a suspended note, then dropped down the octave to begin the tune, putting on our most chocolatey-rich tone. After its fairy tale–like opening phrase, the tune became troubled as our line yearned higher and higher—before gracefully climbing down again to where we started, with a reassuring sense of coming back home. But then, the most glorious moment—the entire string section joined the cellos to repeat the melody. I would feel the whole string section breathing in together as the conductor, Will, gave one of his welcoming gestures to invite us all to join in. All forty of our bows snugly in sync, we gladly obeyed, and the roof seemed to lift off the rehearsal room to allow space for the melody to rise. This was one of the moments that made it all worthwhile, one of the few places where I would exist solely within the music for the duration of the tune, watching and listening acutely to make sure I was perfectly together with my section, and within this hyper-alert state luxuriating in this glorious melody for the minute or so that it lasted.

We were rehearsing this movement one sunny August afternoon, and as we approached the melody, I started to anticipate the pleasure of playing it. But just as we were lingering over the first note, about to plunge into the main part of the melody, the conductor stopped us to give an instruction. I had to stop playing, even while every fibre of my being screamed to keep going. But the rest of my section had put their bows down and were awaiting his directions. Nobody seemed to feel the level of embodied frustration that I did at being stopped in mid flow.

This process of stopping and starting required a high level of embodied restraint from participants. We would cultivate such intensely pleasurable moments as described earlier but then be required to stop immediately on the conductor's request. Frustration was occasionally evident when people would keep playing for a few notes after the conductor had stopped. In fact, this is a perennial problem with young orchestras that I remember well from my youth orchestra days, with the repeated refrain from conductors of '*please* will you stop when I ask you to?' (also described by Peter Weeks [1996] in his study of rehearsals of a North American youth orchestra). I was impressed that both the NSO and the WCYO were usually far too disciplined to do this. Those in the NSO had spent five to ten years playing in orchestras, becoming habituated to this restraint. And despite its frustrations, this way of working was necessary to achieve the social order that putting together a complex piece of music required.

This chapter and the next explore what went on in rehearsals in the youth choir and youth orchestras in my research (the Young Opera Group rehearsed in a different way, being a stage production; chapter 7 will examine their practices). The rehearsal is at the heart of the experience of being in these groups; Cantando would do only two concerts at the end of a year of intensive weekend or holiday rehearsals. These two chapters therefore examine the rehearsal as a cultural practice, asking the basic ethnographic question: What is going on here? The obvious answer to this question is that the musicians are preparing for a performance. But this doesn't entirely satisfy me. The sheer amount of time that is put into rehearsals in the youth music groups I studied suggests that rehearsals are more significant than performances on some level. Nor are rehearsals necessarily enjoyable; they are characterized by hard work rather than fun. The young musicians would tell me they were exhausted after a day's rehearsal. Conductors made jokes to keep the musicians onside. When rehearsals went well, they could be 'thrilling', but when they went badly they were described as 'the most frustrating thing imaginable'. For my participants, going to a rehearsal was as normal as going to school; most of them went to several a week, and it was not uncommon to have two in a day, even after school. They thus became steeped in 'rehearsal etiquette': the norms of behaviour required of them. Rehearsals are, therefore, important sites for social and bodily learning about the culture of classical music practice, and one of the key sites where this tradition is reproduced.

In the groups in this study, much of this learning was made explicit by conductors, for example, the requirements for punctuality and discipline. But even more was learnt implicitly, becoming the tacit knowledge needed to function in this 'world'—for example, what counts as good-quality music, or what the appropriate social relations are between conductor and musicians. This chapter explores one aspect of this tacit knowledge: the self-restraint required by players in order to bring together sixty people to play a long, complex piece of music, using this example to explore how the body is constructed in classical music practice. In rehearsals, I suggest we are not only preparing for the concert but also learning the habit of experiencing emotions but not acting on them. As described in chapter 2, restraint is a cornerstone of bourgeois identity, linked particularly to ideas of disciplining female sexuality. Today, young people's self-control is making a comeback in the UK with the influx of 'character education' and positive psychology programmes from the US (Allen and Bull 2018; Bull and Allen 2018). But there is a contradiction between this requirement for restraint and control, while also using the body for musical expression, to make sound. The body must be expressive, but also controlled. This balance produces an historically and culturally specific type of body which, as I will demonstrate, is the idealized embodiment of middle-class whiteness. This chapter therefore outlines two mechanisms of control within classical music practice: first, whiteness as control and transcendence of the body is encoded into the aesthetic of classical music through its practices; and, second, the social, embodied organization of the orchestra can be read as symbolizing white, male control over the crowd.

The Structure of Rehearsals

Musicians' common-sense explanations for what goes on in rehearsals revealed a clear structure or formula. Violinist Ellie describe a typical rehearsal:

> I guess you play through the piece, so the conductor will pick out things that need to be fixed, so for example, balance, so he'll usually say, strings you're forte, wind you're mezzo forte. [...] and sometimes do a string bit or a woodwind bit or a brass bit, making sure the rhythm is the same and everyone's making the same sound. If we're echoing each other making sure we're doing it the right way.

This description gives the basic structure of most rehearsals that was shared among my participants, which appears to be standard practice among many classical musicians; for example, it is endorsed as the standard format by Charles Barber in his advice to young conductors (2003, 25). This approach can be summarized as taking place in three phases. In the first phase, the piece of music is played all the way through without (intentionally) stopping (although it might 'fall apart' if some people lose their place in the music and have to stop). In the second phase, the conductor gives detailed criticism to the players about exactly how to play particular parts, going over short passage of the music until the players get it right, often rehearsing one section, such as the cellos, on their own. This is where the bulk of rehearsal time is spent. In the third phase (which might be in the rehearsal but more likely is the performance), the piece is put back together and played through, with all the corrections that the conductor has given having been 'fixed'. The form is therefore whole-parts-whole (-parts-whole-parts-whole ad infinitum depending on how many rehearsals there are).

This formula becomes particularly interesting when we contrast it with ideas of coherence, unity, and time in ideologies of classical music. There is an overwhelming preoccupation in much musicological writing with the organic unity of a musical work: the concept of the structure of a piece of music as forming a complex but logical, interconnected whole, where all the fragments are subsumed to a larger unity and coherence (Goehr 1992, 2; T. Taylor 2007, 3). For Lydia Goehr, this 'ideology' of the 'work-concept' leads to the concomitant belief that performers must be 'true' or 'faithful' to the musical work (1992, 2). And yet, the 'true' meaning of the work does not lie in the written score, nor in any one performance of it, but is instead an imagined ideal. Different interpretations of a musical work in performance are trying to get as close as possible to this imagined ideal in order to let the work itself 'shine through'. Rather than the eighteenth-century concept of music as 'adaptable and functional' whereby notations were merely suggestions for the performer (186), in the nineteenth century musical scores became more and more detailed, and 'the performers [had to] now obey the ideas of unfettered genius' (226).

The ideal of the work-concept also leads to time being organized in a particular way. As Kassabian (2013, xviii) notes, the assumption of an organic whole leads to a mode of engagement with the musical work known as 'structural listening'. In structural listening, at any given moment during the piece, the listener is always aware of where they are in the structure of the whole work. This requires a knowledge of common musical forms that allows the listener to follow the harmonies and melodic development over the course of, say, a fifty-minute symphony. As Christopher Small (1996, 29) suggests, these formal structures of classical music are a way of making sure that we never get 'lost in time'; we always know where we have come from and where we are going, and roughly what will happen in order to get there. Any surprises will come within the given structure.

The ideology of the work-concept—the idea that all the details in the score add up to form an organic unity—shapes the structure of rehearsals and performance in the three phases described earlier. As well as a structure of whole-parts-whole, this is also a process of unity then fragmentation, or of organizing time then chopping up time. In the second, liminal phase, all the details of the musical work must be 'fixed' in place. As Ellie described it, 'Sometimes what happens [in rehearsal] is, we'll do a section, go through the section fixing bits and bobs and then play through the section so that it leads into the next section and then play through the next section and he [the conductor] realizes what's wrong, fixes that'. This word, 'fixing', is one that was often used, meaning to correct mistakes, suggesting a clear sense of right and wrong. However, in relation to the ideology of the organic unity of the musical work, fixing could also mean setting each detail, each note or phrase, in place within the larger whole. This process of 'fixing' forms the bulk of the rehearsal time and is required so that the piece doesn't 'fall apart' in concert; as much as stopping in rehearsals is normal and right, stopping in the concert is abnormal and indicates something has gone wrong. But this fixing also is necessary so that all the details of the work, which have been carefully placed there by the composer, can do the work of creating a larger edifice in sound and in time.

This is what is happening when the conductor stops us in rehearsals to give an instruction or correction to the musicians. On the 'common-sense' level of my participants, it is the reason why it doesn't make sense to keep playing a pleasurable melody simply because it's pleasurable, but why everyone will stop for a detail to be 'fixed'. This is what I am calling the 'content of form' of rehearsals. It is an explanation that my participants would recognize; indeed, if the conductor let a problem go past *without* fixing it, there would be muttered grumblings in the pub after the rehearsal. Following the work-concept as a way of structuring rehearsals ensures that pleasure—and other emotions—are fixed in time and place, within the existing structure of the musical work.

The work-concept ideal therefore structures the social organization of rehearsals, working in tandem with another common-sense idea articulated by musicologist Julian Johnson when he argues classical music allows us to 'transcend ... the bodily' (2002, 112), also evident in musicologist Dahlhaus' (1991, 7) description of instrumental music as 'pure structure' which 'represents itself'. Bodies do not figure in this account; they are simply a vehicle for the 'pure structure'. The visceral frustration that I described in the opening section of this chapter is irrelevant to the musical expression of structure. Indeed, this ideology is powerful enough to maintain order even among sixty teenagers cultivating strong emotions in the same space.

However, transcending the body came at a cost, and one of the rare times when the body was made visible was through its failure: when people fainted, felt ill, got exhausted, felt uncomfortable, or got injured. During one day's rehearsal for Cantando, I saw four singers ask permission to go home due to 'exhaustion' or 'not feeling well'. Others spoke of how they would get to lunchtime in a day's Cantando rehearsal and already feel exhausted. WCYO conductor Olly told us we *should* be exhausted after a day's rehearsal, because it was such hard work. This exhaustion appeared to have an affective dimension as a response to the pressure for rightness despite the difficulty of the music. I asked Olly about one of the young players who had wanted to drop out but had been persuaded to stay on. He explained this boy's difficulty by arguing:

> Well, you've got to be brave. And you've got to see it through and you've got to realize that it doesn't necessarily come easily but it's worth [it]. For some people it isn't, for some people, they simply can't do it, some people don't make that choice and can't do it.

For Olly, then, what was required was mind over matter, will over recalcitrant flesh. But bodies made their presence felt in rehearsals. As well as the body asserting its presence through exhaustion and attrition, classical musicians experience high levels of physical injury. Even the cello tutor George's body made itself known through a shoulder injury he had had for some time which meant he was unable to play during some of the rehearsals. He was clearly worried about it, as he worked as a freelance orchestral musician most of the time, so if he couldn't play, he wouldn't get paid. Indeed, Christina Scharff (2016) found in her study of early-career female classical musicians that half of the sixty musicians in her study had had injuries of some kind through playing, and many had had to stop working for a time as a result. Despite this, in her study participants did not talk about injuries, due to fear of being seen as 'faulty' and losing work. This finding appears typical; a systematic review of research literature found that the best estimates for prevalence of playing-related musculoskeletal disorders alone were up to 47% in adults and 17% in secondary school music students, but studies that included mild complaints as well as serious ones found that as many as 87% of adult musicians experienced such disorders (Zaza, Charles, and Muszynski 1998).

The body's failures are therefore writ large in classical music practice, but the ideology of transcendence cannot take account of them, so they must remain secret to allow the ideal that classical music 'transcends' the body to remain intact. And indeed, the practices described later in this chapter—policing movement, wearing all black, and cultivating a mode of 'controlled excitement'—*almost* did work to efface and transcend the body, while producing beautiful performances that confirm the special status of classical music as expressing 'an aspiration to realize a being not confined to the bodily' (Julian Johnson 2002, 112). But this aspiration is fulfilled at a cost, as classical music is highly demanding of the body and takes its toll in the form of injury and exhaustion. In order to maintain the ideology of transcendence and efface the body, there must be mechanisms for ensuring that it is noticed as little as possible. The next section takes a different perspective on the rehearsal by examining ways in which bodies were organized in order to achieve transcendence.

How Is the Body Effaced or Transcended?

The main way the body was effaced was through policing its movements and requiring it to be still. The most explicit account of this came from violinist Alice. Over lunch one day, Alice told a story about a rehearsal with the National Children's Orchestra during which she was sitting on the outside of the first violins, tapping her foot to keep in time while playing a complicated rhythm. The conductor stopped the orchestra and, without saying a word, marched down the line of first violins and stamped on her foot. Still remaining silent, he walked back up to the podium to resume the rehearsal. During that afternoon's rehearsal I found myself tapping my toe inside my shoe to keep my place on the offbeats. I remembered Alice's story and stopped tapping.

This stillness was required only for European repertoire, and bodily movement was encouraged or even choreographed for non-European music. In the New Symphony Orchestra, we played a Latin American piece made popular by the

Simon Bolivar Youth Orchestra (which, as Baker (2014) describes, choreographs very carefully the musicians' apparently exuberant Latin American bodily movements). The conductor decided that we would follow that famous orchestra by adding some choreographed moves while we were playing. Andy, who was introduced at the start of chapter 3, was adamantly against it, arguing that it didn't work in conjunction with the more 'serious' music in the programme such as the Dvořák cello concerto. Maybe he thought the proximity of the body polluted its seriousness somehow. 'I said, I will not play if we do it. [...] we're a classical orchestra'. The conductor backed down and included only one move at the end, where we crouched down as the music suddenly went quiet, and then gradually straightened up as the music got louder. Even this was too much for Andy, who half joked: 'I died inside. Even in the concert I died inside'.

There was a similar contestation over when and how to move one's body in Cantando. During the more 'serious' music such as pieces by Vaughan Williams, Purcell, or Britten, the choir stood still, letting the music emerge without putting any bodily expressivity in the way of the sound and words. For the performance, they wore all black, as is the norm for orchestral and choral musicians. In the concert, singing in the half-shadows in a gloomy Victorian church, it was almost as if they were trying to camouflage their bodies so that the sound would appear to be coming from nowhere, enhancing its ethereal beauty. Any bodily movement or expressivity would have detracted from this effect.

Wearing all black is therefore another mechanism for effacing the body. While Charles Rosen (2002, 118) suggests that this dress code draws attention to musicians' historic status as members of the servant class, the signification of musicians wearing black has changed over time. Lise Vaugeois suggests it is a way of 'muting the individuality' of performers, while also 'minimizing the relationship between the physical production of sound and the aural effects of the music' (2014, 200). Similarly, in the musical groups in my study, it had two main significations. Firstly, it camouflaged the body, making it as unobtrusive and unnoticed as possible, working as another mechanism for achieving transcendence. However, this worked most successfully for male musicians; as Lucy Green argues, performing classical music while being female is a sure way to make the body visible. When we hear a man playing the drums, we hear *the music* on the drums, but when we hear a woman playing the drums, we hear a *woman* playing the drums; the female gendered body makes the body visible where previously it wasn't (Green 1997, 79–80). Indeed, as Lisa McCormick notes, in classical music competitions female performers were on a constant knife edge to determine what was acceptable for them to wear, one competitor saying she was careful that what she wore didn't 'distract from the music' (2015, 195). The visual element was clearly part of the 'text' that was read by judges and audiences, but it had to 'appear natural', which was a particular challenge for women, who are more likely to be sexualized than men (199, 201, 209). Secondly, wearing all black in the styles required for classical music performances is a way of signifying class. As described in chapter 4, for women, classical music's concert attire makes visible its associations with respectable middle-class femininity. Classed associations are also present for men, who wear either all black or 'dinner jackets'. The latter are also associated with middle- and upper-class modes of dress, as this costume is required in spaces such as some Oxford or Cambridge formal dinners, or events associated with other middle- and upper-class professions such as the law.

Even in black, however, bodies could be made visible again through movement. When Cantando started rehearsing a Duke Ellington medley, the body no longer needed to be camouflaged by stillness. This piece was outside the boundaries of 'serious' classical music repertoire, following the conductor, Richard's, determination to branch out beyond the narrow range of music that classical choirs usually perform. Richard gave the choir members instructions to move their bodies more, telling them they were holding themselves like they were still singing Purcell, suggesting a 'gentle swaying', and telling them 'you've got to loosen up'. They had stopped in between numbers in the medley for him to give some points, and there was an irony to being told 'you've got to loosen up' before being given very precise instructions about how to sing all the details in the music. When they started again, a few moved fairly comfortably, but most looked quite self-conscious, and some didn't move at all. They seemed to want to follow Richard's instructions, but they didn't know how to switch from 'singing Purcell' mode to a different form of embodiment. One singer, Holly, joked later: 'You're like, come on guys, pretend you're some black people, and move! Oh! It's really funny watching, because they're singing so beautifully but they're standing here looking so serious'. Richard grumbled that 'trying to get this choir to move even an inch is impossible'.

Holly's comment suggests that bodily movement during the Duke Ellington medley was about making visible its racial associations. In the NSO, as described earlier, movement was introduced for a Latin American piece but not for 'serious' (European) repertoire. However, the clearest example of movement/non-movement as a racialized dichotomy could be seen in some arrangements of 'African' songs sung by Cantando. Richard choreographed the choir with marching and clapping movements and at one point suggested that they march as though they were carrying a very heavy load. Some of them did so in an exaggerated fashion for a few steps, imaginary bundles slung over their backs, sinking with every step, in a seeming parody of what they might imagine an African 'other' to be. This music *requires* bodily movement to maintain the distinction from more 'serious' repertoire. There was a clear divergence, therefore, in the way the body was positioned in European and non-European music. Expressive movement was not only allowed but required in the latter, while in European repertoire the body had to remain still, to be effaced in order to be transcended. These different forms of embodiment also reinforced the boundary-drawing around repertoire described in chapter 2. 'Proper' or 'serious' music was demarcated by stillness, whereas 'cheesy' or 'fun' music was marked out by movement. But most importantly, this was a racialized dichotomy, in that the body was effaced only in repertoire that was associated with white identities. Whiteness is, in this way, encoded into some repertoires and not others; and the repertoire coded as white is also that which is seen as more 'serious' and with greater emotional depth, as chapter 8 explores.

This portrayal by a predominantly white group draws on racialized stereotypes to depict an imagined, essentialized 'African' 'other'. This example is both a straightforward racist trope and a white fantasy of 'otherness'. As Toni Morrison (1992) describes, depictions of racialized others by white people allow us to understand whiteness better. What is being 'othered' here is bodily suffering and enslavement, drawing on familiar tropes of black suffering and people of colour as more closely tied to the body (Ahmed 2002). Whiteness is therefore produced as a quality that is identified by transcending or effacing the body, and as free rather than enslaved. Furthermore, it is important to note that these 'African' songs were consciously used as a way of broadening the choir's repertoire beyond the usual narrow classical repertoire (a common practice among classical choirs, although less so among orchestras). bell hooks describes this as 'eating the other' (1992, 21)—appropriating the culture/bodies of people of colour for white people's pleasure or status or to feed their 'enterprising' spirit (Dyer 1997, 31). While hooks argues that 'the message that acknowledgment and exploration of racial difference can be pleasurable represents a breakthrough, a challenge to white supremacy, to various systems of domination' (1992, 39), it is notable that twenty-five years after she wrote this, classical music has not found a more critical way to engage with racial difference.[1] hooks goes on to say that 'the over-riding fear is that cultural, ethnic, and racial differences will be continually commodified and offered up as new dishes to enhance the white palate—that the Other will be eaten, consumed, and forgotten' (39). Indeed, Skeggs (2003, 1) positions white middle-class appropriation of black culture as a way of resourcing the middle-class self and accumulating capital.

The groups in my study did, on the whole, engage with race as 'eating the other'. The only ways in which race was present or acknowledged was, as discussed earlier, in the occasional use of non-European repertoires, which were choreographed differently onto the body than European repertoire. This lack of explicit discussion of race makes the embodied differences unnoticed and unspeakable, and therefore more powerful. By contrast, as hooks argues, 'Mutual recognition of racism, its impact both on those who are dominated and those who dominate, is the only standpoint that makes possible an encounter between races that is not based on denial and fantasy' (1992, 28). This means that singing 'African' songs is not what is problematic here (other than the undifferentiated assumption of

---

[1] See also Vaugeois' (2014, 185) discussion of the use of 'redface' in classical music institutions in colonial Canada, which she describes as 'producing pleasing fantasies about the colonial subject'. This practice has been used in opera until recently; the Metropolitan Opera in New York made headlines when it dropped 'blackface' productions of Verdi's *Otello* in 2015 (Woolf 2015).

'African' as an identity), but rather the 'fantasy' depiction of 'African' people as marching under a very heavy load. Music can and should be shared between cultures, but this needs to include a critical discussion about the kind of dialogue, denial, or fantasy that is occurring through it. However, the movement/non-movement dichotomy was not the only way in which whiteness was encoded into the practices of classical music.

Controlled Excitement: The Body as a Site of Contradictions

I asked Holly, who was frustrated at her non-moving choir colleagues, what she thought this stillness was about. She answered:

> Probably concentration actually. [...] especially when you're singing without music, you're really aware of what everyone else is doing, when you've got to come in, and you kind of almost forget to move.

Her assumption here seems to be that movement is something added in later, rather than being an integral part of the 'musicking' itself (Small 1998); she is concentrating on getting all the details of the music 'itself' correct, an endeavour that becomes a cerebral one in this account. There is a contradiction, then, between the concentration required to coordinate all the requirements of playing this music, and the sense that you are supposed to also be physically expressive. For, despite all of the disciplining into stillness as described earlier, the idea that the body *should* be expressive remained. For Andy, who so strongly objected to the choreography of the Latin American piece in the NSO, it was only because the movement was coordinated that he objected. 'I move a lot when I play', he told me. 'I just think people should look like they're enjoying it'. Others echoed this, arguing that it is important that the audience can see you enjoying yourself and then has permission to enjoy themselves. Bodily movement could also help with getting it right. Olly, the conductor of the WCYO, complained to the orchestra during one rehearsal that 'with these rhythmic passages I see many of you playing like this'—he gave a comical demonstration of standing stiffly while blowing an instrument. Instead, he went on, 'I want to see that you are feeling the rhythm in your bodies, in some way'. This was a pedagogic point; we weren't playing in time, and he was trying to help us to get it right.

However, George, the cello tutor for the WCYO, made precisely the *opposite* argument for a similar offbeat rhythmic passage that we rehearsed in a cello sectional. He suggested that we should limit our movements to feel the offbeat so that we would 'conserve our energy'. 'No one would say that you shouldn't move, it's part of playing music', he argued, 'but you make a better sound if you don't move around so much'. These contradictory orders even became a joke between George and Olly during a string sectional rehearsal. 'Sit up straight—but relax', George quipped, smiling. Olly upped him one with 'Be calm, but get it right'. George had to turn it into a parody at this point: 'Do this, but also do that, but don't do that too much, and make sure you do this—and smile!' It was a joke, but it also was true. We needed to get every detail of articulation, phrasing, and bowing correct, while being energetic, excited, and passionate. This was no mean feat when the potential for mistakes was seemingly infinite. Violinist Alice joked, 'It's amazing how often I get the bowing wrong, given that there's only two options: up or down!'

The musicians therefore tended to agree in principle that some movement was good, but they were somehow frozen into stillness by the concentration that Holly described as necessary to get all the details right. Indeed, this mode of embodiment was made explicit by Olly when he called for 'a disciplined balance of control and excitement' in one rehearsal. We were playing a piece by Shostakovich, and he pointed out that the strings weren't using the full length of our bows. 'Violins', he said, making one of his typically dry jokes, 'I want you to go home and get out a tape measure, and measure how long your bow is, and look at how much of it you're actually using'. The music needed to sound more 'exciting', he said; this technical tip would help to produce that effect. But we were never to lose control; 'controlled excitement' was what we needed, he told us.

This juxtaposition of measurement and excitement calls to mind Elias' 'controlled de-controlling of emotional control' (qtd. in Wouters 1987, 422). Wouters, in his comparative study of Dutch etiquette books from the 1930s to the 1980s, uses this phrase to describe the expectation that people should be capable of restraining or channelling petty or dangerous feelings if needed. Featherstone takes up this idea to argue that this 'controlled de-control' (2007, 80) is an attribute of an emerging middle-class self in the late twentieth century that distances itself from the 'grotesque other' amid a 'sense of disgust at direct emotional and bodily expressivity' (79). This suggests that 'controlled de-control' is a building block of the middle-class boundary-drawing that I described in chapter 2; loss of self-control and *uncontrolled* emotions would jeopardize one's status as a bona fide member of the middle classes. There is evidence that this disposition is gendered, as an almost identical phrase is used by Fiona Measham (2002) in her discussion of the ways in which drug use is gendered in the UK. She found that women sought a 'controlled loss of control' when taking either legal or illegal drugs and suggests that this 'taps into broader social attitudes around gender' whereby loss of control in public risks women's respectability, self-presentation, and personal safety (Measham 2002, 349). Classical music, for middle-class women, could be seen as a space that allows safe, respectable thrill-seeking.

This 'controlled excitement' is achieved in classical music through technical means. Indeed, the better you were technically, the more exciting the music could become. The body was simultaneously instructed in a thousand technical details, while we were also being told to put energy and excitement into our playing. In theory, the technical instructions would enhance our capacity to play passionately or with excitement. But the net effect, as Holly described, was of intense concentration in order to get all of these details right. This led to a particular form of embodiment of 'controlled excitement', which bears similarities to other accounts of white bodies as 'controlled', such as Christy Kulz's (2017) study of an East London secondary school which details pupils' understandings of racialized identities. One of the teenagers in Kulz's study, a boy called Joshua, of Nigerian heritage, came up with what he called 'the three C's' as a way to explain why white pupils were disciplined less often than ethnic minority pupils: they were 'controlled, compact, and concise', he observed (2017, 98). In this way, as Kulz argues, non-white bodies can become (more) white by exhibiting the modes of bodily comportment that perform whiteness.

In addition, as Richard Dyer notes, whiteness draws on the 'mystery' of the body put forward in Christianity as both present and absent; 'what makes whites different ... is their potential to transcend their raced bodies', 'a need to always be everything and nothing, literally overwhelmingly present and yet apparently absent' (1997, 15). The problem of the body in performing classical music—it needs to be present in order to make sound, but it needs to be transcended in order to allow the spirit of the musical work to shine through—reflects the paradox of whiteness. Indeed, controlled excitement exemplifies Dyer's explanation of white sexuality, in that white people must act on heterosexual urges in order to reproduce their race, 'yet they must also control and transcend their bodies' in order to express 'the qualities of "spirit" that make us white' (27, 30). These qualities of spirit include the 'something that is not of the body which may be variously termed spirit, mind, soul or God', as well as the Christian 'spirit' as existing outside the body, making us never reducible to our physical existence even while the holy spirit exists within the body (of Christ) (16). Similarly in the 'work-concept' the essence or spirit of the musical work does not exist in the score, or in any one performance or recording of it, but is instead an imagined ideal, also never reducible to physical existence (Goehr 1992). In order to realize this 'spirit', the body must be both present and absent, both controlled and also expressive. In this way, ideas of whiteness are both drawn on and reproduced through classical music practice. While these signifiers were seldom named, the young musicians in my study, even the few who were not white, performed a white identity as 'controlled, compact, and concise'. Musicians' bodies encoded whiteness into European repertoires by being controlled and still, yet still expressing 'spirit' and emotion, while never letting emotional excitement get in the way of technical control. The very aesthetic of classical music therefore encodes whiteness.

The Orchestra as a Bourgeois Fantasy of Male Control

The stillness that is the bodily norm in classical music is not an absence but is productive of a particular set of social relations. These social relations are made visible by bringing the body and its affects back into the frame of analysis. This lens allows a different perspective on my rehearsal sites as scenes where powerful affects such as fear, excitement, pleasure, and striving are being cultivated. These included the emotions of the Romantic repertoire that my participants loved, as well as those related to the social relations of rehearsal and the challenge of playing this difficult music. In this light, the mechanisms for keeping the body still can be reread as mechanisms for stopping the spread of these affects: for *containing* affect, ensuring that restraint is practised and these powerful emotional states are not acted on. Similar ideas were circulating in the decades following the institutionalization of the orchestra, and at the same time that music education was being institutionalized. The orchestra's social relations and modes of practice therefore carry the legacy of ideas about the 'mass' or 'crowd' from the late nineteenth century. This history suggests a different reading of what is going on in rehearsals than the common-sense one suggested by my participants.

Amid fears of social disorder, late nineteenth-century writers such as Gustav Le Bon (1960 [1895]) and Gabriel Tarde (2011 [1890]) formulated a psychology of crowds. Ideas of 'contagion' and the unconscious (Le Bon 1960, 30) were important to this psychology, suggesting that powerful emotions would spread and cause the crowd to form a 'collective mind' (24) that would lead it to act as one being. As Lisa Blackman (2012) describes, the crowd was given 'primitive' and female characteristics, with Le Bon suggesting that those who were likely to be swayed by the crowd were those who 'embodied the attributes which connected the human with the animal' (1960, 36). However, the 'inhibition' or 'will' of the leader rendered him able to stand up against these powerful affects and stop them from spreading. The conductor could be seen to exemplify this willpower, and indeed the method of early twentieth-century conductor Arthur Nikisch includes descriptions of using 'mesmerism' in order to control the crowd (Holden 2003, 16). This recalls the ideas of hypnosis, the unconscious, and the power of suggestion that underpinned the crowd psychology of Le Bon and Tarde (Blackman 2012).

In the decades leading up to these debates at the end of the century, the model of the 'mass' of the orchestra (and, to a lesser extent, the choir) being controlled by the 'Napoleonic' ideal of the conductor was coalescing into the form by which we know it today (Bowen 2003, 103). The formative period for the development of the orchestra was the late eighteenth and early nineteenth centuries. However, the cult of the conductor emerged in the early to mid-nineteenth century as orchestras grew larger and started to become professionalized. Earlier in the century, it was the norm for the keyboard player or first violinist to lead (Bowen 2003, 97). The first conductor to face the orchestra rather than the audience, without an instrument, was Gaspare Spontini, who brought 'military discipline' to the Berlin Opera in the 1820s and 1830s. His performances were renowned for their 'precision and dynamic extremes' (Bowen 2003, 103–4), an early precedent for Olly's 'controlled excitement'. In London in the 1830s and 1840s, as William Weber (2004, 59) describes, the role of conductor was typically rotated between the members of an orchestra, but this old-fashioned method was overtaken by Mendelssohn's regime in the 1840s (Bowen 2003, 106).

The conductor's role in labour relations was also becoming evident, as Mendelssohn increased pay and introduced pensions for his musicians; he was also known for improving musical standards by getting rid of the bad players, introducing the 'private rehearsal' rather than holding rehearsals publicly, and instigating the stop-start method of rehearsal with frequent interruptions and corrections (Bowen 2003, 106). With the influence of Liszt and Wagner from the mid-century onwards, the maestro-conductor archetype was established (107). Across the pond, in Boston in the 1880s, impresario and entrepreneur Henry Lee Higginson in his newly founded Boston Symphony Orchestra paired musical control with control of labour. Higginson's musicians would lose their contracts if they played with any other orchestras, and he dismissed musicians immediately if they were not playing up to his standard (DiMaggio 1986, 54). A trend towards increasing control and precision in the music was occurring alongside and through stricter and more codified conditions of employment for musicians. While these developments were, of course, the result of a wide array of social, economic, and musical factors, there is an interesting synchrony between the increasing control of the orchestra and fears of the *lack* of control of crowds. Such ideas of the crowd reflected the ideology of their time: that the working classes, women, children, and racialized others were more susceptible to suggestion or emotion than the middle-class white man, whose self-control allowed him to be the point at which affects stopped. Today, therefore, the social organization of the orchestra can be seen as a form of cultural memory preserving these fears of the unruly crowd.

Indeed, the orchestra figures in wider culture as a prominent socio-cultural model of, and metaphor for, control. A key site in which the idea of the conductor and his control is influential is the corporate world (Logie 2012). According to Spitzer (1996), a range of metaphors have been used to describe the orchestra since the seventeenth century—as an army, a machine, and a civil polity—and in recent decades the orchestra as a corporation controlled by the CEO/conductor could have been added to these, as well as the orchestra as the mass or unruly crowd. The power exhibited by conductors over large groups of people makes them an object of fascination for business leaders; management studies journals appear to be the main place where discussions of the social relations of the orchestra take place.² This cross-fertilization between business leaders and orchestras can be seen most clearly through leadership workshops run by prominent conductors (Logie 2012, 35); I participated in such workshops during my working life as a musician, and indeed the conductor of the WCYO, Olly, ran them himself. This fascination is, Logie suggests, ironic given that 'the profession of conductor is one of the last bastions of totalitarianism in the civilized world' (39). It is possible to make sense of this through the fantasy of control over the corporation/crowd that the conductor represents. The conductor must retain control over himself and his workers, who also represent the working-class masses/crowd. This reading gives a different perspective on the social learning that takes place in rehearsals. The musicians are rehearsing restraint, and the conductor is the embodiment of the willpower that is needed to stand up against these powerful affects, stop them from spreading, and in this way maintain a particular model of social order.

Pleasure and Control

This historical reading of the orchestra as symbolizing male control over the unruly masses helps to make sense of the embodied experience of rehearsals in the musical groups in my study. In rehearsals, most of us became the mass, willingly and easily. Particularly during orchestral rehearsals, which were more 'bitty' than choral rehearsals due to having so many more separate parts, we might have no clear sense of why we were repeating a particular passage, especially if we were struggling to play our own parts. The conductor would have the full score with all the parts in front of him, whereas we would have only our individual part, so we did not share his overview of the whole work. While some people would stay alert, following the process, many people would simply zone out. Looking around me, in WCYO rehearsals, I would see lots of bodies slumping in their seats during the stop-start period of rehearsal. One of the violin tutors told off the violinists for 'zoning out' instead of counting their bars of rest (i.e., bars when they weren't playing). There is a dangerous edge to zoning out; if you aren't ready to play when needed, you risk being humiliated in front of the group, and so orchestral rehearsals seemed to inculcate a mode of attention of switching off then suddenly jumping to attention when you need to play. We would simply wait for the instruction from the conductor—'cellos, basses, and percussion from six bars before letter M'—play that section, then zone out again when the conductor moved on to someone else. In this way we would lose ourselves in time during rehearsals, or rather, we would only be saved from being lost in time by the strict punctuality

---

² See, for example, *Business Horizons* (Vredenburgh and Yunxia He 2003), *Leadership Quarterly* (Hunt, Stelluto, and Hooijberg 2004), *Business Strategy Review* (Kerres 2012), or *Journal of Management Inquiry* (Strubler and Evangelista 2009), as well as the discussion in Logie (2012, chap. 3).

of the timetable; we never ran overtime on the rehearsal schedule by more than a couple of minutes.

Within this slumping, zoning-out, giving-up-control state, there would be periods of intense emotion such as fear or excitement. Unlike the fear of humiliation described in the previous chapter, this fear was cultivated and enjoyed by some of the musicians as part of the 'thrill' or excitement of the music. In a conversation in the pub after an NSO rehearsal, we were talking about a Stravinsky piece we'd been rehearsing. Rosie, a flautist, said that she purposefully hadn't practised the piece in advance, so as to get the excitement of playing it through for the first time and not knowing if she was going to get it right or not. Owen, sitting with us, agreed that he also enjoyed this kind of tension/fear/excitement. The excitement involved relying on your skill to see if you could get through a passage without making a mistake, especially when the music was going past quickly. I experienced this exhilaration when we rehearsed the Tchaikovsky violin concerto with the soloist for the first time. We got to the third movement, and the violinist, with a cheeky grin, started playing much faster than expected; we scrambled to keep up with him. The rhythmic impetus of our offbeats further increased the feeling of being on the edge of our seats. After a few bars we all settled into a tempo together, and I could enjoy the thrill of being carried along so fast. The adrenalin was running through my body and my heart rate increased, my body having suddenly snapped into hyper-alertness in response to what had happened.

In rehearsals, we cultivated such strong, embodied emotional and affective states. They gained much of their power from occurring in such large groups, of around forty people in Cantando, and fifty to sixty in the orchestras. Being able to trust the conductor to stay in control of these powerful affects allowed us to enjoy them safely, without fear of the group losing control. However, not all the musicians gave up control to the same degree. Some of the young men in both orchestras told me they would study the full score in advance and maybe bring a copy to rehearsals. This practice was also, in part, about level of experience; the more experienced and committed musicians were more likely to get to know the full score, but overall this did appear to be a gendered practice, as several younger boys also mentioned this to me, while none of the young women did. Through knowing the full score, they could follow what the conductor was doing when he was rehearsing a different section of the orchestra and see how their own part fitted into the whole, while also enjoying a fantasy of becoming the conductor, which, as chapter 6 shows, was an aspiration more likely to be expressed by young men than young women.

There was also a *pleasure* in staying in control through knowing the whole. It was of a different kind to the indulgent pleasure I described at the opening of this chapter. This was pleasure in knowing the totality, and in seeing the perspective of parts to whole. The sensory, indulgent pleasure of playing a nice tune or making a big sound could also be enjoyed by those who were partaking of this more cognitive form of pleasure, but within the knowledge of the whole structure. Indeed, conductor Olly encouraged us to join him in taking this holistic perspective, saying, for example, 'even while you're in it you have to be able to at the same time stand back from it'; part of his pedagogic mode was to invite us to share in his viewpoint of the structure of the whole, teaching us that 'the music should be transparent' and we 'should be able to stand back from it, look down on it and see all the parts and how they fit together'. Similarly, Will told me he wanted to become a conductor partly because of 'a fascination with being able to make music like that, to be able to essentially play every instrument in the orchestra'.

These two modes of pleasure, pleasure-as-indulgence, and pleasure-as-control each have a different mode of engagement with the body. Pleasure-as-indulgence was all about embodied pleasure and cultivating powerful affective states, such as the fear, adrenalin, or excitement described earlier. Indeed, the sensual pleasure of playing a Rachmaninov melody, as I described at the start of this chapter, was almost disdained by classical musicians for being too enjoyable. Pleasure-as-control was a mode of standing back from, or above, the process in order to see how your part fits into the whole in time and in sound. The latter form of pleasure was more legitimized in rehearsals, even encouraged by Olly, while the former type had to be kept in its place.

This is, therefore, an alternate reading of rehearsals to my participants' common-sense understanding of what was going on. For them, rehearsals followed the logic of the work-concept which structured time and social experience. However, if the body is brought back into the frame of analysis, we can see a different perspective on classical music in practice, not as 'pure structure' that 'represents itself' (Dahlhaus 1991, 7) but as a practice that claims autonomy from the social while in fact producing an historically and culturally specific mode of embodiment. In following the logic of the work-concept whereby the 'spirit' or essence of the work exists outside any material rendition of it, classical music practices articulate ideals of whiteness whereby the spirit exists outside the body. In order to 'transcend' the body and channel this spirit or essence, its injuries must be silenced, its movement must be stilled, and its passions must be controlled.

Conclusion: A Bourgeois Aesthetic?

The historical lineage that I have traced in this chapter suggests links between forms of social organization in classical music and those thrown up by the shift to modernity in the nineteenth century that parallels classical music's rise. However, rather than a simple homology between musical and social 'planes of mediation' (Born 2012, 266), I have suggested that the practices of the orchestra work as a form of cultural memory that preserves these modes of social organization over time. In this light, classical music rehearsals in the groups in my study show the musicians practising a form of public order required in modernity: piecing together a large, complex structure that involves a lot of bodies.

Reading this in light of one possible genealogy of this mode of control, its channelling of fears of unrest in the late nineteenth century, it becomes clear that this form of bodily discipline is not politically neutral. The stillness that is required to 'transcend' the body in classical music is productive of a particular kind of politics. As a political actor, a still body doesn't riot. It watches, thinks, and feels—but emotion is always under cognitive control. While few would argue against the idea that self-control is a necessary human capacity for living in society, the form of self-control exhibited here is uncritically obedient, a type of control imposed from without rather than from within that relies on the conductor to impose order and so neglects more reflexive forms of self-directed discipline.

In rehearsals, therefore, we are performing a fantasy of social order, of a functionalist society where all the parts fit into the whole. To use a metaphor from conductor Olly, the orchestra is 'an extremely good model for a company and the CEO is the conductor'. However, to make this fantasy work, either we have to aspire to become the conductor and exert this control, or we have to relinquish control completely and 'zone out'. This model of social organization is, furthermore, an outdated one; functionalism, the idea of society as an organic unity, does not allow for social change, and the unity it assumes cannot be found in reality. Instead, the orchestra preserves ideas of controlling the masses from the late nineteenth century, and these ideas are passed on through the modes of social organization that are required to perform the repertoire from this period.

Encoded within this fantasy of social order are historical and contemporary ideas of whiteness. Not only is the white male controlling the masses, but musicians are rehearsing modes of embodiment associated with whiteness, most notably 'controlled excitement', while reproducing a hierarchy between European and non-European repertoires through the different ways in which these repertoires are choreographed onto the body. The 'controlled excitement' that the young musicians were required to perform echoes theorizations of whiteness that suggest whites 'control and transcend our bodies' in order to express 'the qualities of "spirit" that make us white' (Dyer 1997, 27, 30). This 'controlled excitement' forms an historical lineage with the mid-nineteenth century, when the forms of social organization and the repertoire associated with this musical aesthetic were being composed. 'Controlled de-control of the emotions' is not, therefore, as Featherstone suggests, a new form of middle-class boundary-drawing in the late twentieth century (2007, 80) but is an essential component of this form of historical and contemporary subjectivity.

In these ways, classical music's history is present in its contemporary practices, and its classed and raced legacies cannot be dismissed as belonging to the past. Indeed, as Mari Yoshihara argues, despite its discourses of universalism, 'far more than other art forms, classical music professes an ideal of rootedness in the music's historical and cultural origins', which are, of course, white European (2008, 190). For the Asian American musicians in Yoshihara's study, despite their 'belief that classical music is a pure, autonomous art form—"absolute music"—that stands outside and above the sphere of politics' (64), they were still subject to subtle forms of exclusion and stereotypes of the Asian musician as technical automaton who lacked true musicality (87; see also Leppänen 2015, 23). Similarly, Taru Leppänen's study of media representations of the Sibelius Violin Competition found that, despite classical music's rhetoric of universality, for Asian musicians 'it was almost impossible to attain the most valuable qualities of Western art music, despite their excellent technical qualities' (2015, 30).

What my research adds to these studies is the finding that race is present in classical music not just through its representation and discourses, but that the very practices that are required to produce the aesthetic of classical music encode and reproduce whiteness through the historical continuities I have identified. Furthermore, the forms of sociality I have described in this chapter are not just about the social relations *around* the music but are intertwined with the aesthetic of the music, in that the practices required to produce this aesthetic are classed and raced. In particular, 'controlled excitement' was formative of—and required by—the aesthetic of the nineteenth-century and early -twentieth-century Romantic repertoire that the groups in my study were playing such as Rachmaninov, Shostakovich, Mahler, Vaughan Williams, Dvořák, and Sibelius. This can be seen through the continuity between 'controlled excitement' and the aesthetic Bowen attributes to prototypical nineteenth-century conductor Gaspare Spontini of 'precision and dynamic extremes' (2003, 103–4). This aesthetic requires high levels of technical skill to play its complex repertoire and difficult instruments with the precision and attention to detail that the ideals of beauty require. The forms of social organization that are required for large-scale musical works such as Romantic symphonies train musicians in these particular modes of embodiment. Non-European repertoires, such as the Duke Ellington medley that Cantando were rehearsing, were subjected to the same logic of precision and detail as classical music, as Lucy Green (2003) has described; thus, despite the way their choreography demarcated them as different to European repertoire, they effectively became classical music through the practices that they drew on. As I will discuss in the conclusion to the book, the encoding of classical music's history in the social relations and practices that are required to produce its aesthetic means that in order to diversify classical music, the aesthetic itself will need to change.

The next chapter, examining the authority of the conductor, continues to explore the space of rehearsals, showing how the embodied intimacy that the conductor builds with musicians is used to gain their consent. It focuses on the gendered social relations of rehearsals, showing how this intimacy was experienced differently by young men and young women.

CHAPTER 6

'Sometimes I Feel Like I'm His Dog'

GENDERED POWER AND THE ETHICS OF CHARISMATIC AUTHORITY

The scene: a school hall filled with around forty teenagers and a few adults. The teenagers, dressed in casual clothing but still looking smart, are standing in two rows in a semicircle, holding musical scores and looking at the man in front of them. He faces them, talking, gesturing, and singing musical examples. A younger man sits slightly to one side behind a small brown piano. Two women, also holding scores, hover around the edges of the choir, and I am sitting at a table to one side. The conductor, Richard, finishes his instructions and tells the choir to start singing from the top of page five. The piece is Purcell's music for the funeral of Queen Mary. The pianist gives a note for each of the five parts, and Richard raises his hands, all eyes in the room trained on him. He lifts his hands to indicate to the choir that they should be ready to sing, then gestures to the bass section, whose members mirror his in-breath. He mouths the words with them as they start singing, his body and hands drawing the sound out of them. Then he gestures towards the tenors for them to sing; his face exaggerates the vowel shapes of each word, and the young men's faces mirror his expressions. The altos have been waiting alertly for their turn; Richard brings them to life with another gesture; the sound builds further—he welcomes the second sopranos in, and then finally the sopranos join the lament, the richness of the layers of sound at such close proximity assailing me like a wall of sorrow.

This chapter examines the embodied authority of the male conductor and explores how this authority was experienced differently by young men and young women. It describes how this mode of authority draws on qualities that are already carried by middle- and upper-class men, and are therefore accessed more easily by them. Existing research on interactions between conductors and orchestras has predominantly been carried out with professional orchestras rather than among youth music groups and has emphasized the ways in which the conductor's authority and charisma are constructed, recognized, and negotiated (Adenot

2015; Faulkner 1973; A. Lewis 2012; Logie 2012; Ponchione 2013; Ravet 2016).[1] This literature is primarily microsocial, focusing on how musical action is made possible within the social space of the orchestra. Two exceptions to this small-scale focus explore the gendered nature of these interactions: Patricia O'Toole's (1994) Foucauldian autoethnographic study of choir rehearsals and Brydie-Leigh Bartleet's (2008) ethnography of professional women conductors which examines ways in which women are positioned as 'other' on the podium, including through gesture, dress, and leadership styles. My study supports and develops O'Toole's and Bartleet's findings by demonstrating the relevance of class as well as gender in shaping the types of bodies that can carry authority comfortably, as well as examining how young people experience male authority. In addition, the research just cited primarily examines orchestral rather than choral practice, but as I demonstrate, the distinctive mode of embodied authority found in the British cathedral choral tradition intensifies the embodied power of the conductor.

This chapter therefore presents a new perspective on the construction of conductors' authority by examining its workings in youth music sites, foregrounding the classed and gendered attributes of the body of the conductor. There are crucial differences between examining music-making in professional and in youth music groups. In youth music groups there are two forms of inequality between the musicians and the conductors that are less present in professional groups: inequality of age and of expertise. These differences mean that the gendered power of the conductor is strengthened in youth music sites, and such inequalities raise questions of the ethics of charismatic authority in classical music education.

The Structures of Charisma

I interviewed and observed four conductors as part of my research. Richard, as mentioned previously, was the conductor of the youth choir, a professional conductor in his forties. Olly was a highly successful professional conductor, also in his forties, who had recently been brought in to conduct the county youth orchestra courses as a way of trying to revitalize their dwindling numbers. The second youth orchestra in my study, the New Symphony Orchestra, had two different conductors during the time I played with them. They booked young conductors who wanted to get experience and would work without being paid. One of these was Adam, who appeared older than his twenty-one years. He had recently finished a degree at Oxford University and was trying to establish himself as a freelance musician and conductor. The other, Will, in his mid-twenties, was well on the way to a successful professional career. All were white British except Will,

---

[1] There is also a large body of work within management studies and business literatures on this topic, as discussed earlier.

who was from East Asia; all had attended Oxford or Cambridge universities except Olly, who went to one of the highly selective London conservatoires. In the absence of wider demographic data on professional conductors, it is not possible to say whether these backgrounds are typical, but it is notable that all these men went through elite forms of education, suggesting that this is likely to be a typical route into the profession.

These conductors used their authority in different registers in my research sites. These modes of authority draw on and reproduce the ways in which gendered authority and power operate in society. Common to all of them is a particular form of intimacy which is enabled by music as non-linguistic, embodied communication. Also common to all three modes is the carefully deliberate construction of the craft of conducting, built on the pre-existing affordances of the middle-class male body. Bodily gesture, posture, tone of voice, and use of emotion were all carefully channelled by conductors in order to get particular effects from the musicians.

THE PEOPLE MANAGER

The two younger conductors in my research, Adam and Will, worked to a model that might be called the 'people manager'. Will in fact described his entire role in terms of 'managing personalities', an idea which frames the conductor-orchestra relationship as one of equals. This was manifested in how careful he was about singling out individuals for correction in front of the group, sometimes giving instructions to players in the breaks rather than in front of the whole orchestra, as he was aware of the possibility for humiliation which this involved.[2] This seemed to be a way for conductors to reconcile being in a position of authority while also making this authority socially acceptable, both to themselves and to others.

It was from these two young men that I got a sense of how the embodied craft of the conductor was constructed. Downplaying the possibilities for power and authority inherent in their role, they instead focused on embodied strategies for maintaining the cooperation of the musicians. Adam told me, for example, that his conducting teacher had told him never to catch anyone's eye in the orchestra. This appeared to be a technique to maintain the omniscience of the conductor. To catch someone's eye might have created a real bond of intimacy between the conductor and an individual player, whereas we—the musicians—had to feel like we were being watched all the time without ever establishing a direct, personal connection with him.

Another tactic which both Adam and Will described was 'reading' the atmosphere of the rehearsal room and using tone of voice and a careful tactfulness to maintain

---

[2] This was similar to the 'more collegial approach to authority' that Brydie-Leigh Bartleet (2008, 43) describes women using on the podium in her ethnography of women conductors.

the delicate balance of the rehearsal, where feelings such as excitement, boredom, frustration, and competitiveness were constantly being cultivated or managed. Will, for example, maintained his composure perfectly even when a player threatened to walk out of a rehearsal after a dispute with his section. This mode of practice foregrounds conducting as a craft which is explicitly learnt; in fact, all of this careful tact and managing of relationships perhaps existed because Will was highly aware of the power dynamics which were possible, and he was working to defuse them.

These techniques are, for the most part, not taught or learnt explicitly; as Nicholas Logie describes in his study of professional conductors' understandings of leadership, only five out of his thirty-one respondents had explicitly learnt leadership strategies (2012, 190–91). In his survey of conductors' training manuals, Logie found that technique and musicianship were discussed in detail, but discussion of leadership was 'generally obscured by terms such as inspiration, passion, charisma, projection', and as a result, conductors in his study had mainly learnt their leadership skills through experience (57). Such informal modes of learning are likely to further entrench existing inequalities in the conducting profession by giving advantage to those who already have the embodied attributes that are seen to be required.

THE CHARISMATIC CHARMER

A different mode of authority, the 'charismatic charmer', was exemplified by Olly, a music college–educated conductor. Beautifully dressed in floral shirts, cufflinks, smart jeans, and highly polished shoes, he had the orchestra eating out of his hand within minutes of the first rehearsal, with his dry jokes and genial, didactic manner. I came home from my first day's fieldwork with him and wrote in my notes how 'I was just enjoying being in his presence'. Similarly to Will and Adam, Olly relied on tact to make sure that when he had to give correction to individual players, it wouldn't be humiliating for them. It was easy to forget that he was in a position of authority because, as with the 'people managers', he relied on the trust and willingness of the young musicians. Their typical mode of openness made it very easy for adults to gain their trust. However, when I interviewed Olly, one lunchtime in between rehearsals, I was taken aback when, as soon as we started the interview, this warm, open, demeanour abruptly disappeared and he immediately became very serious and focused, in what appeared to be a complete personality change. The charm was clearly his conductor persona: a tool for getting and keeping the orchestra onside. He was explicit about this in the interview, saying, 'Well, you know, it's entirely deliberate, and it's twenty years of experience of knowing how to put them at their ease.... If you create a nice atmosphere kids want to do it'. This highly effective 'charm' persona, while used benignly by Olly, raises questions about the use of charisma as a form of power when there is an imbalance of age and expertise, as I will discuss later.

Humour was an integral part of Olly's charm. It seemed to me as though jokes were necessary to leaven the boredom of rehearsals, which involved long periods of waiting while other sections of the orchestra were being rehearsed. Humour was such an important part of the repertoire of conductors that Jeanette, one of the vocal coaches in Cantando Youth Choir, told me she thought this was why there were hardly any female conductors, because this use of humour was gendered. Indeed, in their study of the culture of young men in schools, Mary Jane Kehily and Anoop Nayak found that 'humour is a technique for the enactment of masculine identity' (1997, 70). It is not surprising, then, that as Stephanie Schnurr describes, 'numerous studies have emphasized the various valuable functions of humour for leadership performance' (2008, 300). Jeanette reflected that she had never in her thirty-year career worked with any female conductors. Ironically, she told me, 'Oh, I'm not a conductor,' even though she had for years conducted a choir at one of the schools where she taught singing. Similarly, many of my participants had worked with female music teacher–conductors in school ensembles. However, school music ensembles usually did not count as 'serious' music-making among my participants, and concomitantly this identity was valued less highly than the full-time professional conductor role held by the male conductors in my study.

Olly's humour did indeed create a pleasant atmosphere, but it couldn't entirely override the potential for humiliation which the power dynamic between conductor and musicians created. He was usually very careful with making his jokes gentle and giving corrections tactfully, but even so, sometimes I felt shame for the person he was giving the instruction to. In one rehearsal, when he was trying to get the clarinets to play louder, he said to the two young women playing clarinet, 'It sounds, clarinets, like you're vacuum cleaners with the setting on "suck" instead of "blow"'. I saw one of the clarinetists go red even as she laughed, along with the rest of the orchestra, at his joke. I laughed—because it was funny, and because everyone else was laughing—but at the same time I also cringed, relieved that it wasn't me who had received that comment.[3]

This gentle humour was one aspect of Olly's charisma, which required him to maintain careful control of the high level of emotions in the rehearsal room. Rather than being susceptible to the influence of the group, the conductors in this study would 'read' the atmosphere of the group in order to carefully shape it. In contrast to the susceptibility and openness of the musicians, the conductor became the 'self-enclosed, bounded individual' who is the limiting point at which emotions are contained, whose 'will and inhibition fortify ... against social influence processes' (Blackman 2012, 37). These attributes form a continuity with hegemonic masculinity's 'tight control over emotions' (Connell 2005, 128), as well boys' greater sense of agency and confidence than girls' (Francis, Read, and

---

[3] This kind of tension/humiliation is recounted in other studies of orchestral rehearsals, such as that by Adenot (2015, 4).

Skelton 2012, 78; Stables and Stables 1995). In this way, as described in the previous chapter, powerful emotions can be experienced in the group without fear of a total loss of control; the conductor, with his awesome power of will, is the point at which these emotions are contained.

THE CULT OF PERSONALITY

The third mode of authority was the 'cult of personality'; this is the phrase one of the tutors used to describe it to me. This was the most obviously authoritative mode and generated the most discussion from my participants. This mode of authority occurred in orchestras as well as choirs, but it was exemplified by conductors in the British cathedral choral tradition. The conductor of the youth choir in my study, Richard, had been trained in this tradition, having attended a cathedral choral school as a boarder from the age of eight. He himself was critical of the tradition in many ways, consciously changing his practices to avoid reproducing its narrowness, but despite this he couldn't escape recreating some of its modes of practice. Singers in Cantando described his mode of working as being familiar to them from having worked with other conductors in this tradition, or having trained as cathedral choristers as children. In describing this mode of authority, therefore, rather than simply describing an individual, I am taking 'Richard' as an exemplar of this culture of practice.

This tradition was based on the authority of masculine charisma. The young people told me that Richard is really 'inspirational' and 'amazing'; that 'he's always got the right answer, straight away, or if he [doesn't] he always makes a decision'; and 'he's not afraid to tell people when they're wrong', 'if you're not sure he'll just tell you what to do'. Jeanette, one of the vocal coaches with Cantando, described to me the norms of this tradition. They include what she described as a strongly hierarchical 'pecking order' with the conductor at the top; the conductor's technique of 'getting moody' to get the choir to do what he wants and to keep the group in a state of fear; and a sexualized (in this case heterosexual) culture of innuendo and humour. Jeanette saw this modus operandi as necessary for attaining the high standards of musical excellence which are intrinsic to this musical culture (as described in chapter 3), but she was uncomfortable with aspects of it that were used by conductors she worked with. Most problematic for her was the sexualized humour in this culture, which in the rehearsals I observed was gendered, with jokes being made about women and girls. This humour involved things like reading sexual innuendo into the words of a song, or in one rehearsal I observed as Richard instructed the choir, 'your larynx should wobble like this' and made a reference to Jimmy Savile.[4]

---

[4] Jimmy Savile was a well-known English TV and radio personality who, after his death in 2011, was revealed to have been a prolific sexual offender.

One singer, Francesca, thought that Richard deliberately calculated when to make a joke in order to bring about a particular response, and so his jokes were never as spontaneous as they appeared. In particular, when he made sexualized jokes, they were, she thought, 'actually calculated to make us feel like he's treating us as adults'. When Richard made a crude joke in rehearsals, everyone would laugh, but in the private space of interviews, a few of the young women expressed their discomfort with this. Holly told me that when this happens, 'I don't know how to react. I kind of smile ...'. These jokes created an atmosphere in which women's bodies were sexualized, which played into the dynamic of the choir, which I explore later, of the musicians mirroring the conductor's body, with women's bodies therefore necessarily having to be 'corrected'. This sexualized humour was something that is, Jeanette told me, 'in that world. The trouble is you can't get away with that any more and if anything shows that it's the whole Mike Brewer thing—things have to change'.[5] Indeed, Francesca described how 'there are a lot of male conductors who do rule by that ... conduct by that kind of personality, half flirting, half ... um, ah, dominating'.

Francesca thought Richard's awareness of exactly what he was doing at every point was part of a broader scheme of what she called 'emotional manipulation': 'Often, the emotional manipulation is positively gentle, more along the lines of the stuff that Richard does of ... if he's being a bit short with us then making a joke and making everyone feel better and moving on with the rehearsal'. In this way, humour was used to control the atmosphere of the group. This humour, as well as the tact which was often used, was both an alternative to and the flip side of the humiliation which was always the unspoken possibility in rehearsals. Tact was a way of trying to ensure that someone wasn't humiliated in front of the group, by correcting them in front of sixty-odd people. Tone of voice appeared to be an important part of this tact, and of establishing gendered authority. Richard gave instructions with an intonation which suggested there was no doubt that they would be followed—and indeed there wasn't. Richard was in no doubt that the choir would do what he told them; if they didn't, he would change to a sharp tone of voice and say, 'I've told you twice to do x, now I expect you to do it,' and the genial, welcoming atmosphere in the room would immediately disappear, bodies would realign themselves to attentive upright postures, and any shuffling noises or movements would abruptly stop. In an interview he described this in paternalistic terms to me: 'I've said, several times—I've been quite gentle and nice, and I've warned them, this needs to be in place, and then something went wrong

---

[5] Mike Brewer was a celebrated British choral conductor. Several of my participants had sung under him in the National Youth Choir of Great Britain. He was convicted in 2013 of historic child sexual abuse of a pupil while working at Chetham's School of Music, a specialist secondary school for music, one of thirty-nine teachers at Manchester's two classical music education institutions who were investigated under suspicion of sexual abuse (Pidd 2013). For a discussion of workshops I organized with the music education sector to discuss these issues, see Bull (2016b).

again today, so I said, right, now I'm telling you, you're making me cross, because you know this'.

The three modes of authority that I have described all drew on similar techniques to ensure loyalty to authority, differing mainly in the extent to which the conductors tried to camouflage or downplay their power. Taken together, these techniques had the effect of disavowing any power imbalance in the relationship between musicians and conductor.[6] The young musicians also maintained this sense of equality through emphasizing their agency within the rehearsal process, such as having the power to ask questions. Singer and string player Helen asserted, 'I'll ask Richard questions all the time [in rehearsals]'. However, in the rehearsals I observed or participated in, very few people asked questions or spoke, and when they did, they asked for clarification of details in the score or technical points that deferred to the conductor's expertise, rather than making substantive or interpretive suggestions[7], in contrast to accounts of relations between professional musicians and conductors that emphasize 'shared ownership' of musical interpretation (A. Lewis 2012). Helen's comment illustrates that it was important for the musicians and singers to retain the possibility of asking questions—the sense of agency—even if they did not exercise it. The same disposition of making a choice to obey could be seen in a comment that Will made. He described how he wanted all his gestures to have the feeling of welcoming the musicians to play with/for him. In keeping with his managerial ethos, this would allow them to feel that they were accepting his invitation rather than obeying his command.

Intimacy of Gaze, Gesture, and Breath

Use of the body and the voice, a topic to which I will now turn, was integral to all three modes. Charisma, and the social and musical control which it was intended to bring about, was also achieved through the physicality of the conductor, in a process of mirroring which was described to me by a focus group of the nineteen-to-twenty-one-year-old singers. Already, before this discussion, I had become fascinated by Richard's physicality during rehearsals. He had a solidity to him, a groundedness combined with an openness to his torso that allowed him to gesture with his arms to cajole sounds out of the choir, while staying fixed in a sturdy posture. The singers described to me how the posture of the conductor was all-important because they, the choir, would be mirroring him; in order to create a

---

[6] This is similar to Logie's findings that conductors 'diminish[ed] the significance of all forms of power (both positional and personal) and emphasize[d] the compelling power of the music' (2012, 125).

[7] Similarly, Roger Palmer (2008, 213), in his study of adult amateur classical music groups, 'observed very little questioning of the musical directors' and tutors' authority and only rarely heard them seek members' opinions about musical or interpretative issues'.

good sound with your body, posture as a singer was integral. As one of the singers described in the focus group:

> SINGER: The conductor will be taken as an example by those who are singing. So the conductor has to remain the most energetic and the best posture and the most on focus and everything, throughout the whole thing, because if Richard slumps, I bet you the choir will slump a bit, and if Richard starts to flag, everyone will start to flag. If Richard's mood goes a bit [laughing slightly] everybody else gets a bit ...
> ANNA: You notice that?
> SINGER: Oh yeah, absolutely [agreement from others].

Note the laughter when they talk about Richard's mood. Sometimes during rehearsals, especially in the afternoons if the choir's focus was slipping, or when things were starting to get stressful coming up to a performance, I would notice him start to get impatient with them, the genial good humour slipping away and a slight threat of anger becoming audible in his tone of voice. In particular, the rehearsal before the concert was always a risky time. One singer, Toby, told me that he had been expecting Richard to get angry during the final rehearsal, as he had done the previous two years, but this time he hadn't. This was said in a matter-of-fact way which suggested that the conductor's anger is an accepted part of this kind of music-making. Jeanette was uncomfortable with this and remembered 'that feeling, the tension involved' from singing in cathedral choirs when she was younger. 'Sometimes when [the] kids are new and they don't know Richard, when he gets a bit snappy, [...] you can feel the kids who don't know him and don't know the choir very well, just doing that feeling of, oh my god, oh my god, that tension thing.'

The conductor's mood, therefore, is read and mirrored by the choir through his physicality and tone of voice. It appeared that the way in which some conductors used anger or the threat of anger was carefully calculated, similarly to their use of jokes. In an NSO rehearsal the day before a concert, conductor Adam's mood shifted from relaxed and genial to brusque and slightly impatient. At the start of the rehearsal we launched straight into a fast, difficult passage in the Sibelius symphony we were playing. I wondered if Adam was trying to scare us. He was irritable all morning, being unnecessarily harsh, with a hint of more anger underneath. At the break one of the violinists, Jessica, talked about the conductor of an orchestra at one of the UK conservatoires who, if someone talks in rehearsal, dismisses them from the orchestra on the spot; there is always another player to replace them. 'But', Jessica went on to say, 'he's really good, though'. This is reminiscent of the tactics of impresario Henry Lee Higginson in setting up the Boston Symphony Orchestra in the 1880s, as noted in the previous chapter; musicians would be dismissed instantly if they weren't playing up to standard (DiMaggio

1986, 54). In 2014, the UK classical music world was abuzz with gossip about an eminent conductor who had punched a member of the London Symphony Orchestra. According to Norman Lebrecht (2014), the conductor in question wrote a letter of apology and continued to work with the orchestra. Such authoritarian behaviours by conductors thus became the stuff of legend, contributing to the charismatic aura of the conductor. These conversations inflected our experience of being in this orchestra; we were aware that this kind of ruthless behaviour was possible for a conductor, so it was possible for our conductor.

Why was this unpredictability of mood so powerful? The hint of anger or impatience which Adam (uncharacteristically) exhibited during the rehearsal mentioned earlier has to be contextualized within the strong bond of trust that developed between musicians and conductors in all of the groups I worked with. This was visible both in how earnestly the young people would try their best to follow the conductor's instructions, concentrate hard, and get all the details right, and in how they spoke about the conductors, one singer saying, for example, that 'there's a kind of trust that Richard definitely knows best'. This trust or earnestness amounted to a mode of embodied, affective openness or susceptibility among the young musicians. This meant that a couple of sharp words were enough to get a response from the group.

Furthermore, the 'moodiness' that conductors sometimes used as a rehearsal strategy occurs within the intimacy of the non-verbal, embodied relationship between musician and conductor. At the centre of this—literally—is the conductor's gaze and his physical gestures. In his gaze was both a promise and a threat: the threat that if you make a mistake you might get a 'look', and similarly the promise that if you get it right when the rest of your section makes a mistake, you might be noticed for playing well. I was in Will's line of sight during one week's NSO rehearsals. I was constantly looking up at him to make sure I was playing with his beat, and as his gaze ranged across the orchestra, I felt as though he was often looking at me. I found myself hoping that this was because he had noticed how well I was playing, or that I'd got a difficult passage exactly right. This response to being 'played' by the conductor was surprisingly powerful, and baffling; I had nothing to prove as a musician and no need to impress Will in any way. Yet I still craved his approval. The social structure of the orchestra meant that I was just as susceptible to his charisma as the young musicians I was studying.

This social structure—the way of organizing musicians and conductor in embodied social relationships with each other and in space—was one of the key ways this dynamic was created. As well as the conductor's gaze, there were points when it felt like he was a puppeteer, playing our instruments and our bodies with his gestures. In particular during a pizzicato section in a Rachmaninov symphony (plucking the string rather than using the bow), which requires very precise timing to get the whole section playing together, we had to watch Adam's fingers intently, mirroring our hand gestures on the string with his hand movements. My awareness at such moments was expanded to include the whole cello section—or sometimes all of the string players—but at the forefront of that focus was a hyper-alertness to every micro-gesture of his hands, body, and eyes, my breathing becoming shallow with the effort of concentrating. There was an added physical intimacy of playing without the bow, but instead directly touching the string with my fingers. The conductor would give us a delicate hand gesture for each note; it was almost as if we were trying to be his fingers, or he was inhabiting our hands. The physicality of the gesture was the same for him and for us, as though he was playing our bodies. This also worked on the level of the breath. Even as string players, we would be instructed to breathe together with the conductor's upbeat gesture. In Cantando, this mirroring of the breath was even more intimate, as the choir would mirror Richard's in-breath at the same time as his hand gestures. Adam reflected in interview on how he experimented with changing his hand gestures slightly and how the sound he got back from the orchestra changed with these slight differences. This embodied intimacy in gaze, gesture, and breath had the effect of almost allowing the conductor to inhabit our bodies and draw the sound out of us. Our expression and our sound became his.

Gendered Mirroring: The Embodiment of 'Rightness'

The mirroring of the conductor described earlier occurred even more intensely in choirs than in orchestras. This was in a large part because singers' bodies are their instruments, and so not only is posture an important part of making a good sound, but there is no physical barrier between their bodies and the conductor's body. This extended to facial expressions, as Richard would give instructions or demonstrate what the singers' eyes and eyebrows should look like as they were singing. This close attention to all aspects of posture, breathing, and facial expression meant that Richard often commented explicitly on the way individuals were standing, for example, saying to one young woman, Amy, 'Stand as if you know this piece, you look a bit unconfident'. This postural mirroring was inevitably gendered in that the female singers were trying to imitate the physicality of the male conductor, in a context where women's bodies were joked about as being sexualized. This was particularly difficult for the young women who were less confident, such as Emily, who described to me in an interview the effect this postural correction of others had on her:

> Janey is very young, she's just turned fourteen I think. Richard twice, in front of everyone personally was quite vindictive towards her I thought, and she didn't come to the next couple of rehearsals, and that's understandable because that would've really knocked me. [...] sometimes it would just be, she's standing and he would be like, don't stand like that, [...] you look like the hunchback of Notre Dame, or

something [...] it's kind of quite a dangerous situation to be in because you're so focused on not being picked on and embarrassed in front of everyone that you focus really hard on doing everything right, like, every aspect from your body language, to the way you hold your book, to the way you sing.

Emily focuses intently on doing everything 'right' so as to avoid getting picked on, but in a context where her body is mirroring Richard's stance, gesture, breath, and facial expressions. This experience calls to mind Rebecca Coleman's (2013) work on interactive mirrors, which describes how the body is experienced differently through a screen or mirror which reflects one's body back to oneself with differences or enhancements. As a singer, watching the conductor and being 'played' by him resembles this experience of looking at an interactive mirror, and yet for the young women in the group this meant seeing in the mirror a male body which they could never hope to match perfectly. Indeed, accounts of postural corrections from a few of the young women suggested that women's bodies were, in this practice, inherently in need of correction to try to more accurately mirror the perfect humanity of the white male body of most conductors.

Emily, who was seventeen at the time, had explained to me earlier in the interview that she always wore four-inch heels, as she was uncomfortable with her body. This was a way of making her feel better about herself; taking them off made her feel very self-conscious and ill-at-ease:

> [The conductor] did pick on me once in front of everyone when I was—like at the very beginning when I just joined. I said I like to wear heels, and I think I compromised and I wore the tiniest heels and he picked on me in front of everyone and said, no heels, he made me feel like a floozy, basically, it's not the first time it's happened, but it was quite embarrassing in front of everyone else, and just after I'd joined as well, I didn't want that to be their immediate impression of me, and so I took my shoes off and since then I've always done rehearsals in bare feet or in flats, but it wasn't comfortable for me at all.

In fact, one of the vocal coaches always wore heels, so the extent to which this was about the posture required for singing was debatable. This emphasis on posture thus inadvertently became a mode of imposing an ideal of physicality on the singers. It became the standard of the embodiment of 'rightness' by which all female bodies were judged as not right; as Emily put it, 'I don't have the automatic posture thing,' which could be read as 'I don't have the embodied confidence and/or the male body that is required'. The correction that was discussed in chapter 4, as experienced more intensively by those in less privileged class positions, was also used in this way to correct the female body into not being female.

'You Know That He Will Have Heard It': Fear and Surveillance

The imperative towards rightness that Emily describes was, she went on to say, motivated by fear: 'I'm definitely quite afraid of Richard'. This fear appeared to be the flip side to the enormous respect and trust, almost reverence, that the singers tended to have for Richard. With this level of consent—almost hero worship—from the group, Richard didn't really need to use fear or humiliation tactics. It appeared, however, to be an accepted part of the cathedral choral culture, as Francesca, who was a veteran choral singer, described:

> In one of the choirs I sing with, we're required to put all our markings in before we come to rehearse, and to have looked through all the music. And at one point I had had so much on that I hadn't managed to finish off the markings, and this became obvious [...] and the conductor said, oh Francesca I don't think you've got that in, and I said, I'm really sorry, I haven't had time to finish off the markings, and the response was [he went] completely silent for a good ten seconds, and then he said, 'Thank you for telling me that, I wish you hadn't told me that'. Which completely devastated me, and I just ... I really ... I felt absolutely tiny as a result of that. And it wasn't that my failure to put in the markings had any impact on the rest of the choir. It was that in order for the very slick machine to keep going the response to not doing what was expected had to be that belittling.

In fact, Emily, who knew Francesca well, described how 'she doesn't really have anything to fear because she's so clever and she has a really great voice, and I think that I have a lot more flaws as a singer than she does'. Even for such a confident, articulate young woman as Francesca, however, this power could make her feel 'absolutely tiny'.

This fear was partly produced by the surveillance of the conductor. The following exchange between Katherine and Hannah describes how it felt to work under Richard (the italics are mine):

> KATHERINE: I like it that he's so demanding, he pushes us. Sometimes I get frustrated because, he'll be like, we sing something and he sort of stops us, he keeps stopping us and saying 'you've got to do this' and you think, well, it sounds the same, what exactly are you wanting to change? And then we suddenly get it, and he says 'yes, that's it' and it sounds exactly the same to me, and I was just like, how is that ... it's just like a slight pitching in a tenor or something, because he's just so good at hearing the

holistic sound, the overall sound, but actually knowing what everyone's voice ... *he knows* who is not quite there.

HANNAH: *He knows* what needs to be done to get the blend perfect.

KATHERINE: And *he knows* exactly who it is that isn't quite with it. And that can be quite ...

HANNAH: Scary!

KATHERINE: Intimidating, at times, because you know, you know if you're tired or something, you know that he will have heard it.

I was struck by their repetition of the phrase 'he knows'. They knew that every sound they made with their bodies would be scrutinized and judged by Richard. This contributed to their openness towards him, as there was nowhere they could hide their mistakes or failures.

Any criticisms of Richard's mode of working emerged only in private, in my interviews with the women and involved in this group. In public the structure of hero worship was strongly upheld; Richard was hugely respected by the singers, and for many he was the main reason they sang in this choir. For one singer, Francesca, the authoritarian aspect of choral singing culture meant that she was thinking of giving up some of the choirs she sang in. However, despite her clear and insightful critique of the social relations of choral singing, she was heavily invested in it. She explained that it isn't possible to perform this kind of repertoire without a conductor; the complex musical structures need a central organizing authority, linking the aesthetic of classical music inextricably with this form of social organization. Even though she preferred singing without a conductor, her love of choral singing meant that she felt obliged to work with them. This echoed a more general acceptance among the young musicians that the aesthetic demands of the music they wanted to play and sing required this mode of social organization. It was seen as an intrinsic part of classical musical practice, and they appreciated the high standards of music-making that they achieved with many of these conductors.

Gendered Identifications with Authority

The tactics described here of gendered mirroring, sexualized humour, omniscience, and fear of humiliation were experienced differently by young men and young women in Cantando. These differences drew on the ways they were positioned differently within its heterosexualized culture, as well as the different modes of identification and desire which were available to the young men and young women as a result of gendered patterns in wider society. In a discussion group interview with some of the seventeen- and eighteen-year-olds in the group,

I heard a stark example of these different modes of identification. After the participants had spent most of the discussion talking about how much they loved working with Richard, the adulation reached fever pitch when a young woman, Mollie, admitted that 'sometimes I feel like I'm his dog!—but in a good way'. Not wanting to be outdone, a young man in the group, Dan, exclaimed, 'It's like being in the military—but better than the military!'

These comments reveal differently gendered patterns of identification. Mollie, who declared that she feels like Richard's dog, is able to identify with a pattern of gendered domination and submission, which her comment that this is 'in a good way' suggests she enjoys. This mode of desire, to submit herself wholly to him, appears to be both acceptable and pleasurable for her. By contrast, the mode of identification which Dan draws on when he declares that it's better than 'being in the military' is a homosocial one, a model of authority from what is traditionally a closely bonded, male-only group. Like Mollie, he wants to submit his entire persona wholly to this authority. However, Dan's mode of identification is differently gendered to Mollie's; the conductor's power is one that he can identify with, and identify being or becoming, while for Mollie the position of submission, while pleasurable, gives her less possibility of identifying with becoming powerful. The flip side of this pleasure in submission, for some of the young women in this group, was the fear and humiliation described earlier, by Emily and Francesca. The rehearsal methods of authority and correction—a discipline which was relished by some—were experienced as humiliating and belittling by others, but these emotions were expressed to me only by young women, not by any of the young men.[8]

The role of conductor was, therefore, a mode of authority which was difficult for the young women in my study to inhabit. A few of the young women, including Emily, said they would like to try conducting, but most of them (unlike the young men) said they weren't interested, 'didn't have the skill', or had tried and failed. Helen, for example, described how her body just couldn't do it:

> We did some conducting lessons, and I was really bad, I just looked like I was doing ballet [...]. I think you can either do it or you can't, in terms of physically, it's almost a look, just a way of moving, the kind

---

[8] This analysis has similarities to previous research, both within music education and outside it. Francis, Read, and Skelton (2012, 77–78) found that high-achieving girls were likely to focus on teachers as authority figures who could legitimate their achievements, while boys would instead evaluate their teachers; girls were judged by teachers while boys judged teachers. In music education, Long et al.'s (2014) survey-based study of masterclasses, where a prominent musician gives a public lesson to a performance student, found girls more likely than boys to find such classes intimidating and unfriendly. Finally, Armstrong (2011, 9) found that in the music technology classroom, teachers' interventions were differently configured depending on whether the pupil was male or female. Therefore, my findings are continuous with existing gendered patterns.

of physicalization. It either looks like it comes very naturally, or not really. And I don't think—it's not a question of musicality. I think it's almost just a physical—can you ... can you get the motion, almost. It's really weird. But I can—I wasn't very good and I don't think I'd ever be able to try it again, like I wouldn't be able to conduct a choir.

The 'kind of physicalization' that Helen lacks echoes the 'automatic posture thing' which Harriet describes: the embodied, gendered confidence that Richard epitomized, and unconsciously seemed to expect of all the members of his choir. Marin Alsop, who memorably in 2013 was the first woman to conduct the Last Night of the Proms, and was subjected to gendered abuse as a result, stated in an interview: 'I've really worked hard at trying to, sort of, de-genderize my gestures' (Woolfe 2013). By contrast, Will described how 'the technique, fortunately, has always come quite naturally to me, [...] from all the conducting lessons I've had, I've never really had to change my technique'. These different accounts demonstrate how the 'craft' of conducting is built on the pre-existing affordances of the middle-class male body. Further evidencing this point, it is notable that attention to gesture is foregrounded in both conducting manuals and empirical studies of conductors. As Garnett describes, 'The idea that the conductor should "look like the music" runs through the literature of both choral and orchestral conducting'; conductors require the ability to 'become the embodiment of the composition' (2017, 103). An expressive, confident body is the sine qua non for the beginning conductor. However, as I will discuss in chapter 7, young women are much more likely to experience poor body image than young men, and indeed several of my participants disclosed such issues to me, which further decreased their ability to inhabit embodied authority. This increased the gap between the young men, who were able to imagine being Richard, and the young women, who were not. The young women had the option of either finding pleasure in their submission, as Mollie does, or simply trying to avoid humiliation.

Masculinity, Expertise, and the Ethics of Charismatic Authority

In recent years, male power has been under scrutiny as never before following revelations of sexual harassment and abuse by high-profile figures such as Jimmy Savile and Harvey Weinstein. In the arts sector, Nisbett and Walmsley provide evidence from the UK and Australia of the influence of charismatic leaders, cautioning that charisma can 'supplant ethics, strategy and reason' (2016, 8). It is, therefore, an appropriate moment to ask how charismatic authority, such as that of the conductor, can be used responsibly in classical music.

As outlined earlier, the authority of conductors in this study was built on the pre-existing affordances of the middle- or upper-class male body. However, as well as the gendered power imbalance visible in my research sites between (male) conductors and musicians, another important imbalance—more visible in the younger orchestras in my study than in the NSO—was expertise. Young people's hero worship of some of their conductors stemmed, in part, from the conductor's expert knowledge and ability to get them to play or sing better than they would otherwise. This shows the *enabling* power of the conductor-as-facilitator that, with a more equal balance of power, would be a wholly positive attribute. However, technical expertise is not a neutral attribute, but has also been associated with masculinity (Savage 2010, 19; Connell 2005, 193), and therefore can be seen to exacerbate the gendered inequality between conductor and musicians. In contributing to the 'cult of personality', expertise also increased the susceptibility and vulnerability of the young musicians to the conductor's charisma. This is not to say that expertise is problematic; instead, expertise needs to be understood as one facet of the power imbalance that I have described in this chapter, rather than being seen as a neutral 'good'.

This is one way in which the aesthetic of classical music contributes to the social relations I have described here. The difficulty of the repertoire being played or sung and the level of detail which it is possible to achieve through this way of working allow for high levels of expertise to be deployed. Indeed, the value placed on high standards of music-making worked to legitimize this mode of authority. In this way, the very aesthetic structures of classical music, as institutionalized by the nineteenth-century bourgeoisie and codified in the musical score, can be seen to contribute to the mode of gendered authority I have described in this chapter. As Lambeau describes, the musical score is not a 'neutral' agent, but rather:

> Any musical text (whether written or being created in real time according to specific conventions) sets out somewhat pre-defined roles which increase or restrict the musician's freedom depending on how they are appropriated in the group context. Hence, if the architecture of a musical text can affect the interpersonal relationships in a group, it must be acknowledged as having psychosociological impact: for example, executing a work written for a large corps automatically requires a group to have centralised musical direction and thus a hierarchical framework, just as the existence of unequal musical roles (i.e., solo vs. accompaniment) can lead to social inequalities (individualisation, depersonalisation) with harmful effects, and so on. (2015, 14)

Similarly, among my participants, this mode of authority was seen as necessary for the aesthetic demands of the repertoire and traditions of practice where large-scale, complex pieces are the 'great' works which musicians aspire to perform, and which are seen to need this central organizing mind and body of the omniscient conductor.⁹ This tradition produced a musical and emotional experience which was only possible within this group setting.

However, as Lambeau points out, the musical text leads to certain social inequalities that may have harmful effects, and this raises ethical questions. In my research as well as in the academic literature (Baker 2014; Durrant 2000; O'Toole 1994), there are many accounts of how conductors' power is not used responsibly. In relation to sexual harassment and power, quite apart from the sexualized humour that I observed and heard about during my research, the academic literature on conductors uses the metaphor of seduction to describe conductors' authority. Adenot, in her empirical study of professional conductors and orchestras, concludes that 'ultimately, managing the group also seems to involve a form of seduction' (2015, 10), and Durrant (2000) entitled an article 'Making Choral Rehearsing Seductive.' These examples suggest that sexualized understandings of conductor-musician relations are normalized.

Therefore, a revision of this mode of socio-musical organization is needed, especially when used in pedagogic settings. An ethics of conductors' power has to start from the point that, whether or not charismatic authority is used benignly, it is still a form of power. In my research sites, one effect of this power was to instil in the young musicians the norms of accepted practice of classical music such as the hierarchy of musical value described in chapter 2; the ideology of fidelity to the composer's intentions (Goehr 1992); and, on a darker note, the bullying described in chapter 4. In short, it can work against critical thinking. On the other hand, charisma can be a hugely positive force that facilitates uplifting, fulfilling, and joyful musical experiences. How, then, is it possible to ensure that it is deployed responsibly? The work of the music education organization Sound Connections on young people's voice provides more democratic models for music education. By scaffolding young people's participation in decision-making structures at all levels of a musical organization and encouraging critical discussion of the very questions of class, gender, and authority that this chapter raises, charisma can be used as a positive force. This development does, however, mean that the normal ways of working of classical music pedagogy—where the learning objectives, never explicitly stated, are solely an 'excellent' performance—need to be changed. The rehearsal methods that are common in professional musical practice are not necessarily appropriate for pedagogic spaces. Instead, the question of how

---

⁹ There are a small handful of orchestras that work without a conductor, such as the Orpheus Chamber Orchestra in New York, Spira Mirabilis in Europe, and Lahti Symphony Orchestra in Finland, as well as the Persimfans orchestra in the Soviet Union in the 1920s. One of the major issues with working in this way appears to be that it takes much longer to rehearse this music without a conductor. However, some of the youth music groups in this study spent a lot of time on rehearsals, so for them, the barriers to changing this way of working are more about a powerful culture of practice than any practical reasons. Furthermore, this strong belief in the necessity of having a conductor is, in part, produced by the complexity of the musical material.

young people's voice can be fully incorporated into classical music pedagogy needs to be further explored and experimented with.

Conclusion

The authority of conductors in my study was built on the pre-existing affordances of the privileged male body; it appeared to be easier for middle- and upper-class men to inhabit this role than others. The confidence that is required by conductors is a classed and gendered embodied resource as well as an individual attribute, and unsurprisingly all four of the conductors interviewed for my study were middle or upper class (with women or lower-middle-class conductors in my study working as music teachers rather than as professional conductors). The 'natural' technique of the middle- or upper-class (male) body means potential conductors from this group can build on the ways in which their bodies have been socially constructed throughout their lives to be autonomous, agentic, and able to speak with authority. As Reay, Crozier, and James (2011, 12) note, confidence and entitlement are distinguishing feature of the middle classes, historically and today. This is not limited to men; Maxwell and Aggleton describe how privileged young women in their research were 'able to draw on a strong "I-voice"' (2013, 7; see also Forbes and Lingard 2015, 124). It is notable, then, that even some of the very confident young women in my study such as Helen were still unable to access the bodily attributes of the conductor, and Scharff (2015) found that only around 1.4% of professional conductors in the UK are women. It is the embodied confidence of middle- and upper-class masculinity, therefore, that forms the basis for the conductor's power as a bodily craft. However, as well as confidence, research on conductors and conducting continually draws on and reproduces gendered discourses of risk, control, humour, and expertise that are building blocks for masculine identities (Bordo 2003; Connell 2005; Laurendeau 2008; Lupton 2013; Savage 2010; Seidler 1989).

Gender and class not only were visible in the conductor's body but also were apparent in the ways in which young people in my study experienced his authority. The young musicians enjoyed and welcomed their conductor's authority, even in its more ruthless manifestations. Publicly, the acceptance and openness of the young musicians to the conductor's leadership amounted to a deep form of trust. Their trust towards adults in positions of authority over them is continuous with a wider middle-class trust in institutional authority; by contrast, minority ethnic and working-class young people are less likely to display such trust (see, for example, McShane 2018). This trusting openness and the sense of intimacy it brought about, along with the reliance on non-verbal communication between conductor and musicians, meant that even his smallest gesture would bring about a response. This was exacerbated in Cantando Youth Choir, where young women's bodies were sexualized and more likely to be subjected to correction. These interactions, in conjunction with young people's existing gender and classed senses of self, meant that the gendered identities of the young people—young men as aspiring to inhabit authority, and young women as subject to authority—tended to be reinforced.

The final two empirical chapters of this book foreground the role of sound in creating powerful emotional experiences. Being within the sound of an orchestra or choir creates a sensory, embodied experience which makes young people want to participate in these practices. In addition, sound, as mediated through the body, plays a role in forming the powerful identity that goes with being a classical musician. Chapter 7 focuses particularly on the experience of some of the young women in the Young Opera Company.

CHAPTER 7

'Instead of Destroying My Body I Have a Reason for Maintaining It'

YOUNG WOMEN'S RE-IMAGINING OF THE BODY THROUGH SINGING OPERA

One typical rehearsal for the Young Opera Company's production of *The Magic Flute* takes place on a sunny Sunday afternoon in May in the music block of a state secondary school. The whole cast and chorus are there, comprising around forty teenagers aged twelve to nineteen, sitting on tables or on the floor, some doing homework and listening to their iPods, others watching the rehearsal while they are not needed. I am sitting behind the grand piano in the corner of the room, playing the orchestral part; the director, Sophia, perches on the edge of a table, stopping and starting the scene that is unfolding to give instructions to the cast.

We come to a scene which is described both in the musicological literature (Kerman 1988) and by my participants as the emotional heart of the opera: the aria that the princess Pamina sings when she has been rejected by Prince Tamino. Emily, who is playing Pamina, sings of her grief in an aria that another cast member later described to me as 'spine-tingling'; it is slow, in a minor key, and heartbreakingly expressive. The atmosphere in the rehearsal room shifts from one of working on details, mistakes, fixing things, to an extraordinary feeling of everyone listening. The quality of attention becomes palpable. As I accompany her on the piano, there is enjoyment in giving careful attention to every note. Her vocal line climbs up to an ethereal, eternally sad high B flat, a note which almost seems to shimmer in its glacial strength and delicacy—then ends. The whole room stays silent as I play the coda which ends the aria, putting every expressive possibility into the phrase. I finish, and everyone applauds, the only time in today's rehearsal. Emily herself has a tentative, uncertain air as she sings; a seriousness which fits well with the melancholy of the song. She doesn't seem to notice the attention the aria has garnered and afterwards obediently takes notes from Sophia, the director.

This chapter takes the experiences of some of the young women in the Young Opera Company as a starting point to explore what happens in a social and musical encounter with an anti-feminist, racist cultural text. This reading emerged because my fieldwork revealed that, for many of the young women, the powerful embodied experience of singing opera was one of the most formative parts of this experience. However, this led to a contradiction between, on one hand, the experience of making expressive sound with their bodies as giving them a sense of power, control, and embodied confidence and, on the other hand, the strongly gendered text of the opera through which this embodied practice took place which undermined their emergent empowered voices. Weaving these dissonant experiences together was Mozart's opera *The Magic Flute*, a stalwart of the classical music canon. It was one of the most musically satisfying experiences I had had for a long time to rediscover Mozart's gorgeous melodies and well-proportioned musical structures by playing the piano for this production. And yet, as Catherine Clément vividly describes, the text of the opera, in the music, the words, and the plot, is a story of women's voices being silenced: 'If there is an opera that clearly shows, with all its verbal and musical power, the crushing symbolics of men over women, it is *The Magic Flute*' (1997, 95). Making sense of this production as both a social and an aesthetic experience was fraught with contradictions. However, as I will describe, the text of the opera was less formative of the social experience than might be expected. Young people responded strongly to the characterizations created by the music and the text, accepting its dichotomy of evil versus virtuous femininity, with virtue coded as whiteness. Despite these readings that were congruent with the musical-dramatic text itself, the text was destabilized by the process of producing it, and changes were made to it. These factors would suggest that the text can be, and is already being, changed in order to make it less politically problematic. My participants' strongly held ideas of fidelity to the score and to 'what Mozart would have wanted' inhibited such changes, but their respect and admiration for the adults running the production and the comments about the text and the production that they made to me suggest that a critical space could have been further opened up.

'In Singing, It's My Space Which Is Just Me': Young Women, Body Image, and the Voice

There was a recurring theme in the accounts of some of the young women in the Young Opera Company of the experience of opera singing countering their negative sense of body image. For three of the young women—Emily, Sara, and Megan—this was particularly powerful. Emily, the young woman playing Pamina, was an elegant, serious seventeen-year-old who attended one of the top private schools in the city. She had learnt piano from age five and cello from age nine, then started singing lessons at twelve. Her parents divorced when she was nine, leaving her feeling 'in between' socially because her mother was from a working-class background but her father was upper class, and 'at home we're quite poor but [...] with my accent people assume I'm quite wealthy'. She linked this 'in-between' position to a lack of confidence: 'There's always a sense of. being insufficient with someone like me'. She told me how she initially didn't want to be good at opera singing, 'because I knew that it wasn't cool', preferring to sing pop music, but eventually with the help of her singing teacher she 'came to terms with the fact that this is how my voice sounds best, as an opera singer'. Following her teacher's advice, she auditioned for *The Magic Flute*, despite having never seen an opera before. As she told me, 'I think I had no idea of what I was getting myself into ... I didn't know what I was auditioning for'.

Emily found the rehearsal process, which took the best part of a year, challenging, as her shyness and fear made singing and acting in front of others difficult. This shyness stemmed from childhood:

> All through my childhood I never spoke to anyone, I was extremely shy, and very self-conscious and I still am, [...] and for like the first six months of the opera, like ... it was extremely difficult for me to be able to get up in front of anyone and do the singing or the acting or anything like that. Very difficult.

The physical experience of singing in an operatic style, which uses the core muscles and full lung capacity, meant that Emily had to make a loud noise with her body: 'When I sing properly everyone always shuts up but I don't know if they're shutting up because they don't like it or because they're just stopping to listen. It's hard to tell'. Nevertheless, despite the 'times when it was really, really difficult' being involved in the opera, Emily now describes it as an 'amazing' experience which has 'given me such a boost of confidence'. Part of this boost has been body confidence: 'I tend to wear four-inch heels every day [...] it's part of my self-conscious thing, I'm not really very happy with my body so, it makes me feel better to be taller. [...] It just makes me feel like, thinner and less inferior than boys'. By the end of the opera, however, she felt 'a lot more comfortable in my body'. and she carried her increased body confidence into the rest of her life.

Unlike Emily, for Megan this shift in the experience of the body while singing was only temporary. When I met her, Megan was eighteen and in her final year at sixth form college. Fidgeting as she spoke, Megan mentioned towards the end of our interview:

> Well, actually, I've had a bit of like, body consciousness ... but then when I sing I feel like OK with the size that I am because it makes a big sound, so it's actually accepting in that way, because it's like, OK I'm

not stick thin and I'm not a skinny minny, but listen, I can make a huge sound, and it's like, it's pretty good. That's true, to be honest, I wasn't going to say it, but there it is.

Her reluctance to speak about her body consciousness points towards the difficulty and shame associated with admitting to it, even though such negative feelings towards one's body are endemic among young people, especially women (APPG 2012). However, as I spoke to more of the young women involved in this production, this link between singing and bodily expressivity and confidence emerged as a theme. For Hannah and Katherine, two close friends whom I interviewed together, singing gave them a sense of freedom and control over their bodily expression which they didn't find with playing instruments. This was such a powerful experience that they had both decided to go to music college to study opera. Jeanette, the vocal coach with the Young Opera Company who also taught singing to some of these girls, made explicit the link between taking up space through singing and eating disorders:

> I was teaching someone recently, middle twenties, who was saying to me, we were talking about posture and things and she was saying how difficult she found it to allow herself to expand. And I realized, in trying to explain to her that women in particular [...] we're not allowed to take up space, [...] so I think that personally ties in with eating disorders, I want to disappear, to be smaller, there to be less of me, because there is too much of me.

As discussed later in this chapter, this echoes Susan Bordo's cultural analysis of eating disorders, whereby 'the steadily shrinking space permitted [to] the female body seems expressive of discomfort with greater female power and presence' (2012, 250). This expansion through voice and sound is therefore working against powerful beliefs about women's bodies taking up space.

However, the most powerful account of how singing altered the experience of the body came from Sara. Now nineteen, she had been anorexic earlier in her teens, but because of singing, 'instead of destroying my body I have a reason for maintaining it.' Similarly to Hannah's and Katherine's accounts, Sara described how since her voice is part of her body, unlike an instrument, she has control over it:

> SARA: In singing, it's kind of my space which is just me [...] it's my voice, it's part of my body. [...] And I've had quite a few mental health issues over the past few years and I'm still not doing great with that, but one thing was I was diagnosed with anorexia, and my only reason for recovering and now staying in recovery is for my voice. Because if you don't

eat, you die—well I don't care, but if you don't eat, you can't sing and yes I do care! So it really is, it's my only ...

ANNA: So you could almost say it's saved your life.

SARA: Oh I say that, definitely. Yeah, there's no way I would've been able to recover for myself, I did it for my singing, because ... and I still do it, it's not something you just recover from like flu, it goes on and in several years' time I will still be in the same place. But I maintain my weight and I keep eating and I try not to restrict certain food groups for my voice, it's not for me.

Sara separates her 'self' from her voice; this is common parlance among opera singers, as described in Paul Atkinson's ethnography of the Welsh National Opera, where singers talk about 'the voice' as an 'independent agent':

> The voice exists, and is something that has to be found and used.... The [singers'] accounts are developed as if the singer and the voice were two different identities or agencies that have developed more or less independently ... the voice can almost have a life of its own, independently of the perceptions and intentions of the singer. It reveals its true identity as a voice, or as a type of voice, in a way that does not depend on the will of the performer. The voice determines what the singer will sing, rather than the singer's determining what the voice will produce. (2006, 179)

The materiality of the voice is thus formative in and of itself, in its potentialities, which a teacher hears and works with. During my fieldwork I had two singing lessons with Jeanette, experiencing both the feeling of power at the expansion of self through voice and sound and also the bodily disruption that this entailed. I was comfortable with singing from years of involvement in choirs, but I have not done much solo singing. The sensations resulting from following Jeanette's instructions were uncomfortable; there was an unease, even an edge of fear, at the unfamiliar feeling of making such a big sound, which surprised me. Part of this reluctance was the usual frustration of learning a new bodily technique, in which the body feels gauche and awkward yet also curious at its hitherto undiscovered capacity. This sense of awkwardness—almost feeling like my body was not my own—was compounded because this new bodily technique was also about producing a sound. As soon as I got into the higher register—from a D or E an octave above middle C and upwards, the part of the voice that you can only access if you have a lot of breath and support in the gut—there was an exhilarating, scary, somewhat alien feeling that my voice had taken over and annihilated the rest of me with its volume and intensity of sound. There was a dizzying resonance in my head, an enormous volume of air needed in my belly, and a sense of drawing the sound up from the ground. No wonder that one of the sopranos in *The Magic Flute* had complained of feeling faint and lightheaded during a rehearsal where she had to sing a string of high notes in a row. My body had become solely breath, resonance, and noise.

This uncomfortable yet exhilarating experience, read alongside Sara's, Megan's, and Emily's accounts presented earlier, suggests that singing opera allows an alternative bodily 'imaginary' (Weiss 1999). Weiss suggests 'that human beings tend to have multiple body images and that these body images overlap with one another and are themselves constructed, reconstructed, and deconstructed through a series of ongoing, intercorporeal exchanges' (1999, 165). Following Weiss' idea of overlapping body images, it seems that these young women had a double sense of the voice as within one's own control, formed within the materiality of one's body, but also as expanding the sense of the body beyond the boundaries of the skin to take up a much larger space. Weiss goes on to describe how 'accepting the possibility of radical bodily transformation (and positively identifying with this possibility) involves a corresponding destabilization of the body as a *given*', and imagining or experiencing oneself differently 'will also allow one to explore and test out new and unforeseen *bodily* capabilities' (74). In these examples, the voice (and, in this sense, the body) acts back on the self, with a power or agency of its own, enabling these young women to experience an unforeseen and unfamiliar sense of power and control over their bodies. Not only is this re-imagining of the body exciting for them as individuals, but Weiss also suggests that it has the potential to bring about social change by 'undermining social constraints on what bodies can and can't do' (74). What, then, are the conditions that enable this radical re-imagining of the body, and what kinds of social change might it enable?

'I Feel Powerful, You Just Fill the Room with Sound': Being Heard in Public Space

The voices of the young women in the Young Opera Company were co-produced between the materiality of their bodies and various mediating forces: their relationships with their teachers; the tradition of classical music practice in which they were learning; the repertoire and roles of the operatic canon; and the broader institutional conditions of the opera industry, as discussed later in this chapter. In addition, the spaces of performance and rehearsal played a role in imagining the body differently through sound. The sound that the operatic voice produces was too large to work in the private spaces of a bedroom or living room. Instead, it required public space as a condition of its production. But for these young women, being encouraged and facilitated to make a loud noise with their bodies in large public spaces was not part of their usual lives. The performance venues for this group included a five-hundred-seat concert hall, a large Victorian church, and even a shopping mall in the centre of town. Performing in these most public of public spaces, with only one's body as an instrument, required these young women to imagine the sound which their body made as reaching out to the furthest corner of the room—in effect, re-imagining their bodies as filling that space. This required a differently imaginative sense of the body to their usual body image. Megan told me, 'When the room feels huge and then you fill the room, you just fill the room with sound. [...] I have this whole cartoon image going on of sound waves going out and filling the room'.

The space itself, therefore, is an integral part of this re-imagining of the body, which does not work in the same way in private space. Megan was nervous about being heard practising at home or at school, in spaces where this sound was out of place:

> When I'm totally alone that's OK, but even at home my walls are thin and there are people who can hear, and my neighbours often say, that sounds good, and at college there are always people around, and the rooms aren't soundproof, and there's been times when you're singing and people down the corridor make comments and you can hear them and that's horrible. I just stop, sometimes I can't go on, I'm just like, no, that's enough for now, and it's left on such a bitter taste but I can't do it any more, that's too tense.

There is in Megan's account a palpable discomfort and vulnerability at *being heard* which points towards some of the difficulty around cultivating her voice in this way. This discomfort at being heard and therefore being judged existed for some of these young women in tension with the feeling of power at filling public space with sound.

As well as being linked to the architecture of public spaces, this sense of power came from the sense of using all of one's breath and diaphragm and really going for it, as Megan describes:

> Sometimes when I sing a high note I'm like, grr, anchor, DAAAA! [...] Especially if I enjoy it, because I really plonk on the anchor [...] and then my vibrato just goes, then it's like, hello! [laughs] hello note!

In her low notes, she also stated, 'there's a power there' which linked into the altered sense of her body when she sang. All of these young women, therefore, experienced their bodies differently by using a different sensory mode of perception—sound. Rather than experiencing their bodies as objects of shame or inadequacy as a result of their negative body image, they instead were able to be expressive, proud, and confident. Having control over their own embodied expression felt radical or 'freeing' to them. This involved a 'destabilisation of the body as a *given*' and with this the possibility of radical bodily transformation (Weiss 1999, 74), from hiding or disguising something which is shameful, to celebrating and proclaiming one's presence with a sense of pride. As Megan described, singing in this way 'uses everything'—every part of the body—which radically shifts the experience of being in the body. Holly, a singer in Cantando Youth Choir, described how 'it makes me feel really happy, you know. Like especially being a soprano, when you hit these top notes it's a nice feeling hearing it, and actually yeah, the physicality of it, kind of engaging your whole body in singing one piece of music'. The voice thus emerges as a site of potential for feminist re-imaginings of the body.

The social sanctioning of the group was important in providing a space where using one's voice in this way was encouraged and facilitated by adults and peers. This amounted to being given permission to make noise, as Megan described: 'People expect that, that's what you're there for'. She contrasted this with the usual conditions of childhood and young adulthood: 'that engrained thing from when you're a child—don't be loud, don't be messy. [...] And then suddenly it's like, be louder, you're allowed, it's like, great!' Parents, grandparents, schoolteachers, music teachers, godparents, and other adults endorsed this practice by attending performances and showering praise. Singing teachers and conductors inducted the young people into the tradition of practice in classical music, organized and facilitated spaces of rehearsal and performance, and provided them with emotional support in lessons as they learnt to use their voices in this unfamiliar way. For, despite how good it felt to sing in this way once they knew how to do it, this was not something that came naturally to either Megan and Emily. They both described reluctance and difficulty in the process of learning to sing. Coping with the sense of physical disruption which re-imagining the body in this way entailed, which also required continual instruction and correction from teachers, conductors, and directors, therefore relied on the supportive and trusting relationship with a singing teacher, as described in chapter 3.

The co-production of women's voices and public space is particularly important because of the historical construction of the public sphere as a masculine space (Fraser 1990). The associations of publicness with masculinity and the private sphere with femininity still have profound implications for the representation of women in public. The claiming of public space through sound by these young women, therefore, is to some extent a reversal of the broader conditions of women in society, although this assertion needs to be inflected by my participants' (mostly) middle-class position, which gave them the sense of entitlement to inhabit such spaces, even if not to be noisy in them.

It is possible to trace a link between these ideas of overcoming body consciousness through making sound and a lineage of bourgeois femininity's ailments of interiority: anorexia, hysteria, and neurasthenia.[1] As Elaine Showalter describes, from 1870 to 1910 (a period which overlaps with the formative period

---

[1] As Darmon (2009) points out, the link between social class and anorexia today is not clearly understood in the research literature, despite epidemiological evidence from the UK confirming that middle- and upper-class girls have a higher prevalence of anorexia (McClelland and Crisp 2001).

for music education institutions which I described in chapter 2), as middle-class women were beginning to inhabit public institutions and demand political rights, these 'female nervous disorders ... became epidemic' (1987, 18). These disorders would become the bread and butter of psychoanalysis, which theorized them as expressing an interiority that has been unconsciously repressed. This interiority was sometimes exteriorized in sound; a defining characteristic of an hysterical attack was the victim sobbing and laughing (130). Contemporary commentators argued that this was related to women's unsatisfied sexual and maternal drives, rather than their social conditions, as later feminist analyses have emphasized (131). Indeed, Susie Orbach narrates one way of understanding anorexia as being a protest against the social conditions of femininity: acting the 'good girl' and 'agreeing' to take up only a little space in the world, but retaining control by taking this act to a pathological extreme (1993, 10).

Furthermore, as Susan Bordo's socio-cultural analysis of eating disorders describes, eating disorders represent a 'desperate fixation on our bodies as an arena for control' (2003, 141). Bordo identifies three sets of cultural norms that create the cultural conditions that lead to eating disorders: separation of mind and body; contemporary bourgeois cultural norms of 'fantasies of absolute control' (151); and fear and disdain for traditional female roles, alongside a 'deep fear of "the Female"' and the voracity it symbolizes (155). Two of these cultural norms have already been identified in this book: the cognitive control of mind over body that classical music requires (Gustafson 2009), and the fantasy of absolute control that I have argued is symbolized by the role of the conductor (chapter 5). The third, the 'fear of the woman as too much'—too loud, with too much emotion—symbolizes women's lack of restraint and insatiable hunger/sexuality (Bordo 2003, 161). Earlier in the chapter, Megan described her engrained sense from childhood of 'don't be loud'—and yet here was a space where she was encouraged to be loud. Despite this encouragement, the 'fear of the woman as too much', represented by the character the Queen of the Night, as discussed later, was for my participants the limit to acceptable femininity.

The contradictions around classical music practice that this production crystallizes are now starting to become clear. These young women were finding a space of freedom through encouragement by teachers and other adults towards making a big sound with the body and taking up (sonic) space. This is a strong contrast with Orbach's interpretation of eating disorders as making one's body smaller, and helps to explain why singing was a space that countered negative body image and eating disorders. Despite the control that classical music requires and engenders—mind over body, and conductors/composers over performers/musicians—these young women's voices were not fully controllable as their physical materiality had its own qualities of volume, strength, timbre, and range. Furthermore, the sound produced by their voices was unmistakably female in its pitch and timbre, signifying a loud assertion of female identity, against Bordo's explanation of eating disorders as encompassing a fear of the female. For Emily, Megan, and Sara, the effect of this re-imagining was powerful, shifting the way they experienced their bodies. However, this claiming of space was only allowed to occur under heavily controlled circumstances, and in conflict with classical music's pedagogy of correction, detail, and competition.

Competitiveness and Criticism

Learning to sing in an operatic style required openness to being shaped by a teacher. In chapter 3 I discussed Megan's experience of being 'crafted' by Jeanette in her voice lessons, a process that required her to open herself up to self-critique as well as criticism or direction from others. She found both of these extremely difficult. Her self-criticism was something she thought had probably increased since she started learning classical singing at age fifteen, when she was going through a 'confidence crisis', 'and now it's part of it, part of learning'. The process of taking instructions from the director of the Young Opera Company exacerbated these difficulties for Megan, who explained:

> Someone's criticizing you—they're not, they're directing you, they're saying, 'you should be over here' or 'you should be standing still', but I've immediately turned it to 'should', [...] I can't help it. So even if [the director]'s saying you know, 'turn round here', I hear that as 'you haven't turned round, you're doing it wrong', and it's just, that's just the way I am.

This experience of self-critique was by no means unique to Megan. Rather, it was prevalent among the young people I spoke to, among whom, unsurprisingly, judgements of oneself and others were made frequently. Isabelle, another singer, found that her level of internal self-critique increased exponentially as soon as she started a music performance course at university:

> There were just so many people who were literally doing the same songs as me, right next to me, straight after me, or had performed the same recital straight after me, and I was like, I'm not going to be [...] better than them.

Being double cast in the opera production, singing the same role as Emily, exacerbated this effect on Isabelle:

> I think, oh god [I'm] not going to be better than that. It just makes me not want to do it, so that's what makes me practise over and over again. [...] It's really really bad, I don't know what it is, no matter if someone's younger or older than me, I'll still be like, I want to be better!

It was not so much that being involved in classical music introduced a level of self-critique which was previously absent; rather, it reinforced and exacerbated patterns of self-critique and competitiveness that already existed for many of the young people in my study. Patterns of hard work and repetitive practice could easily turn into obsessive perfectionism, fear, and anxiety. This was reinforced by the stopping and starting, correcting and critiquing, instructing and directing which formed the main substance of lessons and rehearsals. By contrast, another young woman in the group, Elizabeth, who said she was 'quite critical of myself', described herself as 'quite a confident person, in life, I don't tend to put myself down that much'. She saw her habit of self-critique as a positive, necessary quality. Instead, for Elizabeth, judgement was externalized onto others 'all the time'. In these ways, making judgements of one's own and others' performances was a skill that was being learnt and practised in these groups.

The potential for this critical judgement was exacerbated in the Young Opera Company production by many of the roles being double cast, with two singers learning exactly the same part. Most of the young people assured me they didn't feel in competition with whoever they were double cast with, but they also described how this lack of competitiveness, brought about by the positive atmosphere that leaders Sophia and Jeanette created, was a contrast to other sites of youth classical music. Indeed, this shows the power of teachers and leaders in creating or changing the culture for young people's musical participation. Francesca described how youth music is

> quite competitive in terms of, everyone's developing and growing and so you judge yourself by the people around you, and the whole question of who gets solos and that kind of thing can become very, very fraught. [...] I think a good deal of the critique [...] is genuinely intended and presented as a way of being better, [... but] from my own experience it's very easy to internalize it as 'I'm not good'.

This competitiveness can be seen as externalizing the self-critical judgements that classical music practice requires in order to get to a high standard. Notably, even though Jeanette described her pedagogy as 'affirmation, affirmation, affirmation', showing a keen awareness of the critical nature of this practice, this still made few inroads on what Megan described as her 'constant' self-critique in rehearsals: she told me that she just 'wouldn't hear' the positive comments but would remember only the critical ones.

Furthermore, these inner critiques appeared to be gendered, in that it was usually young women who told me about them. This finding can be explained in relation to the concept of post-feminism. Rosalind Gill (2007) describes a 'postfeminist sensibility' whereby feminist discourses are now part of the cultural field through being drawn on but also subverted or depoliticized in the media. Both Gill and Angela McRobbie argue that this leads to 'a higher or deeper form of exploitation' for women than during second-wave feminism, because the objectifying male gaze is internalized to form a new disciplinary regime (Gill 2007, 258). McRobbie describes how women are constantly told that they live in a gender-equal world while trying to negotiate an unequal one, and this leads to forms of 'illegible rage', a spectrum of problems, including self-harm, eating disorders, mental distress, and binge drinking (McRobbie 2008, 95).[2] It is middle-class girls who are most subject to such discourses of 'having it all' thanks to their success in education. For women, these contradictions manifest as inner-directed self-competition (McRobbie 2015, 7) and as a constant monitoring of the 'unruly' body, even while this is presented as something that is freely chosen (Gill 2007, 255). Similarly, research on girls' perfectionism and high achievement shows their powerful but unspoken fear of failure; Walkerdine, Lucey, and Melody describe how the middle-class girls in their study were racked by a fear of failure 'that those around [them] could not bear to hear about because they too held that fear' (2001, 131; see also Allan 2009; Allan and Charles 2014).

These habits of self-criticism, perfectionism, and competition among young women in my study are, therefore, continuous with their experience outside of classical music. These link with wider neoliberal gendered structures as explored by Christina Scharff in her study of early-career female classical musicians in the UK and Berlin. Scharff found a similar pattern of self-directed criticism and externalized competition, even though many of her participants upheld a performance of femininity by distancing themselves from competitive discourses (2017, 130). She argues that this self-criticism is an internalized form of the competition that is demanded by neoliberalism, and that it is likely to be exacerbated in creative professions because of the perpetual self-improvement that is required. My study supports this reading and also finds that the particular pedagogies of classical music, which rely on high levels of detailed direction from adults and constant evaluative judgements, exacerbate this tendency. However, the strong relationships of trust within the one-to-one teaching relationship that some young people reported appeared to negate or at least contain this propensity. The bodily experience of singing was also a powerful countervailing force. Nevertheless, in some ways classical music practice was continuous with the wider social world of middle-class normative femininity. The women running the Young Opera Company, Sophia and Jeanette, were often successful in creating a space where young women could develop embodied confidence, but they were working against a musical tradition that lends itself only too well to the relentless self-criticism that many of the young people described.

However, as I have argued throughout this book, classical music's homology with middle-class forms of selfhood is always partial as it also creates a space

---

[2] Practices of self-criticism and perfectionism have been linked to body dysmorphia and anorexia among middle- and upper-class adolescent girls; see, for example, Evans et al. (2004).

where their opposite can be experienced: freedom and community (Eagleton 1990). The intimate support experienced in some of the young people's relationships with teachers is an example of this. In addition, Lisa McCormick's (2015) study of classical music competitions, which she argues are more about international 'civility' than about competing, points towards instability around the notion of competitiveness within classical music; it is compulsory but also on some level unacceptable or disavowed through discourses that suggest classical music is a space of freedom, set apart from such mundane concerns. Nevertheless, in the context of the Young Opera Company, the confidence and power that these young women found through singing in an operatic style were limited by the ways in which competitiveness and self-critique were ever-present, and this was continuous with gendered structures outside of these musical spaces.

The Conditions of Producing the Voice: The Musical Canon and Opera Industry

This transformative experience of singing was mediated by the music and plot of *The Magic Flute*. It was also constructed within the institutional conditions of the opera world, both in the youth music scene and in the 'symbolic ecology' of classical music that featured heavily in the imagined futures of these young women. This symbolic ecology was an imagined version of the institutional ecology described in chapter 2, dominated by the Royal Opera House and other high-profile cultural institutions. My participants were aware of these institutions largely because of the ways in which adults within the classical music world—Sophia, Jeanette, Richard, and others—talked about them.

Against the potential for opera singing to subvert normative femininity, particularly in relation to body image, in the Young Opera Company's production of *The Magic Flute* the text and the institutional conditions of the opera world came together to confirm hegemonic gender roles of normative bourgeois femininity as sexually vulnerable, objectified, and suffering. Indeed, the ideals of bourgeois femininity were dramatized and sometimes uncomfortably re-inscribed through the staging of this opera. The power of this message was further entrenched by the ideology of being faithful to the written score, which set strict limits for what changes it was possible to make.

Isabelle, who was just about to go to music college to study singing in the hope of becoming an opera singer, told me her experience of the music theatre and opera industry thus far had turned her into a feminist: 'I still think the whole opera and music industry thing it's men before women [...] and I think it's also pretty women over people who aren't considered pretty'. She was also highly aware of the 'sexual economy' of classical music (Yoshihara 2008, 109) that this power imbalance entails:

> I had a singing lesson with a tenor [...] and he said, I'll give you some advice, don't let anyone make you do something you don't want to do, just don't let them do it, they can't force you to do it, don't let them ... [...] and he sort of looked at me, he said, you're an attractive girl and looks go a long way. Don't let anyone ...

Since late 2017, these kinds of accounts have suddenly become public knowledge, thanks to high-profile sexual harassment scandals in Hollywood, Westminster, and other fields. Isabelle's perspective is borne out by a recent survey of members of the UK's Incorporated Society of Musicians, which found that across 250 respondents, 59.6% had experienced some form of discrimination, nearly two-thirds of these accounts being of sexual harassment, including 'groping from instrumental teachers', 'inappropriate advances and sexual comments from older colleagues', and being a victim of indecent exposure from a 'famous musician' (Incorporated Society of Musicians 2017, 4–5). Despite this, the opera industry was immensely appealing to many of the young women involved in this production. Sara, Katherine, Hannah, and Isabelle all planned to train as opera singers after school or university, and Emily was beginning to consider it after her experience of this production.

However, this sexual harassment and objectification did not just take place within the institutional culture of the opera and classical music world, but was present within the text of *The Magic Flute* as well. In one scene, Isabelle's character had to lie on the stage while the evil slave master, Monostatos, sang an aria about how he is going to rape her; she had to pretend to be asleep while he paced around her body and leant over her. She told me how 'it just freaked me out the first few times he did it. Even now [...] it's really disorientating'. The music is a breathlessly fast aria in a major key, and while the scene is supposed to be comic rather than dramatic, the tempo and high energy of the orchestral accompaniment meant I found myself enjoying playing it on the piano during rehearsals. Robbie, playing Monostatos, the would-be rapist, had very good diction, and all his words, in the director's translation, could be clearly heard, such as 'She's lying there so luscious, I'll be damned if I hold fire!', and 'I've got what it takes as well' (complete with hip thrusts). Francesca commented on the dramatic power of this scene, noting that it was 'one of the scenes that has come together in our particular production the best', which is 'a genuine problem' because 'it's believable and compelling [...] but not comfortable at all'. The powerful message that Isabelle received from the text of *The Magic Flute*—that young women are sexually vulnerable—was reinforced both by the musical success of the scene and by her experience of the wider practices of the opera industry. In this way, the potential for opera singing to be a transformative, empowering space for young women was undermined by disempowering messages within the text and from the industry.

Representing Femininity

The two main female roles in the opera, the princess Pamina and her mother the Queen of the Night, were experienced fairly uncritically by my participants as good and evil. The music itself contributed to this, as Pamina's goodness was made emotionally appealing through the beauty of her melodies, which are characterized by smooth vocal lines and slow tempi that show off the arcs of Mozart's beautifully constructed phrases. In the scene described at the beginning of this chapter, the chromatic, expressive intervals of Pamina's aria represent female suffering as 'rightness' (see chapter 4) or, at least, as beauty. Furthermore, not only is this aria written in a range in which only women can sing, but it is in a fairly high part of the female voice. This was the part of the voice which I experienced in my singing lessons as feeling the most powerful, due to the greater volume and resonance that were possible on the high notes. The tone quality in this range, sometimes called the 'head voice' or 'head tone', exemplifies the 'purity' of tone which Jeanette described to me as the ideal she looked for in a voice. This purity, and the deep emotional response that it effected in my participants, seemed to index an idealized mode of femininity, played out through the character of the virginal, suffering princess.

The bel canto aesthetic that is required for singing opera also indexes *white* femininity, as Gustafson describes (2009, chap. 7). Following Barthes, she argues that the 'grain of the voice' discloses a bodily presence (123). In the 'Western musical tradition' the upper body is both the 'origin' of vocal sound and also the site of reason, while the lower body is associated with unreason (127). By contrasting the bel canto style of singing that is required in classical music with a different method of vocal production, 'belting', Gustafson argues that these different types of sound draw on racialized systems of classification. Bel canto singing emphasizes the head tone, where sound is produced higher in the body, 'emphasiz[ing] restraint and polish that downplays the chest and vocal folds' (129). Against this, belting uses a mode of vocal production that comes from below the neck, 'projecting the image of the whole body as the heart of the voice' (129). Drawing on data from music education curricula and psychoacoustic experiments in the US during the twentieth century, Gustafson describes how these different types of sound indexed different racialized bodies, the bel canto tone signifying a white body through its associations with reason and the head, and vocal production from below the neck signifying 'lower instincts' and the 'lower social body', including people of colour (123). This reading is borne out by the importance in opera (bel canto) singing of avoiding physical gestures, such as with the hands, while singing. If the voice is coming from the site of reason—the head—then the body must not be emphasized. Gustafson goes on to argue that in bel canto singing, the voice's grain 'is judged as a quality of the soul rather than as a message from the body' (128) so that the music can appear to be coming from outside the body, from a more spiritual realm. This analysis, as well as her wider argument that classical music prioritizes cognitive control, supports my theorization of the body in classical music as being disciplined so that it can be transcended (as discussed in chapters 1 and 5). The powerful affective responses among my participants that Pamina's arias brought about confirm white, respectable bourgeois femininity as the ideal for young women.

By contrast, the other main female role in the opera is the Queen of the Night, whose 'unnatural' femininity, as many commentators have described, is present in the music itself in the second act. Her vocal line, especially in the famous aria which leaps to ridiculously high notes that most sopranos can't reach, follows the stereotype of excessive or hysterical female madness being portrayed as musical excess, as McClary (2002, 111, 114) describes. She is the epitome of female irrationality; 'excessive ornamentation dissolves her words into inaudibility and meaninglessness' (Subotnik 1991, 137), and 'she speaks not at all to reason ... a madwoman cut off from everyone else' (Clément 1997, 73). Indeed, she could be seen to symbolize femininity as 'too much' as discussed earlier in Bordo's analysis of eating disorders (2003, 161).

How do women respond to such denigrations of themselves? asks Marcia Citron. She argues:

> A female receptor often ends up being forced to adopt a male point of view and thereby take a stand against herself and effectively participate in the conspiracy. She identifies against herself as she is swept up and sutured into male narratives and patterns of desire. (1993b, 74)

To a large extent, Citron's assertion was borne out by my participants' readings of the Queen of the Night and Pamina, although it was not simply the text that created this identification but the relative continuity between the text and the wider social and institutional conditions of femininity they lived under. The Queen of the Night was seen by all my participants as a strong character but as irredeemably evil; even her shift from good to evil as described in the musicological literature was not identified by them (Subotnik 1991). The Queen showed the limits to what was allowed in making sound in public space; none of them could sympathize or identity with her. Even Sara, who played this role, channelled someone in her life who had been abusive to her in order to successfully represent the character. The Queen, the only representation of female power in the opera, signified an illegible version of femininity as irrational, mad, and evil. The 'cultural axes' that support the culture of eating disorders (Bordo 2003) were not, therefore, being challenged in this production.

Participants' readings of Pamina, the princess, were more nuanced and varied, perhaps due to their similar age and social position to her, and reflected their own personalities and life experiences. Elizabeth, a confident young woman heading for Oxford University, saw Pamina as 'an anti-moral'—an example of how *not* to behave. By contrast, Emily saw Pamina as a strong character for surviving everything that she'd been through. Pamina's embodiment of idealized, respectable femininity also drew out contrasting discourses. In the Young Opera Company production, Pamina's costume (chosen by director Sophia) was a floaty white dress, which made her look every inch the virtuous virgin. Hannah and Katherine agreed that this made her 'too perfect' for them to identify with, and for Francesca, Pamina's 'major characteristic is that she's trapped', these young women distancing themselves from identification with Pamina. For the two young women playing Pamina, it was more difficult to do this. Isabelle, one of the Paminas, mentioned that she spent most of the opera on her knees, and Emily, the other Pamina, told me she had bruises and scratches on her knees because of this positioning of Pamina as physically submissive throughout. Both of these young women noticed this characterization, but it was never explicitly discussed as part of the production; rather, director Sophia emphasized Pamina's one moment of agency in the opera as evidence of the feminist values of the production.

As is evident in the frequent references to Pamina's beauty in the libretto, appearance is an important facet of the kind of femininity that is endorsed in this text, further reinforcing normative ideas of respectable femininity as requiring conventional attractiveness (Gill 2007, 246). Her white dress symbolized idealized femininity, but in real life this identity requires not only the 'aesthetic labour' of disciplining the 'unruly body' (Elias, Gill, and Scharff 2017; Gill 2007) but also a careful balancing act between being perceived as attractive and being vulnerable to sexual objectification or violence (Holland et al. 2004), against the reality that all women are vulnerable to sexual assault, regardless of age or appearance (Ministry of Justice, Home Office, and Office for National Statistics 2013). The continuity between the text of *The Magic Flute* and wider social conditions of femininity is shown by the warning Isabelle received from a teacher, mentioned earlier in the chapter, and the scene where Monostatos tries to rape Pamina. As Holland et al. describe, femininity is an 'unsafe sexual identity', and conventionally feminine behaviour puts young women at risk of unsafe sexual activity (2004, 5). The congruence between the text and production of this opera as well as the institutional conditions of the wider industry are clear: that this version of femininity is an essential part of the role of female opera singer, both in and out of character.

Destabilizing the Discourse of Authenticity

Given the transformative potential of singing in an operatic style for some of these young women, it is important to ask whether there is potential to rework the canon and reform the working practices and institutional culture of classical music to enable a progressive mode of practice for opera, and for classical music more generally. Such a renewal, however, is heavily inhibited by the discourse of 'fidelity' or authenticity to the musical score (Goehr 1992; Leech-Wilkinson 2016). This question of authenticity, often referred to as being faithful to the intentions of the composer, shaped the limits of possibility for changing the text and its associated practices. This was particularly interesting in the Young Opera Company's production of *The Magic Flute* in that there had been various changes made to the text to make it suitable for the young cast. Sophia's translation altered the libretto to expunge some of the more blatantly sexist and racist elements from the text, and since the Temple of Wisdom couldn't be cast as intended as men only, due to a lack of boys in the cast, it became a temple inclusive of female and male priests. This required rewriting some of the harmonies to fit women's voices, for a section constituting about a minute of music. This rewriting was on the edge of what changes were considered acceptable in relation to discourses of authenticity. In addition, due to difficulties in finding enough players for the orchestra, performances took place with a smaller orchestra than Mozart intended. The technical difficulty of playing the music meant that the young people in the orchestra could not always manage perfect technical renditions of the music, thus also affecting the fidelity to the score. In other Young Opera Company productions I played the orchestra part on the piano for performances, a common practice for smaller-scale opera performances.

Considering that all these changes had already been made, it might seem that further changes would be possible and even desirable. Indeed, as musicologist Richard Taruskin grumbles, 'Absolutely no one performs pre-twentieth-century music as it would have been performed when new. This may be so easily verified that it is a wonder anyone still believes the contrary' (1995, 164). However, when I discussed this with the cast and adults in the production, it emerged very strongly that all of them thought it was crucially important to stage the opera 'as Mozart intended', in a 'traditional' way. Sarastro, for example, most people agreed, had to be a man. Sophia, despite trying to write a feminist translation, was very keen that for their first time learning this opera, as an important part of the operatic canon, the young people needed to get to know it 'straight': 'They have to learn the reality of *Magic Flute* first. And then they can go and twist it and change it'. This assumption of an authentic work of art existing prior to any interpretive 'twists' was belied by the changes, as just described, that Sophia herself had made to the production. However, she justified these in terms of having to get rid of the 'offensive' elements: 'I don't want to take [the cast] too far from the original, except where the original is actually offensive, to them, the audience, and to me, before they have a chance to learn the original'. Changes to the libretto and the music therefore followed strongly circumscribed rules as to what constituted the parameters of this imagined originary text which must be preserved.

The young people followed Sophia in defending this fidelity, justifying it in different ways. Robbie thought 'maybe a female Sarastro would be great, but there's also the idea of comfort zone, and I think that would make it a bit—not avant-garde, but a bit less out of the familiar, and that might be upsetting for some people'—not upsetting for himself, he hastened to add, but even so, 'I would prefer sort of a more traditional take on it'. Isabelle argued, 'I think you learn so much from singing things that were written so long ago. […] If it was written now, it's always a fusion or a development of other things, new music or theatre', seeing in *The Magic Flute* an authentic text from which more recent culture has developed. Francesca, who was the radical voice among my participants, said she would like to do an all-female production, not as a subversion of the composer's intentions but instead seeing an all-female version as 'gender neutral', which, she argued, 'might be closer to what Mozart intended'. Staying 'true' to the intentions of the composer was therefore a clear theme. The contradiction between the radical potential of opera singing as bodily practice, and the reproduction of gendered norms and traditions, was unlikely to find a space for disruption or synthesis in the Young Opera Company. Because the text and story were mainly seen as a dramatic structure which served as a vehicle for the 'sublime' music, they had to remain intact in order to serve the music, as this was the rationale for putting on the opera. The potential to rework the canon to support rather than undermine the re-imagining of the body was therefore severely limited due to this powerful discourse of authenticity.

However, despite this attachment to fidelity, the meaning of the musical text was already destabilized by the process of producing it. Many of the cast recounted back to me the interpretations that Sophia, the director, had given of the opera, having accepted them uncritically. But around this scaffolding some developed sophisticated understandings of the motivations and histories of the characters, with especially strong relationships with the characters they were playing themselves. Some would even use 'I' to describe their character's experience; for example, Toby, who played the leader of the Temple of Light Sarastro, said, 'I think I'm more powerful than the Queen of the Night', identifying himself in the first person as his character. As Robbie, who played the evil servant Monostatos pointed out, 'I've sort of had to live [the opera], a bit', over the year they'd rehearsed it. This length of engagement allowed him to inhabit his character over time, developing an intimate understanding of Monostatos' motivations.

However, against scholarly readings of the meaning of the text and the musico-dramatic structure of this opera (Kerman 1988; Subotnik 1991; Stuckey 1995), as well as the ideology of the organic whole of the 'work-concept' as described in chapter 5, the opera was not experienced as a unified whole by most of the participants. The plot and dramatic structure were not entirely unimportant, in that they were the rationale for putting on a production in this form, but these took their place within the tapestry of influences which went into making up the experience as a whole. The production was rehearsed in scenes, so that many of the cast would know in great detail the scenes they themselves were in, while having little idea what went on the rest of the time. The convoluted, almost dream-like 'fairy-tale' plot exacerbated this sense of fragmentation. Instead, particular sections or arias appeared to stand out for different people as their favourite part of the music or drama. The scene described at the beginning of this chapter, Pamina's aria, was one such scene of affective intensity which several people mentioned as memorable. The meaning of *The Magic Flute* for the young people in this production was overall much more influenced by the characterizations of each role than by the musical-dramatic structure as a whole, although the music itself entered into these characterizations, as discussed earlier, representing Pamina, for example, as beautiful and suffering and Sarastro as wise and balanced.

The role of the musical text in this production is therefore somewhat contradictory. Its 'greatness' was the rationale for forming the Young Opera Company in the first place (as was spelled out in the programme for the performances), but it became a different object through the process of producing it. The possibilities for changing the text were severely constrained by the discourse of authenticity, but despite this there were still quite a few changes made. Overall, affective moments and powerful characterization were much more important than the structure of the opera as a whole in creating meaning for the young people in the production. This suggests that textual analyses of canonic works such as *The Magic Flute* need to be complemented by attention to the ways in which the text is used, today, as lived experience. This instability opens up ways forward for musical texts to be re-configured to allow young women's transformative experience of singing opera to become part of a wider project of empowerment and gender equality, rather than constrained by representing conventional femininity.

Conclusion: The Radical Potential of the Aesthetic?

This chapter has assessed the encounter between the young women of the Young Opera Company and a profoundly anti-feminist musical text, Mozart's *The Magic Flute*. As Mark Banks (2017) argues, our research needs to take into account the cultural object itself as well as the practices and socialities that surround it. With classical music, this means that the musical text should be assessed in the context of a particular social, affective, aesthetic encounter with it. As various authors have explored, this encounter is unpredictable, as the aesthetic experience does not exist separately to the conditions of its production and reception (Banks 2017; Born 2010; Hennion 2001; Stewart 2012). To apply this understanding to studying inequalities in classical music, as I argued in chapter 1, a multi-scalar approach is needed (Born 2017), taking into account both the individual, embodied level of practice and face-to-face encounters, and also institutional, structural, and imagined mediations of the social, as well as the 'internal goods' of the aesthetic object itself (Banks 2017).

This chapter primarily evaluates this production in relation to one of the questions raised in chapter 1: Can classical music provide a space for women to find an expressive voice that they may lack in wider society? Christina Scharff's study found that this was indeed possible (2017, 44), and Lucy Green's historical survey of women's music-making in the UK similarly suggests that classical music's 'autonomy' from the social has in fact 'preserved a space in which women solo instrumentalists have been able to pursue musical careers without being repeatedly judged according to interruptive delineations of patriarchally defined femininity' (1997, 62). However, for singers, according to Green, the picture is different: 'the relative success of women singers throughout history represents no simple freedom, but, rather, reveals the proximity of singing to patriarchal definitions of femininity' (50).

From my evaluation of the Young Opera Company's production of *The Magic Flute*, it is certainly the case that some of the young women found an expressive voice and an embodied confidence that they lacked more widely, despite their (mostly) professional middle-class backgrounds. However, at the same time their music-making was, as Green describes, 'affirm[ing] and reproduc[ing] patriarchal definitions of femininity' (1997, 46). For the young women in this chapter, singing opera offered a double bonus: the reward of social legitimacy for investing in normative bourgeois femininity, as well as the intoxicating sense of bodily power that comes with singing and the radical experience of feeling entirely in control of one's own body. They were allowed to have a voice and take up space only if they did so within the parameters of normative bourgeois femininity. They also needed a heavy investment of encouragement from trusted adults to take up this space.

As Gail Weiss (1999) points out, there is potential for social change in imagining the body differently. In the text of the opera, in the wider institutional conditions of the opera world, and in this production the young female body remained an object to be controlled, directed, objectified, and shaped; a body which was experienced as insufficient, vulnerable, too fat, kneeling, trapped, and suffering; and yet it was liberated—temporarily—through the voice to become powerful, uncomfortably loud, expressive, and to-be-listened-to, demanding attention. However, the subversive potential of this re-imagining of the body remained an individualized experience, never connecting into broader social and institutional structures such as the gender norms of these young women's lives. In fact, the production reinscribed normative femininity by representing the limits of acceptable femininity in the character of the Queen of the Night, who could be seen to represent the version of the female that inspires fear (Bordo 2003). The uncritical acceptance of the Queen as evil, and of Pamina (despite more complexity around interpretations of her character) as pure and good, means that despite the transformative embodied effects of singing opera, it did not disrupt the cultural conditions that contribute to the body image issues my participants reported.

This chapter has focused on gender inequalities, but as Subotnik notes, the musical material and plot of *The Magic Flute* also reify class and race inequalities under an ostensible message of equality (1991, 147). These themes were uncomfortably visible in the rehearsals for the Young Opera Company, and yet despite this, there was more potential for equality in this production than in other groups in my study, in part because there are lower barriers to entry for singing than for playing an instrument. In addition, Sophia was also adamant that there should be no fees for participation in order to allow the group to be more inclusive. These factors meant that young people from a wider range of social backgrounds were singing in the chorus. However, most of the lead singers were from professional middle-class backgrounds as the difficulty of the solo parts required singers to have had one-to-one lessons, drawing on the long-term, future-oriented investment that is one of the main mechanisms through which classical music creates a segregated middle-class space.

Nevertheless, this chapter points to routes towards renewal for classical music more widely. While its canonic repertoire is problematically gendered, classed, and raced, this can be countered in two ways. First, particularly in a music education/youth music context, critical discussions of the musical text and how young people experience it are urgently needed. As described earlier, many of the young people's comments showed a critical engagement with the text, particularly with Pamina's characterization. This needed more space for discussion to allow them to make sense of the production for themselves and to critically discuss its racism, sexism, and classism, as critic Tim Ashley (2008) also suggests. Adults involved in these productions had a large amount of influence over young people's attitudes and engagement with classical music, and this influence is a clear starting point for bringing about social change.

Second, classical music's ideologies of the unity of the musical work and fidelity to the score were challenged by this production and should be further disrupted. The musical work was not experienced as a unified structure by the young people involved in this production, but was still a powerful experience for them. This suggests that cuts, amendments, and changes (which are more common in opera than in instrumental music; see, for example, Coser 1978) could be introduced without losing the power of the experience. In addition, fidelity to the score was already undermined by rewriting a short passage of harmony to fit with the voices available, as well as using an amateur, pared-down orchestra for the performances. Indeed, any one rendition of a particular work is always already unfaithful to the score in many different ways. This opens the door towards altering the musical text to re-imagine the social world that is created within the opera. This would also mean re-inscribing the ways in which we hear aesthetic beauty through the music. The spine-tingling beauty of Pamina's famous aria, in this production, was constructed in part *through* its presentation of bourgeois femininity.

If we reject the characterization that comes with the aria—which may include amending the musical material itself—its meaning and its beauty might change. This is a risk we need to take. Musical texts are already experienced in different ways in different aesthetic encounters. This undermines arguments for authenticity or fidelity to the score and opens up possibilities for rethinking *The Magic Flute* for the twenty-first century through radical re-imaginings of the musical text, both musically and dramatically.

CHAPTER 8

A Community-in-Sound

CONSTRUCTING THE VALUED SELF

This final empirical chapter moves away from examining the experience of producing sound for individuals towards sound as creating community. It explores how sound helped create and spread powerful shared affects through the embodied experience of being part of a community-in-sound. Teresa, talking about her first experience of playing in the National Youth Orchestra in her early teens, described the power of the orchestra the first time she heard it:

> The National Youth Orchestra as a whole was an amazing experience, I remember the first piece we played, the Prokofiev *Romeo and Juliet*, there were sixteen double basses in this orchestra, so they were [she sings the opening] it was like, amazing! I was blown away by the sound, I remember I didn't come in, because I was like, this is *amazing*, because I'd never been in a proper big orchestra, or a really good orchestra, so it was an amazing experience.

In this description, Teresa keeps repeating how 'amazing' this experience was to try and convey this sense of awe. This chapter explores this sense of being 'in sound' and asks how this powerful sonic affect connects these young people to a valued identity. Being a classical musician was, for many of them, a powerful identity, as evident in their striving for improvement, their desire for correction, their strong friendships, the ways in which they disciplined themselves and sought to be disciplined by others, and above all their love for this music. This powerful identity spurred them to carry out the boundary-drawing work around classical music that I have described throughout this book. It created a sense of being special and valued and contributed towards a desire to safeguard the repertoire, practices, and socialities of this cherished tradition.

Many factors contributed to this deeply held identity. This chapter explores one of the most powerful: the embodied, sonic experience of playing this music.

It links this experience with the emotional identifications that the young people brought to it and with the ideas of value that they read into it. The most powerful of these identifications was the experience of 'emotional depth' which they tended to attribute to classical music. This is an important way in which classical music is valued over other types of music. It was narrated as a subjective experience, but I suggest that this was brought about in part through conditions that were external to the self. Most notably, it occurred through being part of what I am calling a 'community-in-sound' whereby the sound itself opened up the body to emotional experience. Other factors also contributed. These were the historical construction of classical music as autonomous from the social and affording access to a deep part of the self; the acoustic aesthetic of the music that requires a certain mode of listening; and the physical experience of playing with others in grand spaces. These conditions worked together to interpellate these young people as subjects of value who had the emotional depth required to understand and love this music. By recognizing the music as valuable and learning to see themselves as people who recognized its value, they therefore accrued some of the value that society (still) accords classical music, participating in the quintessential middle-class practice of accumulating and storing value over time (Barlow et al. 1995).

Emotional Depth as Interiority

Owen, who was introduced in chapter 2, described how when he played in his first orchestra, having previously played only in brass bands, 'it was pretty much immediate, like, this is what I want to do'.

> ANNA: It was about the music, the type of music, the people, or ... ?
> OWEN: Just everything about it, it sort of enticed me, I think. I'd not really had that kind of experience of doing such a big collective thing with different people, different personalities.
> ANNA: Was it bigger and more diverse than being in a [brass] band?
> OWEN: Yeah, and I think the fact that you could actually respond to the music in terms of the depth of the music, emotional depth. [...] It's quite a personal thing, I think.

Owen described how the first orchestral piece he played was by Mendelssohn, to which he had the reaction, 'this is what I want to do'. In response, I described to him how I suddenly got into Brahms at age eighteen (Owen's age), listening to the piano quartets obsessively, feeling as though the contours of unknowable parts of myself were being traced in Brahms' melodies. Owen knew exactly what I was talking about, telling me that 'the first composer that happened to me with was Mahler'. I was struck that he put this in the passive voice; it was something that *happened* to him. And yet, he had actively cultivated this 'happening'. After his first experience with Mendelssohn at age thirteen, he had put in a lot of effort in order to get to know and understand classical music, listening to recordings of Mahler's Second Symphony and Richard Strauss' Alpine Symphony while he did his homework. 'It's not something that I responded to immediately', he described; the 'epic scale' of these long, complex pieces required investment on his part to learn to love them. At first he just 'got' 'bits and pieces', but eventually he was able to 'respond' to the 'emotional depth' of the music. However, he was clear that this 'personal thing' of responding to the 'emotional depth' of the music first occurred *socially* within a 'big collective' of 'different people'. This was the initial 'call' that led to his wanting to learn about this music. As Blackman describes, drawing on Jean-Luc Nancy, 'Our very sense of interiority emerges through our relations with others, human and non-human and in that sense we are always more than one and less than many' (2012, 184). This deep personal response was drawn out of Owen *within* the collective, formed by and through it.

This discourse of 'depth' was echoed by some of my other interviewees. For example, when I asked Ellie about her listening habits, she told me she didn't listen to music a lot. 'Classic FM I'll listen to, vaguely, but I just can't find that depth in music that ... unless it's classical music'. Similarly, Jenny couldn't understand why people listened to commercial pop music, saying, 'I think people love it so much, but really there's no depth to it. I don't necessarily now think that's a bad thing because it's for enjoyment, so if it brings joy to people then fair enough, but when it's really deep music ...'. Jenny is suggesting here that classical music, because of its depth, is about more than simply enjoyment, but similarly to Ellie, she runs out of words when trying to articulate what this depth in music does. Enjoyment or pleasure is not enough, and these words do not adequately describe the experience my participants are trying to access. Instead, I suggest that the discourse of 'depth' connotes a seriousness and an importance that enjoyable musics such as pop music do not allow.

Other researchers on classical music have also noted this discourse. For example, in a study of orchestral audiences in the UK, Crawford et al. found that they saw classical music as affording a 'fundamental and deeper appreciation of the music', by contrast with the lack of depth of pop music (2014, 11). Similarly, McCormick's study of international classical music competitions found that expressions of 'deep emotions' and 'deep feeling' in performances were valued by jurors (2015, 177, 184). The opera fanatics studied by Benzecry, who explores 'love' for classical music as a metaphor, were found to value depth as a quality of singers' voices, suggesting that there might be particular sonic qualities to the experience of depth (2011, 86), and the amateur classical musicians in Palmer's study (2008, 211) described their music-making 'as engaging *deep* aspects of their psyches and spirit'.

This discourse points towards the existence of a particular 'ontology of the human', as Charles Taylor (1989, 92) describes it: a distinction between inner and outer. As part of an exploration of the sources of morality under modernity,

Taylor argues that 'we think of the depths of the unsaid, the unsayable, the powerful inchoate feelings and affinities and fears which dispute with us the control of our lives, as inner. We are creatures with inner depths'. This sense is 'in large part a feature of our world, the world of modern, Western people' (111). Modernity saw the process of our 'disenchantment' with the world wherein we began to see ourselves as separate from the 'cosmic order'; 'the human agent was no longer to be understood as an element in a larger, meaningful order. His [sic] paradigm purposes are to be discovered within' (193). As discussed in chapter 1, Mellor and Shilling (1997) locate the emergence of this interiority slightly earlier, with the emergence of Puritanism after the Reformation, following Max Weber (2001), and link it into a 're-formation' of the body, away from understanding the sacred through the 'fleshy body' and towards the 'disembodied transcendence of the sublime'. This required 'an 'inner' search for God' rather than a communal, embodied invocation of the sacred (Mellor and Shilling 1997, 100, 106). The work of art brings us 'into the presence of something which is otherwise inaccessible, and which is of the highest moral or spiritual significance' (C. Taylor 1989, 420).

This shift in the 'ontology of the human' is reflected in changing patterns of listening in the nineteenth century that created the conditions for accessing and cultivating 'inner depth' through classical music. James Johnson pinpoints a shift that occurred among the 'aesthetic sensibility' of bourgeois concert audiences in France between 1800 and 1820 from favouring 'programmatic' music where the music portrayed a 'single, objective meaning' for each passage such as a storm or a love quarrel, towards 'absolute' music, a more 'romantic approach' that 'refused to assign any determinate meaning whatever to music' (1996, 207). This shift towards 'absolute' music involved the 'interiorization of experience' through which listening, rather than being a communal experience, became enclosed 'in a private space closed off from community and inaccessible to language', creating 'a new experience, one deeper, more personal, more powerful' (273–74). My participants' identification of the 'depth' of Romantic repertoire shows the resilience of this discourse and experience. Similarly, a recent defence of classical music by musicologist Laurence Kramer (2009) stakes its argument for classical music's value on its ability to channel this form of subjectivity. Kramer argues that 'each of us has a private core of being to call our own', and 'when we listen intently to music, it is the inner self that hears' (2009, 19). Classical music is important in accessing our 'deep inner selves' (19) because it allows for a 'special type of listening' of sustained attention (10).

However, as Beverley Skeggs argues, this sense of interiority or 'inner depth' is 'only available to the privileged few and is premised upon the exclusion of others' (2003, 56). The bourgeois, reflexive self was built through 'cultural technologies of telling the self' such as the novel or the confessional autobiography or journal beloved of early Puritans (122; see also C. Taylor 1989, 184). By contrast, for the working classes, 'telling the self' was enforced as a mode of establishing or displaying respectability, for example, to obtain poor relief (Steedman 2000; Savage 2010). In this way, to be someone who had an inner self that could be narrated to others was a classed resource, a form of 'possessive individualism' that has historically been afforded to those who could possess property (Skeggs 2003, 17). Such individuals were able to possess a sense of ownership over themselves, their lives, and their destinies, and they were allowed to narrate their experience freely, as a story that makes sense over time. This pattern of classed subjectivity is clearly visible in the late Victorian literature that parallels the formative historical period for classical music education institutions. One among many possible examples is Anthony Trollope, who gives his middle-class characters a self-reflexive, inner voice, often a moral one, that his working-class characters lack. A full and complex sense of subjectivity, which brings accompanying moral capacities for self-determination, is primarily afforded to the bourgeois (or, in Dickens, the aspiring bourgeois) subject.

For the young people in my study, being someone who can understand classical music *and love it* means that they are demonstrating this kind of interiority. Owen's comment—that on playing in an orchestra for the first time he knew immediately that this was what he wanted to do—suggests that he recognized himself in the music because he *wanted* to have this kind of interiority. Before this, he had played in brass bands and 'was never interested in orchestras, I just wanted to play in bands', following in his grandfather's footsteps; he was even thinking of joining the military as a musician. And yet, after his first experience of playing in a Saturday morning orchestra run by the local music service, this all changed.

Classical Music as Cultural Technology for Knowing the Bourgeois Self

The recognition of 'inner depth' as a classed resource that has historically been afforded to some groups over others casts a different light on my participants' recognition of an emotional depth in classical music which other musics lack. It suggests a reading of classical music as a cultural technology for knowing the bourgeois self (drawing on Skeggs 2003, 122; see also DeNora 2000). This can be theorized through highlighting the connection between these affects of 'deep' emotion and discourses of the unity and structure of the musical work that I explored in chapter 5, through which large-scale tonal structures provide a mechanism or technology for dealing with time. This 'technology' of tonality also assumes and reproduces particular ideas of the self.

As introduced in chapter 1, McClary (2001) and Citron (1993a) outline a reading of the musical subject (for example, in sonata form) as amenable to analysis as a *social* subject, rather than simply as musical material that requires formal, structural analysis. This can be seen most clearly in the development of tonal structures in the seventeenth and eighteenth centuries. In sonata form, the dominant tonal structure by the nineteenth century, the first or masculine subject (Citron 1993a) progresses through its harmonic journey before 'taming' (1993a,

21) the second or 'feminine' subject' into the 'home' key for the final section of the piece. Tonality can be seen as the corollary of the sense of an inner core or self which endures and develops despite going through various emotions. This is a form of narrating the self by way of a journey that parallels the development of a new 'centered subjectivity' (McClary 2001, 73). This new-found stability of tonality occurs alongside the early novel, which Skeggs also describes as a formative bourgeois technology of telling the self.

Tonality can be read, therefore, as reflecting the emerging sense of an enduring self in the seventeenth and eighteenth centuries. The form of selfhood that is being assumed and produced is one that can see its past and its future progress laid out in a knowable formal structure. This requires being able to hold large-scale temporal structures in mind (up to an hour or more) and still locate oneself between past happenings and future unfoldings. As McClary suggests, 'Tonality teaches listeners how to project forward in time, how to wait patiently but confidently for the pay-off' (2001, 67). If the capacity to imagine possible future(s) and invest in their unfolding is a classed resource, then tonality and its formal structures could be seen as one way of learning or practising this ability. As Barlow et al. (1995) describe, accruing, storing, and institutionalizing resources for the future is a defining feature of the middle classes. This is not because working-class people do not wish to do this, but sometimes it is not possible to invest in the future. Certainly it makes less sense to focus on the long term when the short-term future is difficult or precarious. Furthermore, as Skeggs (2003, 146) notes, long-term investment is about imagining a future self that is valued. If the future that is imagined is uncertain, then investing in it makes less sense.

McClary's theorization of the musical subject as a social subject has been convincingly criticized by DeNora (2005), among others, as being too text-based. DeNora argues that McClary's reading fails to take into account the local conditions of cultural production of the text such as concerns of patrons or the possibilities of new technologies at the time of writing (DeNora 2005, 20–21). However, while there is 'no one-to-one connection between musical forms and the world of ideas' (22), DeNora's overall argument concurs that in the early nineteenth century 'art forms which depicted action and experience over time (rather than static forms such as sculpture or painting) took on a new social function, moulding of subjectivity and the self' (25). In her analysis of the concerto in early nineteenth-century Vienna, she argues that it 'was a form that was produced and received as a lesson in new forms of agency' (26).

There is, then, no necessary homology between a bourgeois social subject and the musical subject(s) that characterize many of classical music's large-scale works. However, it is possible to draw out a tentative homology between the imagined futures of my participants and the practising of self-into-structure that Owen describes through gradually familiarizing himself with large-scale complex works in order to gain access to a new middle-class world and a new form of subjectivity. More generally, a sense of projection of the self into the future was visible among my participants. Chapter 3 described Bethan's blithe confidence that 'everyone here is going to have bright futures'. She had learnt that practising was 'a good way to get into that kind of mindset where you just keep going and what you do pays off'; the discipline of practising every day helps, she said, with the discipline of doing your homework every day. She was about to go to Oxford, so it had worked for her thus far. Similarly, Alice's mother had started her on the violin as a purposeful technique to learn this daily discipline, a drip-drip investment in a future of being able to play well, which takes years to pay off, an important lesson for middle-class children to learn. As discussed in chapter 1, Lareau (2011), Walkerdine, Lucey, and Melody (2001), Vincent and Ball (2007), and others have demonstrated differences between middle-class and working-class child-rearing practices, in which the middle-class mode of 'concerted cultivation' approaches the child as a future-oriented project to be developed through investing in their potential capacities. Working-class parents, as Annette Lareau argues, are more likely to see the child as complete in themselves rather than focusing on the adult they will become (2011, 748). As a result, Lareau suggests that working-class parents tend to be less concerned that their child invest in enrichment activities, and of course may not have the financial means to do so. Indeed, classical music could be a quintessential example of a middle-class future orientation, requiring parents to be able to imagine their child being able to play the violin in five or ten years in order to rationalize ferrying them to lessons and concerts, encouraging them to do their practice, and paying for lessons and instruments.

Musical structures of tonal development and progress can be seen, therefore, to have resonance with a middle-class approach to imagining and investing in a particular future. As McClary further describes, with the beginnings of centred subjectivity, similarly to the novel 'for the duration of an aria (or sonata movement ...) all activity seems to operate under the control of a single governing impulse' (2001, 73). This inner core or self is also therefore *controlling* the development of the musical material and bringing it together into a unified whole. Studying the full score, or becoming a conductor, is a manifestation of this drive for omniscience.

A final point of similarity between my participants' lives and tonality as a tool for developing 'centered subjectivity' can be found in the ways that they narrated themselves in interviews. As noted earlier, 'telling the self' emerged as a classed technology whereby for the bourgeoisie it was a technique for religious reflection but for the working class it was, and often still is, an 'enforced narrative' (Steedman 2000; Jackson 2015). Being able to narrate one's past, present, and future in a coherent manner has a clear relation to the unfolding of musical structures over time where the musical subject that appears in the first section then reappears throughout the piece, possibly fragmented, in different keys, inverted, but finally re-emerges in the home key, clearly recognizable. Indeed, Kramer argues that classical music enables a 'performance of inner coherence' (2009, 224) assuming this model of subjectivity.

This 'inner coherence' could be seen in the way that most of my participants were very comfortable and fluent at narrating their 'musical biographies' (my opening question for interviews). The ease of their telling of the self suggests strongly centred subjects who have clear aspirations and life trajectories (France and Roberts 2017, chap. 3). Indeed, these (relatively) smooth transitions and coherent narratives constitute one of the invisible norms of the white middle classes (Forbes and Lingard 2015; Maxwell and Aggleton 2013; Walkerdine, Lucey, and Melody 2001), although as Allan (2010, 40) reveals, there are tensions within this performance of success for upper-middle-class girls. By contrast, studies of marginalized young people have found it impossible to use interviews for research. Potential participants were suspicious of surveillance, and if an interview was attempted, they would give the story they thought they were supposed to tell (Jackson 2015; McShane 2018).

While many of my participants did narrate struggles of various kinds, for most there was a sense that the reproduction of their class position through embarking on a fulfilling professional career was possible and likely. I am suggesting that this mode of future-oriented subjectivity can be rehearsed through imagining self-into-structure, learning that the turbulent development section in sonata form gives way to an inevitable return to the home key. In both cases, it is assumed that the status quo will be reproduced (even while it is 'transformed by encounters with difference' (hooks 1992, 22)). This is not simply an homology, however; as Born and Hesmondhalgh describe, music may form an imaginary identification that prefigures potential or emergent identities as well as reproducing existing identities (2000, 35–36). Owen's account suggests that classical music's large-scale structures can be used as a cultural technology for recognizing or becoming what he calls a 'proper middle-class' person. Learning classical music can, in this way, be a way of learning to be middle class.

Constructing Interiority through Interpellation: 'It Evokes Something in You'

This interiority and emotional depth was attributed to and cultivated by some social groups and not others. In particular, it was available to those who were literate and had access to certain technologies. The tonal structure of classical music, which cultivates the ability to see past and future laid out in a knowable formal structure, can be seen as one of these technologies of the self. Among my participants, this mode of subjectivity of interiority and depth was especially audible in the Romantic repertoire that they loved. Such responses to this music constitute a form of interpellation, in Althusser's (1971) terms, wherein participants recognize themselves as subjects who are able to experience this 'depth' of emotion in the music. This response cannot easily be verbalized but is experienced on an embodied level. This appeared to be Owen's experience when he described how, in joining an orchestra, 'everything about it, it sort of enticed me'. Similarly, Hannah and Katherine responded as follows when I asked if they had anything in common with other young people who played classical music, other than the music.

> HANNAH: I think it's just literally the music and how you react to it.
> KATHERINE: Yeah, I don't know if there's anything else.
> HANNAH: And it evokes something in you and finding someone else who also gets really passionate about like, a symphony or something, when you listen to something and get moved by music, not everyone has that and I think that's the mark of a musician, is when you can hear that.

Hannah says it 'evokes' something in her; for Owen it 'entices' him. Hannah comments that 'not everyone' 'gets really passionate' about the music or gets 'moved by music'; 'that's the mark of a musician'. There is a recognition in these comments that those who can experience the emotions evoked by this music have something that other people do not. This 'something', I am arguing, is this sense of 'emotional depth', and the ability to access this affective experience is tied to the historical construct of the bourgeois Western masculine self.

Why is this a mode of interpellation rather than simply being one music that that these young people like among others? Firstly, Althusser argues that interpellation or the hailing of the subject involves a process of recognition; people recognize themselves as subjects through being constituted by ideology (1971, 161). This describes Owen's moment of recognition that 'this is what I want to do'. They also recognize *each other*; as Hannah describes, when you find 'someone else who also gets really passionate about like, a symphony or something', there is a mutual recognition of a particular mode of subjectivity. Thus we have a process encompassing 'the mutual recognition of subjects and Subject, the subjects' recognition of each other, and finally the subject's recognition of himself' (Althusser 1971, 168). The 'Subject' Althusser is speaking of here is 'an absolute, unique, Subject' whose prototype is God. In classical music, it is the composer who is the Subject. As Althusser describes, therefore, 'there can only be subjects on the condition that there is an absolute, unique, Subject (God) who interpellates other subjects into being—these subjects mirror the Subject' (167). The deification of the composer (Nettl 1995) and the reverence towards his Word in the form of the score make more sense within this theorization.

Secondly, Althusser describes interpellation as occurring in part through the discipline of ideological state apparatuses. The disciplining of the classical music 'apparatus'—the daily 'practice' and the minor rituals that this practice involves—helps create the subject. Finally, Althusser emphasizes that this subjectivity has to be freely chosen. Some people playing classical music *don't* recognize themselves in the music; it fails to interpellate them. They may carry on playing it for other reasons such as parental pressure or the sociability of it, without getting this 'depth'—and then suddenly 'get' it, or not. Similarly, as Eagleton describes, the new bourgeois subject takes on 'structures of power', which become internalised 'structures of feeling'—but this internal structure of freedom is experienced by the subject as being 'something I just happen to feel' (1988, 300, 333).

The mechanisms through which the historical formation of bourgeois subjectivity is inscribed onto individuals are subtle. There is a tension between these young people's accounts of immediate recognition of something that 'entices you' and the longer-term socialization that must go into acquiring readiness to be interpellated by this sonic and social experience. Accounts that centre on the moment of recognition can reinforce assumptions that there is something universal in classical music that calls out to all those who hear it and obscure the ways in which people must recognize this identity as valuable in order to hear and answer the call. As Judith Butler describes, subject formation through interpellation must be preceded by a 'readiness' or 'anticipatory desire' for this to happen (1997, 111). The conditions of possibility for this 'readiness' are created through a variety of forms of socialization: listening to classical music in the home; recognizing it as a signifier that is associated with respected social and cultural institutions; or, for new middle-class and working-class participants, identifying classical music as an escape route from the identity they were born into towards one that will enable travel, prestige, and access to middle-class spaces. One of the mechanisms by which this interpellation occurred, to which I now turn, was the experience of being part of a 'community-in-sound' that opened up the subject through the senses.

Community-in-Sound: Affective Materiality and the Suspension of Subjectivity

In a previous study of audience members at classical music concerts (Bull 2009), several people started crying during interviews while trying to explain why classical music was so meaningful to them, one telling me, 'It's beyond words, I would explain it if I could, but oh, I can't ...'. An even more immediate visceral reaction was recounted by singing teacher Jeanette, who was trying to explain to me why she thought it was so important to introduce people to opera:

> I love opera [...] when I go to see *Tosca*, I don't know what happens when it comes to the third act, but the minute the tenor starts singing, I cry, and I don't know why I cry. I cried the first time I saw it [...] it's an unnameable reaction, it's just something the music does, it's about music, and it's really funny, when I hear that music it makes me cry. [...] Just something in that music that's soaring and yearning and—chokes me, it chokes me.

The 'unnameability' of this emotion for Jeanette could be seen as a different iteration of the 'emotional depth' discussed earlier, but one which is expressed through an involuntary bodily response. In his ethnography of opera fans in Buenos Aires, Claudio Benzecry describes the same embodied response among his participants, arguing that this initiation through bodily attachment to opera leads towards a 'passionate engagement' where 'fans shape themselves as worthy selves through a laborious, sustained, long-term engagement with opera' (2011, 84). Fans even claim a spiritual or moral superiority through what Benzecry called 'moral listening', a 'process of learning in order to be emotionally moved and affected by opera, which, they believe, consequently makes one a better person' (95). This process all starts with the body; in Benzecry's study, 'passionate fans spoke as if music had taken their body over, occupying the space where the core of the self used to be with such force as to make them forget who they are' (88). Here I build on Benzecry's study to explore in more detail the bodily experience of being part of a community-in-sound and the moral projects of the self that this enables.

Jenny described one such moment in Sibelius' Second Symphony, which we had played together with the New Symphony Orchestra. After the orchestra had spent the previous forty minutes of the symphony in a long, slow buildup, finally the majestic theme is allowed to be heard all the way through. But after this joyous release, the brass sound a warning, while the violins start a high tremolo—a shimmering sound—as suddenly the bottom seems to fall out of the world that has been created over the course of the symphony. The cellos and basses start playing a pizzicato (plucked) line, moving inexorably down, while the violins' line moves further upwards, away from them. A chasm between these high and low sounds opens up before, finally, the brass and wind in all their power and grandeur come in to fill it, providing the awe-ful, satisfying ending to the symphony that is needed. For Jenny, this moment was 'ecstasy':

> The Sibelius ... I cried in one of the last performances because, oh it's so good! [...] There's a D in the last movement, [...] where the basses and cellos are [*she sings it*] they're pizzing, and the strings are really high and the violas come in. It's really high, all typical Sibelius, high strings, then pizz in the bass [*sings it*] I ... whenever I listen to it, oh my god, like ecstasy, it's so good!

This emotional response of 'ecstasy' was often articulated in relation to being within the sound of the group. Teresa, with whom I began this chapter, and Jack, quoted next, described being speechless with awe at their first experience of playing with the National Youth Orchestra. Jack stated:

> When you go into your first tutti rehearsal with like twenty-strong string sections, like, what's it quadruple wind and everything, and we

were playing Shos Five [Shostakovich's Fifth Symphony], so imagine the beginning of Shos Five with 'da-daaaa-da-daaaa-da-daaaa-da-daaaa' [*he sings it*]—it was ...

At this point, Jack waved his hands in the air as he searched for the words to convey the immensity of the combination of this massive sound and this dramatic, terrifying music. This experience of awe at the sound in these groups is an important aspect of the process of interpellation described earlier in the chapter. The materiality of the sound acts on the body, and this is combined with the powerful affective qualities of the music being played, which act in *immaterial* ways on the psyche, following Lisa Blackman's (2012) distinction between the materiality and the immateriality of affect. These physiological and psychological processes do not occur separately, however; this embodied sense of being 'in sound' is crucial to constructing the affective power of the experience.

In order to theorize sound as affective materiality, I draw on Suzanne Cusick's (2013) harrowing accounts of four prisoners' detention as suspected terrorists by US authorities as well as Julian Henriques' (2011) work on 'sonic dominance'. Cusick's essay focuses on the use of music as a tool for psychological and physical torture. She describes how music, often played very loud and for long periods of time, affected the four prisoners by 'jamming' their sense of subjectivity and interiority. This disrupted any sense of knowing their world through sound, both the exterior world of the prison which they would make sense of through piecing together sounds and the interior world of their thoughts. One prisoner described how he would constantly talk to himself with his fingers in his ears to try to retain his link with himself, throughout the hours and days of musical torture, only then to lose this fragile sense of self once the music stopped. Another described how he lost his ability to think: 'Nothing comes to your head; it's just that the experience you're going through is so intense' (Cusick 2013, 287). Cusick theorizes this loss of subjectivity by thinking about how interpellation works through sound, suggesting a model of subject formation in which the acoustic call and response, and being able to control 'our interventions in our acoustic environment,' is fundamental to subjectivity. Therefore, being unable to hear yourself or your world disrupts this process of ongoing construction. Cusick also draws on work on the materiality of sound which describes our immersion in a vibrating world; what we describe as sound is one aspect of a constant vibration. She uses both of these frameworks to interpret the moments of 'psychological shock or paralysis', as the CIA manual describes it (279), where the 'world that is familiar to the subject' explodes (290).

This mode of 'psychological shock or paralysis' appears to be a more invasive, non-consensual version of Henriques' idea of sonic dominance, formulated in the dance halls of Kingston, Jamaica, where the collective experience along with the sound systems create 'the visceral experience of audition, immersed in auditory volumes, swimming in a sea of sound.... There is no escape, not even thinking about it, just being there alive, in and as the excess of sound' (2011, xv). As just noted, in Cusick's account, Prisoner Y describes how 'the experience you're going through is so intense ... that it takes you away from everything else, everything else besides it' (2013, 287). In a similar vein, Benzecry's opera fans 'spoke as if music had taken their body over, ... mak[ing] them forget who they are' (2011, 88).

Clearly, there are important differences between the use of sound against people's will in order to destroy their sense of self, as in Cusick's account, and my participants' openness and willingness to be interpellated into the identity of classical musician. What I want to take from these accounts is the way in which sound can be used to suspend or even interrupt subjectivity, bringing enforced attention to the present moment in the immediate body, with 'no escape', so that it 'takes you away from everything else'. This can be a process of opening up the self through sensory experience to confirm or create a new identity. Recall Teresa's account from the beginning of this chapter: 'I was blown away by the sound, I remember I didn't come in, because I was like, this is *amazing*'. The sensory experience was overwhelming and equates to a similar suspension of self through the experience of being 'in sound'.

However, unlike the amplified sounds which Cusick and Henriques describe, classical music eschews amplification. Indeed, an acoustic aesthetic is one of its defining features, which plays a role in the boundary-drawing which delimits the 'proper', as discussed in chapter 2; having to amplify classical instruments, for example, for an outdoor concert, is seen as compromising the music. And yet, even this acoustic sound still works on the body in a visceral way, as I have been describing in this chapter. But unlike the undeniable physicality of the sound system Henriques describes, with its almost painfully deep bass, classical music inhabits the body in a way which allows the sense that it is being transcended. The 'ecstasy' described by Jenny is a particular affordance that is facilitated by eschewing amplification. Listening to acoustic sounds requires close attention to hear the contrast between very quiet and loud sounds, and very high or low sounds, almost as though creating a sonic analogy of the body being both present and absent. Even when my participants narrated how the sound worked on them, it was never in such a way as to draw attention to their bodies. The sense of the sublime—the sacred as located *outside* the body (Mellor and Shilling 1997, 3)—is reinforced. The affects that are attached to these processes, for my participants, tended to be those of awe and the sublime, such as Jenny's experience, described in her earlier comment: 'oh my god, like ecstasy, it's so good!'

These sensations are compounded and exteriorized by the effect of 'muscular bonding', as William McNeill calls 'the human emotional response to moving rhythmically together in dance and drill' (1995, vi). Drawing on his own experience of drills in the US Army, McNeill traces a history of this 'muscular, rhythmic dimension of human sociality' (156) which leads to a 'blurring of self-awareness' and a 'strange sense of personal enlargement; a sort of swelling out, becoming bigger than life, thanks to participation in collective ritual' (8). This account describes a phenomenon called 'entrainment', the synchronization of autonomous bodies that hold rhythms, which can occur on intraindividual, interindividual, or intergroup levels (Clayton, Sager, and Will 2005). As Clayton notes, reviewing experimental literature on interindividual entrainment, 'Group coordination ... does seem to have measurable effects on group bonding' (2013, 33–34), an idea that he notes was first described by Durkheim in his account of ritual celebrations in *The Elementary Forms of Religious Life* (Clayton 2013, 33).

Therefore, as well as the effects of sound on the body, entrainment through embodied synchronized rhythms contributed further to this sense of community-in-sound. When I was playing with the New Symphony Orchestra, at times the whole cello section or the whole string section would play together, and even though I was playing as loud as I could, my sound was lost in that of the group. Playing loudly required large physical gestures, for example, in a Sibelius symphony all the string section were using every inch of our bows to play a grand melody in unison. What I had thought of as simply really liking that melody was in fact constructed partly through the 'muscular bonding' or entrainment which was occurring at that moment. It was an extremely simple melody, almost banal, but the physical pleasure of playing it in unison with forty other string players gave a wonderful feeling of being lifted or carried within the group for its duration.

Playing quietly together had a similar effect but required an even more focused mode of concentration, listening for the detail of being exactly together, so that everyone in the cello section changed bow direction at exactly the same moment as though we were one player. The sound was working on us in this musical passage by requiring an intense focus on the most quiet sounds. This state of sensory hyper-alertness to what was going on was sometimes combined with playing a melody that evoked this response of emotional depth in me. I would feel an enormous tenderness for particular corners of a phrase as the melody wound its way through tension and release, moving higher, to its eventual resolution. But during this deep sense of satisfaction and delight, the sensory hyper-alertness remained in the foreground. My attention was therefore always exteriorized to the group around me, and yet the music was touching that place of 'inner depth', that 'unnameable' interiority that could be called a self.

In this way, interiority is *externalized* as performed-and-heard sound just as, as described earlier, external heard sound is interiorized as depth. The interiority that my participants experienced as so personal to themselves is made external—made audible—and shared in sound and bodily movement, creating a strongly bonded group. Musical practice is, therefore, a mechanism or cultural technology for opening up bodies and acting on and between them in powerful ways. This can be a huge relief after the pressure of being the individualized, competitive self the rest of the time; no wonder it is experienced as intensely emotional. The suspension of subjectivity in sound I have described works as a sonic *invasion* of our bodies and their personal space, but also as a sonic *extension* of the body, as Julian

Henriques (2011) describes, 'expand[ing] and augment[ing] the body's potential for connection and extension' (Blackman 2011, 247).

These processes combine to create a powerful experience that I have labelled 'community-in-sound'. By this term, I refer firstly to the material role of sound in breaking open the subject, facilitating this experience of connection. This is both physiological and volitional, requiring a willingness to open up to this experience, a trust in the group, and a letting go towards re-imagining the body as part of a larger whole. Secondly, this term describes the ways in which sound works on the body to shape subjectivity. The interpellation of the subject of value described earlier is facilitated by this process of suspension of subjectivity through sound, and in this way, the affective properties transmitted through sound are not only material but also can have a psychological or immaterial dimension, as Lisa Blackman (2012) argues. Thirdly, this term describes the experience of bourgeois community that classical music enables. Community-in-sound exists in dialectic with the future-oriented, accumulative individualism that characterizes the bourgeois self. It allows a horizontal connection between bodies and a brief experience of community which contrasts with the social relations of authority and hierarchy that snap back into place once the moment is over. In this way, the fantasy of bourgeois community that Eagleton (1990) describes as being enabled by the aesthetic can be lived out for a brief period of time. Within this space, both freedom and connectedness are experienced.

Being Affected in the Right Way: Legitimate Culture and Becoming a Subject of Value

What are the effects of this exteriorizing of interiority in sound? They are not entirely predictable (Banks 2017; Born 2017; Stewart 2012), and are surely diffuse and subtle, for example, reinforcing the sense of inner depth this music works upon. However, one clearly identifiable effect for my participants was to contribute to the formation of a powerful identity as a musician, as string player Fred described:

> I think NYO [National Youth Orchestra] makes you realize, do I really want to do music or not? I think everyone has a period in NYO where they think I definitely want to do music. I definitely came back from a course once where I was like, I've got to do music.

Fred eventually made the 'difficult decision' not to study music after he left school, but instead went to an elite university. However, it is testament to the power of this practice that this was not a straightforward decision for Fred, threatening to disrupt his smooth transitions. This potential for classical music to interrupt middle-class social reproduction reveals an interesting tension within middle-class identity, between desiring order and reproducing their own class position but also, following Eagleton, being drawn towards a space that signifies freedom—the aesthetic. A study by Yoshihara (2008) study showed that following a career in classical music, despite its associated prestige, could lead people into lower-earning or less successful careers than they might achieve if they followed a more conventional career route, suggesting classical music has the power to disrupt classed reproduction.

The feeling of 'being in the zone' or 'flow' (Banks 2014a; Jordan, McClure, and Woodward 2017; Scharff 2017) could also contribute to intensifying these experiences of community and identity formation. Singer Francesca described an experience like this:

> FRANCESCA: I think in a world-class performance the audience should forget who they are and the performers should forget who they are and you're all concentrated within the music.
> ANNA: Has that happened to you?
> FRANCESCA: Yeah. A couple of times. Once when I've been singing, with [an adult choir] we did *Israel in Egypt* [an oratorio by Handel] a couple of years ago, I did a solo, there's a duet, and it was the biggest thing I'd ever done. It was in Whitchester Cathedral [...] and it had been occupying my thoughts for literally weeks. [...] There was a massive fugue, and I got to the end, we were in the last few bars, and ... I realized that I didn't want it to end at all, I would have been happy to carry on singing with that group and that music—it felt like forever, and that was really really exciting.

This experience of forgetting the self and simply existing in the moment is by no means unique to classical music. While 'being in the zone' has mainly been theorized within the discipline of psychology, recent accounts from sociology have explored the social effects and affordances of this state, for example, Banks (2014a) asks whether it is a means to exploit creative workers more successfully. Supporting this position, Scharff found that these moments of intense pleasure and oneness with the audience experienced by the classical musicians in her study gave them a reason for enduring precarious and uncertain conditions of labour (2017, 161). In the preceding example, 'being in the zone' contributes to the sense of the self being opened up and connected with others through the music. This further strengthens the creation of identity and community occurring through participation in this music.

However, what is crucial here, and the point that brings together the significance of this chapter, is, as Skeggs and Wood argue, that 'affect really matters when it is connected to an idea that is loaded with value' (2012, 228). I have described the powerful affects that are cultivated and formed within this musical practice, and how they create intense forms of identity and sociality. But the crucial factor of difference with Henriques' dance halls, or with many other affective musical experiences, is that my participants' musical practices are connected to ideas of legitimate cultural value. This was described in chapters 1 and 2, where I laid out the 'institutional ecology' of youth classical music, its central (if contested) place within music education curricula, and its privileged status in funding.

This privileged status is most obvious, perhaps, in the architecture of classical music's performance spaces: the symbolic and physical spaces of practice. Francesca, in the preceding extract, describes singing at age seventeen or eighteen in an enormous fifteenth-century cathedral, where sound resonates for some seven or eight seconds amid the vast crenellations and distant gargoyles of the space. Our concerts with the New Symphony Orchestra took place in a modern five-hundred-seat concert hall that cost the best part of £1000 to hire for the concert. These spaces form a 'symbolic ecology' of places and people around which my participants' imagined world of classical music was constructed, complementing the 'institutional ecology' described in chapter 3. Young people attended performances and played in major classical music venues such as the Royal Albert Hall, which allowed them to imagine a symbolic world to which they belonged. During rehearsals, conductors would refer to symbols of greatness, such as St Paul's Cathedral or the Berlin Philharmonic Orchestra (supposed to be the best orchestra in the world). Groups from both the Young Opera Company and the New Symphony Orchestra took trips to London to go to the Proms. The singers or musicians could then aspire to perform in these venues or with these groups. As I argued in chapter 7, creating sound in these large public spaces works on the body in a particular way. I am suggesting, therefore, that a sense of value is also accumulated by my participants through performing repeatedly in these kinds of venues; this is not just a one-off, special experience but a regular occurrence which gives participants the sense of a *right* to these spaces.

Skeggs and Wood go on to argue that 'ideology is secured once an investment is made in gaining value' (2012, 232). Recall how Owen, after his first experience of playing in an orchestra, would listen to Mahler and Strauss symphonies while doing his homework in order to learn the repertoire and the language of this music. For him, the 'hook' or 'call' came as a sudden moment of realization when, as he told me, he thought, 'Why for the past year and a half [since starting to play horn], why have I shunned this? I realized it is so much better than playing brass band music' which doesn't have 'any real depth to it'. When young people encounter classical music, it is already constructed as conferring a particular mode of personhood, that of interiority or depth. For those who recognize this as a valuable form of subjectivity, this means they *want* to recognize themselves in it and be given the right to inhabit these grand spaces and imagine themselves as denizens of this symbolic ecology. Owen's journey between his lower-middle-class home town and 'proper middle-class' classical music friends makes his account particularly important as this was a choice he had to make rather than something that was the norm for his friends and family. For him as an individual, this is a wonderful journey, but it has taken him away from his family and home town. As with many journeys of class mobility, it is an individual rather than a collective journey (Power et al. 2010). The 'call' beckoned him towards a new world, with the promise from Mendelssohn, Mahler, and Richard Strauss that he, too, could be this type of subject.

Conclusion: The Political Work of Affect

The distinctive aesthetic of classical music, with its acoustic sounds, dynamic extremes, and large-scale works (in terms of both duration and number of musicians), creates and enables the social experience described in this chapter. Through this aesthetic, is affective experiences are generated through, and connected with valued forms of selfhood and privileged institutional structures (see Leys 2011, 451). The experience of depth that I have described in this chapter is narrated through the discourse of an 'unnameable' musical response, but also through the discourses of complexity, unity, and cognitive control described in chapter 5. In addition, this chapter helps to explain the overwhelming emphasis on using acoustic rather than amplified sounds in the classical music aesthetic. As Julian Henriques argues, amplification makes the body undeniably present by a 'sonic invasion' of our bodies (2011, xvi). By contrast, classical music's almost exclusive use of acoustic sounds allows an experience of the sublime that works on the body while appearing not to.

Classical music is by no means unique among musical genres in being able to interpellate subjects in the way described in this chapter. This process of recognition occurs in different ways in different genres of music, and here I have described how the process works for this music in this particular social group. My participants clearly perceived their engagement with classical music as different to the way they experienced other genres of music such as pop music, which they saw as lacking emotional depth. I have argued that this sense of 'interiority' or 'depth' that my participants described hearing in classical music forms a connection to historical accounts of bourgeois selfhood. Classical music's tonal structures can therefore be seen as a cultural technology for coming to know the bourgeois self by learning how to see the self as a stable core which develops and can be invested in over time. It is onto these differences that much of the edifice of the privileged status of classical music is built and institutionalized. This sense that this music touches parts of the self which other genres of music do not reach, and does this through large-scale, complex structures, is part of what supports its status as different or special. In conjunction with the institutional forms of value described in chapter 2, this belief creates a powerful political force.

Teresa, whose account of being 'in sound' was provided at the beginning of this chapter, was turned down for the NYO the subsequent year. After more rejections, she eventually refused to audition again, despite her parents' encouragement. While her love for this music remained, she had found the whole experience of being in the NYO 'really stressful', describing sectional rehearsals as 'the worst things *ever*—I just found them *so* intimidating and I felt like I couldn't play anything'. She became convinced she wasn't good enough to pursue music as a career, a decision which, at age twenty, she was '100% happy with'. Teresa had experienced being interpellated into this musical identity, which allowed her into the warmth of community and the satisfaction of achieving and performing, but also the stress of competition, and then eventually rejection and exclusion. This trajectory exemplifies the social relations of classical music practice as described in chapters 3 to 6. These social relations constitute a political norm of community—one of hierarchy, exclusions, and competition—as being the naturalized order. When you fail your next audition, as Teresa did, you are excluded from that part of the community. This was an exclusion that she endorsed as correct and justified because her standard of playing wasn't high enough for her to be in the group. However, she still plays in amateur orchestras, and her love for this music—as constructed through the affective, communal experience of playing it—has stayed with her. The powerful identification that this music engenders in many of the young people in this study forms a firmer bedrock than can be shaken by failing a few auditions.

I have described in this chapter a dialectical or liminal space of 'community-in-sound' that contrasts with the competitive individualism that was often experienced by participants outside of this space. However, this space of freedom (Eagleton 1990) is only available to some, and Teresa's account shows some of the limits to this community. The experiences of loss of self or ecstasy that Francesca, Jenny, and others describe are built on the condition of possibility of years and years of hard work and investment, both from themselves and from teachers and parents. For the young women singing opera, described in the previous chapter, this experience of bodily transformation occurred more quickly (as singing requires a different kind of technique to instrumental playing). What all these accounts of bodily transformation or freedom have in common is that this transformation does not lead anywhere other than the performances themselves. For my participants, this was enough. These experiences are individually satisfying, and satisfying on the level of the group. However, from a broader critical perspective, they can be seen to link people more strongly into the culture and norms of this world rather than to connect with others outside the middle-class group they are playing with. The community, history, and identity that classical music allows people to connect with are those of the white European middle classes (as Benzecry (2011, 191) also found in his study of opera lovers in Buenos Aires). Classical music is, in this way, hugely valuable for those who experience it, but its ideas of aesthetic beauty both require and simultaneously camouflage the exclusionary mechanisms that are at work. And so it remains the practice and passion of the middle and aspiring middle classes.

Conclusion

I wrote this book to try to make sense of some of the paradoxes and contradictions that I experienced as a classical musician—contradictions that eventually became so weighty I stopped playing. Indeed, the doubts that I described in the opening to this book can now be made sense of as expressing fundamental contradictions within (my) bourgeois identity, such as a sense of social responsibility pushing me towards engagement with the world, while at the same time wanting to retain classical music as a space of freedom outside of the world of politics, inequality, and suffering. However, perhaps the starkest contradiction in this musical tradition is this: within the cultural and institutional framework of youth classical music, many of the young people in my study found an expressive voice, a strong sense of identity, and a supportive and intimate social scene. But the practices and tradition that provided these benefits were, at the same time, upholding hegemonic structures in the form of Eurocentric, Enlightenment hierarchies that legitimized the value of some and confirmed the lack of value of others. This paradox—that the pleasure of playing beautiful music is reproducing gendered and classed structures of domination—was uncomfortably mirrored in the Young Opera Company's production of *The Magic Flute*. The plot centres on the triumph of masculine European rationality in the form of Sarastro and his Temple of Wisdom over the evil, hysterical Queen of the Night. This story is all sung in melodies and harmonies of such beauty that I was still humming them with pleasure months after the production ended. And yet, the opera presents no viable way of inhabiting a female identity; female power is represented as the evil Queen of the Night, while Pamina, the female protagonist, is subject to sexual violence, imprisonment, and powerlessness.

These are only some of the many paradoxes that characterize this musical tradition. Another is that the body is disciplined, ordered, and indeed required for creating sound, and yet it has to be concealed and transcended to ensure that the presence of the body doesn't corrupt the spirit of the music. The music is hard work—but it has to sound easy. The rhetoric of universal greatness conceals the truth that this music is the expression of a particular cultural value system at a particular time. And finally, the Romantic repertoire that my participants adored stemmed from a movement that carried a strong antibourgeois critique at its inception, but this critique has been neutralized and the repertoire co-opted to reproduce bourgeois subjectivities of investment, order, hierarchy, and control. These contradictions support Eagleton's argument about the ambivalence of the aesthetic in modernity: that while it is a necessary safety valve to uphold bourgeois society, providing the middle classes with the space of solidarity and community that their everyday world lacks, this space always threatens to act back on their carefully ordered world by bringing its powerful emotions and sense of freedom into day-to-day life.

Overall, I have argued that classical music education cultivates a form of selfhood that is recognized as valuable. This value derives from classical music's history, institutions, and contemporary cultural associations, as well as from the resonances of this form of selfhood with qualities that are valued by the middle classes: emotional 'depth' and an inward, individualized sense of self; self-control and willingness to work with authority; strongly gendered norms of behavior, most notably female respectability; and technical expertise. As such, classical music education can be understood as a cultural technology for forming a middle-class self. The value of classical music is invisible partly because those who are attributed value because of it *do not realize* that this is happening; as Skeggs (2003) describes, it is only those who have had to fight against being positioned as valueless for whom this value is visible. Classical music's value is upheld through a quintessentially middle-class practice: closing off spaces where it is stored. However, unlike in other spaces of middle-class boundary-drawing such as private schooling or gated communities, the boundaries are denied. Rather than existing in physical space, they can be found in the aesthetic of the music which requires years of investment of time, money, and effort to be able to successfully embody, and which is seen as 'autonomous' from the social world rather than doing this political work of exclusion.

In this study I have outlined the ways in which classical music, as practised in my research sites, is linked to middle-class forms of identity, selfhood, and history. These can be broken down into four 'articulations' (S. Hall 1985) between the normative practices of classical music (as viewed through its education practices) and the middle classes. As discussed in chapter 1, these articulations are somewhat contingent and require work to uphold, and as such they are, at different times, stronger or weaker. The first articulation between classical music and the middle classes is the formal modes of social organization that the music requires. These include the strong authority of the teacher and conductor, clear boundaries around participation and repertoire, and musicians' clearly demarcated place within hierarchical structures. These formal modes of social organization are demanded by classical music's canon of repertoire in which the score spells out exactly who is involved. Anyone who has informally played or sung classical repertoire will recognize the experience of having the wrong number or type of musicians. If, for example, you are 'bashing' through string quartets with friends, but you have two friends who are cellists, one cellist has to sit out and listen (unless you happen to have the parts for the only well-known piece of music for string quartet with an extra cello—Schubert's String Quintet). This is one way that the aesthetic—through the canon of repertoire, and the practice of being 'faithful' to the composer's intentions—dictates the practices of classical music.

These formal modes of social organization also extended to clear boundaries around participation and around repertoire. As discussed in chapter 3, participation in all the groups in my study was regulated, either through auditions or through young people being required to have attained a particular standard of playing (measured by grade exams); it is clear who is included and who is not. Similarly, boundary-drawing around repertoire, as discussed in chapters 2 and 5, drew distinctions between 'proper' or 'serious' repertoire, and 'cheesy' or 'jazzy' repertoire. These boundaries were delineated through racialized modes of embodiment whereby European classical music was performed with a still body while non-European musics choreographed the body into movement and visibility.

This formality is not intrinsically linked to the middle classes, but despite the contingency of this 'articulation', the link can be clearly traced empirically. Studies of working-class musics and cultures, historically and today, describe more dialogic, informal modes of participation. Maria Barrett's (2016) study of the Royal Court Theatre in Liverpool, which, unlike most theatres, attracts a large working-class audience, found that a large part of the popularity for audiences there was the informality and the 'banter' between performers and audience, as well as the opportunity for audiences to join in on musical numbers. This description is reminiscent of Victorian music hall (Bailey 1986), as well as accounts of creative hedonism and antipretentious humour identified among working-class cultures (Skeggs 2005, 88). By contrast, many middle-class forms of culture are characterized by clear distinctions between audience and performers, and cultural venues that are not only socially but also sonically sealed from the bustle of urban life, mirroring middle-class boundary-drawing processes more generally.

These formal modes of consuming culture allow for distinctive emotional experiences. While Barrett and Bailey describe audiences talking about pleasure, entertainment, enjoyment, or other communal forms of emotion as part of their experience of music, I have described how 'controlled excitement' and 'emotional depth' characterized the emotional experience of playing and listening to classical music. 'Deep' emotions are accorded greater weight than enjoyment or entertainment, and they index a valued form of selfhood. When the middle classes do let their hair down, it is in bounded ways that do not disrupt their everyday life. 'Controlled excitement' is an emotional disposition that allows strong emotional experiences to be contained within a clear structure. While Featherstone (2007) has suggested that this 'controlled de-control' of the emotions is a characteristic of an emerging middle-class fraction in late modernity, I have traced it, through classical music's aesthetic of 'precision and dynamic extremes' (Bowen 2003, 103–4), back to the development and institutionalization of classical music's practices in the early to mid-nineteenth century.

The second articulation between classical music and the middle classes is its reliance on the historical and contemporary modes of embodiment of the white middle classes. Firstly, 'controlled excitement', as well as being an emotional disposition, was a mode of embodiment that required the capacity to maintain total technical control while cultivating strong emotions. Secondly, classical music requires young women to perform a 'respectable' female identity. The importance of respectability as a classed identity has been traced back to the gendered relations of the nineteenth-century bourgeois family wherein restrained female sexuality was the linchpin of respectable bourgeois identity (McClintock 1995; Nead 1988; Skeggs 1997), and is still an important marker of class for women in the UK that dictates whether women are believed, taken seriously, or treated respectfully (Jay 2015; Nicholls 2018). Chapter 7 showed how classical music allowed young women to inhabit female respectability in a more empowering way, through the transformative experience of singing opera. However, even here the contradictions and limitations of respectable femininity were inscribed into the musical and dramatic text of the opera.

Another mode of embodiment that was apparent among the young people in my research sites was an openness and trust towards adults in positions of authority, as described in chapter 6. This trust could be described as a bodily porousness, rather than as a form of agency or a deliberate choice to trust conductors or teachers. It meant that the young people would respond to even the smallest sign from their conductor, so that any gesture, tone of voice, or instruction would act powerfully on them regardless of whether they admired or feared him. This trust was also conferred upon myself as a researcher, with most of the young people willing to participate in interviews and to talk openly about their lives. By contrast, studies of working-class and ethnic minority young people have found that trust in figures of institutionalized authority such as teachers, police, or social workers is much less forthcoming. For example, Brian McShane's (2018) study of young black men in South London describes how they held their bodies in a closed way that performed the lack of trust they had in him, as a youth worker, or other adults in official positions. The trust and openness that characterized most of my participants are striking in comparison.

A third articulation between classical music and the middle classes is the imaginative dimension of bourgeois selfhood that can be read through examining the scene. As described in chapter 1, Georgina Born (2017) argues that music 'mediates' the social world via four 'planes', one of which is the 'imagined communities' that are conjured up through listening to music or participating in a musical scene. In chapter 1 I noted previous research in which the orchestra is imagined as an idealized community or social utopia. In chapters 5 and 6, I explored the classed, gendered, and racialized dimensions of this imagined ideal community, in particular the orchestra as a bourgeois fantasy of male control. This social structure is very telling of the middle-class relationship with authority. As Reay, Crozier, and James (2011) describe, one of the characteristics of the

British middle classes, historically and today, is a sense of responsibility. For these people who are used to being responsible for everything and who are required to be in control of their emotions, of their diaries, of their futures, and of every other aspect of their lives, there is an enormous relief in being able to give up control to the conductor. However, because of the power differences between the conductors and the young people in my site—of age, musical expertise, and experience, and for the young women, gender—this authority relationship could easily become toxic and dysfunctional. This relationship also reflected the ways in which the young people ascribed authority to certain figures, playing out a fantasy of order and control.

This control can be enabling as well as constraining. It allows the aesthetic to function as an imagined realm of freedom, providing a vision of social belonging and solidarity that the individualistic bourgeoisie may feel they lack (Eagleton 1990). It enables a sense of connectedness and community that dovetails with the psychological experience of 'flow' or 'being in the zone'. In rehearsals, competitiveness and community vied with one another. Fear of making a mistake and being judged was commonly expressed, and self-criticism or competition with others was the norm, but sometimes in rehearsals the atmosphere would shift and a wonderful sense of community would arise. In the UK, however, it is usually a white middle-class community that is being created, and therefore it is solidarity among this group that is being cultivated rather than connections with those in different social positions. Within this experience of belonging and togetherness, the aesthetic as a realm of freedom is reached through transcending the everyday world and the body, reproducing ideals associated with the Christian soul and the white body.

Finally, linking these three 'articulations' together, the aesthetic of 'getting it right' and classical music's affordances for precision and detail provide the rationale for these processes of sociality, embodiment, and imagination. As described in chapter 7, and also discussed by other authors (Kingsbury 1988; Goehr 1992; Leech-Wilkinson 2016), being 'faithful' to the composer's intentions was a strongly held ideal among both adults and young people in my study. This fidelity required sticking as closely as possible to the directions on the score, and as a result, rehearsals involved high levels of attention to detail. The reliance on non-amplified sounds which supports listening closely to tiny details contributes to this aesthetic of getting it right. Playing precisely in tune and together is seen as a marker of a good-quality performance, unlike some other genres where mistakes or wrong tuning can be turned into an expressive gesture (J. Bennett 2015; Walser 1997). Knowledge of what constitutes getting it right is a body of expertise that is codified in classical music's educational institutions, such as the exam boards and conservatoires, and this cultural knowledge is a form of value that is stored and passed on over time. A telling contrast comes from Byron Dueck's study of working-class indigenous musical communities in Canada in which he describes an ethic of 'non-interference' in music teaching whereby the child/pupil explores and develops musically at their own pace, in their own direction (Dueck 2013, personal communication). This ethic of 'non-interference' contrasts strongly with the ethic of correction that predominates in classical music pedagogy. It also demonstrates how the classed differences in parenting practices described by Lareau (2011) and others (Vincent and Ball 2007; Byrne 2006; Faircloth 2014; Walkerdine, Lucey, and Melody 2001) are visible in music pedagogies themselves (a link that is explored by Clare Hall and Sally Savage (2016)).

Furthermore, the instruments required to play classical music's canon take years, if not decades, to become proficient in, and the canonic repertoire often demands a high level of technical ability. My participants had been playing their instruments for between five and fifteen years. Even in the WCYO, the younger of the two orchestras in my study, we were playing highly demanding music that required technical proficiency on an instrument, ability to read staff notation fluently, and high levels of aural and ensemble skills. In this way, the aesthetic demands of the music are a sufficient barrier to keep out anyone who is not able or willing to make this long-term investment. These years of practice, lessons, and other forms of investment contribute to making 'classical musician' into a strongly held identity; for some of my participants this identity was the most important part of who they were. This long-term investment also contributes to forming strongly bonded social groups that tended to be fairly homogeneous in their social characteristics, as described in chapter 3. A further factor working against inclusivity is the fear of making mistakes and being judged, but the emphasis on 'getting it right' that generates this fear is crucial in order to be able to attain the high musical standards that the repertoire, instruments, and conventions of this aesthetic demand. In this way, the music itself does the boundary-drawing work that keeps the majority of young people outside the middle classes from participating.

There are, therefore, powerful barriers to wider participation that are created by the aesthetic of classical music's canonic repertoire as found in my research sites, but these barriers are inextricable from what creates beauty in this tradition and so cannot be removed without making fundamental changes to the culture of practice. In addition, widening participation is inhibited by the sense that there is something of value, usually described in musical terms, that needs to be safeguarded within this tradition. This defence of value on musical grounds, as Lucy Green (2003) describes, draws on certain assumptions about what is more generally valuable in music, and one of the characteristics of classical music that is used to assert its value and judge other genres as less valuable is structural complexity or sophistication. As well as the assumptions outlined by Green, a further way in which classical music was valued by my participants was because of its ability to draw on and create a form of selfhood that is experienced as deep interiority. This contributes to forming the value both of classical music and of the person who can appreciate it. A lineage can be traced that links this form of selfhood with an older bourgeois subjectivity—a self where 'deep' emotional experience is valued, and experienced inwardly yet communally, and for whom it makes sense to invest in long-term assets and rewards.

The distinctive aesthetic of classical music therefore contributes towards creating inequalities in classical music practice through the four 'articulations' described earlier. However, this intertwining of the social and the aesthetic also makes it difficult to talk about inequalities because critical discussion is often perceived as an attack on the 'music itself'—the very thing that is meaningful and special to participants, and that is deeply formative of their very selves. The pleasure of self-realization through artistic practice (S. Taylor and Littleton 2012) and the intense sociabilities and experience of 'being in the zone' afforded by classical music's spaces of performance and rehearsal work against allowing space for critique because it is too difficult to gain distance from such a powerful source of one's meaning and identity. But unless we are critical of the patterns of inclusion and exclusion that are formed through the practices that are required by classical music's aesthetic and the modes of social organization that are written into the scores of its canonic repertoire, this closed world cannot be opened up to a wider range of people.

Implications of This Study

While this study has explored the youth classical music scene in a small city in England, my theorization of classical music and class contributes to a wider understanding of how classical music, as a genre, is shaped by and in turn shapes social inequalities, and also to understanding the middle classes in the UK today. Although this study was narrowly focused in time and place, my findings tentatively point towards a depiction of a wider culture of classical music for two reasons. Firstly, my participants' descriptions of their links with musical institutions nationally (and, in some instances, internationally) showed that this culture of practice was continuous with wider institutional, social, and musical sites in the UK and further afield. Secondly, throughout this book I have drawn out points of similarity (and some differences) with studies of other cultures of classical music that, I would suggest, show that there is a shared culture within this genre, despite some local differences (Baker 2014; Yoshihara 2008; McCormick 2015; Sagiv 2013; Hall 2011; Perkins 2011; Wagner 2015). However, the understanding of class that I have based my study on is, in many ways, particular to the UK, and so it is important to note that economic inequality may form a different articulation with cultures of class in different countries. Further attention is needed to the ways in which classical music refracts and intersects with other cultures and how classical music's culture travels across time and space, especially the role of British musical institutions in influencing musical cultures and standards in the Commonwealth as well as the growth of classical music in East Asia today.

How might this method of looking at musical practices to understand inequalities be helpful for studying other genres? Rather than relying on individual accounts of transformation or transcendence, I would suggest that we need detailed empirical accounts of aesthetic experience and cultural production that pay attention to social inequalities both internal and external to the process of producing/consuming music, that is, how inequalities occur within the rehearsal/performance process as well how inequalities from the wider world affect cultural production. In addition, comparative work across different genres that are produced and consumed by different social groups would be able to help reveal how musical aesthetics are shaped through social and embodied practices which draw on classed patterns. Through examining such classed patterns within cultural and educational institutions, the ways in which strongly socially stratified patterns of musical taste shape inequalities in production can also be addressed (Oakley and O'Brien 2015).

It is likely that there are parallels between the culture of classical music that I have described here and other, similarly institutionalized and classed genres of music. For example, one of the practices that I have identified in classical music is the long-term investment that is required in order to be able to play the difficult instruments and repertoire, and this long-term investment may also contribute to class inequality in other genres. The ways in which the aesthetic forms a barrier or boundary that allows such genres to retain prestige is apparent in Indian classical music, as Alaghband-Zadeh describes, where the 'old middle-class' values of listeners are reflected in what they most enjoy in the music itself: 'those features that they interpret as traditional or that they associate with the past', such as the slow parts that require patience to listen to, rather than virtuosic, 'gimmicky' musical innovations (2017, 212). Similarly, the patterns of classed investment and imagined futures that I have described among my participants are similar to those identified in Nylander and Melldahl's (2015) study of applicants to an elite jazz school in Sweden. The jazz profession is, however, still more open than classical music to musicians who have come through different pedagogic routes, as Banks, Ebrey, and Toynbee describe in their study of black British jazz musicians, who tended to learn informally, within a tradition of domestic music-making that included informal instrument playing and performing for family (2014, 12). Furthermore, Banks and colleagues found that jazz education 'unlike classical music [was] not institutionally embedded', so would-be musicians had to find their own routes into the profession (15) rather than following standardized 'progression routes' (Lonie and Sandbrook 2011). These studies give a wider framing for my discussion of classical music's distinctive history of institutionalization and the social organization of its canonic repertoire and formalized pedagogies, and how these contribute towards its inequalities in education and the profession.

Aside from the contributions this book makes to the sociology of music, it also sheds light on the structure and practices of reproduction of the middle classes in the UK today, in two main ways. Firstly, it demonstrates some of the ways in which gender is a crucial structuring mechanism in forming fractions of the middle classes. Examining the pathways of the young musicians in this study (as discussed in more detail in Bull 2018), it demonstrates the structuring role of gender in forming young people's classed pathways, and thus in class formation. In chapter 3, I introduced three groups or 'ideal types' among my participants, showing how their gender and class positions mapped onto their imagined futures. The 'bright futures' group, young men and women from professional and upper-middle-class families, comprised those who had decided not to pursue a career in classical music. The second group, the 'masters of the musical universe', were young men also from professional middle-class families who were pursuing careers in classical music because they had been promised positions of prestige within the classical music industry. The third group, the 'humble and hard-working' young musicians, were the young people from working-class or lower-middle-class backgrounds, and young women from professional middle-class families, who chose classical music as a career even though they were highly uncertain of the possibility of success.

These pathways can be explained, to some extent, by Bourdieu's (1983) theorization of middle-class fractions in his work on the field of cultural production. As outlined in chapter 1, the field of cultural production occupies a 'dominated' position within the field of power, and therefore it makes sense that those in the most dominant social positions—the white middle-class young men—would eschew a career in this field unless they knew they would be in positions of power. However, it is here that the gendered patterns that I found among my participants' pathways through classical music need more explanation than Bourdieu's theory allows, given his relative neglect of women or gender (Adkins 2004, 3). My research shows that middle-class young women were more likely than middle-class young men to pursue a career in classical music rather than following professions that would offer greater economic rewards. This pattern can be explained through two factors. Firstly, as discussed in chapter 7, young women found within classical music an encouragement towards public expression that they welcomed. Playing music written by men while being led or conducted by men was not seen as detracting from this. Tied up with such narratives of embodied expressivity was the idea of artistic practice as a form of self-realization, as described by Stephanie Taylor and Karen Littleton (2012, 31, 58); similarly, among my female participants, there were accounts of wanting to pursue a career as a musician for therapeutic reasons and/or for personal development. Secondly, the associations of classical music with respectable femininity meant that the identity of 'classical musician' was often a socially approved choice for young women. The expressive voice that classical music offers could be developed in the context of performing a respectable and valued female gender identity. By contrast, for the young men, the sense of entitlement that is cultivated by learning classical music was not realized in the career opportunities that are on offer, and so many of the young men in this study took this sense of confidence and entitlement with them into other fields.

Therefore, for young women in my study, aiming for status in, or even just entry into, the field of cultural production rather than the wider field of power made more sense than it did to the young men. If we see Bourdieu's theorization of the field of cultural production as a theory of class fractions, this example shows the role of gendered pathways and identities in reproducing the structure of the middle classes. Further evidence comes from Yoshihara, who notes that in both the US and East Asia, learning classical music is still seen as a means for women to make an upper-middle-class marriage (2008, 103). In the creative industries more widely, McRobbie argues that 'passionate work' is a distinctive mode of gender re-traditionalization (2015, 141). In her research, this was visible through young women's willingness to work long hours for very little pay in the hope of gaining a foothold in the field of creative work. My study confirms this gendered pattern within cultural work, as well as revealing the strongly held gender roles of the middle class as exhibited in the differences between what young men and young women felt entitled to and the choices they made. The gendered identifications and imaginaries of these middle-class young people were outlined in chapter 6, which showed that young men aspired to *become* the conductor, whereas young women not only could not imagine inhabiting this role but could be fearful of him, while also being at risk of being sexualized. The choices revealed by these pathways can therefore be seen to reflect a deeper gendered structure of identity among the middle classes. Finally, as well as classical music reproducing middle-class gender roles, these gendered pathways are necessary to reproduce classical music as a tradition. In my study, women were more likely to take on the unpaid, voluntary administrative labour that allows the exams, concerts, youth orchestra rehearsals, and other everyday practices of classical music to function. This labour in turn supports men to continue in positions of prestige and authority.

The second way in which this study contributes to understanding the middle classes in the UK today is through demonstrating ways in which classical music education still works as a form of legitimate culture that can confer cultural capital, enabled by its institutional ecology. However, the possibilities for generating cultural capital through classical music education—in terms of a valued identity and sense of self-worth that could be converted into other resources—differed according to the class position of my participants, the instrument they played, and the pathway they took through the institutional ecology I have described. The youth classical music scene offered access to exclusive educational spaces, strong social networks with other privately educated young people, the opportunity to escape from their local area, and the development of confidence and authoritative speech. Therefore, for the young musicians who were already part of the professional class or upper middle class, participation in classical music did not substantially add to what they already had. For others—some of those in the professional middle class as well as the young people in lower-middle-class or working-class positions—classical music helped to consolidate their class position or worked as a tool for social mobility by giving them access to the resources listed earlier. This social mobility, as has been documented in relation to other areas of social life (Friedman 2014b; Loveday 2014), could be a double-edged sword, as to varying extents young people carried their classed dispositions with them. Some felt that their place within this world was precarious because it was dependent on their musical ability, which could lead them to pursue punishing practice regimes and contribute to mental health problems (see chapter 4).

For cultural capital to be effective, its status signals have to be shared among a wide group of people (M. Lamont and Lareau 1988). A key argument of this book is that the institutionalized nature of classical music is crucial in determining its value. As discussed in chapter 2, a particularly British ecology is evident in the Victorian music education institutions, the music exam boards and the conservatoires, which provided a framework around which other aspects of the 'institutional ecology' of classical music were organized. These institutions, particularly the grade exam boards through their success in credentializing musical standards, enable this value to be widely recognized. This ecology, building on its roots during the height of the British Empire (Johnson-Hill 2015), also allows knowledge of classical music to work as a shared signal internationally. This is an example of the middle classes institutionalizing their resources to enable them to retain their value and be passed on to future generations (Barlow et al. 1995).

However, while classical music was not valued as a form of youth culture among my participants' peers at state schools, and indeed could even be a source of stigma (as also noted by David Clarke (2012, 173)), once at college or university (from age seventeen onwards), they reported that this attitude among peers started to shift. But by investing in a form of culture that could accrue institutional support rather than affording value as a form of youth culture, the young people played a longer game. This was, for the most part, not intentional; they engaged in classical music without expecting that it would ever be convertible to economic value. Therefore, investment in classical music is an uncertain form of capital; it conferred very clear, tangible benefits on some young people, such as a music scholarship to a private school, while for others, classical music was simply an expression of their social position. In my study, young people invested in it for the social networks of other sociable geeks, the musical enjoyment, and the sense of identity it conferred, as well as because their parents wanted them to, rather than for the material rewards. Other studies have suggested that parents invest in classical music education for their children for a variety of reasons, not always clearly defined (Byrne 2006; Rollock et al. 2015). And, of course, many other high-status activities such as elite sports confer similar advantages. Classical music is one of many such ways of accumulating social resources. It has particularities: for example, it is a less regulated sector than sports; it attracts a different type of young person, the sociable geek; and the socialities of classical music, as described earlier, are different to those of many sports. However, there are many similarities, such as the role of national prestige in driving high standards and the strong authority of the coach/conductor, and so it would be productive for understanding how extracurricular resources affect class formation to undertake comparative research examining music and sport together.

Challenges and Directions for Music Education Practice and Policy

Cultural policy debates are often characterized by a dichotomy between access and excellence (O'Brien 2013; Hesmondhalgh et al. 2015). As it currently stands, classical music education is often about widening access *to* excellence, for example, with El Sistema–inspired programmes aiming to give disadvantaged children access to high culture (and, in doing so, to transform them). Instead, a more radical meaning of 'access' from the 1960s and 1970s needs to be mobilized (O'Brien 2013, 41) which challenges versions of artistic and cultural practice that allow privileged groups in society to accrue and pass on resources. This leads to difficult normative questions around excellence, elitism, and talent, notably, at what point does the pursuit of excellence or talent begin to detract from the wider social good? 'Excellence' and 'talent' are terms that have been critiqued in recent discussions both within music education and across the arts more widely (Banks 2017; Hunter and Micklem 2016; Duffy 2016; Lonie and Sandbrook 2011). For Henry Kingsbury:

> The very meaning of musical 'talent' is inextricably linked to power relations ... an attribution of 'talent' brings a positive value to a perceived social inequality ... the invocation of 'talent' contributes significantly to the reproduction of a structure of inequality in social power. (1988, 79)

Kingsbury does not develop this statement in relation to wider social inequalities, but I would suggest that recognizing differences in ability is not intrinsically problematic but becomes so only where it magnifies other social differences, or if it naturalizes and normalizes inequality. Within a musical scene, the question of what levels of inequality are acceptable is one that needs to be a subject of ongoing debate. In music education, the imperative to nurture exceptional talent and contribute to national prestige has for a long time vied with the possibility for high levels of cultural participation, as outlined in the divisions between the Tonic Sol-fa movement and the music exam boards in chapter 2. Personally, I would rather live in a society without virtuosi but also without people who feel entirely musically disenfranchised. Of course, it is not a zero-sum game. However, the culture of classical music described in this book produces highly skilled musicians but also legitimizes hierarchy, competition, and exclusion. As it stands, therefore, ideals of participation and excellence sit uneasily alongside one another. This does not necessarily have to be the case, but the imperative towards narrow, exclusionary models of excellence is driven by a range of factors: by teachers, who teach as they were taught (R. Wright and Davies 2010, 46; Sagiv and Hall 2015; Philpott 2010, 89); by conservative assessment models both in and out of school (Fautley 2015; Philpott 2001, 160); by the powerful influence of higher education music institutions, both universities and conservatoires (Dibben 2006; Perkins 2013, 20); by parents who want to accrue value of various kinds for their children (Byrne 2006; Rollock et al. 2015); and by young people themselves who want to find their social niche and, as described in this book, often have a strong sense of hierarchies of valued identities. This broad set of interests makes it a challenge to bring about change.

In addition to these concerns, classical music education and practice can also have effects on a wider social level, outside of music. For example, as chapter 3 demonstrated, musical hierarchies of ability can also contribute to the formation of social hierarchies. Such hierarchies within classical music education may reflect inequalities in society more widely but can also act back on social inequality by either legitimizing or questioning it. A litmus test towards exploring these questions could be to ask whether developing individual ability also perpetuates social divisions, and whether musical 'excellence' in a particular programme is being used as a currency of class or other inequalities, for example, by allowing certain groups to accrue and store value. While inherited differences in musical ability undoubtedly exist, high levels of parental/adult investment can masquerade as 'talent' or excellence, and in classical music education musical ability rests on long-term investment, which is currently premised on being middle class. However, in a society with higher levels of opportunity for music education for everyone and institutional recognition of a wider variety of types of musical expression, excellence would be less able to be used for class advantage. This is in part a question of institutional recognition and validation. As Banks (2017) describes, selection into higher education arts institutions is at particular risk of being unmeritocratic. This is because the 'ineffability' of talent (Banks 2017, 76) 'as something that is recognized when it is heard' (Juuti and Littleton 2010, 491) means that the right socialization and training, conferred through social and economic advantage, can be misrecognized by institutions as talent, leading to classed and racialized patterns of exclusion (Banks 2017; Burke and McManus 2009; Koza 2008).

With these normative and social justice questions in mind, I now turn to key points of intervention for policymakers[1] to work against classical music education being used as a currency of class, and towards turning it into a space that enables critique and creative dialogue with other social groups, while still keeping

---

[1] By the term 'policymakers', I include government and public organizations but also the private and charitable groups that make up a large part of classical music's institutional ecology.

music-making at the heart of music education. Firstly, it is necessary to recognize the uneven weighting of the music education ecology, in terms of resources as well as institutions, towards classical music. This draws on the historically informed approach laid out in chapter 2 that examines provision across music education charities as well as public provision and higher education. These institutional patterns are an example of middle-class social closure through accruing resources in elite spaces, a perennial problem in tackling inequality and social cohesion more generally. This rebalancing of musical institutions is therefore also a strategy for rebalancing social resources to combat the ways the middle classes store their value. In order to do this, the private/charity sector may need to be more strongly regulated or incentivized towards inclusion, and/or the state sector needs to have *more* innovative, well-resourced, and successful programmes than the private sector in order to be able to retain public support. In addition, the state's role of rebalancing resources across the sector can include supporting innovative work by music education charities, within many of which there is a strong commitment to music education as a public good.

New Labour took an important step towards rebalancing this ecology by setting up Youth Music, a music education charity for disadvantaged young people that supports a wide variety of music genres, in 1999. Trinity College London's new Arts Awards is also an important intervention, although no data is available on its social class uptake (Hollingworth et al. 2016). In addition, since the introduction of music education 'hubs' in England in 2012, the wider ecology of music education is playing a larger part in public provision, and Fautley and Whittaker report that, as a result, hubs 'are diversifying from the Western Classical canon which has held sway for a long time' (2017, 45). However, as the richest music education charities are classical music ones (although they may offer a wider range of types of music), there is a high risk that the values of classical music continue to be privileged over other genres across music education. Therefore, further steps are needed to rebalance the institutional ecology so that genres and musical identities other than classical music are equally well supported. The challenge lies in working skilfully with a mixed ecology that incentivizes diversification of the privatized institutional ecology for classical music to ensure wider recognition of other genres, while channelling increased funding within the public sector towards an ecology that recognizes multiple progression routes and vernacular musical codes.

Secondly, music educators and academics have for a long time been making the case for greater recognition of children's and young people's musical lives outside of formal education (A. Lamont et al. 2003; Banks 2014b; Lonie and Dickens 2014). By contrast, a music education policy that focuses on instrumental tuition as its main intervention (the 'give every child a violin' approach) perpetuates class divides in music education by reproducing the norms—and exclusions—of classical music, particularly as teachers are likely to come from a classical background and often lack the skills to be able to effectively deliver large-group teaching

(Hallam 2016). Whole-class instrumental teaching should not therefore be the central plank of a music education policy. Instead, as well as offering instrumental teaching, recognition and support needs to be given to music-making in a wider variety of forms and genres, including more creative and technology-focused forms of music-making, including electronic music, DJ'ing, and dance, as well as instrumental tuition, and to allow young people to choose their musical path. Indeed, the majority of working-class children now claim to mainly play other instruments than those offered by the classical orchestra, or pop music instruments such as the electric guitar (Hume and Wells 2014). As Mark Banks notes, these other instruments 'appear to include the kind of smart and mobile technologies that allow for social and DIY music production, without the cost of lessons or conventional instrumentation'. As a result, 'much of the music-making undertaken by ordinary children goes unheralded or unnoticed' (Banks 2014b). Instead, music education should support the forms of music that children and young people are already engaged with as well as opening up new possibilities.

Thirdly, cultural and education institutions need to lead on change within classical music education and the profession. Most urgently, as Scharff (2015, 18) notes, data on inequalities needs to be routinely collected and made public. This is an issue across the cultural sector, as Romer reports, as 'the number of [Arts Council England's] National Portfolio Organisations choosing not to reveal diversity information remains a major issue' (2018). As well as data gathering, the ongoing work that many classical music education institutions are doing on rethinking selection processes, curricula, and pedagogies needs to be extended and developed. There is a lot to be done to increase fairness in selection processes in music education, and lessons can be learned from research by Burke and McManus (2009) in art colleges and moves towards contextual admissions in higher education more widely (Boliver et al. 2017; see also Banks 2017, chapter 4). To support this, curricula need to be diversified. The example given in chapter 2 of the current ABRSM syllabus for the grade eight piano exam, which includes no music by female composers, only one non-European composer, and only five pieces written since 1950 (ABRSM 2017), gives a sense of the scale of the challenge.

However, an example of reforming musical standards to work towards class equality can be seen in a recent restructuring of the Harvard University music degree programme. Describing standards as 'a very amorphous and ideology-laden concept', Anne Schreffler, director of undergraduate studies in Harvard's music faculty, introduced pluralist pathways through the university's music degree programme, removing the requirement for certain core music theory modules in order to allow students who had not had ten years of music education in childhood to be able to major in music (Robin 2017). The reforms garnered a heated response on social media and from other academics, who criticized Harvard for failing to teach students vital skills (Robin 2017; Pace 2017), and through this contributing towards a broader shift 'away from specialist theoretical training as a de-skilling of the musicological profession' ('"Can Musical Conservatism

Be Progressive?"' 2018). This example feeds into a broader ongoing discussion asking, 'What should university study of music consist of?' discussed in a recent edited volume (Rodriguez and Heile 2017). Such debates show that the classical music world is far from reaching consensus on the effects of, and ways forward on questions of, excellence, quality, and standard.

Within institutions, however, music educators themselves can adapt pedagogies and organizational cultures to mitigate the unequal resources that young people bring with them into music education, and to work against the ways in which social hierarchies can be passed on through this tradition. One example in this book of an attempt to create a culture that supports equality was the National Youth Orchestra abolishing hierarchy in the string sections, as discussed in chapter 3. These musical hierarchies did indeed encourage social hierarchies among my participants, and potentially legitimized high levels of social inequality in wider society, which are associated with a wide range of negative outcomes (Pickett and Wilkinson 2010). However, this move was not effective (at least, according to my participants) because the young people themselves did not agree with the politics of the decision. Indeed, it was based on a contradictory position: they were being told they were elite because they had been accepted, via audition, into the NYO. The social world of classical music, as well as the wider world of middle-class education and individual investment into their futures, had taught them to be competitive. They had worked hard to get where they were and had been told they would be rewarded for their hard work. Therefore, it didn't make sense when one of the rewards they had been promised was suddenly revoked. For this decision to be effective, it would have to be accompanied by a broader discussion with the young people of the reasons why it was being taken. The potential for creating spaces of critical deliberation in classical music education was also argued for in chapter 7, which showed that young people were formulating their own ideas of the characterization of Pamina in *The Magic Flute*, but would have benefitted from a facilitated space to explore these further.

This leads onto my final point: for reasons relating to inclusivity but also to safeguarding, classical music education urgently requires more sophisticated ways of including young people's voices, as called for by Spruce (2015) and Zeserson et al. (2014). As this book shows, young people's voices can be conservative, defending existing hierarchies and inequalities, and it is striking that the classical music culture described here is one that produces such a strong defence of tradition, hierarchy, and authority. For this reason, young people's voices must not be an add-on but need to become an integral part of pedagogies and institutional cultures that allow a multiplicity of voices (Spruce 2015, 298). Crucially, this needs to take place within a framework that makes visible the ways in which some voices are amplified and others are silenced, rather than simply listening to those who have thrived within a particular model. This emphasis on voice also needs to be used to adapt the 'master-apprentice' model of one-to-one teaching, where teachers still 'continue to teach along the lines of convention, giving little credence to the need for change' (Sagiv and Hall 2015, 117; see also Perkins 2011; Gaunt 2010). Adult-driven, correction-oriented modes of pedagogy are not the only, or the best, way to learn music; there are many examples of musical pedagogies, whether self-directed or taught, that do not require such high levels of control and that are being adapted to classical music, including multiple creativities (Burnard 2013); intercultural education (Burnard, Mackinlay, and Powell 2016); multiple teachers (Haddon 2011); group teaching (Daniel 2008); the 'master-less studio' (Lebler 2007); and 'listening pedagogy' (Gouzouasis and Ryu 2014). These methods have the potential to contribute towards music education becoming a more democratic space, even if this democracy may lead to unanticipated outcomes.

This focus on young people's voices is also needed to address concerns over abuse in music education, whether sexual, emotional, or physical. Revelations of sexual abuse in classical music education (Pace 2013; Pidd 2013; Baker 2014) show that, as with other areas of society characterized by strong authority, hierarchies, and economies of prestige, classical music has a problem with sexual violence and sexual harassment (Incorporated Society of Musicians 2018). There is, however, a surprising lack of research exploring the patterns and mechanisms by which abuse occurs in music education. Reframing institutional cultures to support and scaffold young people's voices within education institutions is one way in which abuse can be prevented and detected, by showing young people that they will be listened to and believed, and by encouraging them to have a voice about issues that concern them. However, as chapter 4 demonstrated, for the young people in my study, emotional abuse was an accepted and normalized part of the culture of classical music education. This normalization shows that a focus on pupil voice on its own is not enough but needs to be accompanied by sector-led statutory regulation. Necessary interventions include specific guidance on the issues that arise in music education; standardized, accredited, and recognized child protection training that can be carried between institutions within the music education sector; and minimum regulatory standards specific to music education (although see Musicians' Union (2018); Bull (2016b)). This is a particular challenge given the diverse and lightly regulated nature of the sector in the UK, but lessons can be learnt from similar challenges that have been faced by the sports education sector.

Overall, there needs to be a recognition in music education policy that not all social and musical identities are equally valued—in education, in policy, by young people themselves, and by other mainstream social institutions—and the unspoken value of classical music continues to generate further rewards for the already-privileged young people who participate in it. Opportunities abound for young people whose parents have invested in making sure their child is musically 'talented'. This allows many young people to develop a deeply held identity that is a hugely important part of their lives and sense of self. But as the music education sector is currently structured, this strong identity means that they uphold the boundaries of classical music and the rules that they have learnt about what is valued in this genre. This contrasts with narratives in policy documents that focus on opportunities for all, and on multiple pathways towards excellence (Lonie and Sandbrook 2011). While the pluralistic provision of music education in the UK makes policy implementation difficult, policymakers need to find ways to ensure recognition and value for a wide range of musical genres, with an awareness that musical genres also constitute social groupings.

The ways in which the classed and gendered identities described in this book intersect with racialized identities are an urgent area for further investigation in classical music. While I have identified a congruence between the practices of classical music observed in this study and a particular strand of Protestant whiteness, there are clearly complex intersections between race, class, and gender within classical music practice that deserve further attention and can contribute to ongoing work theorizing the intersection of class and race (O. Khan and Shaheen 2017). For example, initiatives that create opportunities within classical music for black and minority ethnic young people such as London Music Masters and the Chineke! Orchestra's youth education programme should be studied to explore whether and how the practices within classical music that I have associated with whiteness are being disrupted. In addition, the ways in which classical music's practices and pedagogies marginalize or exclude disabled and neuro-diverse musicians is starting to be addressed by other researchers and activists through similar critiques to those I have made (Howe et al. 2016; Lubet 2009; Straus 2006).

Such progress is a challenge in a climate of 'austerity' where music education in general is underfunded and sidelined in schools, and youth services more generally have been massively cut (De St Croix 2017). However, the context of austerity and increasing inequality means that the segregation of classical music in privileged spaces is all the more dangerous, as it works against social mixing and social cohesion. The best defence for better public funding for music education is, therefore, not the outdated mantra that every child should have a chance to learn an instrument, but that a public system has more power to sustain and develop more representative, cross-cultural, and innovative musical cultures. Indeed, this occurred in publicly funded music education programmes in the 1980s (Cleave and Dust 1989; J. Lewis 2013). To this end, classical music institutions could usefully draw on examples of interfaith work that aim to overcome divisions in society by establishing two-way dialogues between classical music and other genres and groups, where classical musicians are just as interested in learning about other musical cultures as they are in bringing classical music to others.

These points need to nuance debates on 'excellence' and access. The Cold War era of elite competitions over national prestige in classical music that led to an elitist ecology of specialist music schools (Pace 2015b) is now over, and many of classical music's institutional structures for supporting 'excellence', such as specialist music secondary schools, need to be similarly questioned. Models of music education that foreground virtuosic instrumental ability are outdated. Instead, music education institutions and policy need to support the development of musicians who can create and play music across genres; as Dawn Bennett's (2008) research shows, professional musicians need to be able to play in a variety of genres. Musicians also need to have at least a passing competence in using sound technologies, and to be literate in reading different types of written notation (not necessarily or only staff notation) and also in using music software. This will involve technical competence on instruments for *some* musicians, but developing a broader set of skills will inevitably mean fewer hours in a practice room. There will of course always be those musicians for whom instrumental or vocal skill is an all-consuming passion, but institutional structures and training routes need to valorize the creative musician with a wide set of competencies, rather than the current conservatoire 'superstar' system that pits students against each other in a hierarchy (Perkins 2011).

Opening Up Classical Music's Aesthetic

In order to address inequalities evident in classical music education and its cultural institutions, we need to disrupt the aesthetics of the music itself rather than continuing to produce perfect versions of the canonic repertoire. The boundary-drawing that I have described, which safeguards classical music's cultural prestige, needs to be loosened, and the 'treasures' guarded by it must be let out for us to play with. Of course, composers and musical activists in the 1960s and 1970s have already done this, and many still are (Ross 2008; N. Williams 2015). But through the mechanisms I have described in this book—the interpellation of 'deep' subjectivity; the powerful, rich institutional ecology; the camouflaging of social boundaries as musical ones—these moves were sidelined and have not led to lasting change. Indeed, the direction in recent years has been more towards reinforcing classical music's hegemony, particularly in music education, as can be seen from the National Plan for Music Education and the proliferation of El Sistema–style programmes. Indeed, in the latter, far from being an emancipatory force in this new breed of music education programme, classical music can be seen on a structural level as reinforcing the same patterns of exclusion and inequality as mainstream schooling which sociology of education has been exposing and critiquing for some decades (Reay 2017). Against the discourse in policy and music education practice that classical music education just needs more investment in order to open up this cultural practice to everyone, I am arguing that classical music has stronger links with the middle class than just the economic—that the practices themselves are associated with key traits of bourgeois identity. This does not mean that this music cannot be reclaimed or resignified, but that both the practices and the aesthetic of classical music have to change if classed, raced, and gendered hierarchies are not to be reproduced alongside musical ones. This requires a loosening of musical boundaries in order to open up the social boundaries.

One way forward on these questions in fact already exists in policy, in the form of Arts Council England's Creative Case for Diversity:

> The Creative Case is based upon the simple observation that diversity, in the widest sense, is an integral part of the artistic process. It is an important element in the dynamic that drives art forward, that innovates it and brings it closer to a profound dialogue with contemporary society. (Arts Council England 2011, 7)

There are particular challenges for classical musicians in addressing the Creative Case for Diversity, and this policy remains underexplored among classical music practitioners and organizations. While for many musicians, the challenge of diversity and innovation is appealing and exciting, the practice of doing creative processes differently has not generally been linked with possibilities for diversifying classical music. In addition, this shift in terminology from cultural diversity to 'creative diversity' has been criticized by Malik (2013) as allowing a move away from political questions to creative ones, which might obscure patterns of inequality. Furthermore, this policy also assumes that a diverse creative process will make the creative *product* stronger, while as chapter 6 shows, authoritarian models that reproduce gender and racial oppression may lead to an excellent aesthetic product. As this book has argued throughout, classical music's history plays an important role in its lack of diversity today, so that a major difficulty in diversifying classical music is that its standardized norms are to a large extent *required* by the ideals of aesthetic beauty within the genre.

Despite these problems, I see potential in the Creative Case for Diversity for classical music to open its social and aesthetic boundaries, and to move away from 'monologism' to allow more musical and social dialogue with other groups (Spruce 2015, 297). Of course, the devil is in the detail, but innovative work by other authors and practitioners is already looking at this question (Burnard 2013; Cain 2015; Gaunt and Westerlund 2013; Laurence 2010; Spruce 2015). Towards this end, the tradition and practices of classical music—its aesthetic, pedagogies, repertoire, and institutions—need to change and adapt in order to address the inequalities that this tradition helps legitimize and perpetuate.

Appendix

INTERVIEWEES

Young musicians

Pseudonym	Mother's occupation	Father's occupation	Ethnicity	Type of secondary school	Class fraction
Andy†	Nurse	Dry-liner	White	State	Working class/new middle class
Helen	Singing teacher	Vicar/dean of higher education institution	White	State	Professional middle class
Miriam	Civil servant, used to work in family food business	Manager, agricultural supply store chain	White	State	New middle class
Nilanka*	Academic	Academic	British Asian	Music scholarship to private school	Professional middle class
Alice*	Dentist	Unknown	White	Music scholarship to private school	Professional middle class

Pseudonym	Mother's occupation	Father's occupation	Ethnicity	Type of secondary school	Class fraction
Adam	Not working outside the home	Company director	White	State	Upper middle class
Jonathan	Accountant	Firefighter and factory safety inspector (two jobs)	White	State	New middle class
Jack*	Not working outside the home	Runs IT company	Mixed race (East Asian/White)	Private	Professional middle class
Fred*	Financial analyst	Retired pharmacologist	White	Music scholarship to private school	Professional middle class
Jenny	Runs B&B	Stepfather: business consultant	White	Specialist, music secondary school	New middle class
Owen	Deputy town clerk	Deputy bursar at higher education institution	White	State	New middle class
Elliet	Not working outside the home	Runs IT company	Mixed race (East Asian/British)	Private	Professional middle class
Laurie	Doesn't work since having children; used to be a nurse	Solicitor	Mixed race (East Asian/British)	Music scholarship to private school	Upper/upper middle class
Jonty	Priest	Unknown	White	State	Professional middle class
Holly	School lab technician and garden designer	Chartered accountant	White	State	Professional middle class

Thomas*	Piano teacher	Engineer	White	State secondary, then music scholarship to public school for sixth form	Professional middle class
Sam*	'Involved with various charities'	Lawyer	White	Private	Upper middle class
Lisa	Flute teacher	Saxophone teacher	White	State	Professional middle class
Francesca	Secondary school teacher	Dean of higher education institution	White	Private	Upper middle class
Toby	Child psychologist	Urban planner, city council	White	State	Professional middle class
Robbie	School lab technician	Vicar	White	State	Professional middle class
Elizabeth	Surgeon/academic	Off work with long-term illness	East Asian	State	Professional middle class
Sara	Teacher	Unknown	White	Music scholarship to private school	Professional middle class
Katherine*	Primary school teacher	n/a (single mother)	White	State	Unclear
Hannah*	Secondary school teacher	Academic	White	Private	Professional middle class

Pseudonym	Mother's occupation	Father's occupation	Ethnicity	Type of secondary school	Class fraction
Emily	Teaching assistant (used to be a teacher)	Managing director	White	Private	'In between'
Fergus	Medical editor	Runs R&D company	White	State	Professional middle class
Nathan	Language teacher at a university	Computer programmer, private sector	White	State	Professional middle class
Isabel	Midwife	Town planner, county council	White	State	Professional middle class
Rosie*	Secretary for husband's company	Agricultural consultant	White	Private	Professional middle class
Beth*	Secretary for husband's company	Agricultural consultant	White	Private	Professional middle class
Amy*	Academic	Lawyer	White	State	Professional middle class
Bethan*	Statistician	Architect	White	State	Professional middle class
Teresa	Receptionist	Academic	White	State and private	Professional middle class
Susanna	Not working outside the home	In telecoms, private company	White	State	Professional middle class
Will	Owns a shipbuilding company	Civil servant in East Asia	East Asian	Public	Upper class
Megan	Head teacher	Artisan baker	White	State	Professional middle class

Teachers, Conductors, and Administrators

Name	Role	Group
Tristram*	Conductor	Cantando
Danny*	Accompanist	Cantando
Jeanette†	Vocal tutor	YOC, Cantando
Linda	Administrator	Cantando
Olly	Conductor	WCYO
Christine	Administrator	WCYO
Kate	Administrator	WCYO
Sophia	Director	YOC
Gregory	Chorus master	YOC

* Denotes interview as carried out in a pair with the participant listed immediately above or below.

† Denotes more than one interview carried out with this participant.

REFERENCES

ABRSM. 2017. 'Piano Grades: Requirements and Information'. 2017. https://gb.abrsm.org/fileadmin/user_upload/syllabuses/pianoSyllabusComplete17.pdf.
———. 2018. 'Marking Criteria 2018'. https://gb.abrsm.org/fileadmin/user_upload/syllabuses/Marking_criteria_2018__A4_website__instruments.pdf.
Adenot, Pauline. 2015. 'The Orchestra Conductor'. Translated by Maggie Jones. *Transposition. Musique et Sciences Sociales*, no. 5 (s2): 1–14. http://transposition.revues.org/1296.
Adkins, Lisa. 2004. 'Introduction: Feminism, Bourdieu and After'. *Sociological Review* 52 (s2): 1–18. https://doi.org/10.1111/j.1467-954X.2005.00521.x.
Adorno, Theodor W., and J. M. Bernstein. 2001. *The Culture Industry: Selected Essays on Mass Culture*. Routledge.
Ahmed, Sara. 2002. 'Racialised Bodies'. In *Real Bodies: A Sociological Introduction*, edited by Mary Evans and Ellie Lee, 46–63. Basingstoke: Palgrave.
———. 2004. *The Cultural Politics of Emotion*. New York: Routledge.
Alaghband-Zadeh, Chloë. 2017. 'Listening to North Indian Classical Music: How Embodied Ways of Listening Perform Imagined Histories and Social Class'. *Ethnomusicology* 61 (2): 207–33.
Allan, Alexandra. 2009. 'The Importance of Being a "Lady": Hyper-femininity and Heterosexuality in the Private, Single-Sex Primary School'. *Gender and Education* 21 (2): 145–58. https://doi.org/10.1080/09540250802213172.
———. 2010. 'Picturing success: young femininities and the (im)possibilities of academic achievement in selective, single-sex education'. *International Studies in Sociology of Education* 20 (1): 39–54. https://doi.org/10.1080/09620211003655630.
Allan, Alexandra, and Claire Charles. 2014. 'Cosmo Girls: Configurations of Class and Femininity in Elite Educational Settings'. *British Journal of Sociology of Education* 35 (3): 333–52. https://doi.org/10.1080/01425692.2013.764148.
Allen, Kim, and Anna Bull. 2018. 'Following Policy: A Network Ethnography of the UK Character Education Policy Community'. *Sociological Research Online* 23 (2): 438–58. https://doi.org/10.1177/1360780418769678.
Althusser, Louis. 1971. 'Ideology and Ideological State Apparatuses. Notes towards an Investigation'. In *Lenin and Philosophy and Other Essays*, 121–73. New York: Monthly Review Press.
APPG. 2012. 'Reflections on Body Image: Report from the All Party Parliamentary Group on Body Image'. https://www.berealcampaign.co.uk/assets/filemanager/documents/appg_body_image_final.pdf.
Armstrong, Victoria. 2011. *Gender and Composition in the Music Technology Classroom*. Burlington, VT: Ashgate.
———. 2013. 'Women's Musical Lives: Self-Managing a Freelance Career'. *Women: A Cultural Review* 24: 298–314. https://doi.org/10.1080/09574042.2013.850598.

Arts Council England. 2011. 'What Is the Creative Case for Diversity?' http://www.creativecase.org.uk/domains/disabilityarts.org/local/media/audio/Final_What_is_the_Creative_Case_for_Diversity.pdf.

———. 2012a. 'Directory of Music Education Charities'. Unpublished.

———. 2012b. 'In Harmony Commissioned Grant Guidance for Applicants'. http://www.artscouncil.org.uk/media/uploads/pdf/In_Harmony_commissioned_grant_guidance_final.pdf.

Ashley, Tim. 2008. 'Opera Critic Tim Ashley on Why Mozart's Magic Flute Is Racist—and It's Time Directors Admitted It'. *The Guardian*. 9 July. http://www.theguardian.com/music/2008/jul/09/classicalmusicandopera.comment.

Atkinson, Paul. 2006. *Everyday Arias: An Operatic Ethnography*. Oxford: Rowman Altamira.

Atkinson, Rowland, Simon Parker, and Roger Burrows. 2017. 'Elite Formation, Power and Space in Contemporary London'. *Theory, Culture and Society*, July, 0263276417717792. https://doi.org/10.1177/0263276417717792.

Bacqué, Marie-Hélène, Gary Bridge, and Michaela Benson. 2015. *The Middle Classes and the City*. , Basingstoke: Palgrave Macmillan.

Bailey, Peter. 1978. *Leisure and Class in Victorian England: Rational Recreation and the Contest for Control, 1830–1885*. Abingdon, Oxon: Routledge.

———. 1986. *Music Hall: The Business of Pleasure*. Popular Music in Britain. Milton Keynes: Open University Press.

Baker, Geoffrey. 2014. *El Sistema: Orchestrating Venezuela's Youth*. New York: Oxford University Press.

———. 2017a. 'IDB Study Sheds Doubt on El Sistema's Claims of Social Inclusion and Transformation'. *Geoff Baker* (blog). 17 April. https://geoffbakermusic.wordpress.com/el-sistema-older-posts/idb-study-sheds-doubt-on-el-sistemas-claims-of-social-inclusion-and-transformation-short-version/.

———. 2017b. 'New Year, Old Problems: Rolex Man in Vienna'. *Geoff Baker* (blog). 17 April. https://geoffbakermusic.wordpress.com/el-sistema-older-posts/new-year-old-problems-rolex-man-in-vienna/.

Baker, Geoffrey, Anna Bull, and Mark Taylor. 2018. 'Who Watches the Watchmen? Evaluating Evaluations of El Sistema'. *British Journal of Music Education*, June, 1–15. https://doi.org/10.1017/S0265051718000086.

Banks, Mark. 2014a. '"Being in the Zone" of Cultural Work'. *Culture Unbound* 6. http://www.cultureunbound.ep.liu.se/v6/cul14v6_capitalism.pdf#page=229.

———. 2014b. 'More Children Making Music, But Are Lessons Too Conventional?' *The Conversation*, 19 September 2014. http://theconversation.com/more-children-making-music-but-are-lessons-too-conventional-31752.

———. 2017. *Creative Justice: Cultural Industries, Work and Inequality*. Lanham, MD: Rowman and Littlefield International.

Banks, Mark, Jill Ebrey, and Jason Toynbee. 2014. *Working Lives in Black British Jazz*. Manchester: Jazz Services. http://hummedia.manchester.ac.uk/institutes/cresc/sites/default/files/WLIBBJ%20NEW%20FINAL.pdf.

Barber, Charles. 2003. 'Conductors in Rehearsal'. In *The Cambridge Companion to Conducting*, edited by José Antonio Bowen, 17–27. Cambridge Companions to Music. Cambridge: Cambridge University Press.

Barlow, James, Peter Dickens, Tony Fielding, and Mike Savage. 1995. *Property, Bureaucracy and Culture: Middle-class Formation in Contemporary Britain*. New ed. London: Routledge.

Barrett, Maria. 2016. 'Our place': class, the theatre audience and the Royal Court Liverpool. PhD. University of Warwick.

Bartleet, Brydie-Leigh. 2008. 'Women Conductors on the Orchestral Podium: Pedagogical and Professional Implications'. *College Music Symposium* 48: 31–51.

Bazalgette, Sir Peter. 2014. 'We Have to Recognise the Huge Value of Arts and Culture to Society'. *The Guardian*. 27 April. http://www.theguardian.com/culture/2014/apr/27/value-of-arts-and-culture-to-society-peter-bazalgette.

Beck, Ulrich. 1992. *Risk Society: Towards a New Modernity*. Theory, Culture and Society. London: Sage.
Becker, Howard Saul. 1982. *Art Worlds*. Berkeley: University of California Press.
Beckles Willson, Rachel. 2009. 'The Parallax Worlds of the West-Eastern Divan Orchestra'. *Journal of the Royal Musical Association* 134 (November): 319–47. https://doi.org/10.1080/02690400903109109.
Bennett, Dawn. 2008. *Understanding the Classical Music Profession: The Past, the Present and Strategies for the Future*. Aldershot: Ashgate.
Bennett, Joe. 2015. 'BB King Was Great Because He Played "Out of Tune"'. *The Conversation*, 15 May. http://theconversation.com/bb-king-was-great-because-he-played-out-of-tune-41910.
Bennett, Tony, Mike Savage, Elizabeth Bortolaia Silva, Alan Warde, Modesto Gayo-Cal, and David Wright. 2008. *Culture, Class, Distinction*. London: Routledge.
Benson, Michaela, Gary Bridge, and Deborah Wilson. 2014. 'School Choice in London and Paris: A Comparison of Middle-Class Strategies'. *Social Policy and Administration*, June. https://doi.org/10.1111/spol.12079.
Benzecry, Claudio E. 2011. *The Opera Fanatic: Ethnography of an Obsession*. Chicago: University of Chicago Press.
Blackman, Lisa. 2008. *The Body: The Key Concepts*. Oxford: Berg.
———. 2011. "This Is a Matter of Pride: The Choir: Unsung Town and Community Transformation." In *Reality Television and Class*, edited by Helen Wood and Beverley Skeggs, 237–49. London: Palgrave Macmillan.
———. 2012. *Immaterial Bodies: Affect, Embodiment, Mediation*. Theory, Culture and Society. London: Sage.
Bohlman, Philip Vilas. 1989. *'The Land Where Two Streams Flow': Music in the German-Jewish Community of Israel*. Champaign: University of Illinois Press.
Boliver, Vikki, Claire Crawford, Mandy Powell, and Will Craige. 2017. 'Admissions in Context: The Use of Contextual Information by Leading Universities'. Sutton Trust.
Bordo, Susan. 2003. *Unbearable Weight: Feminism, Western Culture, and the Body*. 2nd rev. ed. Berkeley: University of California Press.
———. 2012. 'Beyond the Anorexic Paradigm: Re-thinking "Eating" Disorders'. In *Routledge Handbook of Body Studies*, edited by Bryan S. Turner, 244–55. Routledge International Handbooks. London: Routledge.
Born, Georgina. 2010. 'The Social and the Aesthetic: For a Post-Bourdieuian Theory of Cultural Production'. *Cultural Sociology* 4 (2): 171–208. https://doi.org/10.1177/1749975510368471.
———. 2012. 'Music and the Social'. In *The Cultural Study of Music: A Critical Introduction*, edited by Martin Clayton, Trevor Herbert, and Richard Middleton, 2nd ed., 261–74. Abingdon, Oxon: Routledge.
———. 2017. 'After Relational Aesthetics: Improvised Music, the Social, and (Re)Theorizing the Aesthetic'. In *Improvisation and Social Aesthetics*, edited by Georgina Born, Eric Lewis, and Will Straw, 33–58. Durham, NC: Duke University Press.
Born, Georgina, and Kyle Devine. 2015. 'Music Technology, Gender, and Class: Digitization, Educational and Social Change in Britain'. *Twentieth-Century Music* 12 (2): 135–72. https://doi.org/10.1017/S1478572215000018.
Born, Georgina, and David Hesmondhalgh. 2000. 'Introduction: On Difference, Representation, and Appropriation in Music'. In Born, Georgina and Hesmondhalgh, David (ed.s). *Western Music and Its Others: Difference, Representation, and Appropriation in Music*, 1–58. Berkeley: University of California Press.
Bourdieu, Pierre. 1977. *Outline of a Theory of Practice*. Cambridge: Cambridge University Press.
———. 1983. 'The Field of Cultural Production, or: The Economic World Reversed'. *Poetics* 12 (4–5): 311–56.
———. 1984. *Distinction: A Social Critique of the Judgement of Taste*. Translated by Richard Nice. Cambridge, MA: Harvard University Press.
———. 1986. 'The Forms of Capital'. In *Handbook of Theory of Research for the Sociology of Education*, edited by John Richardson, 241–58. New York: Greenwood Press.

———. 1987. 'What Makes a Social Class? On the Theoretical and Practical Existence of Groups'. *Berkeley Journal of Sociology* 32: 1–17.

———. 1990. *The Logic of Practice*. Cambridge: Polity Press.

Bowen, José Antonio. 2003. *The Cambridge Companion to Conducting*. Cambridge Companions to Music. Cambridge: Cambridge University Press.

Brackenridge, C., and K. Fasting, eds. 2002. *Sexual Harassment and Abuse in Sport: International Research and Policy Perspectives*. London: Whiting and Birch.

Brackenridge, Celia. 1997. '"He Owned Me Basically ...": Women's Experience of Sexual Abuse in Sport'. *International Review for the Sociology of Sport* 32 (2): 115–30. https://doi.org/10.1177/101269097032002001.

Bratton, J. S. 1986. *Music Hall: Performance and Style*. Popular Music in Britain. Milton Keynes: Open University Press.

Brown, Wendy. 2009. *Edgework: Critical Essays on Knowledge and Politics*. Princeton, NJ: Princeton University Press.

Bull, Anna. 2009. 'An Ethnographic Study of Concert Audiences at the Cambridge Summer Music Festival'. Unpublished manuscript.

———. 2016a. 'El Sistema as a Bourgeois Social Project: Class, Gender, and Victorian Values'. *Action, Criticism & Theory for Music Education* 15 (1): 120–53.

———. 2016b. 'Safeguarding and Youth Voice in Music Education'. *Dr Anna Bull* (blog). 28 November. https://annabullresearch.wordpress.com/2016/11/28/safeguarding-and-youth-voice-in-music-education/.

———. 2018. 'Uncertain Capital: Class, Gender, and the "Imagined Futures" of Young Classical Musicians'. In *The Classical Music Industry*, edited by Chris Dromey and Julia Haferkorn, 79–95. London: Routledge.

Bull, Anna, and Kim Allen. 2018. 'Introduction: Sociological Interrogations of the Turn to Character'. *Sociological Research Online*, April. 1360780418769672. https://doi.org/10.1177/1360780418769672.

Bull, Anna, and Christina Scharff. 2017. '"McDonalds" Music' versus "Serious Music": How Production and Consumption Practices Help to Reproduce Class Inequality in the Classical Music Profession'. *Cultural Sociology* 11 (3): 283–301. https://doi.org/10.1177/1749975517711045.

Burke, Penny Jane, and Jackie McManus. 2009. '"Art for a Few": Exclusion and Misrecognition in Art and Design Higher Education Admissions'. National Arts Learning Network. http://www.ukadia.ac.uk/en/projects/projects--research/admissions-research.cfm.

Burnard, Pamela. 2012. *Musical Creativities in Practice*. Oxford: Oxford University Press.

———. 2013. *Developing Creativities in Higher Music Education: International Perspectives and Practices*. Abingdon: Routledge.

Burnard, Pamela, Elizabeth Mackinlay, and Kimberly Powell. 2016. *The Routledge International Handbook of Intercultural Arts Research*. Abingdon: Routledge.

Butler, Judith. 1997. *The Psychic Life of Power: Theories in Subjection*. Stanford, CA: Stanford University Press.

Butler, Tim, and Garry Robson. 2003. *London Calling: The Middle Classes and the Re-making of Inner London*. Oxford: Berg.

Byrne, Bridget. 2006. 'In Search of a "Good Mix": "Race", Class, Gender and Practices of Mothering'. *Sociology* 40 (6): 1001–17. https://doi.org/10.1177/0038038506069841.

Cain, Melissa. 2015. 'Musics of "The Other": Creating Musical Identities and Overcoming Cultural Boundaries in Australian Music Education'. *British Journal of Music Education* 32 (1): 71–86. https://doi.org/10.1017/S0265051714000394.

'"Can Musical Conservatism Be Progressive?": 2nd Annual Conference of the Critical Theory for Musicology Study Group'. 2018. 12 January. https://criticaltheoryformusicology.files.wordpress.com/2018/01/ctfm-2018-conference-programme.pdf.

Cantor, David, Bonnie Fisher, Susan Chibnall, Reanne Townsend, Hynshik Lee, Carol Bruce, and Gail Thomas. 2015. 'Report on the AAU Campus Climate Survey on Sexual Assault and Sexual Misconduct'. Association of American Universities. https://www.aau.edu/

uploadedFiles/AAU_Publications/AAU_Reports/Sexual_Assault_Campus_Survey/AAU_Campus_Climate_Survey_12_14_15.pdf.
Chan, Tak Wing, and John H. Goldthorpe. 2005. 'The Social Stratification of Theatre, Dance and Cinema Attendance'. *Cultural Trends* 14 (3): 193–212. https://doi.org/10.1080/09548960500436774.
———. 2007. 'Social Stratification and Cultural Consumption: Music in England'. *European Sociological Review* 23 (1): 1–19. https://doi.org/10.1093/esr/jcl016.
Charity Commission. 2017. 'Charity Overview'. 17 November. http://apps.charitycommission.gov.uk/Showcharity/RegisterOfCharities/CharityWithPartB.aspx?RegisteredCharityNumber=292182&SubsidiaryNumber=0.
Citron, Marcia J. 1993a. 'Feminist Approaches to Musicology'. In *Cecilia Reclaimed: Feminist Perspectives on Gender and Music*, edited by Susan C. Cook and Judy S. Tsou, 15–34. Urbana: University of Illinois Press.
———. 1993b. *Gender and the Musical Canon*. Cambridge: Cambridge University Press.
Clarke, David. 2012. 'Musical Autonomy Revisited'. In *The Cultural Study of Music: A Critical Introduction*, edited by Martin Clayton, Trevor Herbert, and Richard Middleton, 2nd ed., 172–83. Abingdon, Oxon: Routledge.
Clarke, John. 2015. 'Stuart Hall and the Theory and Practice of Articulation'. *Discourse: Studies in the Cultural Politics of Education* 36 (2): 275–86. https://doi.org/10.1080/01596306.2015.1013247.
'Class, Race and Classical Music—Listen to the LMM Debate'. 2014. 16 April. http://www.youtube.com/watch?v=hQBtZXtTayA&feature=youtube_gdata_player.
Clayton, Martin. 2013. 'Entrainment, Ethnography and Musical Interaction'. In *Experience and Meaning in Music Performance*, edited by Martin Clayton, Byron Dueck, and Laura Leante, 17–39. Oxford: Oxford University Press.
Clayton, Martin, Rebecca Sager, and Udo Will. 2005. 'In Time with the Music: The Concept of Entrainment and Its Significance for Ethnomusicology'. In *European Meetings in Ethnomusicology* 11:1–82. Romanian Society for Ethnomusicology. http://dro.dur.ac.uk/8713/1/8713.pdf.
Cleave, Shirley, and Karen Dust. 1989. *A Sound Start: The Schools' Instrumental Music Service*. National Foundation for Educational Research Library. Windsor: NFER-Nelson.
Clément, Catherine. 1997. *Opera, Or, The Undoing of Women*. London: I. B. Tauris.
Coleman, Rebecca. 2013. 'Sociology and the Virtual: Interactive Mirrors, Representational Thinking and Intensive Power'. *Sociological Review* 61 (1): 1–20. https://doi.org/10.1111/1467-954X.12002.
Connell, R. W. 2005. *Masculinities*. 2nd ed. Cambridge: Polity Press.
Coser, Rose Laub. 1978. 'The Principle of Patriarchy: The Case of "The Magic Flute"'. *Signs* 4 (2): 337–48. https://doi.org/10.2307/3173030.
Coughlan, Sean. 2017. 'Cambridge "Less Posh Than Bristol"'. *BBC News*, 2 February, sec. Education and Family. http://www.bbc.co.uk/news/education-38842482.
Cox, Gordon. 1993. *A History of Music Education in England, 1872–1928*. Aldershot: Scolar Press.
Crawford, Garry, Victoria Gosling, Gaynor Bagnall, and Ben Light. 2014. 'An Orchestral Audience: Classical Music and Continued Patterns of Distinction'. *Cultural Sociology*, July. 1749975514541862. https://doi.org/10.1177/1749975514541862.
Crompton, Rosemary. 2015. *Class and Stratification*. 3rd ed. Cambridge: Polity Press.
Cusick, Suzanne G. 2013. 'Towards an Acoustemology of Detention in the "Global War on Terror"'. In *Music, Sound and Space: Transformations of Public and Private Experience*, edited by Georgina Born, 275–91. Cambridge: Cambridge University Press.
Dahlhaus, Carl. 1991. *The Idea of Absolute Music*. Chicago: University of Chicago Press.
Daniel, Ryan. 2008. *Group Piano Teaching*. Riga: VDM Verlag Dr. Mueller.
Darmon, Muriel. 2009. 'The Fifth Element: Social Class and the Sociology of Anorexia'. *Sociology* 43 (4): 717–33. https://doi.org/10.1177/0038038509105417.
Daubney, Ally, and Duncan Mackrill. 2018. 'Changes in Secondary Music Curriculum Provision 2012-16'. Accessed 14 January 2019. https://www.ism.org/images/files/Changes-in-Secondary-Music-Curriculum-Provision-2012-16_Summary-final.pdf.

Davidoff, Leonore, and Catherine Hall. 2002. *Family Fortunes: Men and Women of the English Middle Class 1780–1850*. Rev. ed. London: Routledge.
DeNora, Tia. 1995. *Beethoven and the Construction of Genius: Musical Politics in Vienna, 1792–1803*. Berkeley: University of California Press.
———. 2000. *Music in Everyday Life*. Cambridge: Cambridge University Press.
———. 2003. *After Adorno: Rethinking Music Sociology*. Cambridge: Cambridge University Press.
———. 2005. 'The Concerto and Society'. In *The Cambridge Companion to the Concerto*, edited by Simon Keefe, 19–32. Cambridge: Cambridge University Press.
———. 2006. 'Music and Self-Identity'. In *The Popular Music Studies Reader*, edited by Andy Bennett, Barry Shank, and Jason Toynbee, 141–47. London: Routledge.
Dent, H. C. 1977. *The Training of Teachers in England and Wales, 1800–1975*. London: Hodder Arnold H&S.
Department for Business, Innovation and Skills. 2013. 'Pupils on Free School Meals Attending Music Colleges—A Freedom of Information Request to Department for Business, Innovation and Skills—WhatDoTheyKnow'. https://www.whatdotheyknow.com/request/pupils_on_free_school_meals_atte#incoming-414358.
De St Croix, Tania de. 2017. 'Youth Work, Performativity and the New Youth Impact Agenda: Getting Paid for Numbers?' *Journal of Education Policy* 33 (3): 1–25. https://doi.org/10.1080/02680939.2017.1372637.
Dibben, Nicola. 2006. 'The Socio-cultural and Learning Experiences of Music Students in a British University'. *British Journal of Music Education* 23 (1): 91–116. https://doi.org/10.1017/S0265051705006765.
DiMaggio, Paul. 1986. 'Cultural Entrepreneurship in Nineteenth-Century Boston'. In *Nonprofit Enterprise in the Arts: Studies in Mission and Constraint*, 41–62. New York: Oxford University Press.
Dueck, Byron. 2013. *Musical Intimacies and Indigenous Imaginaries: Aboriginal Music and Dance in Public Performance*. New York: Oxford University Press.
Duffy, Stella. 2016. '"Great Art for Everyone"—The Problem Is in the Title'. *Not Writing But Blogging* (blog). 29 February. https://stelladuffy.wordpress.com/2016/02/29/great-art-for-everyone-the-problem-is-in-the-title/.
Durrant, Colin. 2000. 'Making Choral Rehearsing Seductive: Implications for Practice and Choral Education'. *Research Studies in Music Education* 15 (1): 40–49.
Dyer, Richard. 1997. *White*. London: Routledge.
Eagleton, Terry. 1988. 'The Ideology of the Aesthetic'. *Poetics Today* 9 (2): 327–38.
———. 1990. *The Ideology of the Aesthetic*. Oxford: Wiley-Blackwell.
Ehrenreich, B., 1990. *Fear of Falling: The Inner Life of the Middle Class*. New York: HarperPerennial.
Ehrlich, Cyril. 1985. *The Music Profession in Britain since the Eighteenth Century: A Social History*. Oxford: Clarendon.
Elias, Ana Sofia, Rosalind Gill, and Christina Scharff, eds. 2017. *Aesthetic Labour: Rethinking Beauty Politics in Neoliberalism*. London: Palgrave Macmillan.
'El Sistema Global Program Directory'. n.d. Sistema Global. Accessed 6 January 2018. http://sistemaglobal.org/el-sistema-global-program-directory/.
Etheridge, Stephen. 2012. 'Brass Bands in the Southern Pennines, 1857–1914: The Ethos of Rational Recreation and Perceptions of Working-Class Respectability'. In *Class, Culture and Community: New Perspectives in Nineteenth and Twentieth Century British Labour History*, edited by Anne Baldwin, Chris Ellis, Stephen Etheridge, Keith Laybourn, and Neil Pye, 37–54. Newcastle-upon-Tyne: Cambridge Scholars Publishing.
Evans, John, Emma Rich, and Rachel Holroyd. 2004. 'Disordered Eating and Disordered Schooling: What Schools Do to Middle Class Girls'. *British Journal of Sociology of Education* 25 (2): 123–42. https://doi.org/10.1080/0142569042000205154.
Faircloth, Charlotte. 2014. 'Intensive Parenting and the Expansion of Parenting'. In *Parenting Culture Studies*, edited by E. Lee, J. Bristow, C. Faircloth, and J. Macvarish, 25–50. Basingstoke: Palgrave Macmillan.
Faulkner, Robert R. 1973. 'Orchestra Interaction: Some Features of Communication and Authority in an Artistic Organization'. *Sociological Quarterly* 14 (2): 147–57. https://doi.org/10.1111/j.1533-8525.1973.tb00850.x.

Fautley, Martin. 2015. 'Music Education Assessment and Social Justice: Resisting Hegemony through Formative Assessment'. In *The Oxford Handbook of Social Justice in Music Education*, edited by Cathy Benedict, Patrick Schmidt, Gary Spruce, and Paul Woodford, 513–24. New York: Oxford University Press.

Fautley, Martin, and Adam Whittaker. 2017. 'Key Data on Music Education Hubs 2016'. Birmingham, UK: Birmingham City University. http://www.artscouncil.org.uk/sites/default/files/download-file/key_data_music_report.pdf.

Featherstone, Mike. 2007. *Consumer Culture and Postmodernism*. Los Angeles: Sage.

Feeny, Antony. 2016. 'Economic Ear: Classical Music Gets a Raise, but Other Arts Rise Even Further'. *Classical Music*. London: Rhinegold. 13 December. http://www.rhinegold.co.uk/classical_music/economic-ear-classical-music-gets-raise-arts-rise-even/.

Feld, Steven. 1990. *Sound and Sentiment: Birds, Weeping, Poetics, and Song in Kaluli Expression*. 2nd ed. University of Pennsylvania Press Conduct and Communication Series. Philadelphia: University of Pennsylvania Press.

Forbes, Joan, and Bob Lingard. 2015. 'Assured Optimism in a Scottish Girls' School: Habitus and the (Re)Production of Global Privilege'. *British Journal of Sociology of Education* 36 (1): 116–36. https://doi.org/10.1080/01425692.2014.967839.

France, Alan, and Steven Roberts. 2017. *Youth and Social Class: Enduring Inequality in the United Kingdom, Australia and New Zealand*. London: Palgrave Macmillan.

Francis, Becky, Louise Archer, Jeremy Hodgen, David Pepper, Becky Taylor, and Mary-Claire Travers. 2016. 'Exploring the Relative Lack of Impact of Research on "Ability Grouping" in England: A Discourse Analytic Account'. *Cambridge Journal of Education* 47 (1): 1–17. https://doi.org/10.1080/0305764X.2015.1093095.

Francis, Becky, Barbara Read, and Christine Skelton. 2012. *The Identities and Practices of High Achieving Pupils: Negotiating Achievement and Peer Cultures*. London: Bloomsbury.

Fraser, Nancy. 1990. 'Rethinking the Public Sphere: A Contribution to the Critique of Actually Existing Democracy'. *Social Text*, no. 25/26: 56. https://doi.org/10.2307/466240.

Freire, Paulo. 2000. *Pedagogy of the Oppressed: 30th Anniversary Edition*. New York: Continuum International Publishing Group.

Friedman, Sam. 2014a. *Comedy and Distinction: The Cultural Currency of a 'Good' Sense of Humour*. Culture, Economy and the Social. London: Routledge.

———. 2014b. 'The Price of the Ticket: Rethinking the Experience of Social Mobility'. *Sociology* 48 (2): 352–68. https://doi.org/10.1177/0038038513490355.

Friedman, Sam, Mike Savage, Laurie Hanquinet, and Andrew Miles. 2015. 'Cultural Sociology and New Forms of Distinction'. *Poetics* 53 (December): 1–8. https://doi.org/10.1016/j.poetic.2015.10.002.

Frith, Simon. 1996a. 'Music and Identity'. In *Questions of Cultural Identity*, edited by Stuart Hall and Paul Du Gay, 108–27. London: Sage.

———. 1996b. *Performing Rites: On the Value of Popular Music*. Oxford: Oxford University Press.

Fuller, Sophie. 1998. 'Women Composers during the British Musical Renaissance, 1880–1918'. King's College, University of London. http://citeseerx.ist.psu.edu/viewdoc/download?doi=10.1.1.692.5558&rep=rep1&type=pdf.

Gamsu, Sol. 2016. 'Education, Class and the City: A Comparison of Circuits of Education in Sheffield and London'. King's College London.

Garnett, Liz. 2017. *Choral Conducting and the Construction of Meaning: 'Gesture, Voice, Identity'*. Abingdon: Routledge.

Gaunt, Helena. 2010. 'One-to-One Tuition in a Conservatoire: The Perceptions of Instrumental and Vocal Students'. *Psychology of Music* 38 (2): 178–208. https://doi.org/10.1177/0305735609339467.

Gaunt, Helena, and Heidi Westerlund. 2013. *Collaborative Learning in Higher Music Education*. New ed. Farnham: Ashgate.

Gay, Peter. 1998. *The Bourgeois Experience: Victoria to Freud*. London: HarperCollins.

Gill, Rosalind. 2007. *Gender and the Media*. Cambridge: Polity Press.

Gillett, Paula. 2000. *Musical Women in England, 1870–1914: Encroaching on All Man's Privileges*. New York: St Martin's Press.

———. 2004. 'Entrepreneurial Women Musicians in Britain: From the 1790s to the Early 1900s'. In *The Musician as Entrepreneur, 1700–1914: Managers, Charlatans, and Idealists*, edited by William Weber, 198–220. Bloomington: Indiana University Press.

Gilmore, Samuel. 1987. 'Coordination and Convention: The Organization of the Concert World'. *Symbolic Interaction* 10 (2): 209–27. https://doi.org/10.1525/si.1987.10.2.209.

Goehr, Lydia. 1992. *The Imaginary Museum of Musical Works: An Essay in the Philosophy of Music*. Oxford: Clarendon Press.

Gouzouasis, Peter, and Jee Yeon Ryu. 2014. 'A Pedagogical Tale from the Piano Studio: Autoethnography in Early Childhood Music Education Research'. *Music Education Research* 17 (4): 1–24. https://doi.org/10.1080/14613808.2014.972924.

Green, Lucy. 1997. *Music, Gender, Education*. Cambridge: Cambridge University Press.

———. 2003. 'Why "Ideology" Is Still Relevant for Critical Thinking in Music Education'. *Action, Criticism, and Theory for Music Education* 2 (2): 1–24. http://act.maydaygroup.org/articles/Green2_2.pdf.

———. 2005. 'Musical Meaning and Social Reproduction: A Case for Retrieving Autonomy'. *Educational Philosophy and Theory* 37 (1): 77–92. https://doi.org/10.1111/j.1469-5812.2005.00099.x.

Gregg, Melissa, and Gregory J. Seigworth, eds. 2010. *The Affect Theory Reader*. Durham, NC: Duke University Press.

Griffiths, Matt. 2014. 'Music Education Must Move beyond Classical and Become More Inclusive'. *The Guardian*, 11 August, sec. Culture Professionals Network. http://www.theguardian.com/culture-professionals-network/culture-professionals-blog/2014/aug/11/music-education-inclusive-funding-hubs.

Gunn, Simon. 1997. 'The Sublime and the Vulgar: The Hallé Concerts and the Constitution of "High Culture" in Manchester c. 1850–1880'. *Journal of Victorian Culture* 2 (2): 208–28. https://doi.org/10.1080/13555509709505950.

Gustafson, Ruth. 2009. *Race and Curriculum: Music in Childhood Education*. New York: Palgrave Macmillan.

Haddon, Elizabeth. 2011. 'Multiple Teachers: Multiple Gains?' *British Journal of Music Education* 28 (special issue 1): 69–85. https://doi.org/10.1017/S0265051710000422.

Hall, Clare. 2015. 'Singing Gender and Class: Understanding Choirboys' Musical Habitus'. In *Bourdieu and the Sociology of Music Education*, edited by Pamela Burnard, Yiva Hofvander Trulsson, and Johan Soderman, 43–60. Farnham: Ashgate.

———. 2018. *Masculinity, Class and Music Education: Boys Performing Middle-Class Masculinities through Music*. London: Palgrave Macmillan.

Hall, Clare, and Sally Savage. 2016. 'Thinking about and beyond the Cultural Contradictions of Motherhood through Musical Mothering'. In *Music of Motherhood*, edited by Martha Joy Rose, Lynda Ross, and Jennifer Hartmann, 32–50. Bradford, ON: Demeter Press.

Hall, Stuart. 1985. 'Signification, Representation, Ideology: Althusser and the Post-structuralist Debates'. *Critical Studies in Media Communication* 2 (2): 91–114.

———. 2005. 'Encoding/Decoding'. In *Media and Cultural Studies—Keywords*, edited by Meenakshi Gigi Durham and Douglas M. Kellner, rev. ed., 163–73. Malden, MA: Wiley-Blackwell.

Hall, Stuart, and Tony Jefferson. 1993. *Resistance through Rituals: Youth Subcultures in Post-war Britain*. London: Psychology Press.

Hallam, Susan. 2016. 'Whole Class Ensemble Teaching (WCET) Final Report'. Music Mark. https://www.musicmark.org.uk/wp-content/uploads/WCET-Final-Report.pdf.

Hallam, Susan, and Andrea Creech, eds. 2010. *Music Education in the 21st Century in the United Kingdom: Achievements, Analysis and Aspirations*. Bedford Way Papers 34. London: Institute of Education, University of London.

Hallam, Susan, Lynne Rogers, and Andrea Creech. 2008. 'Gender Differences in Musical Instrument Choice'. *International Journal of Music Education* 26 (1): 7–19. https://doi.org/10.1177/0255761407085646.

Hanquinet, Laurie, Henk Roose, and Mike Savage. 2014. 'The Eyes of the Beholder: Aesthetic Preferences and the Remaking of Cultural Capital'. *Sociology* 48 (1): 111–32. https://doi.org/10.1177/0038038513477935.

Hanquinet, Laurie, and Mike Savage, eds. 2015. *Routledge International Handbook of the Sociology of Art and Culture*. New York: Routledge.

Harding, Sandra G. 1996. 'Rethinking Standpoint Epistemology: What Is "Strong Objectivity"?' In *Feminism and Science*, edited by Evelyn Fox Keller and Helen E. Longino, 235–48. Oxford Readings in Feminism. Oxford: Oxford University Press.

Hargreaves, David J., and Nigel A. Marshall. 2003. 'Developing Identities in Music Education'. *Music Education Research* 5 (3): 263–73. https://doi.org/10.1080/1461380032000126355.

Harper-Scott, J. P. E. 2012. *The Quilting Points of Musical Modernism: Revolution, Reaction, and William Walton*. Cambridge: Cambridge University Press.

Haslam, Nick. 2014. 'Class Stereotypes: Chavs, White Trash, Bogans and Other Animals'. *The Conversation*, 25 February. http://theconversation.com/class-stereotypes-chavs-white-trash-bogans-and-other-animals-22952.

Hays, Sharon. 1998. *The Cultural Contradictions of Motherhood*. New ed. New Haven, CT: Yale University Press.

Hebdige, D. 1981. *Subculture: The Meaning of Style*. London: Routledge.

Hennion, Antoine. 2001. 'Music Lovers Taste as Performance'. *Theory, Culture and Society* 18 (5): 1–22. https://doi.org/10.1177/02632760122051940.

Henriques, Julian. 2011. *Sonic Bodies: Reggae Sound Systems, Performance Techniques and Ways of Knowing*. London: Continuum.

Herbert, Trevor, ed. 2000. *The British Brass Band: A Musical and Social History*. 2nd ed. Oxford: Oxford University Press.

Hesmondhalgh, David. 2013. *Why Music Matters*. Chichester: Wiley.

Hesmondhalgh, David, Kate Oakley, David Lee, and Melissa Nisbett. 2015. *Culture, Economy and Politics: The Case of New Labour*. Basingstoke: Palgrave Macmillan.

Hess, Juliet. 2016. 'Interrupting the Symphony: Unpacking the Importance Placed on Classical Concert Experiences'. *Music Education Research*, June, 1–11. https://doi.org/10.1080/14613808.2016.1202224.

Hewett, Ivan. 2014. 'Music Education: A Middle-Class Preserve?' *Telegraph*, 6 November. http://www.telegraph.co.uk/culture/music/music-news/10891882/Music-education-a-middle-class-preserve.html.

Hill, Liz. 2014. 'Pressure Mounts on Councils to Cut Music Education Funding'. *ArtsProfessional*, 17 April. http://www.artsprofessional.co.uk/news/pressure-mounts-councils-cut-music-education-funding.

HM Government. 2015. 'Working Together to Safeguard Children'. March. https://www.gov.uk/government/uploads/system/uploads/attachment_data/file/592101/Working_Together_to_Safeguard_Children_20170213.pdf.

Hobsbawm, Eric, and Terence O. Ranger. 1992. *The Invention of Tradition*. Cambridge: Cambridge University Press.

Hodgkins, Chris. 2013. 'Arts Funding, Opera and All That Jazz'. *The Guardian*, 19 January, sec. Music. http://www.guardian.co.uk/music/2013/jan/21/arts-funding-opera-jazz.

Hoher, Dagmar. 1986. 'The Composition of Music Hall Audiences'. In *Music Hall: The Business of Pleasure*, edited by Peter Bailey, 74–92. Popular Music in Britain. Milton Keynes: Open University Press.

Holden, Raymond. 2003. 'The Technique of Conducting'. In *The Cambridge Companion to Conducting*, edited by José Antonio Bowen, 3–16. Cambridge Companions to Music. Cambridge: Cambridge University Press.

Holland, Janet, Caroline Ramazanoglu, Rachel Thomson, and Sue Sharpe. 2004. *The Male in the Head: Young People, Heterosexuality and Power*. London: Tufnell.

Hollingworth, S., A. Paraskevopoulou, Y. Robinson, E. Chaligianni, and A. Mansaray. 2016. 'Arts Award Impact Study 2012–2016: A Report for Trinity College London'. London: London South Bank University.

hooks, bell. 1992. *Black Looks: Race and Representation*. Boston: South End Press.

Howe, Blake, Stephanie Jensen-Moulton, Neil William Lerner, and Joseph Nathan Straus. 2016. *The Oxford Handbook of Music and Disability Studies*. New York: Oxford University Press.

Hume, Simon, and Emma Wells. 2014. 'ABRSM: Making Music'. ABRSM. http://gb.abrsm.org/de/making-music/#.

Hunt, James G., George Edward Stelluto, and Robert Hooijberg. 2004. 'Toward New-Wave Organization Creativity: Beyond Romance and Analogy in the Relationship between Orchestra-Conductor Leadership and Musician Creativity'. *Leadership Quarterly* 15 (1): 145–62. https://doi.org/10.1016/j.leaqua.2003.12.009.

Hunter, Jo, and David Micklem. 2016. 'Everyday Creativity'. 64 Million Artists. http://64millionartists.com/everyday-creativity-2/.

Ilari, Beatriz. 2013. 'Concerted Cultivation and Music Learning: Global Issues and Local Variations'. *Research Studies in Music Education* 35 (2): 179–96. https://doi.org/10.1177/1321103X13509348.

Incorporated Society of Musicians. 2017. 'Dignity at Work: A Survey of Discrimination in the Music Profession. An Interim Report'. London: Incorporated Society of Musicians. https://www.ism.org/images/files/Dignity-at-work-a-survey-of-discrimination-in-the-music-sector.pdf.

———. 2018. 'Dignity at Work: A Survey of Discrimination in the Music Sector'. London: Incorporated Society of Musicians. https://www.ism.org/images/images/ISM_Dignity-at-work-April-2018.pdf.

Institute of Ideas. 2013. 'One to One Tuition in the Dock? The Crisis in Music Schools'. 19 October. http://www.battleofideas.org.uk/2013/session_detail/7867.

Irwin, Sarah, and Sharon Elley. 2011. 'Concerted Cultivation? Parenting Values, Education and Class Diversity'. *Sociology* 45 (3): 480–95. https://doi.org/10.1177/0038038511399618.

Jackson, Emma. 2015. *Young Homeless People and Urban Space: Fixed in Mobility*. Abingdon: Routledge.

Jackson, Emma, and Michaela Benson. 2014. 'Neither "Deepest, Darkest Peckham" nor "Run-of-the-Mill" East Dulwich: The Middle Classes and Their "Others" in an Inner-London Neighbourhood'. *International Journal of Urban and Regional Research*, May. https://doi.org/10.1111/1468-2427.12129.

James, David, Diane Reay, Gill Crozier, Phoebe Beedell, Sumi Hollingworth, Fiona Jamieson, and Katya Williams. 2010. 'Neoliberal Policy and the Meaning of Counterintuitive Middle-Class School Choices'. *Current Sociology* 58 (4): 623–41. https://doi.org/10.1177/0011392110368003.

Jay, Alexis. 2015. 'Independent Inquiry into Child Sexual Exploitation in Rotherham (1997–2013)'. Rotherham Metropolitan Borough Council. http://www.rotherham.gov.uk/downloads/file/1407/independent_inquiry_cse_in_rotherham.

Jensen, Tracey. 2014. 'Welfare Commonsense, Poverty Porn and Doxosophy'. *Sociological Research Online* 19 (3): 3. https://doi.org/10.5153/sro.3441.

Johnson, James H. 1996. *Listening in Paris: A Cultural History*. Berkeley: University of California Press.

Johnson, Julian. 2002. *Who Needs Classical Music? Cultural Choice and Musical Value*. Oxford: Oxford University Press.

Johnson-Hill, Erin. 2015. 'Re-examining the Academy: Music Institutions and Empire in Nineteenth-Century London'. PhD thesis. New Haven: Yale University.

Jordan, Tim, Brigid McClure, and Kath Woodward, eds. 2017. *Culture, Identity and Intense Performativity: Being in the Zone*. New York: Routledge.

Juuti, Sini, and Karen Littleton. 2010. 'Musical Identities in Transition: Solo-Piano Students' Accounts of Entering the Academy'. *Psychology of Music* 38 (4): 481–97. https://doi.org/10.1177/0305735609351915.

Kane, David, and Jenny Clark. 2012. 'Music Education Charities: The Size and Scope of Music Education Charities in England'. Arts Council England, NCVO Research. http://www.artscouncil.org.uk/media/uploads/music_education_report.pdf.

Kassabian, Anahid. 2013. *Ubiquitous Listening Affect, Attention, and Distributed Subjectivity*. Berkeley: University of California Press. http://site.ebrary.com/id/10669203.

Kehily, Mary Jane, and Anoop Nayak. 1997. '"Lads and Laughter": Humour and the Production of Heterosexual Hierarchies'. *Gender and Education* 9 (1): 69–88. https://doi.org/10.1080/09540259721466.

Kerman, Joseph. 1988. *Opera as Drama*. Berkeley: University of California Press.

Kerres, B. 2012. 'Performing Leadership'. *Business Strategy Review* 23 (1): 56–59. https://doi.org/10.1111/j.1467-8616.2012.00821.x.

Khan, Omar, and Faiza Shaheen. 2017. 'Minority Report: Race and Class in Post-Brexit Britain'. London: Runnymede Trust. http://classonline.org.uk/docs/Race_and_Class_Post-Brexit_Perspectives_report_v5.pdf.

Khan, Shamus Rahman. 2012. *Privilege: The Making of an Adolescent Elite at St. Paul's School*. Princeton, NJ: Princeton University Press.

King, Anthony, and Daniel Smith. 2017. 'The Jack Wills Crowd: Towards a Sociology of an Elite Subculture'. *British Journal of Sociology* 69 (1): 44–66. https://doi.org/10.1111/1468-4446.12254.

Kingsbury, Henry. 1988. *Music, Talent, and Performance: A Conservatory Cultural System*. Philadelphia: Temple University Press.

Kok, Roe-Min. 2011. 'Music for a Postcolonial Child: Theorizing Malaysian Memories'. In *Learning, Teaching, and Musical Identity: Voices across Cultures*, edited by Lucy Green, 73–90. Bloomington: Indiana University Press.

Koza, Julia Eklund. 2008. 'Listening for Whiteness: Hearing Racial Politics in Undergraduate School Music'. *Philosophy of Music Education Review* 16 (2): 145–55.

Kramer, Lawrence. 2009. *Why Classical Music Still Matters*. Berkeley: University of California Press.

Kulz, Christy. 2017. *Factories for Learning: Producing Race and Class Inequality in the Neoliberal Academy*. Manchester: Manchester University Press.

Laing, Dave, and Norton York. 2000. 'The Value of Music in London'. *Cultural Trends* 10 (38): 1–34. https://doi.org/10.1080/09548960009365116.

Lambeau, Céline. 2015. '"As a Chief Needs Men, So Men Need a Chief"'. Translated by Maggie Jones. *Transposition. Musique et Sciences Sociales*, 5 (September): 1–24. http://transposition.revues.org/1364.

Lamont, Alexandra, David J. Hargreaves, Nigel A. Marshall, and Mark Tarrant. 2003. 'Young People's Music in and out of School'. *British Journal of Music Education* 20 (3): 229–41. https://doi.org/10.1017/S0265051703005412.

Lamont, Michèle. 1992a. *Cultivating Differences: Symbolic Boundaries and the Making of Inequality*. Chicago: University of Chicago Press.

———. 1992b. *Money, Morals and Manners. The Culture of the French and American Upper-Middle Class*. Chicago: University of Chicago Press.

Lamont, Michèle, and Annette Lareau. 1988. 'Cultural Capital: Allusions, Gaps and Glissandos in Recent Theoretical Developments'. *Sociological Theory* 6 (2): 153–68. https://doi.org/10.2307/202113.

Lareau, Annette. 2011. *Unequal Childhoods: Class, Race, and Family Life*. 2nd ed. Berkeley: University of California Press.

Laurence, Felicity. 2010. 'Listening to Children: Voice, Agency and Ownership in School Musicking'. In *Sociology and Music Education*, edited by Ruth Wright, 243–62. Farnham: Ashgate.

Laurendeau, Jason. 2008. '"Gendered Risk Regimes": A Theoretical Consideration of Edgework and Gender'. *Sociology of Sport Journal* 25 (3): 293–309.

Lebler, Don. 2007. 'Student-as-Master? Reflections on a Learning Innovation in Popular Music Pedagogy'. *International Journal of Music Education* 25 (3): 205–21. https://doi.org/10.1177/0255761407083575.

Le Bon, Gustav. 1960 [1895]. *The Crowd: A Study of the Popular Mind*. New York: Viking.

Lebrecht, Norman. 2014. 'When a Conductor Hits a Player'. *Slipped Disc* (blog). 26 February. http://slippedisc.com/2014/02/when-a-conductor-hits-a-player/.

Leech-Wilkinson, Daniel. 2016. 'Classical Music as Enforced Utopia'. *Arts and Humanities in Higher Education* 15 (3–4): 325–36. https://doi.org/10.1177/1474022216647706.

Legg, Robert. 2012. 'Bach, Beethoven, Bourdieu: "Cultural Capital" and the Scholastic Canon in England's A-Level Examinations'. *Curriculum Journal*, 23 (2): 157–72.

Lenskyj, Helen. 1992. 'Unsafe at Home Base: Women's Experiences of Sexual Harassment in University Sport and Physical Education'. *Women in Sport and Physical Activity Journal* 1 (1): 19–33. https://doi.org/10.1123/wspaj.1.1.19.

Leppänen, Taru. 2015. 'The West and the Rest of Classical Music: Asian Musicians in the Finnish Media Coverage of the 1995 Jean Sibelius Violin Competition'. *European Journal of Cultural Studies* 18 (1): 19–34. https://doi.org/10.1177/1367549414557804.

Leppert, Richard. 1995. *The Sight of Sound: Music, Representation, and the History of the Body*. Berkeley: University of California Press.

Lewis, Justin. 2013. *Art, Culture and Enterprise (Routledge Revivals): The Politics of Art and the Cultural Industries*. Abingdon: Routledge.

Lewis, Leslie Anne. 2012. 'The Incomplete Conductor: Theorizing the Conductor's Role in Orchestral Interpretation in the Light of Shared Leadership Practices'. PhD dissertation. London: Royal Holloway, University of London.

Leys, Ruth. 2011. 'The Turn to Affect: A Critique'. *Critical Inquiry* 37 (3): 434–72. https://doi.org/10.1086/659353.

Littler, Jo. 2017. *Against Meritocracy: Culture, Power and Myths of Mobility*. Abingdon, Oxon: Routledge.

Logie, Nicholas. 2012. 'The Role of Leadership in Conducting Orchestras'. PhD dissertation. Milton Keynes: Open University. http://oro.open.ac.uk/38069/.

Long, Marion, Andrea Creech, Helena Gaunt, and Susan Hallam. 2014. 'Conservatoire Students' Experiences and Perceptions of Instrument-Specific Master Classes'. *Music Education Research* 16 (2): 176–92. https://doi.org/10.1080/14613808.2013.859659.

Lonie, Douglas, and Luke Dickens. 2014. 'Rehearsal Spaces for Young People: Communities of Practice and the Place of Participation in Non-formal Music Education'. In *Informal Education and Children's Everyday Lives: Geographies, Histories and Practices*, edited by Peter Kraftl and Sarah Mills, 163–96. Basingstoke: Palgrave Macmillan.

Lonie, Douglas, and Ben Sandbrook. 2011. 'Ingredients for Encouraging the Talent and Potential of Young Musicians'. Dartington Hall, Devon: South West Music School. http://www.foundations-for-excellence.org/digi/.

Loveday, Vik. 2014. 'Working-Class Participation, Middle-Class Aspiration? Value, Upward Mobility and Symbolic Indebtedness in Higher Education'. *Sociological Review*, 63 (3), 570–88. https://doi.org/10.1111/1467-954X.12167.

———. 2015. 'Embodying Deficiency through "Affective Practice": Shame, Relationality, and the Lived Experience of Social Class and Gender in Higher Education'. *Sociology*, 50 (6): 1140–55. https://doi.org/10.1177/0038038515589301.

Lubet, Alex. 2009. 'The Inclusion of Music/the Music of Inclusion'. *International Journal of Inclusive Education* 13 (7): 727–39. https://doi.org/10.1080/13603110903046010.

Lupton, Deborah. 2013. *Risk*. 2nd ed. London: Routledge.

Lynch, Michael. 2010. 'Music in the Training Colleges of England and Wales 1872–1899: Perspectives from HMI'. *British Journal of Music Education* 27 (2): 171–84. https://doi.org/10.1017/S0265051710000070.

Malik, Sarita. 2013. '"Creative Diversity": UK Public Service Broadcasting after Multiculturalism'. *Popular Communication* 11 (3): 227–41. https://doi.org/10.1080/15405702.2013.810081.

Martin, Peter J. 1995. *Sounds and Society: Themes in the Sociology of Music*. Music and Society. Manchester: Manchester University Press.

Maxwell, Claire, and Peter Aggleton. 2013. 'Becoming Accomplished: Concerted Cultivation among Privately Educated Young Women'. *Pedagogy, Culture and Society* 21 (1): 75–93. https://doi.org/10.1080/14681366.2012.748682.

McClary, Susan. 1989. 'The blasphemy of talking politics during Bach Year'. In *Music and Society: The Politics of Composition, Performance and Reception*, edited by Richard Leppert and Susan McClary, 13–62. Cambridge: Cambridge University Press.

———. 2001. *Conventional Wisdom: The Content of Musical Form*. New ed. Berkeley: University of California Press.

———. 2002. *Feminine Endings: Music, Gender, and Sexuality.* Minneapolis: University of Minnesota Press.

McClelland, Lisa, and Arthur Crisp. 2001. 'Anorexia Nervosa and Social Class'. *International Journal of Eating Disorders* 29 (2): 150–56. https://doi.org/10.1002/1098-108X(200103)29:2<150::AID-EAT1004>3.0.CO;2-I.

McClintock, Anne. 1995. *Imperial Leather: Race, Gender, and Sexuality in the Colonial Conquest.* New York: Routledge.

McCormick, Lisa. 2015. *Performing Civility: International Competitions in Classical Music.* Cambridge: Cambridge University Press.

McGuire, Charles Edward. 2009. *Music and Victorian Philanthropy: The Tonic Sol-Fa Movement.* Cambridge: Cambridge University Press.

McNeill, William Hardy. 1995. *Keeping Together in Time: Dance and Drill in Human History.* Cambridge, MA: Harvard University Press.

McRobbie, Angela. 2008. *The Aftermath of Feminism: Gender, Culture and Social Change.* London: Sage.

———. 2015. *Be Creative: Making a Living in the New Culture Industries.* Cambridge: Polity Press.

McShane, Brian. 2018. 'The Place of Trust: Young Men, Relationality and Everyday Violence'. PhD dissertation. London: Goldsmiths, University of London.

McVeigh, Alice. 2016. 'Faking It—The Great Unmentionable of Orchestral Playing'. *The Strad*, 27 September. https://www.thestrad.com/faking-it--the-great-unmentionable-of-orchestral-playing/2149.article.

McVeigh, Simon. 2004. '"An Audience for High-Class Music": Concert Promoters and Entrepreneurs in Late-Nineteenth-Century London'. In *The Musician as Entrepreneur, 1700–1914: Managers, Charlatans, and Idealists*, edited by William Weber, 162–83. Bloomington: Indiana University Press.

Measham, Fiona. 2002. '"Doing Gender"—"Doing Drugs": Conceptualizing the Gendering of Drugs Cultures'. *Contemporary Drug Problems* 29 (2): 335–73. https://doi.org/10.1177/009145090202900206.

Mellor, Philip A., and Chris Shilling. 1997. *Re-forming the Body: Religion, Community and Modernity.* London: Sage.

Mendick, Heather, Kim Allen, and Laura Harvey. 2015. '"We Can Get Everything We Want If We Try Hard": Young People, Celebrity, Hard Work'. *British Journal of Educational Studies* 63 (2): 161–78. https://doi.org/10.1080/00071005.2014.1002382.

Mendick, Heather, Aisha Ahmad, Kim Allen, and Laura Harvey. 2018. *Celebrity, Aspiration and Contemporary Youth: Education and Inequality in an Era of Austerity.* London: Bloomsbury.

Middleton, Richard. 1990. *Studying Popular Music.* Milton Keynes: Open University Press.

Miles, Andrew, and Alice Sullivan. 2012. 'Understanding Participation in Culture and Sport: Mixing Methods, Reordering Knowledges'. *Cultural Trends* 21 (4): 311–24. https://doi.org/10.1080/09548963.2012.726795.

Milestone, Rachel. 2007. 'The Town Hall as Music Venue in Nineteenth-Century Stalybridge'. In *Music in the British Provinces, 1690–1914*, edited by Rachel Cowgill and Peter Holman, 295–324. Illustrated edition. Farnham: Ashgate.

Ministry of Justice, Home Office, and Office for National Statistics. 2013. 'An Overview of Sexual Offending in England & Wales'. http://www.ons.gov.uk/ons/rel/crime-stats/an-overview-of-sexual-offending-in-england---wales/december-2012/index.html.

Monk, Craig. 2014. 'Focus on Funding'. *PRS Members Music Magazine*, September, 13.

Moran, Leslie J., and Beverley Skeggs. 2003. *Sexuality and the Politics of Violence and Safety.* New York: Routledge.

Moretti, Franco. 2014. *The Bourgeois: Between History and Literature.* Reprint. Brooklyn, NY: Verso.

Morrison, Toni. 1992. *Playing in the Dark: Whiteness and the Literary Imagination.* Cambridge, MA: Harvard University Press.

Musicians' Union. 2018. 'The MU—Training'. https://www.musiciansunion.org.uk/Home/Advice/Education/Safeguarding-Child-Protection/Training.

Nead, Lynda. 1988. *Myths of Sexuality: Representations of Women in Victorian Britain.* Oxford: Basil Blackwell.

Neale, Stephen. 1980. *Genre*. London: British Film Institute.

Neelands, Jonothan, Eleanora Belfiore, Catriona Firth, Natalie Hart, Liese Perrin, Susan Brock, Dominic Holdaway, and Jane Woddis. 2015. 'Enriching Britain: Culture, Creativity and Growth'. University of Warwick. http://www2.warwick.ac.uk/research/warwickcommission/futureculture/finalreport/warwick_commission_report_2015.pdf.

Nettl, Bruno. 1995. *Heartland Excursions: Ethnomusicological Reflections on Schools of Music*. Music in American Life. Urbana: University of Illinois Press.

Nicholls, Emily. 2018. *Running the Tightrope: Managing Femininities and Identities on a Girls' Night Out*. London: Palgrave Macmillan.

Nisbett, Melissa, and Ben Walmsley. 2016. 'The Romanticization of Charismatic Leadership in the Arts'. *Journal of Arts Management, Law, and Society* 46 (1): 1–11.

Nooshin, Laudan. 2011. 'Introduction to the Special Issue: The Ethnomusicology of Western Art Music'. *Ethnomusicology Forum* 20 (3): 285–300. https://doi.org/10.1080/17411912.2011.659439.

Nylander, Erik, and Andreas Melldahl. 2015. 'Playing with Capital: Inherited and Acquired Assets in a Jazz Audition'. *Poetics* 48 (suppl. C): 83–106. https://doi.org/10.1016/j.poetic.2014.12.002.

Oakley, Kate, and Dave O'Brien. 2015. 'Cultural Value and Inequality. A Critical Literature Review'. Swindon: Arts and Humanities Research Council.

O'Brien, Dave. 2013. *Cultural Policy: Management, Value and Modernity in the Creative Industries*. London: Routledge.

O'Brien, Dave, Daniel Laurison, Andrew Miles, and Sam Friedman. 2016. 'Are the Creative Industries Meritocratic? An Analysis of the 2014 British Labour Force Survey'. *Cultural Trends* 25 (2): 116–31. https://doi.org/10.1080/09548963.2016.1170943.

OED. 2006. 'Practise | Practice, V.' OED Online. December. http://www.oed.com/view/Entry/149234.

Olcese, Cristiana, and Mike Savage. 2015. 'Notes towards a "Social Aesthetic": Guest Editors' Introduction to the Special Section'. *British Journal of Sociology* 66 (4): 720–37. https://doi.org/10.1111/1468-4446.12159.

Orbach, Susie. 1993. *Hunger Strike: The Anorectic's Struggle as a Metaphor for Our Age*. 2nd ed. London: Penguin.

O'Toole, Patricia. 1994. 'I Sing in a Choir but I Have No Voice!' *Quarterly Journal of Music Teaching and Learning* 4 (5): 1–26.

Pace, Ian. 2013. 'The Culture of Music Education Lends Itself to Abuse'. *Times Educational Supplement*, 11 May. https://www.tes.com/article.aspx?storyCode=6333285.

———. 2015a. 'Music Teacher Sentenced to 11 Years in Prison as Abuse Film Whiplash Prepares for Oscars'. *The Conversation* 20 February. http://theconversation.com/music-teacher-sentenced-to-11-years-in-prison-as-abuse-film-whiplash-prepares-for-oscars-37786.

———. 2015b. 'The Origins and Early History of the Five Specialist Music Schools in the UK during the Cold War (1962–1978): Organisation, Ideology and Pedagogical Traditions'. Presented at 'Music education and abuse of children and young people: historical and sociological perspectives', 15 September, Institute of Musical Research, University of London, Senate House.

———. 2017. 'The Insidious Class Divide in Music Teaching'. *The Conversation*, 17 May. http://theconversation.com/the-insidious-class-divide-in-music-teaching-77574.

Palmer, Roger. 2008. 'Questions arising from the views of some members of four amateur classical music organizations'. *International Journal of Community Music* 1 (2): 203–16. https://doi.org/info:doi/10.1386/ijcm.1.2.203_1.

Perkins, Rosie. 2011. 'The Construction of "Learning Cultures": An Ethnographically-Informed Case Study of a UK Conservatoire'. PhD dissertation, University of Cambridge.

———. 2013. 'Hierarchies and Learning in the Conservatoire: Exploring What Students Learn through the Lens of Bourdieu'. *Research Studies in Music Education* 35 (2): 197–212. https://doi.org/10.1177/1321103X13508060.

Pew Research Center, 2008. 'Inside the Middle Class: Bad Times Hit the Good Life'. *Pew Research Center's Social & Demographic Trends Project* (blog). 9 April. http://www.pewsocialtrends.org/2008/04/09/inside-the-middle-class-bad-times-hit-the-good-life/.
Philpott, Chris. 2001. 'Equality of Opportunity and Instrumental Tuition'. In *Issues in Music Teaching*, edited by Chris Philpott and Charles Plummeridge, 156–69. Issues in Subject Teaching Series. London: RoutledgeFalmer.
———. 2010. 'The Sociological Critique of Curriculum Music in England: Is Radical Change Really Possible?' In *Sociology and Music Education*, edited by Ruth Wright, 81–92. Farnham: Ashgate.
Philpott, Chris, and Gary Spruce. 2012. *Debates in Music Teaching*. Debates in Subject Teaching Series. New York: Routledge.
Pickett, Kate, and Richard Wilkinson. 2010. *The Spirit Level: Why Equality Is Better for Everyone*. London: Penguin.
Pidd, Helen. 2013. '39 Manchester Music School Teachers Face Inquiry'. *The Guardian*, 7 May, sec. UK News. http://www.guardian.co.uk/uk/2013/may/07/manchester-music-schools-teachers-investigation?INTCMP=SRCH.
Pieper, Antje. 2008. 'Music and Middle-Class Culture in Early Nineteenth-Century Leipzig and Birmingham'. *Cultural and Social History* 5 (1): 53–73. https://doi.org/10.2752/147800408X267256.
Pitts, Stephanie. 2000. *A Century of Change in Music Education: Historical Perspectives on Contemporary Practice in British Secondary School Music*. Farnham: Ashgate.
Ponchione, Cayenna. 2013. 'Exploring a Metamorphosis: Identity Formation for an Emerging Conductor'. *Arts and Humanities in Higher Education* 12 (2–3): 181–93. https://doi.org/10.1177/1474022212473529.
Power, Sally, Andrew Curtis, Geoff Whitty, and Tony Edwards. 2010. 'Private Education and Disadvantage: The Experiences of Assisted Place Holders'. *International Studies in Sociology of Education* 20 (1): 23–38. https://doi.org/10.1080/09620211003655622.
Press Association. 2012. 'Only Two-Thirds of British Children Live with Both Parents'. *The Guardian*, 29 December, sec. Life and Style. http://www.theguardian.com/lifeandstyle/2012/dec/29/two-thirds-british-children-live-parents.
Prieur, Annick, and Mike Savage. 2013. 'Emerging Forms of Cultural Capital'. *European Societies* 15 (2): 246–67. https://doi.org/10.1080/14616696.2012.748930.
Purcell School. n.d. 'Headmaster's Welcome'. Accessed 28 January 2018. http://www.purcell-school.org/headmasters-welcome.html.
Puwar, Nirmal. 2004. *Space Invaders: Race, Gender and Bodies Out of Place*. Oxford: Berg.
Ravet, Hyacinthe. 2016. 'Negotiated Authority, Shared Creativity: Cooperation Models among Conductors and Performers'. *Musicae Scientiae* 20 (3): 287–303. https://doi.org/10.1177/1029864915617232.
RCM. 2017. 'Expected Standard | Royal College of Music'. 2017. http://www.rcm.ac.uk/junior/howtoapply/expectedstandard/.
Reading Youth Orchestra. 2014. 'History of the Reading Youth Orchestra 1944–1954: Reading Youth Orchestra (RYO)'. http://www.readingyouthorchestra.co.uk/our-history/history-of-the-reading-youth-orchestra-1944-1954/#.VGI2bY-me8Y.
Reay, Diane. 1998. 'Setting the Agenda: The Growing Impact of Market Forces on Pupil Grouping in British Secondary Schooling'. *Journal of Curriculum Studies* 30 (5): 545–58. https://doi.org/10.1080/002202798183440.
———. 2004a. 'Education and Cultural Capital: The Implications of Changing Trends in Education Policies'. *Cultural Trends* 13 (2): 73–86. https://doi.org/10.1080/0954896042000267161.
———. 2004b. 'Gendering Bourdieu's Concepts of Capitals? Emotional Capital, Women and Social Class'. *Sociological Review* 52 (s2): 57–74. https://doi.org/10.1111/j.1467-954X.2005.00524.x.

———. 2004c. '"Mostly Roughs and Toughs": Social Class, Race and Representation in Inner City Schooling'. *Sociology* 38 (5): 1005–23. https://doi.org/10.1177/0038038504047183.

———. 2017. *Miseducation*. Bristol: Policy Press.

Reay, Diane, Gill Crozier, and David James. 2011. *White Middle-Class Identities and Urban Schooling*. Basingstoke,: Palgrave Macmillan.

Richens, Frances. 2016. 'Classical Music Becoming Middle Class, Committee Hears'. *ArtsProfessional*, 9 September. http://www.artsprofessional.co.uk/news/classical-music-becoming-middle-class-committee-hears.

Rivera, Lauren A. 2016. *Pedigree: How Elite Students Get Elite Jobs*. Rev. ed. Princeton, NJ: Princeton University Press.

Robin, William. 2017. 'What Controversial Changes at Harvard Mean for Music in the University'. *The Log Journal* (blog). https://nationalsawdust.org/thelog/2017/04/25/what-controversial-changes-at-harvard-means-for-music-in-the-university/.

Rodriguez, Eva Moreda, and Björn Heile. 2017. 'Introduction'. In *Higher Education in Music in the Twenty-First Century*, edited by Björn Heile, Eva Moreda Rodriguez, and Jane Stanley, 1–10. Abingdon: Routledge.

Rogers, Lynne, and Susan Hallam. 2010. 'Music Services'. In *Music Education in the 21st Century in the United Kingdom: Achievements, Analysis and Aspirations*, 279–94. London: Institute of Education.

Rohr, Deborah. 1999. 'Women and the Music Profession in Victorian England: The Royal Society of Female Musicians, 1839–1866'. *Journal of Musicological Research* 18 (4): 307–46. https://doi.org/10.1080/01411899908574762.

Rollock, Nicola, David Gillborn, Carol Vincent, and Stephen J. Ball. 2015. *The Colour of Class: The Educational Strategies of the Black Middle Classes*. London: Routledge.

Romer, Christy. 2018. 'Arts Council Will "Push NPOs Hard" to Collect Diversity Data'. *ArtsProfessional*, 19 January. https://www.artsprofessional.co.uk/news/arts-council-will-push-npos-hard-collect-diversity-data?utm_source=Weekly-News&utm_medium=email&utm_content=nid-207446&utm_campaign=19th-January-2018.

Rosen, Charles. 2002. *Piano Notes: The World of the Pianist by Charles Rosen*. New York: Penguin.

Ross, Alex. 2008. *The Rest Is Noise: Listening to the Twentieth Century*. London: Harper Perennial.

Sagiv, Dan. 2013. 'Discipline and Pleasure: "Dual Pedagogy" Conserving an Elitist Tradition in the Instruction of Classical Music in Israeli Conservatories'. PhD dissertation. Hebrew University of Jerusalem.

Sagiv, Dan, and Clare Hall. 2015. 'Producing a Classical Habitus: Reconsidering Instrumental Music Teaching Methods'. In *Bourdieu and the Sociology of Music Education*, edited by Pamela Burnard, Yiva Hofvander Trulsson, and Johan Soderman, 113–26. Farnham: Ashgate.

Saha, Anamik. 2017. *Race and the Cultural Industries*. Malden, MA: Polity Press.

Savage, Mike. 2000. *Class Analysis and Social Transformation*. Buckingham, UK: Open University Press.

———. 2003. 'Review Essay: A New Class Paradigm?' *British Journal of Sociology of Education* 24 (4): 535–41. https://doi.org/10.1080/01425690301920.

———. 2006. 'The Musical Field'. *Cultural Trends* 15 (2–3): 159–74. https://doi.org/10.1080/09548960600712975.

———. 2010. *Identities and Social Change in Britain since 1940: The Politics of Method*. Oxford: Oxford University Press.

———. 2014. 'FOCUS: Social Change in the 21st Century: The New Sociology of "Wealth Elites"'. *Discover Society*, 1 December. http://discoversociety.org/2014/12/01/focus-social-change-in-the-21st-century-the-new-sociology-of-wealth-elites/.

Savage, Mike, and Karel Williams. 2008. 'Elites: Remembered in Capitalism and Forgotten by Social Sciences'. *Sociological Review* 56 (1): 1–24. https://doi.org/10.1111/j.1467-954X.2008.00759.x.

Scharff, Christina. 2015. 'Equality and Diversity in the Classical Music Profession'. Kings College London. http://blogs.kcl.ac.uk/young-female-and-entrepreneurial/files/2014/02/Equality-and-Diversity-in-the-Classical-Music-Profession.pdf.

———. 2016. 'Gender and Neoliberalism: Young Women as Ideal Neoliberal Subjects '. In *The Handbook of Neoliberalism*, edited by S. Springer, K. Birch, and J. MacLeavy. Abingdon: Routledge. Routledge Handbooks Online. https://www.routledgehandbooks.com/citation?doi=10.4324/9781315730660.

———. 2017. *Gender, Subjectivity, and Cultural Work: The Classical Music Profession*. London: Routledge.

Scott, Edward. 2018. *'Music Education in Schools' (Library Briefing)*. London: House of Lords.

Schnurr, Stephanie. 2008. 'Surviving in a Man's World with a Sense of Humour: An Analysis of Women Leaders' Use of Humour at Work'. *Leadership* 4 (3): 299–319. https://doi.org/10.1177/1742715008092363.

Seddon, Laura. 2013. *British Women Composers and Instrumental Chamber Music in the Early Twentieth Century*. Farnham: Routledge.

Seidler, Victor J. 1989. *Rediscovering Masculinity: Reason, Language and Sexuality*. London: Routledge.

Sennett, Richard. 1992. *The Fall of Public Man*. London: W. W. Norton.

———. 2009. *The Craftsman*. London: Penguin.

———. 2012. *Together: The Rituals, Pleasures and Politics of Co-operation*. London: Allen Lane.

Service, Tom. 2009. 'Why We Are Shutting Children Out of Classical Music'. *The Guardian*, 2 April, sec. Music. http://www.theguardian.com/music/2009/apr/02/classical-music-children.

Sharp, Caroline, and Adam Rabiasz. 2016. 'Key Data on Music Education Hubs 2015'. Slough: National foundation for Educational Research.

Shepherd, John, and Graham Vulliamy. 1994. 'The Struggle for Culture: A Sociological Case Study of the Development of a National Music Curriculum'. *British Journal of Sociology of Education* 15 (1): 27–40.

Shilling, Chris. 2004. 'Physical Capital and Situated Action: A New Direction for Corporeal Sociology'. *British Journal of Sociology of Education* 25 (4): 473–87.http://search.ebscohost.com/login.aspx?direct=true&db=edsjsr&AN=edsjsr.4128672&site=eds-live.

Showalter, Elaine. 1987. *The Female Malady: Women, Madness, and English Culture, 1830–1980*. London: Virago.

Skeggs, Beverley. 1997. *Formations of Class and Gender: Becoming Respectable*. London: Sage.

———. 2003. *Class, Self, Culture*. London: Routledge.

———. 2005. 'Exchange, Value and Affect: Bourdieu and 'the Self''. *Sociological Review* 52 (s2): 75–95. https://doi.org/10.1111/j.1467-954X.2005.00525.x.

———. 2010. 'Class, Culture and Morality: Legacies and Logics in the Space for Identification'. In *The Sage Handbook of Identities*, edited by Margaret Wetherell and Chandra Talpade Mohanty, 339–59. London: Sage.

Skeggs, Beverley, and Helen Wood. 2012. *Reacting to Reality Television: Performance, Audience and Value*. New York: Routledge.

Small, Christopher. 1996. *Music, Society, Education*. Middletown, CT: Wesleyan University Press.

———. 1998. *Musicking: The Meanings of Performing and Listening*. Middletown, CT: Wesleyan University Press.

Solie, Ruth A. 2004. *Music in Other Words: Victorian Conversations*. California Studies in 19th Century Music 12. Berkeley: University of California Press.

Spitzer, John. 1996. 'Metaphors of the Orchestra: The Orchestra as a Metaphor'. *Musical Quarterly* 80 (2): 234–64. https://doi.org/10.1093/mq/80.2.234.

Spruce, Gary. 2013. 'Participation, Inclusion, Diversity, and the Policy of English Music Education'. In *Reaching Out: Music Education with "Hard to Reach" Children and Young People*, edited by Chris Harrison, 23–31. London: UK Association for Music Education.

———. 2015. 'Music Education, Social Justice, and the "Student Voice"'. In *The Oxford Handbook of Social Justice in Music Education*, edited by Cathy Benedict, Patrick Schmidt, Gary Spruce, and Paul Woodford, 287–301. New York: Oxford University Press.

Stables, Andrew, and Sian Stables. 1995. 'Gender Differences in Students' Approaches to A-Level Subject Choices and Perceptions of A-Level Subjects: A Study of First-Year A-Level Students

in a Tertiary College'. *Educational Research* 37 (1): 39–51. https://doi.org/10.1080/0013188950370104.
Stahl, Garth, Pamela Burnard, and Rosie Perkins. 2017. 'Critical Reflections on the Use of Bourdieu's Tools "In Concert" to Understand the Practices of Learning in Three Musical Sites'. *Sociological Research Online* 22 (3): 57–77. https://doi.org/10.1177/1360780417724073.
Steedman, Carolyn. 2000. 'Enforced Narratives: Stories of Another Self'. In *Feminism and Autobiography*, edited by Tess Coslett, Celia Lury, and Penny Summerfield, 25–39. Transformations: Thinking through Feminism. London: Routledge.
Stewart, Simon. 2012. 'Evaluating Culture: Sociology, Aesthetics and Policy'. *Sociological Research Online* 18 (1): 14.
Straus, Joseph N. 2006. 'Normalizing the Abnormal: Disability in Music and Music Theory'. *Journal of the American Musicological Society* 59 (1): 113–84. https://doi.org/10.1525/jams.2006.59.1.113.
Strubler, David C., and Robert Evangelista. 2009. 'Maestro Neeme Jarvi on Leadership: The Power of Innovation, Stakeholder Relations, Teamwork, and Nonverbal Communication'. *Journal of Management Inquiry* 18 (2): 119–21. https://doi.org/10.1177/1056492609333413.
Stuckey, Priscilla. 1995. 'Light Dispels Darkness: Gender, Ritual, and Society in Mozart's "The Magic Flute"'. *Journal of Feminist Studies in Religion* 11 (1): 5–39. https://doi.org/10.2307/25002242.
Subotnik, Rose Rosengard. 1991. 'Whose "Magic Flute"? Intimations of Reality at the Gates of the Enlightenment'. *19th-Century Music* 15 (2): 132–50. https://doi.org/10.2307/746368.
Sullivan, Alice. 2001. 'Cultural Capital and Educational Attainment'. *Sociology* 35 (4): 893–912. https://doi.org/10.1177/0038038501035004006.
Talbot, Michael, ed. 2002. *The Business of Music*. Liverpool Music Symposium 2. Liverpool: Liverpool University Press.
Tampubolon, Gindo. 2010. 'Social Stratification and Cultures Hierarchy among the Omnivores: Evidence from the Arts Council England Surveys'. *Sociological Review* 58 (1): 1–25. https://doi.org/10.1111/j.1467-954X.2009.01880.x.
Tarde, Gabriel. 2011 [1890]. *The Laws of Imitation*. Charleston: Nabu Press.
Taruskin, Richard. 1995. *Text and Act: Essays on Music and Performance*. New York: Oxford University Press.
Taylor, Charles. 1989. *Sources of the Self: The Making of the Modern Identity*. Cambridge: Cambridge University Press.
Taylor, Nick. 2018. 'The Return of Character: Parallels between Late-Victorian and Twenty-First Century Discourses'. *Sociological Research Online* 23 (2): 399–415. https://doi.org/10.1177/1360780418769679.
Taylor, Stephanie, and Karen Littleton. 2012. *Contemporary Identities of Creativity and Creative Work*. Farnham: Routledge.
Taylor, Timothy Dean. 2007. *Beyond Exoticism: Western Music and the World*. Durham, NC: Duke University Press.
Tregear, Peter, Geir Johansen, Harald Jørgensen, John Sloboda, Helena Tulve, and Richard Wistreich. 2016. 'Conservatoires in Society: Institutional Challenges and Possibilities for Change'. *Arts and Humanities in Higher Education* 15 (3–4): 276–92. https://doi.org/10.1177/1474022216647379.
US Department of Commerce, Economics and Statistics Administration. 2010. 'Middle Class in America'. Office of the Vice President of the United States Middle Class Task Force. http://2010-2014.commerce.gov/sites/default/files/documents/migrated/Middle%20Class%20Report.pdf.
Vaugeois, Lise C. 2014. 'Colonization and the Institutionalization of Hierarchies of the Human through Music Education: Studies in the Education of Feeling'. PhD dissertation. University of Toronto.
Vincent, Carol, and Stephen J. Ball. 2007. '"Making Up" the Middle-Class Child: Families, Activities and Class Dispositions'. *Sociology* 41 (6): 1061–77. https://doi.org/10.1177/0038038507082315.

Vincent, Carol, Sarah Neal, and Humera Iqbal. 2015. 'Friendship and Diversity: Children's and Adults' Friendships across Social Class and Ethnic Difference'. https://friendshipacrossdifference.files.wordpress.com/2015/07/mf-final-dissemination-report.pdf.

Vincent, Carol, Nicola Rollock, Stephen Ball, and David Gillborn. 2012a. 'Being Strategic, Being Watchful, Being Determined: Black Middle-Class Parents and Schooling'. *British Journal of Sociology of Education* 33 (3): 337–54. https://doi.org/10.1080/01425692.2012.668833.

———. 2012b. 'Raising Middle-Class Black Children: Parenting Priorities, Actions and Strategies'. *Sociology* 47 (3): 427–42. https://doi.org/10.1177/0038038512454244.

Vredenburgh, Donald, and Irene Yunxia He. 2003. 'Leadership Lessons from a Conductor-less Orchestra'. *Business Horizons* 46 (5): 19–24. https://doi.org/10.1016/S0007-6813(03)00067-3.

Wacquant, Loïc J. D. 1991. 'Making Class: The Middle Class(es) in Social Theory and Social Structure'. In *Bringing Class Back In: Contemporary and Historical Perspectives*, edited by Scott McNall, Rhonda F. Levine, and Rick Fantasia, 39–64. Boulder, CO: Routledge.

Wagner, Izabela. 2015. *Producing Excellence: The Making of Virtuosos*. New Brunswick, NJ: Rutgers University Press.

Walkerdine, Valerie, Helen Lucey, and June Melody. 2001. *Growing Up Girl: Psychosocial Explorations of Gender and Class*. New York: New York University Press.

Walser, Robert. 1997. '"Out of Notes": Signification, Interpretation, and the Problem of Miles Davis'. In *Keeping Score: Music, Disciplinarity, Culture*, edited by Anahid Kassabian, David Schwarz and Lawrence Siegel, 147–68. Charlottesville: University Press of Virginia.

Weber, Max. 2001. *The Protestant Ethic and the Spirit of Capitalism*. Chicago: Fitzroy Dearborn.

Weber, William. 2004. *Music and the Middle Class: The Social Structure of Concert Life in London, Paris and Vienna between 1830 and 1848*. Revised edition. Farnham: Ashgate.

Weeks, Peter. 1996. 'A Rehearsal of a Beethoven Passage: An Analysis of Correction Talk'. *Research on Language and Social Interaction* 29 (3): 247–90. https://doi.org/10.1207/s15327973rlsi2903_3.

Weiss, Gail. 1999. *Body Images: Embodiment as Intercorporeality*. New York: Routledge.

Williams, Nick. 2015. 'Hoketus: Of Hierarchy and Hiccups'. *Tempo* 69 (273): 5–11. https://doi.org/10.1017/S004029821500008X.

Williams, Raymond. 1976. *Keywords: A Vocabulary of Culture and Society*. Fontana Communications Series. London: Fontana.

Willis, Paul E. 1978. *Profane Culture*. London: Routledge and Kegan Paul.

Wolff, Janet. 1993. *The Social Production of Art*. 2nd ed. New York: New York University Press.

Woolf, Nicky. 2015. 'Decision to Scrap Blackface from Otello Not Complicated, Says Met Director'. *The Guardian*, 22 September. http://www.theguardian.com/music/2015/sep/22/otello-metropolitan-opera-scraps-blackface.

Woolfe, Zachary. 2013. 'Female Conductors Search for Equality at Highest Level'. *New York Times*, 20 December. http://www.nytimes.com/2013/12/22/arts/music/female-conductors-search-for-equality-at-highest-level.html.

Wouters, Cas. 1987. 'Developments in the Behavioural Codes between the Sexes: The Formalization of Informalization in the Netherlands, 1930–85'. *Theory, Culture and Society* 4 (2–3): 405–27. https://doi.org/10.1177/026327687004002012.

Wright, David. 2003. 'Grove's Role in the Founding of the RCM'. In *George Grove, Music and Victorian Culture*, edited by Michael Musgrave, 219–64. Houndmills, Basingstoke: Palgrave Macmillan.

———. 2005. 'The South Kensington Music Schools and the Development of the British Conservatoire in the Late Nineteenth Century'. *Journal of the Royal Musical Association* 130 (2): 236–82.

———. 2013. *The Associated Board of the Royal Schools of Music. A Social and Cultural History*. Woodbridge: Boydell and Brewer.

Wright, Ruth, and Brian Davies. 2010. 'Class, Power, Culture and the Music Curriculum'. In *Sociology and Music Education*, edited by Ruth Wright, 35–50. Farnham: Ashgate.

Yoshihara, Mari. 2008. *Musicians from a Different Shore: Asians and Asian Americans in Classical Music*. Philadelphia: Temple University Press.

Zaza, C., C. Charles, and A. Muszynski. 1998. 'The Meaning of Playing-Related Musculoskeletal Disorders to Classical Musicians'. *Social Science and Medicine* 47 (12): 2013–23.

Zeserson, K., J. A. Saunders, S. Burn, and E. Himonides. 2014. 'Inspiring Music for All: Next Steps in Innovation, Improvement and Integration'. http://discovery.ucl.ac.uk/1476037/1/Inspiring%20Music%20for%20All.pdf.

INDEX

ABRSM. *See* Associated Board of the Royal Schools of Music (ABRSM)
abuse
    definition of emotional, 86–87n.2
    in music education, 190
    in one-to-one pedagogy, 89–90
    and power, 177–78
academia, as white middle-class space, xxv
access
    to classical music education, xv, 185–86
    to music industry by working classes, xix–xx
Adenot, Pauline, 129
administration, of music organizations, 61–62n.3
administrative labour, 183
Adorno, Theodor, xxii–xxiii, xxv–xxvi
aesthetic of music
    boundary-drawing involving, xxix–xxx, 6
    defining, xviii
    ethics of, 71
    intersecting with class values, 16
    of rock music, 13
    in social analysis, 14–15
    and social position, xiii
    See also ideology of the aesthetic
affect, 24–25
    affective intensity, 150–51
    affective materiality, 164, 172
    affective openness, 121
    affective responses, 146–47
    contained by conductors, 105–7
    pleasure and control of, 108, 109
    in rehearsals, 105
    of rightness and wrongness, 81
age, classical music consumption and, xv, 3
Aggleton, Peter, 130
Alaghband-Zadeh, Chloë, 181
A-level music syllabus, 19–20
Allan, Alexandra, 162
Allen, Kim, 75
Alsop, Marin, 127

Althusser, Louis, 162–64
amplification, 167, 172
anorexia, 139–40
Armstrong, Victoria, 9–10, 126n.8
Army, 32
articulation, xxix–xxx, 13–15, 16, 175–76, 177, *See also* Hall, Stuart
artistic field, divisions in, 10
Arts Awards, 187
Arts Councils, xxi, 31–32, 62, 192–93
Asian American musicians
    and bodily practice, 23
    stereotypes about, 110–11
assemblage, of classical music, 13
Associated Board of the Royal Schools of Music (ABRSM)
    diversification of syllabi of, 188
    first syllabus from, 41, 42*f*
    gender of examinees, 40
    modern syllabi of, 43–44
    on social class and classical music participation, xx–xxi
    on social class and instrument selection, 19
    as 'standardizer,' 30
Atkinson, Paul, 136
austerity, and support of music programs, 191
authoritative leadership, 117
autonomous art, 10, 21
autonomy, of classical music, xxv–xxvi, 13

Bailey, Peter, 34–35, 38–39
Baker, Geoffrey, xxii
Banks, Mark, 14–15, 68, 170, 181, 186, 187–88
Barber, Charles. 2003., 95
Barlow, James, 12, 48, 160
Barrett, Maria, 176
Bartleet, Brydie-Leigh, 112–13, 114n.2
Bazalgette, Sir Peter, 46–47
'behemoths' of music education, 29
'being in the zone,' 170

Index

bel canto aesthetic, 24, 146–47
belonging
    in classical music study, 17–18
    in musical groups, 59
    sense of, in classical music organizations, 178
belting, 146–47
Bennett, Dawn, 191–92
Bennett, Tony, xiii
Benzecry, Claudio E., 157, 165
Bernstein, Leonard, 46
Birmingham Centre for Contemporary Cultural Studies (CCCS), 13
Blackman, Lisa, 105, 156–57, 169
Black musicians
    and stereotypes, 9
    See also Gustafson, Ruth; McClintock, Anne
bodily movement
    encouraged for non-European music, 98–99
    permitted in opera singing, 135
    in rehearsals, 98
bodily practice
    classed values reproduced in, xv–xvi
    of classical music, xxix–xxx, 22
    of conducting, 114, 127
    of gendered respectability, 38–39
    middle class values visible in, xii–xiii
    opera singing as, xxviii–xxix
    and respectability, 41
    and social position, xiii
    white ideals embodied in, xxviii
body
    changes in, during opera singing, 136–37, 138–39
    classical music experienced in, 167
    disciplining of, 42–43
    effacement or transcendence of, 98
    expressiveness and control of, 94–95
    failings of, 97–98
    and production of voice, 146–47
    'spirit' as separate from, 104
    transcendence of, and amplification, 172
body image
    multiple and overlapping, 137
    and opera singing, 133, 138–39
Bohlman, Philip, 17
Bordo, Susan, 135, 140–41
Born, Georgina, xviii, 13, 16, 18, 20, 162, 177–78
boundary-drawing, 27–49
    around participation and practice of classical music, xvi, 176
    and class, 4
    by classical music, xxvii
    and gendered respectability, 36
    and institutional ecology of youth classical music, 28
    institutionalizing respectability, 41
    as middle-class practice, 5
    in the present, 44
    and sacralization of music-as-art, 34
    and "systematic" training in music, 39
Bourdieu, Pierre, xvi, 2, 3–4, 5, 22, 35–36, 57–59, 182–83
bourgeois aesthetic, of music, 15
'bourgeois self'
    classical music as way of knowing, 159
    in classical music practice, xv–xvi, xxix–xxx
    instructed by middle-class values, 5
    and middle class, 36–37
    as product of privilege, 158–59
    restraint as characteristic of, 94–95
brass instruments
    and class, 10–11
    pedagogic models for, 27
breathing together, in musical performances, 121–22
Brewer, Mike, 118
'bright futures' group, 64–66, 181–82
British cathedral choral tradition, 117
British New Labour government, 62–63
Brown, Wendy, 5
bullying, by music teachers, 86
Burke, Penny Jane, 188
Burnard, Pamela, 19
business leaders, 106–7
Butler, Judith, 164
Butler, Tim, 10–11
Byrne, Bridget, 7–8

Cantando Youth Choir, xxiii
    bodily movement in, 99, 100
    changes in, 60
    musical education sponsored by, 63
    'proper' and popular music performed by, 46
    views of 'proper' music in, 45
capital
    classical music participation giving access to different types of, xxix
    cultural (*see* cultural capital)
    forms of, 2
    gained by classical musicians, 18, 91
    music standard as, 64
capitalism, 21
career aspirations, 67–68
CCCS (Birmingham Centre for Contemporary Cultural Studies), 13
charisma, structures of, 113
charismatic authority, ethics of, 127
'charismatic charmer' model, 115
'chav' culture
    avoidance of, with classical music participation, 12
    middle-class culture vs., 74
    and participation in classical music, 58
Chernoff, John Miller, 72
Chichester Psalms (Bernstein), 46

Chopin, Frédic, 43
Christianity
    and bodily practice of music, 24
    and musical practices, 23
    and transcendence of body, 104
    views of body in, 24–25
church choirs, 32
Citron, Marcia, 15, 147–48, 159–60
Clarke, David, xxvi, 21
class(es), 1–26
    and bodily practice of classical music, 22
    and boundary-drawing, 4
    changing, with classical music participation, 28
    classical music participation as expression of, 69
    definitions of, in different cultures, 180
    and economic inequality, 2
    friendships within same, 58–59
    and ideology of the aesthetic, 20
    improving, with classical music participation, 72–73
    and 'intensive parenting,' 6
    music as culture, 13
    and parenting, 160–61
    and performance dress codes, 99–100
    and response to conductors, 130–31
    and school choice, 62–63
    social mediation and classical music, 16
    sociological theories of, 2
    stereotypes and classical music, 8
    students' assessment of own, 27
    and value of classical music, 18
    and work ethic, 77–78
    See also specific classes
classed respectability, 74–75
classical music
    bodily practice of, xxix–xxx, 22
    consumption of, by age, xv, 3
    as cultural capital, 2–4
    defining, xvii
    diversification of, 1
    emancipatory potential of, xxv–xxvi
    formal structures of, 96
    as genre, xvii–xviii
    and inequality, xviii
    institutional ecology of, 28
    institutionalization of study and production of, 17
    in music education, 18–19
    perceived emotional depth of, xxix, 157–58, 162–63
    research on, xiii, 26
    'respectable' femininity associated with, 9
    role of, in development of self, 25–26
    and social mediation, 16
    special status of, 47
    and stereotypes, 8
    value of, xiii–xiv, xviii, 3, 8, 18, 170–71, 179–80

classical music institutions
    ecology of, 29, 183–84, 186–87, 191–92
    establishment of, 14
    influence of, on music sector, 32
    'informal economy' of, 31
    lack of research involving, xviii
    need for change in, xiii–xiv, 188
    sacralization of music by, xxvii
    value stored by, xiv–xv, 184
classical music participation
    to alleviate inequality, xxii–xxiii
    boundaries to, 176
    improving social status with, 72–73
    reasons for, 184–85
    and social identity, 20
classical music pedagogy
    alternatives to traditional, 189–90
    correction in, 178–79
    norms in, xv
    one-to-one (*see* one-to-one pedagogy)
    and reflexive self, 4–5
    required for classical music participation, xvii–xviii
classical music practice
    bourgeois ideals upheld in, xxvi
    and gender, 9
    self-criticism exacerbated in, 143
class mobility
    with classical music participation, 72–73, 91
    individualism in, 171–72
Clayton, Martin, 167–68
Clément, Catherine, 133
cognitive control, 24
commodification, of classical music, xxvi
community
    classical music groups as imagined, 16–17
    in classical music performance, 72, 83
    and competitiveness, in rehearsals, 178
    created by classical music, 21
    orchestra as idealized, 177–78
community-in-sound, 155–73
    affective materiality and subjectivity in, 164
    culture and value in, 169
    experience of, xxix
    gaining self-knowledge in, 159
    individualism and competitiveness suspended in, 21–22
    and interiority, 156
    and interpellation, 162
competitive music festivals, 35
competitiveness
    and community, in rehearsals, 178
    and community-in-sound, 173
    encouraged by capitalism, 21
    in opera singing, 141
composition, gender and, 40
concealing labour, 78
'concerted cultivation' model of parenting, 6–7, 160–61

conductor(s)
    as business leader, 106–7
    changing roles of, 105–6
    control exhibited by, 107–8
    mirroring of, 119–21, 122
    orchestras working without, 128–29n.9
    studies on authority of, 112–13
    willpower exemplified by, 105
    women as, 126–27
confidence
    in conducting, 127
    gained by opera singing, 134
    and social class, 86
    social distribution of, 85
'content of form' rehearsals, 97
control
    bodily, 41, 94–95, 135, 136–37 (see also Bordo, Susan)
    exhibited by conductor, 107–8, 112–31
    fantasy of male, 105
    giving up, and gender, 108, 140–41
    loss of, 103
    mechanisms of, in classical music practice, 94–95
    over musical material, 161
    pleasure and, 107
    in rehearsal, 107
    relinquishing, 177–78
    self-control, 94–95, 175
    whiteness as, 104
'controlled de-control,' 103, 110, 176
'controlled excitement,' xxviii, 102, 110, 176, 177
correction
    in classical music pedagogy, 178–79
    as focus of rehearsals, 81–82, 96
    of posture, 122–23
    shame experienced upon, 116
Crawford, Garry, xix, 157
Creative Case for Diversity (Arts Council England), xxix–xxx, 62, 192–93
criticism, in opera singing, 141
crowd psychology, 105
Crozier, Gill, 5, 12, 15–16, 130, 177–78
'cult of personality' model, 117
cultural capital
    classical music as, xxix–xxx, 2–4
    gained through classical music education, 183–84
    and institutionalization of classical music, 184
    in music education curriculum, 19–20
cultural technology
    classical music as, xxix
    large-scale musical structures as, 162
    musical practice as, 168–69
    music education as, 175
    tonality as, 159, 172
culture
    in community-in-sound, 169

consumption of, by classes, 3
    music as, 13
Curwen, John, 35
Curwen, Spencer, 35
Cusick, Suzanne, 166

Dahlhaus, Carl, 97
Darmon, Muriel, 139–40n.1
Davidoff, Leonore, 23, 38–39
Davies, Brian, 19–20
DeNora, Tia, 14–15, 25–26, 68, 160
Devine, Kyle, xix–xx
Dibben, Nicola, xix–xxn.4, 17
discipline, 64–65
diversity
    and artistic innovation, 62
    supporting, in music education, 192–93
domesticity, in late Victorian England, 36–37
dress code, for performances, 99–100
Dudamel, Gustavo, xxvi
Dueck, Byron, 61–62, 178–79
Durrant, Colin, 129
Dyer, Richard, 24, 104, 110

Eagleton, Terry, xxix, 20–22, 163–64, 169, 174–75
East Asian musicians, 9
eating disorders
    cultural conditions leading to, 140
    and opera singing, 140–41
    and social class, 139–40n.1
    and space allowed to women, 135–36
Ebrey, Jill, 181
economic inequality, 2
education
    commitment to, as middle-class value, 5
    level of, and classical music consumption, xix
    music (see music education)
    theories of mixed-ability classes, 61–62n.4
Ehrenreich, Barbara, 4–5
Ehrlich, Cyril, 29
Elias, Ana Sofia, 103
El Sistema, xxii, 16–17, 192
emerging cultural capital, 3
emotional abuse
    definition of, 86–87n.2
    in music education, 190
emotional responses, to classical music, xxix, 164–66, 176
'entrainment,' 167–68
ethics
    of aesthetics, 71
    of charismatic authority, 127
    related to practice, 22–23
ethnography, xxiii
excitement, in rehearsals, 108
exhaustion, during and following rehearsals, 97
expertise, of conductors, 127
expression

and concentration on music, 102
encouraged by teachers, 53–54
through classical music, for women, 43, 182–83
valuing, 10

Fautley, Martin, 187
fear
  and bullying by music teachers, 86–87
  of failure, among females, 142–43
  of female power, and eating disorders, 140
  and gendered power, 124
  of getting it wrong, 85
  and social class, 86
  social distribution of, 85
Fear of Falling (Ehrenreich), 4–5
Featherstone, Mike, 103, 110, 176
Feeny, Antony, xxi
female nervous disorders, 139–40
female sexuality, 36, 41–43, *See also* gendered respectability
femininity
  in musical practice, 8–9
  represented in *The Magic Flute*, 146–48
  representing, in opera singing, 146
feminism, 142–43
fidelity, to musical work, xxviii–xxix, 47, 95–96, 133, 149, 153–54, 178–79, 192
film music, 46
formal structures, of classical music, 96
Francis, Becky, 126n.8
friendships
  and musical ability, 57
  within same class, 58–59
Frith, Simon, xviii, 72
future orientation
  of middle class, 160
  of practice, 22
  projection of self into, 160–61

Garnett, Liz, 127
gaze, of conductors, 121
gender
  and career aspirations, 67–68
  and fractions of middle classes, 181–82
  gendered power experienced by different, 125
  and interactions with teachers, 126n.8
  and musical instrument selection, 33
  and musical practice, 8–9
  and professional musical careers, 66
  reflected in sonata form, 15
  and response to conductors, 130–31
  theorising with class, 9
gendered power, 112–31
  'charismatic charmer' model, 115
  'cult of personality' model, 117
  and ethics of charismatic authority, 127
  experienced by different genders, 125
  fear and surveillance, 124
  and mirroring of conductors, 122
  nonverbal expressions of, 119
  'people manager' model, 114
  in rehearsals, xxviii
  and structures of charisma, 113
gendered respectability
  and boundary-drawing, 36
  in classical music practice, 177
  performed through classical music, 44–45
  in present classical music practice, 74–75
gender norms
  and classical music, 8–9
  of middle and working classes, 9
'getting it right,' xxvii–xxviii, 70–92, 178–79
  and affects of rightness and wrongness, 81
  concealing labour, 78
  and ethics of aesthetics, 71
  social distribution of fear and confidence, 85
  and teaching methods, 86
  through respectability and hard work, 73
Gill, Rosalind, 142–43
Gillett, Paula, 39–40, 41, 43
globalization, classical music and, xvii
Glover, Sarah, 35
Goehr, Lydia, 20, 95–96
grade exams
  and idea of musical standard as variable, 54–55
  influence of, on music sector, 32
  in institutional ecology, 30
  respectability displayed in, 41
Green, Lucy, xxv–xxvi, 8–9, 18–19, 99–100, 111, 152, 179–80
Gregg, Melissa, 24–25
group tuition
  in music education, 7–8
  offered by local authority music services, 30–31
  problems in offering, 187–88
Grove, George, 38–39
Gunn, Simon, 34
Gustafson, Ruth, 24, 146–47

habitus, 22
Hall, Catherine, 23, 38–39
Hall, Clare, 6–7, 9–10, 17–18, 79–80, 85–86
Hall, Stuart, 13
hard work, 73
hard-working, as moral category, 75
Harvard University, 188–89
Harvey, Laura, 75
Haweis, Reverend, 37–38, 43
Henriques, Julian, 166–67, 168–69, 172
Hesmondhalgh, David, xviii, 162
Hess, Juliet, 46
heteronomous art, 10
hierarchies
  in British cathedral choral tradition, 117
  in classical music, xvii–xviii, 174
  See also musical hierarchies; social hierarchies

Higginson, Henry Lee, 106
Hoher, Dagmar, 37
Holland, Janet, 148
hooks, bell, 101–2
Hullah, John, 37–38, 47
'humble and hard-working' group, 66–67, 181–82
humor
  in rehearsals, 94
  sexualized, in British cathedral choral tradition, 117–18
  used by conductors, 116

idealized community, orchestra as, 177–78
identity(-ies)
  as classical musician, xi, 67, 155–56, 172–73
  classical music participation in formation of, 3–4
  and musical ability, 57
  musical hierarchies and formation of, 57–58
  one-on-one pedagogy and formation of, 51–54
  See also self
ideology of the aesthetic
  and class, 20
  and inequality, xiii–xiv
  long-term investment required by, xv–xvi
IHSE (In Harmony Sistema England), xxii–xxiii
Ilari, Beatriz, 6–7
imagined communities, classical music groups as, 16–17
imperialism, 24
improvisation, 84–85
Incorporated Society of Musicians, 31, 145
independent (private) schools, 32
individualism
  in classical music pedagogy, 16
  in class mobility, 171–72
  community-in-sound vs., 173
  encouraged by capitalism, 21
  and musical standard, 59
inequality
  and classical music, xviii
  classical music participation to alleviate, xxii–xxiii
  cultural, xii
  future studies on music and, 181
  and musical ability, 185–86
  music working against, xxiv–xxv
  in out-of-school music education, xvi
  sociological definition of, 2
  students' lack of awareness about, 81
  study of music and, xxvi–xxvii
  in Whitchestershire, xxiv
'informal economy,' of music education organizations, 31
In Harmony Sistema England (IHSE), xxii–xxiii
in-school music education, 19
institutional ecology, of youth classical music, xviii, 28

institutionalization
  of classical music study and production, 17, 184
  of music-as-art, 34
  of respectability, 41
  value stored through, 48
intellectual content, 33–34
'intensive parenting'
  and class, 6
  and formation of self, 4
  and future orientation, 160–61
  and musical ability, 186
interiority
  based on class, 158–59
  and community-in-sound, 156
  constructing, through interpellation, 162
  emergence of, 157–58
  expressed through female nervous disorders, 139–40
interpellation, 162
intimacy, in one-on-one pedagogy, 51–54, 143–44

James, David, 5, 12, 15–16, 130, 177–78
jazz, 181
Johnson, James, 158
Johnson, Julian, xii–xiii, 23, 97
Johnson-Hill, Erin, 40–41
Joyful Messiah (Quincy Jones, arr.), 46
'Junior Departments' of music conservatoires, 29

Kassabian, Anahid, 96
Kehily, Mary Jane, 116
Khan, Shamus Rahman, 80–81
Kingsbury, Henry, 16, 185–86
Kramer, Lawrence, 85, 158
Kulz, Christy, 104

labour
  administrative, 183
  concealing, 78
Labour government, 30–31
Laing, Dave, xxi
Lambeau, Céline, 128, 129
Lamont, Michèle, xvi, 3, 5, 35–36
Lareau, Annette, 3, 6, 160–61
Le Bon, Gustav, 105
Lebrecht, Norman, 120–21
Legg, Robert, 19–20
Leppänen, Taru, 110–11
Leppert, Richard, 37
Littler, Jo, 80–81
Littleton, Karen, 182–83
local authority music services
  establishment of, 14
  in institutional ecology, 30–31
Logie, Nicholas, 106–7, 115, 119n.6
Long, Marion, 126n.8
Loudon, John Claudius, 38–39
Lucey, Helen, 142–43

Magic Flute, The (Mozart), xxviii–xxix, 133, 145, 149, 153, 174
Making Music, 31
Malik, Sarita, 193
management techniques, 106–7
Martin, Peter, 34–35
'masters of the musical universe' group, 66, 181–82
Maxwell, Claire, 130
McClary, Susan, xxix, 15, 159–60, 161
McClintock, Anne, 15–16, 24, 36–37, 75
McCormick, Lisa, 17, 99–100, 143–44, 157
McGuire, Charles Edward, 35
McManus, Jackie, 188
McNeill, William, 167–68
McRobbie, Angela, 142–43, 183
McShane, Brian, 177
Measham, Fiona, 103
Melldahl, Andreas, 181
Mellor, Philip A., 23, 157–58
Melody, June, 142–43
men
　conducting seen as natural for, 130
　gender expectations for, 9–10
　pursuit of classical music careers by, 182–83
Mendelssohn, Felix, 105–6
Mendick, Heather, 75
meritocracy, work ethic and, 80–81
Messiah (Handel), 46
metropolitan habitus, 10–11
middle class(es)
　boundary-drawing by, xiii–xiv
　bourgeois identity of, 36–37
　classical music consumption by, xix
　commonalities among, 4–5
　as cultural entrepreneurs of music, 34–35
　entitlement of, to public spaces, 171
　expansion of music education of, 39–40
　fractions of, xiv, 10, 181–82
　future orientation of, 161
　gaining trust of members of, 177
　gender and fractions of, 181–82
　gender norms of, 9
　morality of, reflected in classical music, xii–xiii, 73–74
　norms of, xiv, 17, 173, 175
　participation in entertainment by, 176
　research needed on, xiv
　responsibility of, 177–78
　restraint as characteristic of, 103
　in United States, 4–5n.1
　of Whitchestershire, xxiv
military, music education by, 32
mixed-ability music groups, 61–62
mood, of conductors, 120–21
morality
　and bodily practice, 23
　of classical music, 73–74
　of music, 42–43
　in music movements, 35–36
　as symbolic boundary, 5
Moran, Leslie J., 47–48
Morrison, Toni, 101
Mozart, Wolfgang Amadeus, xxviii–xxix, 133, 145, 149, 174
music
　as culture, 13
　emotionality and control in, 37
　redemptive powers of, 38
　young women's morality during nineteenth century and, 37
musical ability
　and access to classical music education, 185–86
　and concealed effort, 79–80
　innate and cultivated, 6–7
　judged by others, 82–83
　one-on-one pedagogy necessary for, 71
　as part of identity, 57
　and social groups, 57
musical aspirations
　and decisions about future, 169–70
　of students, 65–67
musical 'excellence'
　cost of, in classical music education, 185–86
　examining current ideas of, 191–92
　and social inequalities, 68–69
　striving for, as ultimate end, 62
musical hierarchies
　removing, 189
　social and, xxvii, 56, 58, 186
musical instruments
　becoming proficient in, 179
　class and selection of, 10–11, 19
　demand for different, 33
　gender and selection of, 8–9, 33
　non-traditional, 187–88
　and sense of self, 71
musical standard, 50–69
　and aesthetic of classical music, xxvii–xxviii
　alternative views of, 188–89
　effect of, on youth's futures, 64
　and flight from public services, 60
　and 'getting it right,' 178–79
　institutionalized in grade exams, 42–43
　moral obligations towards improving, 40–41
　musical and social hierarchies, 56
　and one-on-one pedagogy, 51
　playing with others at higher level of, 54
　recognition of, 54
　required for Junior Departments, 29
　and social space, 57
musical structure, 161
musical work, imagined ideal of, 95–96
Music and Dance Scheme, 31–32
Music and Morals (Haweis), 37–38

music-as-art
  sacralization of, 34
  and 'work concept,' 20
music conservatoires
  influence of, on music sector, 32
  in institutional ecology, 29
  racialised, gendered, and classed inequalities in, xx
music education, 185
  as boundary, 6
  class and gender shaped by, 28
  as cultural technology, 175
  establishment of, 14
  group tuition in, 7–8
  inequality and tertiary, xix–xx
  in-school and out-of-school, 19
  lack of regulation in, 32
  military involvement in, 32
  national curriculum for, 19–20
  'non-interference' strategy of, 178–79
  out-of-school, xvi
  popular and classical music in, 18–19
  Suzuki method of, 6–7
  variety of musical genres in, 186–87, 191
  for various classes, 38
music examination boards, 30
music grade exams, 7–8
music halls, 37
Musicians' Union, 31
music industry, xix–xx
music-making
  and gender, 8–9
  honoring many traditions of, 187–88
  in schools, 116
  in Victorian England, 35
music technology, xix–xx

National Plan for Music Education (NPME), 19–20, 30–31, 192
National Training School for Music, 40n.4
National Youth Brass Band, 31–32
National Youth Choir, 31–32
National Youth Orchestra, 27, 31–32, 189
'natural growth' model of parenting, 6
Nayak, Anoop, 116
Nead, Lynda, 36
Neale, Steve, xvii–xviiin.1
neoliberalism, 5
New Labour, 187
'new' middle class, 10–11
New Symphony Orchestra (NSO), xxiii, 60–61
Nicholls, Emily, 74–75
Nikisch, Arthur, 105
Nisbett, Melissa, 127
non-European repertoire
  bodily movement in, 98–101
  engagement with, 43–44, 101–2
'non-interference' music education, 178–79

non-musical institutions, 32
nonverbal communication
  of gendered power, 119
  in one-on-one pedagogy, 53–54
  in peer interactions, 55
Nooshin, Laudan, xvii
NPME (National Plan for Music Education), 19–20, 30–31, 192
NSO (New Symphony Orchestra), xxiii, 60–61
Nylander, Erik, 181

O'Brien, Dave, xix–xx
one-to-one pedagogy, 6
  alternatives to traditional, 189–90
  artistic interpretations of, 37
  bullying by teachers in, 89–90
  instead of group tuition, 31
  intimacy in, 143–44
  and musical standard, 51
  in opera singing, 141
  as social mediation, 16
  study participants' history of, xxiv
opera singing, 132–54
  and authenticity of music, 149
  as bodily practice, xxviii–xxix
  and body image, 133
  competitiveness and criticism in, 141
  representations of femininity in, 8–9
  representing femininity in, 146
  and sexism, 144
  voice as power, 137
opportunities, available for young musicians, 32–33
Orbach, Susie, 139–41
orchestras
  hierarchies in, 56
  working without conductors, 128–29n.9
O'Toole, Patricia, 112–13
out-of-school music education, xvi, 19

Pace, Ian, 89–90
Palmer, Roger, 119n.7, 157
paradoxes, in classical music practice, 174–75
parenting
  and class, 160–61
  'concerted cultivation' model of, 6–7
  intensive (see 'intensive parenting')
  'natural growth' model of, 6
peers
  musical standard improved or lowered by, 55
  value of classical music among, 184–85
  wrongness judged by, 82–83
'people manager' model of conducting, 114
perfectionism, of young women, 142–43
Perkins, Rosie, 19
philanthropic funding, xxi–xxii
Philpott, Chris, 19

piano
  class status of playing, 40
  as 'modest' instrument, 41
  and respectable femininity, 43
Pickett, Kate, xxiv–xxv
pleasure
  in rehearsal, 107
  of retaining control, 108–9
pleasure-as-control, 108–9
pleasure-as-indulgence, 108–9
policies, concerning music education, 186–87
'popular' music
  boundaries drawn around, 176
  classical musicians' views of, 157
  in music education, 18–19
postfeminist sensibility, 142–43
posture, correction of, 122–23
power
  and abuse, 177–78
  of music teachers, 89–90
  responsible use of, 129–30
  voice as, 137, 152 (see also gendered power)
practice
  definitions of, 22–23
  as work ethic, 75–78
preservation, of classical music, 47
Prieur, Annick, 3
'professional' middle class, 10–11
'proper' music, 44
public funding
  of classical music programs, xxi–xxii
  for music programs, xv
public services, flight from, 60
public space(s)
  for classical music performance, xvi, 171
  opera singing in, 137–38, 139
Purcell School, 31–32

Rachmaninov, Sergei, 93
racialised identities
  and bodily movement in music performance, 100–1
  and classical music practices, 111
  and 'eating the other,' 101–2
  future research on classical music and, 191
  and ideals of cognitive control, 24
  of study participants, xxiv
  See also whiteness
RCM (Royal College of Music), 39
Read, Barbara, 126n.8
Reading Youth Orchestra, xiv–xv
Reay, Diane, 5, 12, 15–16, 61–62n.4, 130, 177–78
reflexive self
  development of, with 'intensive parenting,' 4
  as product of privilege, 158–59
rehearsal(s), 93–111
  bodily movement in, xxviii, 98
  community and competitiveness in, 178
  controlled excitement in, 102
  correction as focus of, 81–82
  future studies on inequality in, 181
  and gendered power, xxviii
  pleasure and control in, 107
  social relations in, 105
  structure of, 95
repertoire
  boundary-drawing around, 176
  changes in, during Victorian period, 34
  social organization required by, xv–xvi
respectability
  and church attendance, 23
  'getting it right' through, 73
  institutionalizing, 41
'respectable' femininity, 9, 177, See also gendered respectability
responsibility, of middle class, 177–78
restraint, in rehearsals, 93–95
rhythms, synchronized, 167–68
rightness
  affects of wrongness and, 81
  lack of, in improvisation, 84
  musical and social, 72
  of social behavior, 90
Robson, Garry, 10–11
Rollock, Nicola, 9
Rosen, Charles, 99–100
Royal Academy of Music, xx, 40n.4
Royal Air Force, 32
Royal College of Music (RCM), 39
Royal College of Music Junior Department, 29
Royal Colleges of Music, 30
Royal Court Theatre, 176
Royal Navy, 32
Rutter, John, 45

sacralization
  of classical music, xiii–xiv
  of music-as-art, 34
Sagiv, Dan, 85–86
Saha, Anamik, xxvi
Savage, Mike, 3
Savile, Jimmy, 117
Scharff, Christina, xiii–xiv, xix, 3, 9–10, 17–18, 33, 66, 97–98, 130, 143, 152, 170, 188
school choice, 62–63
schools
  music-making in, 116
  status of music education within, xvi
  and tertiary music degrees, xx
Schreffler, Anne, 188–89
seduction, conducting as, 129
Seigworth, Gregory J., 24–25
self
  classical music pedagogy and formation of, 7–8, 175
  'intensive parenting' and formation of, 4
  musical instruments and sense of, 71

self (*cont.*)
  projected into future, 160–61
  role of classical music in development of, xxix, 25–26, 180
  valued forms of, xiii–xiv
  voice as separate from, 136–37
self-criticism, of young women, 142–43
self-critique, among opera singers, 141–42
self-knowledge, gaining, 159
self-worth, 3–4
Sennett, Richard, 73, 76, 85–86
'serious' music
  boundaries drawn around, 176
  classical music's classification as, 33–34
  lack of bodily movement in, 98–101
  promoting music education as, 38–39
sexism
  in *The Magic Flute*, 133, 145
  and opera singing, 144
sexual harassment, in classical music environment, 144–45
sexuality, female, 36, 41–43, *See also* gendered respectability
sexualized humor
  in British cathedral choral tradition, 117–18
  used by conductors, 129
sexual violence, in opera and real life, 148
shame
  as affect of wrongness, 83–84
  experienced upon correction in rehearsals, 116
  of getting it wrong, 85
Shilling, Chris, 23, 157–58
Showalter, Elaine, 139–40
Simon Bolivar Youth Orchestra, 98–99
singing, 8–9, *See also* opera singing
Sistema Scotland, xxii–xxiii
Skeggs, Beverley, 3–4, 8, 15–16, 47–48, 64–65, 72–73, 158–59, 160, 170–72
Skelton, Christine, 126n.8
skill development, through practice, 22
Small, Christopher, 96
social aesthetic, 14–15
social capital, 65
social cohesion, 21
social groups, musical ability and, 57
social hierarchies
  in classical music practice, xxiv–xxv, 175–76
  musical and, xxvii, 56, 58, 186
  seen as necessary for classical music, 125
social identity
  and classical music participation, 20
  mediation of, with classical music participation, 17
social justice, xv
social mediation, 16
social mobility
  classical music participation as, 69
  through classical music participation, 183–84

social organization
  formal modes of, xxix–xxx
  rehearsals as idealized, 110
social position
  and aesthetics, xiii
  and bullying by music teachers, 89
  improving, with classical music participation, 91
social relations
  heard through classical music, xiii
  in rehearsal, 105
social resources, gained through classical music participation, 184–85
social space
  homogeneity of, in classical music, 12
  and musical standard, 57
socioeconomic status, of classical musicians, 17–18
Solie, Ruth, 43
sonata form, 15, 159–60
'sonic dominance,' 166–67
'spirit,' as separate from body, 104
Spitzer, John, 106–7
Spontini, Gaspare, 105–6
Sport England, 32
Spruce, Gary, 19–20
Stahl, Garth, 19
'standardizers' of music education, 30
stereotypes
  about Asian American musicians, 110–11
  about Black musicians, 9
  and bodily movement, 101
  and classical music, 8
stillness, bodily
  and body effacement, 98
  of classical music performers, 24
  of listeners, 24, 34
  political effects of, 105, 110
  see also bodily movement
string instruments, 10–11
structural listening, 96
subjectivity, in community-in-sound, 164
Subotnik, Rose Rosengard, 153
Sullivan, Sir Arthur, 40–41
surveillance
  by conductors, 114
  and gendered power, 124
Suzuki method, 6–7
'symbolic boundaries,' 5
"systematic" training, in music, 39

'talent scouts,' 31–32, 79–80
Tarde, Gabriel, 105
Taruskin, Richard, 149–50
Taylor, Charles, 157–58
Taylor, Mark, xxii
Taylor, Nick, 75
Taylor, Stephanie, 182–83

teachers, 126n.8
teaching methods, 86
'telling the self,' 158–59, 161
time investment, in classical music practice, 179
tonality, 159, 172
tone of voice, 118–19
Tonic Sol-fa movement, 35–36, 40–41, 48
Toynbee, Jason, 181
transcendence, provided by classical music, 23
Trinity College London, 30, 40, 187
Trollope, Anthony, 158–59
trust
    in musical group, 169
    of musicians, in conductor, 121, 130–31
    of youth, in authority, 177
tuning, 83–84

unions, for music teachers, 31
United States
    middle classes in, 4–5n.1
    research on boundary-drawing in, 5
unity
    creating, in classical music performance, 72
    of a musical work, 95–96, 153–54
    in rehearsals, 110
'upper- and upper-middle' class, 10–11

value (worth)
    of artistic work, 10
    of classical music, xiii–xiv, xviii, 3, 8, 18, 170–71, 179–80
    in community-in-sound, 169
    in development of self, 175
    of different genres of music, 190–91
values (ethics)
    in classical music, xxiv–xxv
    of middle classes, 5
    in music education, xxii–xxiii, 28–29
Vaugeois, Lise, 99–100, 101n.1
Victorian England
    domesticity in, 36–37
    moral and taste boundary-drawing in, 35–36
violin, 40
visibility, in opera singing, 139
voice
    as power, 137, 152
    as separate from self, 136–37

Wagner, Izabela, 76
Walkerdine, Valerie, 142–43
Walmsley, Ben, 127
Webber, Andrew Lloyd, 46
Weber, William, 34, 105–6
Weeks, Peter, 82–83, 93–94
Weiss, Gail, 137, 152–53
West-Eastern Divan Orchestra, 16–17
'Western art music,' xvii
Whiplash (film), 89–90

Whitchester County Youth Orchestra, xxiii
    entry standards for, 56
    views of musical standards of, 60–61
Whitchestershire, xxiv
Whitchestershire county music service, 31
whiteness
    appropriation of other cultures by, 101
    and bel canto aesthetic, 146–47
    and bodily movement in music performance, 100–1
    and classical music consumption, xix
    and classical music practice, 191
    of composers, in music education, xi–xii
    control and transcendence of body as characteristic of, 94–95
    embodied in bodily practice, xxviii
    embodiment of, 24
    exhibited through control, 104
    ideas of, encoded in rehearsal practices, 110
    in music conservatories, xx
    and transcendence of body, 104
Whittaker, Adam, 187
Whole Class Ensemble Teaching, 30–31, 187–88
Wilkinson, Richard, xxiv–xxv
Williams, John, 46
Willis, Paul E., 13, 14–15
willpower, exemplified by conductor, 105
women
    appropriate work available for, 36–37
    clothing worn by, 99–100
    as conductors, 126–27
    equality for, 36–37
    gendered respectability for, 36
    gender expectations for, 9–10
    musical education of, 39
    at music conservatoires, xx
    pursuit of classical music careers by, 182–83
    seen as more emotional than middle-class white males, 106
    'telling of self' by, 162
Wood, Helen, 170–72
'work-concept,' 20
    and bodily practice of music, 24
    and fidelity to music work, 95–97
    in opera, 150–51
    See also Goehr, Lydia
work ethic
    in classical music practice, 75–78
    as middle class characteristic, 75
    and mistreatment by music teachers, 87–88
    in rehearsal, 94
    rewarded in classical music practice, 90
working class(es)
    access to music industry by, xix–xx
    and concealment of labour, 80
    gaining trust of members of, 177
    gender norms of, 9
    in middle class classical music practice, 183–84

working class(es) (*cont.*)
  parenting views of, 160–61
  participation in classical music during nineteenth century, 34–35, 39–40
  response of, to classical music, xix
  and sense of self, 158–59
Wouters, Cas, 103
Wright, David, xx–xxi, 7–8, 37–39
Wright, Ruth, 19–20
wrongness
  affects of rightness and, 81
  called out, in front of group, 124
  correcting, in rehearsals, 96
  correcting, with practice, 76–77
  lack of, in improvisation, 84
  as process of improvement, 73
  of social behavior, 90
  threat of, for working- and middle-class students, 81

York, Norton, xxi
Yoshihara, Mari, 6–7, 17–18, 23, 110–11, 169–70, 183
Young Opera Company, xxiii
young people
  listening to experiences of, 189–90
  understanding of economic equality by, 2
Youth Music, 187